The Time Traveler's Guide to Medieval England

*A Handbook for Visitors to
the Fourteenth Century*

IAN MORTIMER

A TOUCHSTONE BOOK
Published by Simon & Schuster

New York   London   Toronto   Sydney

Touchstone
A Division of Simon & Schuster, Inc.
1230 Avenue of the Americas
New York, NY 10020

Copyright © 2008 by Ian Mortimer
Originally published in Great Britain in 2008 by the Bodley Head,
a division of Random House UK

Manufactured in the United States of America

ISBN 978-1-4391-1289-2
Book Club Edition

For my wife, Sophie,
without whom this book would not have been written
and whom I would not have met
had it not been for this book.

Acknowledgments

I would like to thank my editors Will Sulkin and Jörg Hensgen, and all their colleagues at Random House who have helped to bring this idea to fruition, and my agent, Jim Gill, for sound advice. I am very grateful also to Kathryn Warner for giving me feedback on the first draft, and to those who accommodated me on various research trips, namely Zak Reddan and Mary Fawcett, Jay Hammond, Judy Mortimer, and Robert and Julie Mortimer. I would also like to record my gratitude for the helpful suggestions which Peter McAdie and Anne Wegner made during the course of editing this book.

By far my greatest debt is to my wife, Sophie. We first met in order to discuss this book in January 1995. I am deeply grateful to her not only for encouraging me to write it but also for subsequently marrying me. We now have three children: Alexander, Elizabeth, and Oliver. I am grateful to them too for teaching me things about life in all ages which one simply cannot learn from a book.

Moretonhampstead, Devon
March 9, 2008

Contents

The past is a foreign country—
they do things differently there.
                    L. P. Hartley, *The Go-Between*

INTRODUCTION

Welcome to Medieval England

What does the word "medieval" conjure up in your mind? Knights and castles? Monks and abbeys? Huge tracts of forest in which outlaws live in defiance of the law? Such images may be popular but they say little about what life was like for the majority. Imagine you could travel in time; what would you find if you went back to the fourteenth century? Imagine yourself in a dusty London street on a summer morning. A servant opens an upstairs shutter and starts beating a blanket. A dog guarding a traveler's packhorses starts barking. Nearby traders call out from their market stalls while two women stand chatting, one shielding her eyes from the sun, the other with a basket in her arms. The wooden beams of houses project out over the street. Painted signs above the doors show what is on sale in the shops beneath. Suddenly a thief grabs a merchant's purse near the traders' stalls, and the merchant runs after him, shouting. Everyone turns to watch. And you, in the middle of all this, where are you going to stay tonight? What are you wearing? What are you going to eat?

As soon as you start to think of the past *happening* (as opposed to it having happened), a new way of conceiving history becomes possible. The very idea of traveling to the Middle Ages allows us to consider the past in greater breadth—to discover more about the problems which the English have had to face, the delights they found in life, and what they themselves were like. As with a historical biography, a travel book about a past age allows us to see its inhabitants in a sympathetic way: not as a series of graphs showing fluctuations in grain yields or household income but as an investigation into the sensations of being alive in a different time. You can start to gain an inkling as to why people did this or that, and even why they believed things which we find simply incredible. You can gain this insight because you know that these people are human, like you, and that some of these reactions are simply natural. The idea of traveling to the Middle Ages allows you to understand these people not only in terms of evidence but also in terms of their humanity, their hopes and fears, the drama of their lives. Although writers have traditionally been forced to resort to historical fiction to do this, there is no reason why a nonfiction writer should not present his material in just as direct and as sympathetic a manner. It does not make the facts themselves less true to put them in the present tense rather than the past.

In some senses this idea is not new. For many decades architectural historians have been re-creating images of castles and monasteries as they appeared in their heyday. Museum curators similarly have reconstructed old houses and their interiors, filling them with the furniture of a past age. Groups of individuals have formed reenactment societies, attempting to discover what it was like to live in a different time through the bold, practical experiment of donning period clothing and cooking with a cauldron on an open fire, or trying to wield a replica sword while wearing heavy armor. Collectively they remind us that history is much more than an educational process. Understanding the past is a matter of experience as well as knowledge, a striving to make spiritual, emotional, poetic, dramatic, and inspirational connections with our forebears. It is about our personal reactions to the challenges of living in previous centuries and earlier cultures, and our understanding of what makes one century different from another.

The nearest historians have come to considering the past at first hand is the genre of "what if?" or "virtual history." This is where historians consider what would have happened if things had turned out differently. For example, what if Hitler had invaded Britain in 1940? What if the Spanish Armada had been successful? While such speculations are open to the obvious criticism that these things did not happen (with the implication that there is no point considering them), they have the great virtue of taking the reader directly to a moment in time and presenting events as if they were still unfolding. This can bring a real immediacy to a narrative. Put yourself in the shoes of the duke of Wellington at Waterloo, or Nelson at Trafalgar: they were only too well aware of the consequences of defeat. So too were their political masters back in England. *They* certainly considered the past that never was; so to reconstruct what might otherwise have happened brings us closer to those leaders in the moments of their decision-making. Just think: if Henry IV had not returned to England in 1399 to remove Richard II from power, we would have had several more years—perhaps many more—of Richard's tyrannical rule, probably resulting in the destruction of the Lancastrian dynasty and all those who supported it. In the spring of 1399 that likelihood was the key political issue and one of the reasons why Henry *did* return. It was also the principal reason why so many men supported him. In this way it is clear that seeing events as happening is crucial to a proper understanding of the past, even if the results are just as speculative now as they were at the time.

Virtual history as described above is only useful for understanding political events; it has relatively little value for social history. We cannot profitably speculate on what might have happened if, say, the Black Death had not come to Europe; it was not a matter of decision-making. But as with a reconstruction of a typical medieval house, virtual time travel allows us a clearer, more integrated picture of what it was like to live in a different age. In particular, it raises many questions which previously may not have even occurred to us and which do not necessarily have easy answers. How do people greet each other in the Middle Ages? What is their sense of humor like? How far away from home do individuals travel? Writing history from the point of view of our own curiosity forces us to consider a number of questions that traditional history books tend to ignore.

Medieval England is potentially a vast destination for the historical traveler. The four centuries between the Norman invasion and the advent of printing see huge changes in society. The "Middle Ages" are exactly that—a series of ages—and a Norman knight would find himself as out of place preparing for a late-fourteenth-century battle as an eighteenth-century prime minister would if he found himself electioneering today. For this reason, this guidebook concentrates on just one century, the fourteenth. This period comes closest to the popular conception of what is "medieval," with its chivalry, jousts, etiquette, art, and architecture. It might even be considered the epitome of the Middle Ages, containing civil wars, battles against the neighboring kingdoms of Scotland and France, sieges, outlaws, monasticism, cathedral building, the preaching of friars, the flagellants, famine, the last of the Crusades, the Peasants' Revolt, and (above all else) the Black Death.

Having emphasized that the focus of this book is fourteenth-century England, a few caveats must be added. It is not possible to recover every detail of the period on the basis of fourteenth-century English evidence alone; sometimes the contemporary record is frustratingly incomplete. Also we cannot always be sure that the manner of doing something in 1320 necessarily held true in 1390. In some cases we can be sure that things changed dramatically: the entire nature of English warfare altered over this period, and so did the landscape of disease, with the catastrophic advent of the plague in 1348. Thus, where necessary, details from the fifteenth century have been used to inform descriptions of the later part of the fourteenth century, and the thirteenth century has been used to inform judgments about the early part. This blurring of time boundaries is only necessary where very difficult questions are raised. For example, we have relatively few sources underpinning our understanding of courtesy and manners in the fourteenth century whereas we have several excellent sources for the early fifteenth. Since it is unlikely that good manners developed overnight, the later evidence has been used as the fullest and most accurate available.

Many types of source material have been used in writing this book. Needless to say, contemporary primary sources are of vital importance. These include unpublished and published chronicles, letters, household accounts, poems, and advisory texts. Illuminated manuscripts show daily life in ways which the texts do not always describe: for example, whether women rode sidesaddle. A wealth of architectural evidence is available in the extant buildings of fourteenth-century England—the houses as well as the castles, churches, and monasteries—and the ever-expanding literature about them provides even more information. In some cases we have documents which complement the architectural record: building accounts and surveys, for example. We have an increasing array of archaeological finds, from excavated tools, shoes, and clothes to the pips of berries found in medieval latrines, and fish bones on the waterlogged sites of ancient ponds. We have a plethora of more usual archaeological artifacts too, such as coins, ceramics, and ironware. The extent to which a good museum can give you an insight into how life was lived in the Middle Ages is restricted only by your own curiosity and imagination.

But most of all, it needs to be said that the very best evidence for what it was like to be alive in the fourteenth century is an awareness of what it is like to be alive in any age, and that includes today. Our sole context for understanding all the historical data we might ever gather is our own life experience. We might eat differently, be taller, and live longer, and we might look at jousting as being unspeakably dangerous and not at all a sport, but we know what grief is and what love, fear, pain, ambition, enmity and hunger are. We should always remember that what we have in common with the past is just as important, real, and as essential to our lives as those things which make us different. Consider a group of historians in seven hundred years' time trying to explain to their contemporaries what it was like to live in the early twenty-first century. Maybe they will have some books to rely on, some photographs, perhaps some digitized film, the remains of our houses, and the odd council rubbish pit but overall they will concentrate on what it is to be human. W. H. Auden once suggested that to understand your own country you need to have lived in at least two others. One can say something similar for periods of time: to understand your own century you need to have come to terms with at least two others. The key to learning something about the past might be a ruin or an archive but the means whereby we may understand it is—and always will be—ourselves.

I

The Landscape

Cities and Towns

It is the cathedral that you will see first. As you journey along the road you come to a break in the trees and there it is, massive and magnificent, cresting the hilltop in the morning sun. Despite the wooden scaffolding at its west end, the long eighty-foot-high pointed lead roof and the flying buttresses and colossal towers is simply the wonder of the region. It is hundreds of times bigger than every other building around it and dwarfs the stone walls surrounding the city. The hundreds of houses appear tiny, all at chaotic angles, and of different shades and hues, as if they were so many stones at the bottom of a stream flowing around the great boulder of the cathedral. The thirty churches—though their low stumpy towers stand out from the mass of roofs—seem humble by comparison.

When you draw closer to the city walls you will see the great gatehouse. Two round towers, each more than fifty feet high, stand either side of a pointed arch, newly built, with a painted statue of the king in a niche above the grand entrance. It leaves you in no doubt about the civic pride of the city, nor its authority. Beyond these gates you are subject to the mayor's jurisdiction. Here reside the king's officers, in the castle on the northeastern perimeter. Here is a place of rule and order. The high circling walls, the statue of the king, the great round towers, and—above it all—the immense cathedral collectively impress you with their sheer strength.

And then you notice the smell. Four hundred yards from the city gate, the muddy road you are following crosses a brook. As you look along the banks you see piles of refuse, broken crockery, animal bones, entrails, human feces, and rotting meat strewn in and around the bushes. In some places the muddy banks slide into thick quagmires where townsmen have hauled out their refuse and pitched it into the stream. In others, rich green grasses, reeds, and undergrowth spring from the highly fertilized earth. As you watch, two seminaked men lift another barrel of excrement from the back of a cart and empty it into the water. A small brown pig roots around in the garbage. It is not called Shitbrook for nothing.

You have come face-to-face with the contrasts of a medieval city. It is so proud, so grand, and in places so beautiful and yet it displays all the disgusting features of a bloated glutton. The city as a body is a caricature of the human body: smelly, dirty, commanding, rich, and indulgent. As you hurry across the wooden bridge over Shitbrook and hasten towards the gates, the contrasts become even more vivid. A group of boys with dirty faces and tousled hair run towards you and crowd around, shouting, 'Sir, do you want a room? A bed for the night? Where are you from?' struggling between them to take the reins of your horse and maybe pretending that they know your brother or are from the same region as you. Their clothes are filthy, and their feet even filthier, bound into leather shoes which have suffered the stones and mud of the streets for more years than their owners. Welcome to a place of pride, wealth, authority, crime, justice, high art, stench, and beggary.

The city described above is Exeter, in the southwest of England, but it could almost be any of the seventeen cathedral cities. You could say the same for many of the large towns too, except for the fact that their churches are not cathedrals. Arriving in every one of these places involves an assault on all the senses. Your eyes will open wide at the great churches, and you will be dazzled by the wealth and the stained glass they contain. Your nostrils will be invaded by the stench from the sewage-polluted watercourses and town ditches. After the natural quiet of the country road, the birdsong, and the wind in the trees, your hearing must attune to the calls of travelers and town criers, the shouts of laborers and the ringing of church bells. In any town on a market day, or during a fair, you will find yourself being jostled by the crowds who come in from the country for the occasion, and who live it up rowdily in the taverns. To visit an English town in the late fourteenth century is a bewildering and extreme sensory experience.

A major town is an intimidating place. Already you will have seen the desiccated remains of thieves left hanging on gallows at windswept crossroads. At the principal gates of a regional capital you will find the heads and limbs of traitors on display. When you enter the city of York (the largest city in the north) you will see the blackened heads of criminals stuck on poles above the city gates, their eyes plucked out by birds. Legs and arms hang by ropes, each the relic of a treasonable plot, now riddled with maggots or covered with flies. These remains remind you of the power of the king, a greater and more ominous shadow behind the immediate authority of the mayor and aldermen, local lords, sheriffs, and judicial courts.

This, you could say, is the landscape of medieval England: a place of fear and decay. But the moment you walk under the shadow of a city gatehouse, you realize it is much more than that. In Exeter, for example, as soon as you enter the great gate of the city, you face the wide and handsome prospect of South Street. Some of the finest houses and inns are here, the gable ends of their steeply angled roofs neatly meeting the street. On your right is the church of Holy Trinity, a cult of special devotion in the late fourteenth century. Farther down you have the handsome town house of an abbot. On your left is a row of merchants' houses, some with their shops open, with silks and other expensive fabrics on show inside the covered shop fronts. For a moment you might notice the uneven surface of the road, which is dust, or mud after it has rained. But then you will be distracted by the amount of activity around you. Ponies and packhorses are ambling through the town, towards the marketplace, laden with grain and guided by peasants from the local farms. Priests pass by, robed in their habits, with crucifixes and rosaries hanging from their girdles. Perhaps a black-robed Dominican friar is preaching to the people at the top of the street, watched by a small circle of admirers. Workers are driving their sheep and cattle into market or steering carts laden with eggs, milk, and cheeses towards the line of shops known as Milk Street.

The city is so *alive*, so full of busy people, that within a short while you have forgotten about the decapitated traitors. And Shitbrook's stench is no longer in the air; now there is a remarkable absence of animal dung in the streets. All is revealed in South Street when you see a servant shoveling up horse dung from the area in front of his master's house. As you walk towards the center of the city, you will encounter more traders' shops tightly packed together in small street-front premises—sometimes tiny rooms of less than forty square feet—but all with their distinctive projecting signs to tell the illiterate their trade. Some are paintings depicting the items on sale, such as a painted knife indicating the shop of a cutler. Others are three-dimensional objects: a bushel on a pole, showing that freshly brewed ale is available, or a bandaged arm, marking a surgeon's premises. At the top of Smithen Street, which leads down to the river, you can hear the clang of blacksmiths hammering away at their forges and shouting in guttural voices at their apprentices to fetch water or bring coal. Others in the same street are setting up stalls, hanging out ironwares such as scissors, rushlight holders, and knives to attract the attention of those coming in from the surrounding countryside. A little farther on you come to Butchers Row, or the Shambles, where the counters of the shops are laden with meat lying exposed in the sun, with joints and carcasses hanging from hooks in the shade of the shop behind. Listen to the *thunk* as the cleaver comes down and strikes the chopping board, and watch as the leather-aproned butcher lifts the red meat onto the scales, balancing it carefully with metal weights until he is satisfied that he, at least, is getting a good deal.

It is here, among the city's shops, that your preconceptions of medieval England will begin to fall apart. Walk into the center of any large town or city and you will be struck by the extraordinary range of costumes, from russet-clad peasants to richly dressed merchants and esquires and their wives, and maybe even a knight or nobleman. Their traveling cloaks might hide the colorful hues of their clothes in grey winter but, in this sunlight, the rich reds, bright yellows, and deep blues are shown off, trimmed with furs according to social rank. Similarly the languages and accents you hear in a city give a cosmopolitan air to the place. Foreign merchants are regularly to be found in the greater towns and cities, but even in the smaller ones you will hear both French and English spoken in the street, and occasionally Latin and Cornish. Over the hubbub of the morning's business you will hear the town crier, calling from the crossroads at the center of the town, or laughter as friends share a joke. Over it all the practiced cries of the street vendors ring out as they walk around with trays of food, calling out "Hot peascods" or "Rushes fair and green," "Hot sheep's feet" or "Ribs of beef and many a pie."[1]

Given the noise and the textures of the place, you may be surprised to learn how few people actually live in the greater towns and cities of England. In 1377 the walls of Exeter encircle six or seven hundred houses where about twenty-six hundred citizens live. But that makes it

The Largest English Towns in 1377[2]

Rank	Place (cities in capitals)	Taxpayers	Estimated Population
1	LONDON	23,314	40,000
2	YORK	7,248	12,100
3	Bristol	6,345	10,600
4	Coventry	4,817	8,000
5	NORWICH	3,952	6,600
6	LINCOLN	3,569	5,900
7	SALISBURY	3,226	5,400
8	Lynn	3,217	5,400
9	Colchester	2,955	4,900
10	Boston	2,871	4,800
11	Beverley	2,663	4,400
12	Newcastle-upon-Tyne	2,647	4,400
13	CANTERBURY	2,574	4,300
14	Bury St. Edmunds	2,445	4,100
15	Oxford	2,357	3,900
16	Gloucester	2,239	3,700
17	Leicester	2,101	3,500
18	Shrewsbury	2,083	3,500
19	Great Yarmouth	1,941	3,200
20	HEREFORD	1,903	3,200
21	Cambridge	1,902	3,200
22	ELY	1,772	3,000
23	Plymouth	ca. 1,700?	2,800
24	EXETER	1,560	2,600
25	Kingston upon Hull	1,557	2,600
26	WORCESTER	1,557	2,600
27	Ipswich	1,507	2,500
28	Northampton	1,477	2,500
29	Nottingham	1,447	2,400
30	WINCHESTER	1,440	2,400

the twenty-fourth largest community in the whole kingdom. Only the very largest—London, with more than forty thousand inhabitants—can properly be called a great city when compared to the largest Continental cities of Bruges, Ghent, Paris, Venice, Florence, and Rome, all of which have in excess of fifty thousand. However, do not be misled into thinking that towns like Exeter are small, quiet places. The inns add considerably to the total, albeit on a continually shifting basis. Travelers of all sorts—clergymen, merchants, messengers, king's officers, judges, clerks, master masons, carpenters, painters, pilgrims, itinerant preachers, and musicians—are to be found every day in a town. In addition you will come across crowds of local people coming in from the countryside to buy goods and services or to bring their produce to the retailers. When you think of the sheer variety of wares and services which the city provides, from metalwork to leatherwork, from the sheriff's courts and scriveners' offices to apothecaries' and spicemongers' shops, it soon becomes clear how the daytime population of a city can be two or even three times as great as the number of people living within the walls. And on a special occasion—during a fair, for example—it can be many times greater.

The total of 100,000 taxpayers in the thirty largest communities indicates that about 170,000 people—about 6 or 7 percent of the population of the kingdom—live in towns. There are about two hundred other market towns in England with more than four hundred inhabitants. In total, about 12 percent of English people live in a town of some sort, even if it be a small town of just a hundred families.[3] It follows that the majority live in rural areas, coming into their local town or city when necessary. The majority walk in, and walk home, carrying whatever they have bought or driving whatever livestock they have to sell. It is this purposeful coming and going of people, this movement, which makes a medieval city feel so vibrant and alive.

Town Houses

The range of people living in a city is matched by the wide variety of buildings to be found within the walls. You have already seen some of the most handsome and prestigious houses, situated on the widest, grandest, and cleanest streets, which are almost always those leading from the principal gates into the center of town. But not all citizens dwell in the luxury of handsome three-storey houses. You will have noticed the small alleys, sometimes no more than six or seven feet wide. They look dark on account of the jetties of upper storeys which close in over the thoroughfare, so that the second and third storeys of houses facing each other come within just three or four feet. Houses here have little light and probably no outside space. Some alleys are barely more substantial than muddy paths. If there are no servants to clear them, and if the householders fail to clean them, before long they become dank, smelly, and altogether unsavory. Walk along one of them in winter, on a murky afternoon in the rain, and your impression of richness and civic pride will soon be washed away. The rain splashes down into wide muddy puddles through which you will have to pass, and the lack of light (due to the lowering clouds and the overarching houses) rinses all color from the scene. Then you see the rivulets of water trickling between the buckets of offal and kitchen rubbish outside a house, carrying the liquid of rotting food into the street. Next time you walk along here in the churned-up mud, the stench of decay will fill your nostrils.

These two- and three-storey buildings are nowhere near the bottom end of the housing hierarchy. If you walk down a few more of these dark alleys, you will see that there are turnings off which are even narrower. The most densely inhabited areas of a city are warrens of tiny lanes and paths, sometimes no more than three or four feet wide. Here you find the poorest houses: low, single-storey rows of old timber buildings, with no proper foundations, subdivided into small rented rooms. You can see that they are old: the shutters hang at angles or have disappeared completely. The shingles (wooden tiles) are slipping from the roofs, which are covered in lichen and moss or streaked with birdlime. The paths and alleys leading to them are little more than stinking drains, effectively open sewers. They are the most dilapidated buildings in the city, but because they are not on a main street, and because they do not threaten civic pride (because no visitors or wealthy people see them), the authorities do not force the owners to keep them in good repair. If a door is open, you may just discern in the gloom a single room divided into two unequal parts, the smaller for the children to sleep in, and the other for cooking and the adults' mattresses. There is often no toilet, just a bucket (to be emptied at Shitbrook). The tenants of these houses spend almost the whole day away from home, at their workplaces; they eat in the street and urinate and defecate where they can, ideally in the municipal toilets on the city bridge. Their children grow up similarly out of doors, playing in the street. They were the urchins who ran up to you when you first approached the city gate.

Walking through the alleys and lanes of a medieval city, you are bound to come face-to-face with a high wall. This is not the great wall encircling the settlement but one of a number of subdivisions you can expect to find—around monasteries, for example, or protecting the houses of rich knights, prelates, and lords. In most cities you will find the precincts of the cathedral area enclosed by a wall, with gates allowing people in during daylight hours and firmly keeping them out after dark. Similarly, the older monasteries, which may date back to Saxon times, tend to be located in the center of the city. All towns have at least one walled-off religious enclosure, and some have more than a dozen. For this reason, space inside even the most extensive city is relatively scarce. Often a third of the whole area inside the walls is given over to the monasteries and religious precincts. Add the tenth or so given over to the royal castle, and a similar area for the parish churches, and it is clear that almost the entire population has to live in half the city—with most of the best sites occupied by the large houses of the wealthy. Hence the immigrant population has to be squeezed into small tenements constructed on the sites of destroyed houses or alongside a churchyard. Few inhabitants of these slums make enough money to move up into the houses of the prosperous traders and freemen of the town.

Walk back to the market square or the main market street of the city and look around. Notice how almost all the houses are narrow and tall. Each is no more than about fifteen or sixteen feet wide. Most are three or four storeys in height, with shutters either side of the unglazed windows. This arrangement of narrow, tall houses means that many merchants can have a frontage on the main marketplace. At ground level you see the heavy oak door to the building. To its side, and occupying most of the front of the house, is the shop front. At night and on Sundays this is closed up and looks like a wooden barricade across a large window. But during trading hours the lower half is hinged down to form a display counter and the upper half is hinged up, and propped, to provide a shelter for the goods. The shop inside may actually be a workshop—perhaps of a leatherworker, jeweler, tailor, shoemaker, or similar craftsman. Other traders—butchers and fishmongers, for instance—tend to work out of doors, standing in front of their counters, using their shops' interiors as storage areas. In either case, the house above is where the trader and his family live. Only the richest merchants—those who specialize in goods transported in bulk, by sea—have separate houses and warehouses. This close relationship of residence and work premises means that many shop buildings have some fine touches of decoration: tiled or slate-hung upper storeys, or projecting wooden beams with carved corner pieces. Some even boast carved and painted coats of arms or heraldic beasts.

And then you turn a corner and see some totally different houses, altogether larger and set sideways onto the street. Your eye is immediately drawn to the pointed gatehouse, with a crenellated stone tower above, or the long wooden house with large oriel windows projecting over the road. These are the houses of the wealthiest and most important citizens. Just as the various types of traders congregate together—the dyers by a watercourse, the cloth merchants in Cloth Street, the butchers in Butchers Row—the majority of the most influential citizens also live close to one another in the widest, most prominent streets. Here you may find the town house of a major financier next to that of a knight or an archdeacon. At the start of the century such houses may well be still made of wood, but increasingly they are being rebuilt so that by 1400 the majority are proud and sturdy stone structures, with chimneys and glazed windows. This is why, when gazing down a street of well-spaced high-status town mansions, you will invariably see one or two covered in scaffolding. Close inspection will reveal that the scaffolding is made up of poles of alder and ash lashed together, supporting planks of poplar, with pulleys for raising and maneuvering stones and baskets of tiles. In this way, the dilapidated remains of the thirteenth century are gradually being swept away, and new and extended structures are taking their place.

These types of accommodation—from the single-room alleyway slums to the tall merchants' houses and the wide stone mansions of the wealthy—do not fully illustrate the variety in building and accommodation in a city. There are, in addition, the smart houses of the canons and other officers within the cathedral precinct, each with its scriptorium, chapel, and library as well as living quarters. In the case of Exeter, there is the royal castle, with its ancient gatehouse (which is already three hundred years old by the time the Black Prince visits it in 1372). There is the guildhall abutting the high street, the bishop's palace adjacent to the cathedral, and the College of the Vicars Choral (who sing Mass in the cathedral) just outside the cathedral close. The finest inns, with their signs displayed above their wide arched gates, are to be found on the main streets. The towers of the town gate-houses also provide accommodation to a select few civic servants. At the bottom end of society, accommodation for some visitors is pro-vided by letting out sleeping space in the barns and stables that are to be found dotted around the city. Many houses are subdivided so that, in a row of three old traders' houses, you might find a dozen poor families. There are also the monastic guesthouses, the friaries, and the hospitals. And as you leave the city itself and pass into the suburbs you will have the distinct impression that, while the residents might be rel-atively few in number, the structures in which they live show greater variety than any modern city, even though the latter has twenty or thirty times as many inhabitants.

One last thing. Before you leave, turn around and look back along the main street. Have you noticed that the roads are practically the only public spaces? There are no public parks, no public gardens, and large open squares are very rare in English cities except where they serve as the marketplace. The street is the sole common outdoor do-main. The guildhall is only for freemen of the city, the parish churches are only for parishioners. When people gather together in large num-bers they meet in the streets, often in the marketplace or at the market cross. It is there that news is disseminated by the town crier, jugglers perform, and friars preach. But the market cross is only the central point in this network of conversations. Gossip is spread by men and women meeting in the lanes and alleys, at the shops, in the market itself, or at the water conduits. It is not just the buildings that make a medieval city but the spaces between them.

London

No trip to medieval England would be complete without a visit to London. It is not just the largest city in England but also the richest, the most vibrant, the most polluted, the smelliest, the most powerful, the most colorful, the most violent, and the most diverse. For most of the century the adjacent town of Westminster—joined to the city by the long elegant street called the Strand—is also the permanent seat of government. To be precise, it *becomes* the permanent seat of government. In 1300 the government is still predominantly itinerant, following the king as he journeys around the kingdom. However, from 1337 Edward III increasingly situates his civil service in one place, at Westminster. His chancellor, treasurer, and other officers of state all issue their letters from permanent offices there. After the last meeting at York (1335), parliaments too are normally held at Westminster. Richard II does hold six of his twenty-four parliaments elsewhere (at Gloucester, Northampton, Salisbury, Cambridge, Winchester, and Shrewsbury), but doing so only strengthens the feeling that Westminster is the proper place for parliamentary assemblies, so that the commons can more easily attend. All these developments, plus London's links with European traders and banking houses, enhance the standing of the capital. Its importance as an economic and a political center at the end of the century is greater than that of all the other cities in England combined.

Visitors arriving in London are overwhelmed by the spectacle— stunned by the sight of so many houses, so many shops, so many wide streets (in excess of twenty feet), and so many markets. They remark on the number of swans gracefully moving up the river, and on the whitewashed arches of London Bridge. They are engrossed by the hundreds of small boats bobbing up and down the Thames. By day the quays seem very busy, with both local and international trade, for ships of a hundred tons can dock here, bringing merchants and their goods from as far as the Baltic and the Mediterranean. Visitors are equally fascinated by the crowds. The forty thousand inhabitants of the capital are joined by travelers and businessmen from all the corners of Christendom. So many of them are dressed in fine velvet, satin, and damask that all you can do is gawp at their finery as they swish into this shop or strut out of that one, attended by their servants.

London, like every city, is a place of huge contrasts. The streets— even the main ones—have tubs of putrid water positioned here and there, supposedly in case of fire but more often than not full of

Ten Places to See in London

1. London Bridge. The nineteen huge arches spanning the Thames constitute one of the engineering marvels of the kingdom. The surface is twenty-eight feet wide, with buildings taking up seven feet on either side. These are cantilevered for an extra seven feet out over the river, with shops opening onto the bridge and merchants' houses above. There is a chapel dedicated to St. Thomas halfway along and a drawbridge for the security of the city towards the southern end. Watch out for the rapids between the arches at changes of the tide; the city youths take bets on shooting them in rowboats.

2. St. Paul's Cathedral. This church, started in the twelfth century and recently extended (finished in 1314), is one of the most impressive in the country. At 585 feet long, it is the third-longest church in the whole of Christendom. Its 489-foot spire is the second tallest in England, dwarfing that of Salisbury (404 feet) and second only to that of Lincoln Cathedral (535 feet). But forget statistics; it is the beauty of the church—especially its rose window at the east end and its chapter house—for which it deserves to be on any list of London sights.

3. The Royal Palace in the Tower of London. You are, of course, familiar with the White Tower, the great building left by William the Conqueror, but most of the visible castle—including the moat—actually dates from the thirteenth century. Here is situated an extensive royal palace, including a great hall, royal solar (private living room), and a multitude of lordly chambers. In addition, a royal mint is based here, as are the royal library and the royal menagerie. Edward III's collection of lions, leopards, and other big cats is kept here from the late 1330s and is continually being supplemented with new animals.

4. London Wall. All great cities are walled but London's wall is special. It rises to a height of eighteen feet and has no fewer than seven great gatehouses: Ludgate, Newgate, Aldersgate, Cripplegate, Bishopsgate, Aldgate, and Bridgegate (the last leading onto London Bridge). These are the city's security at night; their immense oak doors are secured by heavy drawbars. In times of war the citizens can defend their city as if it were an immense castle.

5. Smithfield, just outside the city walls, is home to the main meat market of the city. Needless to say, this is where people regularly meet in the course of shopping. Even more people gather, however, for the three-day fair held here every St. Bartholomew's Day (August 24). As it is still a field, literally, it provides a suitable ground for jousts and tournaments.

6. The Strand runs from the bridge over the Fleet, just outside Ludgate, along the north bank of the Thames to Westminster. Not only does it afford the medieval traveler the best view of the river, it is also where the most prestigious houses are situated. Several bishops have palaces along this street. Most impressive of all is the Savoy, a royal palace which is home to Edward III in his youth. Later Edward passes it on to his son, John of Gaunt, under whom it becomes the most wonderful town house anywhere in the kingdom. However, it is burnt to the ground during the Peasant's Revolt (1381) and remains a burnt-out shell for the rest of the century.

7. Westminster Palace. The ancient great hall, built in the eleventh century, is the scene of many famous feasts. In the last decade of the fourteenth century, Richard II replaces the old twin-aisled layout with an incredible single-span wooden roof, one of the most stunning carpentry achievements of any age, designed in part by the great architect Henry Yevele. Directly across the courtyard you will see Edward III's bell tower, completed in 1367, also designed by Yevele. The bell hanging within it, called "The Edward," weighs just over four tons and is the forerunner of Big Ben. Also within the precincts are the main chambers of the government, namely the Painted Chamber, the Marcolf Chamber, and the White Chamber (the rooms where the Houses of Parliament meet); the Exchequer, the Royal Courts of Justice, and the royal chapel (St. Stephen's). Here too you will find the private royal residences, the Prince's Palace (the chambers of the prince of Wales), Queen Eleanor's palace, and, most importantly, the Privy Palace, where the king spends time with his family and favorites. Edward II keeps a chamber here for his friend Piers Gaveston; Queen Isabella has one for Roger Mortimer.[6]

8. The Church of Westminster Abbey was almost entirely rebuilt by Henry III in the thirteenth century at a cost of more than £41,000 (making it the second-most expensive building in the whole of medieval England).[7] Here Henry III himself is buried, together with two of his fourteenth-century successors: Edward I (d. 1307) and Edward III (d. 1377). The finished but still-empty tomb of Richard II (d. 1399) is also here, awaiting his reburial in the reign of Henry V. Do note the brilliant wall paintings, which do not survive into modern times. Similarly make sure you see the shrine of St. Edward the Confessor, plated with gold and encrusted with precious jewels.

9. Tyburn. Most towns and cities execute their thieves and murderers outside the gates of the castle. London is different. The place for common thieves to be hanged is at the junction of Tyburn Road (the forerunner of Oxford Street) and Watling Street (one day to be Edgware Road). Gallows stand here permanently, beneath the high elm trees which grow beside the Tyburn stream, and executions take place almost every day. The best-attended are those of high-status traitors. Roger Mortimer is executed here in 1330, his naked body being left on the gallows for two days.

10. The Southwark Stews or bathhouses are a tourist attraction of an altogether different sort. Prostitutes are not tolerated in London except in one street, Cock Lane. Hence Londoners and visitors resort to the stews at Southwark, on the other side of the river. Here men may eat and drink; have a hot, scented bath; and spend time in female company. In 1374 there are eighteen establishments, all run by Flemish women. Contrary to what you might expect, there is little or no stigma attached to those who frequent the stews: there are few sexually contracted diseases and the marriage vows only require the fidelity of the female partner; the man may do as he pleases. Some clergymen rail against such immorality, of course, but few directly allude to Southwark. Most of the bathhouses are rented from the bishop of Winchester.

decaying rubbish. The few streets that do preserve some vestige of road surface are so badly paved that the stones serve more to preserve the puddles than to assist transport. Elsewhere the heavily trodden mud seems to last all year. Inhabitants will draw your attention to how "evil smelling" this mud is just after it has rained (as if you need telling). And yet these are not the worst of London's problems. The stench and obstruction of the animal dung, vegetable rubbish, fish remains, and entrails of beasts present problems of public sanitation on a scale unmatched by any other town in England. With forty thousand permanent citizens and sometimes as many as one hundred thousand mouths to feed and bowels to evacuate, it is impossible for a city with no sewage system to cope. You will see rats everywhere. The place is infested with them. Such is the level of detritus, especially in the town ditches, that it is also infested with dogs and pigs. There are frequent attempts to eradicate the wild pig population, but each one bears testimony to the failure of the previous effort. If you cannot get rid of the pigs, what hope is there for eradicating the rats?

The fundamental problem is that of scale. London is a walled city spilling over into its suburbs. There are more than a hundred over-populated parishes. Even after the Great Plague of 1348–49—which kills off the citizens at the rate of two hundred each day—people arrive continually from the countryside to take their place. Thus there is an unremitting stream of residential rubbish. There is also a constant demand for more products. London is a major manufacturing center and so it consumes, among other things, thousands of animal carcasses and hides. The easiest way of transporting these is on the hoof, alive, but this means slaughtering, skinning, and butchering thousands of animals daily in residential areas. At the start of the century you can find tanning—one of the smelliest occupations of all—being carried on next to people's houses. Likewise pelterers (sellers of animal skins) and fullers (cleaners of raw wool) ply their trades in streets alongside spicemongers and apothecaries. The resultant incongruity is like having a perfume shop situated next to a fishmonger's—but far worse, for the smell of rotting meat is associated with diseases in the medieval mind, often for good reasons. You know things are really bad when, in 1355, the London authorities issue an order preventing any more excrement from being thrown into the ditch around the Fleet Prison on account of fears for the health of the prisoners.[4]

The state of London does improve. This is largely due to the efforts of successive mayors and aldermen to clean up the streets. The first step is the establishment of a mechanism for appointing official swine killers, who are paid 4d for each pig they remove. In 1309 punitive fines are levied on those who leave human or animal excrement in the streets and lanes: 40d for a first offense, 80d for a second.[5] In 1310 tailors and pelterers are forbidden from scouring furs in the main streets during daylight hours, on penalty of imprisonment. The following year the flaying of dead horses is prohibited within the city walls. From 1357 there are rules against leaving dung, crates, and empty barrels lying by the doors of houses, and against throwing rubbish into the Thames and the Fleet, the latter river being almost completely blocked. In 1371 all slaughtering of large beasts (including sheep) within the city is prohibited; henceforth they must be taken to Stratford Bow or Knightsbridge to be killed. Finally, the passing of the Statute of Cambridge in 1388 makes anyone who throws "dung, garbage, entrails and other ordure" into ditches, ponds, lakes, and rivers liable to pay a fine of £20 to the king. With that legislation, the idea of parliamentary responsibility for public hygiene has finally arrived, and—in London's case especially—not before time.

Forget, if you can, the noxious smells and obstructive rubbish of the city and concentrate on its virtues. Look at how many goldsmiths and silversmiths there are, how many spicemongers' shops, how many silk merchants' emporia. There are people who will declare that London is a great city because you can get all the medicines you require. There are certainly more physicians, surgeons, and apothecaries here than anywhere else in England. You will also find a communal running water supply—fed through a series of conduits—even though the pressure is sometimes low, as a result of all the siphoning off to private houses. On certain special occasions the conduits are even made to run with wine—for example, on the arrival of the captive king of France in 1357, or to celebrate the coronation of Henry IV in 1399.

Small Towns

You might think that a small settlement with three or four streets and about a hundred houses and twenty or so stables does not deserve to be called a town. You would probably describe it as a village, and—with a population of perhaps just five hundred—a small one at that. You would not necessarily be wrong: there are many places this size which are certainly best described as villages. But similarly there are many such settlements which are undoubtedly towns. What distinguishes them as such is their market.

All the reasons for emphasizing the importance of the city to its hinterland also apply to small towns. If they have a market, people will come to buy and sell. Farmers regularly need new plowshares, for which they must come into town. They also need to sell their livestock and grain. They or their wives need to buy bronze or brass vessels for cooking, and salt, candles, needles, leather goods, and other items. If you happen to live in a remote manor, perhaps twenty-five miles from the nearest city, you do not want to travel that far for minor commodities, such as a few nails to mend a broken trestle. It would take you two days to get there and back and the cost of a night's accommodation. Hence the need for so many small market towns—by 1300 almost nowhere in England is more than eight miles from one, and most places are within six miles. That is a far more manageable journey for the man in need of a few nails or a plowshare.

The small towns of medieval England are unlike the cities and large towns. They do not have eighteen-foot-high stone walls around the perimeter. Nor do they have substantial gatehouses. They tend to be gathered around a marketplace, with the parish church on one side (usually the east), with the houses themselves and their garden walls marking the boundaries. The center is generally the market cross. The other principal structures, apart from the church, are the manor house, the rectory or vicarage, and the inns. You will find no guildhall here, nor a monastery or friary, although it is possible there is a hospital, for the accommodation of poor travelers. If not, there may well be a church house, fulfilling much the same purpose.

The streets are muddy, rutted, and uneven, the center of each one being a drain carrying whatever detritus has been discarded by townsmen and market visitors. As for the marketplace itself, it has probably been partially filled with ramshackle wooden houses. Over the years, lines of market stalls have become rows of two- and three-storey houses in which traders live above their shops. They have little or no outside space. Hence they add to the density of even the smallest town, making the once-spacious marketplace into a series of narrow alleys. The strict orders stopping unsavory trades being carried on in the main streets do not apply in a small town. There is every likelihood that as you glance into the workshops you will see piles of animal entrails being slopped into a bucket. Similarly there are normally no rules preventing roofs from being thatched (unlike in a city or large town). Hence these rows of cheap houses in marketplaces present a huge fire risk, being built of wood and cob (a mixture of clay, straw, dung, and animal hair) with roofs of thatch. When one catches alight, the whole line tends to go up in flames. Unsurprisingly such a conflagration only encourages the lord to build a replacement row on similarly shaky principles. Within a few months, the streets are foul with debris again and the alleys partially blocked by empty barrels and broken crates, the conflagration all but forgotten.

Small towns are not just muddy carbuncles on the medieval landscape. Each preserves at least part of its original open market square, and in summer, when the stalls are all set up, and the shops are open, with the sunlight shining onto the wooden worktops, there is a totally different feel to them. The size of the crowd that gathers on market days will surprise you: several hundred people come in from farms and manors in the surrounding parishes. In addition there are the travelers and the long-distance merchants who journey from market to market selling their wares. Colors abound, music is to be heard in the streets. The alehouses and inns are full to overflowing; there is laughter, shouting, and banter, and much parading of strutting horses. Most of all there is a sense of excitement that leaves you in no doubt that this small community of a hundred houses is not merely a provincial outpost of the trading world but an integral part of it. The holding of a market has transformed this part of the landscape into a hubbub of commerce, discussion, gossip, and news, if only for one day each week.

The Countryside

In summer the roads are dusty. Carts and packhorses trundle along, overtaken by groups of pedestrians and the occasional galloping messenger. If you escape your fellow travelers, the road is quiet. There is suddenly nothing to hear except the birdsong, the rumble and creak of cartwheels, and perhaps the rushing water of a stream or a river. The quiet distance of the hills and fields becomes the focus of your attention.

In the modern world, an English field is a small square patch of ground between two and ten acres. You are used to seeing them all spread out across the hills like a patchwork quilt. They are very different in the fourteenth century. Throughout most of the country—in fact in all areas apart from Devon and Cornwall, parts of Kent and Essex, and the northwest—you will encounter massive, irregularly shaped fields of between seven hundred and twelve hundred acres, with no hedges, fences, or walls. Within each huge field there are individual strips of land, each one of about an acre, marked out and maintained separately by tenants, so that they resemble an enormous set of allotments. These strips are all grouped in "furlongs"—not to be confused with the unit of distance used in more recent times—and the furlongs are surrounded by "baulks," or paths. School history lessons will probably have led you to believe that one in every two or three fields is left fallow every second or third year, but, as you can see for yourself, it is not the huge fields that are left fallow but the individual furlongs within them. Two out of every three furlongs are planted with grain of some sort—mostly wheat, oats, and barley—but every third one is left fallow, grazed in the meantime by cattle, sheep, goats, or pigs.

Around these huge areas of land, bounded by ditches and earth walls, are commons of grassland for sheep, or woodlands to provide firewood and building materials, or wide low-lying meadows in which to grow hay. Commons and meadows are to be found in all areas of England, many thousands of upland acres being given over to grazing sheep. Here and there you will see small fields or enclosures, surrounded either by stone walls or a ditch, bank, and hedge, where the animals are kept when brought in for winter. But such walls and raised hedges are few in number. You could saunter straight off the highway onto the grass verge and into the fields. Many grazing animals do exactly that and trample all over the harvest crops, much to the annoyance of the villagers and the embarrassment of the hayward whose duty it is to protect the crops.

Contrary to what you might expect, the woodland area is not very much greater than in the modern world—that is to say about

7 percent of the land. However, almost every inch of the medieval woodland is managed carefully. Some areas are cornered off and coppiced and then surrounded by high earth banks with hedges on top to stop the deer and other animals from eating the new shoots. The coppiced trees provide poles for charcoal burning, for fences and staves, or just for firewood. Other areas of the woodland are managed for timber, with spaces being cleared to encourage the trees to grow tall and straight. Great oaks are prized commodities, allowing wide structural spans to be crossed with a single beam. There is relatively little fallen wood lying on the ground, especially in those woods near villages. The right to gather sticks and fallen timber is one which the manorial lord often grants to his tenants, and they take advantage of every last twig of it. In many areas it is their sole means of keeping warm through the long winter months. Where there is more fallen wood than the local tenants can use, the rights to gather it are sold. When the forest of Leicester is impassable, the lord sets a price of 1d for six cartloads of dead wood. That sees the forest floor quickly cleared.[8]

You might notice something else as you wander through the wood. Where are the conifers? In medieval England there are just three coniferous species—Scotch pine, yew, and juniper—and juniper is more of a bush than a tree. There are very few evergreens at all—holly is the only common one—so the winter skyline is particularly bleak. Every other pine, spruce, larch, cedar, cypress, and fir you can think of is absent. In case you see pine or fir boards used in a lord's castle and wonder where the trees are, the answer is that they are in Scandinavia: the timber is imported.[9] Nor will you find holm oaks, red oaks, redwoods, Turkey oaks, or horse chestnuts. The trees that cover England are largely those introduced during the Bronze Age and Roman periods mingled with the species which repopulated the British Isles after the last Ice Age: rowan, ash, alder, field maple, hazel, sweet chestnut, whitebeam, aspen, some poplars, silver birch, beech, lime, walnut, willow, elm, and hornbeam. And of course the good old oak. Both forms of oak are common: the small sessile variety that thrives in hilly areas, and the far more valuable pedunculate sort used for building houses and ships.[10]

Now you are looking more closely at the landscape, you might notice some more subtle differences. That squirrel in the trees above you is a red one—the grey variety has yet to reach Britain. In the fields the cattle are smaller than their modern counterparts: *much* smaller. So too are the sheep. The breeding programs to produce large farm animals will not take place for several centuries. The lichens hanging from the boughs above the path through the wood are probably unfamiliar, as many more varieties survive in the unpolluted air. With darkness closing in over the trees, and a long way yet to the next town, you might wonder whether there are still wolves in medieval England . . . Rest assured that there are not. Well, probably not. The modern tradition states that the last English wolf was killed in North Lancashire in the fourteenth century but you are very unlikely to meet it. Ralph Higden, writing at Chester in 1340, comments that there are now "few wolves" left in England.[11] The last set of instructions to trap and kill wolves is issued in 1289, so if you want to see an indigenous wild wolf, you will have to go to the Highlands of Scotland. There are still some wild boar in the aristocratic hunting parks or chases but they too have been brought almost to the point of extinction, so the chances of your being gored by one are remote. The only really dangerous beast to be encountered in the woods and forests of fourteenth-century England is—as you have probably guessed—man. Groups of armed men, like the Folville and Coterel gangs, do roam the forest roads looking for stragglers to rob. But that is a business to consider in the chapter on law and order, not here.

The Changing Landscape

There is a common misconception that the English countryside is unchanging. "As old as the hills" is a phrase one often hears. However, those hills are slowly being developed. Some are being cleared of undergrowth and coming under the plow for the first time. Some are being enclosed within field boundaries, for the more efficient management of large flocks of sheep. The gentle slopes where oats once grew are now increasingly manured carefully so that they can yield wheat. The flat ground is also changing. The Lincolnshire Fens, Somerset Levels, and Romney Marsh are all much smaller than they used to be; many square miles of marshland have been reclaimed through the construction of long drainage ditches. Wheat, oats, and barley grow where once eels were farmed.

There are many factors affecting change in the medieval landscape, and not all of them are of human origin. For example, the silting up of rivers can hugely affect the patterns of economic development and trade in a region. A prosperous port can very quickly become a ghost town, with a ripple effect on the roads and hinterland. Coastal erosion has similar consequences. At the beginning of the century the East Anglian town of Dunwich is one of the most important ports in England. It has a Benedictine priory, two friaries, six parish churches, two chapels of ease, and a church belonging to the Knights Templar. But if you go there in January 1328, be warned: a terrific storm on the night of the fourteenth will destroy part of the town and shift enough gravel and pebbles to block the harbor entirely. Dunwich's importance to shipping is extinguished. If you stay around the area for the next twenty years you will see the rest of the town suffer, economically decaying after the loss of its harbor. In 1347 another almighty storm sweeps away four hundred houses and two parish churches. Go there and you will hear the crashing of buildings as they collapse into the sea and the screams of terrified people trapped by fallen timbers in the darkness, struggling to escape the sea spray and gale.

Climate change is another factor affecting the landscape. At the beginning of the century it is not unusual to buy English wine. Many noble and royal houses have extensive vineyards. Not so a hundred years later. By 1400 the vineyards of England have all gone. The mean temperature for the year has dropped by about one degree centigrade.[12] This does not sound like a very great difference but it represents a severe setback for some communities. The weather is that little bit colder in every circumstance, including when there are rain clouds nearby. The greater rainfall leads to flooded roads and ruined crops. In 1315–17, during the terrible years of the Great Famine (a consequence of prolonged heavy rainfall), animals may be seen drowned in their flooded pastures. Flooding also leads to greater numbers of parasites and a prevalence of crop diseases. If you tour any part of England during the Great Famine you will see the peasants digging and repairing ditches in the hope of saving their crops. Many fail and whole families die as a consequence, killed by the diseases connected with malnutrition. With fewer people left to tend the land, more acres are abandoned and return to waste ground. In this way even a slight variation in temperature can wreak profound changes upon the countryside.

The factor which affects the landscape more than any other is disease. From 1348, waves of plague depopulate rural manors to such an extent that the entire way of managing the land changes. It is not just the people killed by the disease itself who matter. If a manor suddenly has a third of its workforce wiped out, then a third of the lord's rents go unpaid. The lord might demand that the surviving tenants work twice as hard. However, if he is not paying them and the lord of the next manor who is in need of workers is offering to pay them good money for helping with *his* harvest, they are likely to forget their bonds of service to their original lord and move, taking their families with them, even though it is against the law. In this way the lord of a manor might lose not just a third or a half of his manorial tenants but all of them. Then, faced with the prospect of a useless piece of land, he will wonder how he can make money out of it. One solution is to forget about arable farming altogether and let the manor revert to grazing land where a large flock of sheep can be kept. Thus you may see several thousand acres of well-tended grain around a village turn into a grassy down in just a few years, the ruined church tower left as the sole reminder that here was once a community.

Villages

In total more than a thousand villages have been deserted and are in ruins by the end of the century.[13] Thus a visit to England in 1300 is a very different experience from a visit in 1400. Even those communities that continue to thrive are affected by the Great Plague of 1348–49 ("the Black Death," as we refer to it). In the 1350s and 1360s most villages have abandoned houses on the outskirts. Robbed of their valuable timbers, their roofless cob walls are sadly collapsing into the mud and untended grass and weeds. In some places the repairs to a once-prosperous parish church are beyond the means of the parishioners. Rather than replace the roof of one aisle or one chapel, they will pull down the walls and fill in the arches, shrinking the church to suit both their budget and their requirements.

A fourteenth-century village is far from picturesque. Forget postcard images of flowers in pots at the doors of quaint thatched cottages. It is a visual mess in both layout and presentation. The first house you might see has low walls of limewashed cob and narrow windows with external shutters. A broad thatched roof rises from about chest height to twenty-five feet or more, with smoke coming from one of the crude triangular openings—makeshift louvers—built into either end of the ridge. The thatch itself, which probably is laden with moss and lichen, extends out over the walls by a good eighteen inches, giving the whole building the aspect of a frown. The cobbles of the toft (the area on which the house is built) are uneven and have partially sunk into the mud. A small fence runs around the whole house and garden. Adjacent to the house are water butts and piles of firewood. Nearby are a hut containing the privy, a working cart, the remains of a broken cart, a haywain, a thatched stable, a goose house, a henhouse, a barn, and perhaps a small brew house and bake house.

After a few minutes of staring at this conglomeration, you might start to realize how the whole toft, together with its garden, has been arranged. The firewood is located within easy reach of the house. Likewise the privy—a smelly earth closet—is close (but not too close) to the door. The reason the thatch extends so far out over the walls is to protect them from the rain and snow, for they are composed of cob or clay, straw, and animal dung. The henhouse and goose house are positioned where they are in order to keep them safe from foxes and other predators at night. The broken cart is there so it can be repaired or reused for something else: a principle of recycling which applies to almost everything in medieval England. The garden at the rear is where the householder grows vegetables and herbs. The barrels are deliberately placed to collect rainwater—the cleanest water available—as it runs off the roof. Gradually you realize that there is a wholly different aesthetic at work here. Of course there is no need for flowers in a pot to beautify a medieval house. To the medieval yeoman's eye, the beauty lies in having the necessities of life close at hand. To the family which lives here, beauty lies in the smoke issuing from the roof openings and the knowledge that there is plenty more firewood just outside the door.

Once you understand the aesthetic difference between the modern concept of a comfortable home and the practicalities of living in the fourteenth century, you will begin to understand why the village looks as it does. Practicalities take precedence over beauty and thus become ideals, or things of beauty, in themselves. Yes, the houses appear to

have been scattered all over the place, as if each toft were a giant playing card from a pack that the Devil once tossed over his shoulder in a
fit of pique. Nevertheless there is a reason why each one is where it
is. Many stand alongside the lanes which lead to their allotted acres in
the open fields, permitting easy access for the carts and oxen. The mill
stands where it does because the river runs that way. Other houses
are situated where they are because of their wells, or because there
is a frost pocket that chills a certain area of land in winter, or because
a certain area is liable to flood. The village develops in line with the
contours of necessity. Now you can see why medieval parishioners
have no compunction about simply lopping off one aisle of the church
when the population of the village shrinks. The harmonious symme-
try of the church is destroyed, as they realize; but the resultant smaller
building is better suited for the reduced population, and there is a different sort of harmony in that.

Your first impression on reaching the heart of any one English village will be that all the houses look much the same. Whether they are
built individually or in groups, they are almost all single storey and no
more than sixteen feet from front to back—all medieval houses are
just one room in depth. Village houses also tend to have the same style
of construction and roofing as one another. However, across the wider
landscape, this appearance of similarity is misleading. There are differences of size, purpose, and construction methods. And, of course,
there are substantial regional variations. In some parts of the country
stone is more easily available than oak. On Dartmoor, where large
beams cannot easily be transported but stone is plentiful, people live
in granite houses and thatch them with reed or bracken, which needs
to be replaced annually. In parts of Cornwall houses are built of slate
blocks and roofed with slate slabs. In Kent, elm is used in the frames
of a substantial minority of houses.[14] In most regions, stone buildings
are a status symbol. The majority of rural workers live in timber-
framed houses thatched with straw.

Most village houses measure between twenty-five and forty feet
in length, but some are square one-roomed cottages and others
sixty-foot-long yeomen's houses. The latter are handsome two-bay
halls, with a two-storey wing at each end and many outbuildings.
At the other extreme, a widow's cottage may be just a single-storey,
one-room dwelling of about thirteen feet square, with a porch and a

henhouse by the back door. In some regions, especially in the West Country, you will still find longhouses; these can be anything up to ninety feet long, with one end accommodating cattle and the other the farmer's family. Bear in mind that in these remote regions, a village will not necessarily be a series of grouped houses but may well consist of a number of scattered farmsteads, with only a handful of them being in sight of the parish church.

At the start of the fourteenth century there is a great deal of shoddy building. Many rural workers' houses are built cheaply, without proper foundations but with their beams placed straight into the ground. Of course, without a foundation plinth the timbers rot, so houses of this type need replacing every thirty or forty years. Early in the century, however, things start to change. More houses begin to be built with stone foundations, or footings, for timber and cob walls or rebuilt entirely with walls of stone. The roofs are also improved. A technique is developed in some parts of the country whereby the top level of thatch is replaced regularly while the base level is kept in place. Some of this fourteenth-century base thatch lasts so well it may be found in the roofs of houses in modern times, after more than six hundred years—complete with the dried bodies of medieval grasshoppers and ladybirds which happened to be crawling across it when it was cut.

Apart from the church, the highest-quality buildings in any village are those constructed by the lord of the manor. Some of these are stone residences for the lord and his family. But even if the lord does not reside there himself, there will be a manor house or barton set at the heart of his principal farm or demesne (land that he does not rent out but keeps for his own use). Here all the tenants of the manor come to pay their rents, fines, and other dues to the bailiff and to join in the communal meals held at Christmas and on other special occasions, such as harvesttime. The gamut of farm buildings clustered around a manor house may make it appear more like a hamlet—with its huge threshing barns and haylofts, ox houses and brew houses, stables, slaughterhouse, granary, goose house, henhouse, shearing shed, bailiff's house, and workers' cottages.

Of course there are many other individual buildings which make up the rural landscape. In the past, Cistercian monks were keen to build their monasteries in remote places, and although the great age of monastery building has long since gone, their huge and strikingly

Density of Rural Settlement in England in 1377

Region and County	Rural Poll Tax Payers (over 14 years)	Total Population Per Sq. Mile[15]
East of England		
Bedfordshire	20,339	73
Norfolk	88,797	71
Suffolk	58,610	65
Huntingdonshire	14,169	64
Essex	47,962	52
East Midlands		
Rutland	5,994	70
Northamptonshire	40,225	66
South Coast		
Kent	56,557	61
Dorset	34,241	57
Hampshire	33,241	34
Southwest		
Cornwall	34,274	43
Devon	45,635	29
West Midlands		
Staffordshire	21,465	31
Shropshire	23,574	29
The North		
Lancashire	23,880	22
Westmorland	7,389	16
Cumberland	11,841	13

elegant churches still dominate their valley settings. Likewise, although most castles in England are situated within or adjacent to towns, a few do stand in rural areas, guarding roads and harbors. Sir Edward Dallyngrigge's new fortress at Bodiam in Sussex is a good example; so are the Pomeroy family's castle at Berry in Devon and the Talbot family's seat at Goodrich in Herefordshire. You may also notice the open tin mining in the southwest, where deep scars in the hillsides attest to the quarrying and washing of mineral ore, or the vast fishponds situated on the estates of the great monasteries.

For the sake of advising the would-be visitor, perhaps there is just one other essential thing to say. Not all of rural England is the same. In some of the hilly regions it is not possible to use wheeled transport. This means that the character of the landscape is altogether different from lowland England. Building materials are gathered from the immediate vicinity. Being prone to heavy rainfall, and poor for arable farming, the manors have far lower populations. Many abandoned settlements are to be found in these regions after the Great Plague. Also, being poorer and relatively isolated, these manors are normally ignored by their lords. So they do not attract the best master masons to rebuild the churches or manorial buildings, and the structures that are erected are often provincial in character and amateurish in execution. At the other extreme, areas of East Anglia are very flat and fertile, and thus rich. They are also relatively safe, unlike rural areas bordering on Scotland and Wales.

The largest areas of abandoned landscape are to be found in the far north, in parts of Cumberland and Northumberland. Here there *are* parishes and manors, in theory, but for much of the fourteenth century there are few or no people. This is for three reasons: climate change, plague, and the frequent incursions of the Scots. The ruined houses and chapels are left open to the elements. A huge parish like Bewcastle in Cumberland, consisting of more than forty thousand acres, is almost uninhabited. A similar situation prevails in Northumberland. The land is border land, guarded by the valiant Percy family, lords of Alnwick, but for the most part it is empty. Areas like Redesdale, which were once well populated, have been largely abandoned. The massive parish of Simonburn, measuring thirty-three miles by fourteen and covering more than 150,000 acres, is so sparsely populated that its tithes are insufficient to maintain a single priest. No royal tax collectors go there. No one goes there. Battles take place from time to time, and you will find the odd obstinate crofter eking out a living from a smallholding hidden in a valley, but sometimes you can ride for a whole day in this region and see no one. It is simply not worth building a home in a land where there is a strong likelihood that your crops with be burnt, your animals stolen, and you and your family assaulted and killed by the invading Scots. It is certainly a far cry from the villages and small towns in the Midlands and the south, where young children can be found playing in the dust of the street.

2

The People

No one can tell you exactly how many people there are in fourteenth-century England. Estimates tend to be around 5 million in 1300 (give or take half a million) and around 2.5 million in 1400 (give or take a quarter of a million).[1] The one thing that everyone agrees on is that there are far fewer people at the end of the century than at the start: about half as many. The total population shrinks by 9 to 10 percent between 1315 and 1325, by 30 to 40 percent in the Great Plague of 1348–49, and by a further 15 to 25 percent over the rest of the century. Large numbers of children cannot quickly reverse these losses. As you will have seen from the effects on the landscape, it is a traumatic experience for the whole of society. Not until the 1630s will the population get back to 5 million again, and not until the 1740s will it reach 5.5 million.

How long do these people live? It depends on where you are and what sort of wealth you enjoy. Yeomen in Worcestershire in the first half of the fourteenth century can, at the age of twenty, look forward to an average of twenty-eight years more life; and their successors in the second half can expect another thirty-two years.[2] This does not sound too bad: a lifespan of fifty years, more or less. However, this bald figure means that half of all adults die before they reach fifty. And these are the *prosperous* members of Worcestershire society. Poor peasants in the same area can expect to live for five or six years less. And all these figures are for those who have already reached the age of twenty: half the population will die before this age. Life expectancy at birth can be as low as eighteen, as at the Yorkshire village of Wharram Percy.

For this reason the majority of medieval people are relatively young. Between 35 and 40 percent of those you will meet are under

fifteen. At the other end of the age spectrum, just 5 percent of fourteenth-century people are aged over sixty-five. There are many more
youths and far fewer old people. The contrast is most striking when
you consider the median age. If you were to line up every modern
English person in age order, the man or woman in the middle would
be thirty-eight. If you were to do the same in the fourteenth century,
the median would be twenty-one. Half the entire population is aged
twenty-one or less.[3]

This preponderance of young people leads to social differences in
every community and field of activity. The average man or woman
in the medieval street has seventeen years' less experience to draw on
in every aspect of his or her lives. He or she has many fewer elders to
ask for advice. When you consider that societies with youthful populations are more violent, tend to be supportive of slavery, and see nothing wrong in holding brutal combats in which men fight to the death
for the sake of entertainment, you realize that society has changed
fundamentally. The Middle Ages are not comparable with ancient
Rome, but the medieval understanding of a bondman's servitude is
not very far removed from slavery, and the enthusiasm for watching
knights jousting is not totally dissimilar to that of Roman citizens
watching gladiators draw blood. There is just one very important difference: medieval audiences know that their tournament fighters are
voluntarily risking injury and death. They are aristocratic knights fighting for pride and glory, not slaves forced to hack each other to pieces
for the amusement of the bloodthirsty masses.

How do medieval people appear? On the whole they are just
slightly shorter than us. The average man is a little over 5' 7" (171 to
172 cm) and the average woman about 5' 2" (158 to 159 cm). Their feet
are also smaller, most men having shoe sizes (English) of 4 to 6 and
most women 1 to 3.[4] However, you will note that the wealthy tend to
be more or less the same height as you.[5] The poor, on the other hand,
tend to be considerably shorter: a disparity due to genetic selection as
well as diet. This gives the nobleman a clear advantage when it comes
to a fight. Talking of fighting, you are bound to come across men who
have lost eyes, ears, or limbs in the French and Scottish wars, or in less
glorious outbursts of violence. A surprisingly large number hobble
about with leg or foot injuries that have never healed properly, often
a result of an accident at work. In some towns one in every twenty

people is getting by with a broken or fractured limb.[6] Then there are accidents of birth to consider. One bishop of Durham, Louis de Beaumont, is renowned for having two clubfeet. Most people have suffered at some time or another from a disease which has affected their youthful beauty (supposing they had some to start with).

It is generally said that medieval men are in their prime in their twenties, mature in their thirties, and growing old in their forties. This means that men have to take on responsibility at a relatively young age. In some towns citizens as young as twelve can serve on juries.[7] Leaders in their twenties are trusted and considered deserving of respect. At the age of just twenty Edward III declares war on the Scots and leads an army into battle despite being outnumbered two to one. This is not some rash act; he commands the full confidence of his nobles, knights, men-at-arms, and infantry. In the modern world he would still be considered too young even to be an MP. When people declare that "children have to grow up so quickly these days," they should pause and reflect on this fact. Medieval boys are expected to work from the age of seven and can be hanged for theft at the same age. They can marry at the age of fourteen and are liable to serve in an army from the age of fifteen. Noblemen might hold office or be given command of an army before they are twenty. At the battle of Crécy (1346) the command of the vanguard—the foremost battalion of the army—is given to Prince Edward, then just sixteen years of age. It is unthinkable that we would put a sixteen-year-old in charge of a battalion, in combat, today.

As for women, you can advance these "prime," "mature," and "growing old" periods of life by six or seven years. A woman is in her prime at seventeen, mature at twenty-five, and growing old by her mid-thirties. In the words of one of Chaucer's characters, a thirty-year-old woman is just "winter forage." Betrothals of boys and girls take place in infancy, and marriage at the age of twelve is approved of for a girl, although cohabitation usually begins at fourteen. Teenage pregnancies are positively encouraged—another significant contrast with modern England. Most girls of good birth are married by the age of sixteen and have produced five or six children by their mid-twenties, although two or three of those will have died. At that age many of them are widows as a result of the Scottish and French wars. That is, of course, presuming they survive the high risks associated with multiple childbirth.

Having said all this, a tiny number of men and women do live into their eighties. That grizzled old knight Sir Geoffrey de Geneville, the brother of the biographer of St. Louis, is still living in the Dominican Friary at Trim in 1314, at the age of eighty-eight.[8] The shrewd Cornish clergyman, linguist, and translator John Trevisa, who comes into the world in about 1326, has yet to depart from it in 1412, aged eighty-six. The chronicler John Hardyng, born in 1377, writes a chronicle about the triumph of the first Lancastrian king, Henry IV, in 1399 and lives long enough to rewrite the whole story with the opposite political slant for the Yorkist king, Edward IV, in the 1460s. He is still alive in 1464 at the age of eighty-seven. Similar extremes of old age are to be found among the English bishops. The average age at election of those in office in 1300 is forty-three. They live for another twenty-one years, taking them to an average age of sixty-four. Those in office in 1400 are, on average, forty-four at the time of their election. They survive for another twenty-three years, taking them to sixty-seven. Among this group are men like Bishop Skirlaw of Durham and Bishop Burghill of Lichfield, who are still in office at the age of seventy. William of Wykeham is still bishop of Winchester at the age of eighty.

The Three Estates

Medieval society thinks of itself like this: there are three sections of society, or "estates," created by God—those who fight, those who pray, and those who work the land. The aristocracy are "those who fight." They protect "those who pray" and "those who work." The clergy do the praying and intercede on behalf of the souls of the fighters and the workers. "Those who work" feed the aristocracy and the clergy through the payment of service, rents, and tithes. In this way each group contributes to the welfare of society as a whole.

It is a neat concept and particularly attractive to those doing the fighting and praying, who use it to justify the gross inequalities in society. But it is a concept that has been increasingly outdated since the twelfth century. Between 1333 and 1346 it is systematically shredded by the English longbowmen, who, although ranked among "those who work," show that they are a far more potent military force than the massed charging ranks of "those who fight." In those few years, "those who work" become "those who fight," thereby threatening to make the old aristocracy redundant. Nevertheless, despite the inadequacy of the model, it is worth using it, if only because it shows how fourteenth-century people themselves understand their class system.

THOSE WHO FIGHT

> The King

> Dukes, Earls, and Barons
> (50 to 80 "tenants-in-chief")

> Knights (about 1,100)
> Esquires and Gentlemen (10,000)
> (who hold their manors from the tenants-in-chief)

As the above diagram shows, "those who fight" includes several tiers, a pyramid of wealth and military responsibility. At the top of the pile is the king, who is the lord of all the land in the kingdom. Those royal estates which are kept in the king's hand bring in an annual income from which the king pays for the royal household, including the various departments of government. In addition, the king can seek extra money to finance military expeditions through subsidies and other taxes, subject to the approval of Parliament.

In the second tier are the lords. There are three ranks: dukes, earls, and barons.[9] The title of duke takes precedence, being invented in 1337 for Edward III's eldest son, Edward of Woodstock, later known as the Black Prince. It is normally a royal title: three of the four dukes created before 1377 are the king's sons. More common are those great lords in the next tier of precedence: the earls. Their number fluctuates between seven and fourteen over the century. The lowest rank of aristocracy is the baronage: the number of barons fluctuates between forty and seventy.

All these lords hold their principal estates *directly* from the king and are thus known as "tenants-in-chief." They normally receive a personal summons to attend each parliament. They constitute the House of Lords. When it comes to fighting, they are all technically bound to serve the king with their retinues at their own expense for forty days each year. In effect, however, those who are willing to serve the king do so for as long as they are required and are compensated for their expenditure accordingly.

Lordly status loosely correlates with income. In theory each earl should receive at least £1,000 from his estates. Most have between £700 and £3,000. The richest is Thomas of Lancaster, who has five earldoms and an income of about £11,000 in 1311. This is exceeded by only two people over the whole century. Second on the fourteenth-century "Rich List" is Queen Isabella, who allocates to herself 20,000 marks (£13,333) per year in 1327–30. First place goes to John of Gaunt, duke of Lancaster, whose gross income from his English and Welsh estates in 1394–95 is in the region of £12,000, in addition to a pension from Castile of about £6,600.[10] Most barons have an income of between £300 and £700, but in a few exceptional cases—Lord Berkeley, for instance—a baron may receive as much as £1,300 per year.

The third tier in the feudal hierarchy is made up of lords of manors held *indirectly* from the king—that is to say, held by local lords from the tenants-in-chief. These local lords do not receive a personal summons to attend parliaments, although they may be elected to represent their country as "knights of the shire." They are not "lords" in the sense of having a baronial title but merely lords over their manorial tenants. In theory all of them with an annual income of £40 or more—about eleven hundred men—should be dubbed knights by the king. Those who are not are called "esquires" (provided they are entitled to bear coats of arms, due to their descent from a knight; otherwise they are just "gentlemen").

The foregoing does not account for all manorial lords. Many lordships are in the hands of clergymen or institutions, such as monasteries or university colleges. Many old manors have been divided between co-heiresses, and so a "lord of the manor" might be the holder of just a quarter of a knight's fee, perhaps less than a thousand acres, yielding as little as £5 per year. There are about ten thousand men who fall into this category of local gentry, with incomes of £5 to £40 per year.[11] To what extent they should be considered among "those who fight" is open to debate. Nevertheless, their legal status and family connections give them influence among their peers and power over their tenants and bondmen, so do not be fooled by their lack of wealth into thinking they are of little consequence.

The Social Hierarchy

Laity (landed and rural men)	Laity (urban)	Clergy
Dukes		Archbishops
Earls		Bishops
		Abbots summoned to Parliament,[12] the prior of the Hospitallers, and the Master of the Templars (to 1308)
Barons		Abbots of lesser abbeys
		Priors of the larger priories, and priors of the mendicant orders (friars)
Knights	Mayors of cities and incorporated towns	Canons of cathedrals, archdeacons, and priors of lesser priories
Esquires and gentlemen with £200 or more income from land	The richest merchants, with more than £1,000 capital, and aldermen of cities and incorporated towns	Other higher clergy and wealthy rectors (normally of multiple parishes)
Esquires and gentlemen with £100 income from land	Middling merchants with £500 capital or more	Rectors of single parishes

Franklins/yeomen	Merchants with less than £500 capital; some professionals (e.g. physicians, lawyers, and a few master masons/ master carpenters)	Vicars of parishes
Husbandmen (freemen)	Shopkeepers, local traders, skilled workers, and freemen of towns	Chaplains, friars, and minor clergy
Villeins (unfree)	Laborers	Hermits
Domestic servants	Domestic servants	
	Beggars	

Those Who Pray

The hierarchy of the English clergy is similar to that of the secular lords. There are spiritual noblemen—archbishops, bishops, and the abbots of the major religious houses—and subordinate levels: archdeacons, deans, canons, and the lesser clergy.

Top of the pile in England are the archbishops of Canterbury and York. Of these two, the archbishop of Canterbury takes precedence. His province extends over fourteen of the seventeen English dioceses and all four of the Welsh ones.[13] Each diocese is presided over by a bishop, who is directly subordinate to the archbishop. The archbishop of York is not subordinate to the archbishop of Canterbury but is obliged to yield precedence to his southern counterpart. His province covers the three other English dioceses (Carlisle, Durham, and York). There are a few other men dressed in ecclesiastical robes who are designated bishops. These are suffragan archbishops and bishops appointed by the pope and given exotic titles such as "Archbishop of Damascus," "Bishop of Chrysopolis," or "Archbishop of Nazareth," but their authority comes from the pope; they are not part of the English church hierarchy.

With regard to the pope, you need to bear two things in mind. The first is that for most of the century the pope is not based in Rome but in Avignon, in the south of France. The second is that, from 1378, there are actually two popes. These divergences from the norm all arise from a bitter argument between Pope Boniface VIII and King Philip of France around 1300. After Boniface's death in 1303 the dispute is temporarily patched up by his successor, Benedict XI, but even in death Boniface continues to irritate the French king. The next pope after Benedict, Clement V, is a Francophile and does his best to placate Philip by creating many more French cardinals. In addition, he establishes himself and the papal court at Avignon. The extra French cardinals consistently elect French popes, who appoint more French cardinals, who in turn elect more French popes until 1378. In that year the Great Schism occurs in the Church. The Scots, French, and Spanish support the election of yet another French pope, Clement VII, who remains at Avignon. The English, Italians, and most of the German countries which make up the Holy Roman Empire regard Clement as an antipope and instead support the election of Pope Urban VI, who returns to Italy and nominally bases his court at Rome. So, in a nutshell: until 1305 there is just one pope, based in Rome. From 1305 to 1378 there is just one pope and he is at Avignon. From 1378 to the end of the century there are two popes, one at Avignon and the other in Rome, and the English recognize only the latter.

The reason why this is important is that the pope appoints every archbishop, bishop, and archdeacon in Christendom, including the British Isles. This gives him huge influence. When an English bishop dies, the king can write to the pope asking for his nominated candidate to be appointed, but the choice remains the pope's. Needless to say, the French popes (who have authority in England before the schism of 1378) are not always swayed by the requests of English kings. There are other problems too. The Avignon popes are far happier appointing hangers-on at Avignon to positions of ecclesiastical authority than distant Englishmen whom they might never have met. Thus many archdeacons and canons in the English church are foreigners, and many of these never visit England but simply pocket the money accruing from their English appointments. Finally, England is at war with France. Resentment against the French popes is understandably high.

Like their secular counterparts, most archbishops and bishops are tenants-in-chief, holding manors directly from the king. Each English bishop receives a similar amount to an earl: a sum between £3,500 per year (Canterbury) and £400 per year (Rochester). The bishop of Ely enjoys an income of about £2,500 in 1300; the bishop of Worcester has about £1,200.[14] In a few cases, the comparison between bishops and earls runs even closer. Some of the men who occupy these episcopal thrones are the sons of noblemen and hanker after a life of action. Bishop Hatfield of Durham is given command of the rearmost division in the march across Normandy during the Crécy campaign (1346). Archbishop Zouche of York similarly demonstrates his valor, jointly leading an English army to victory at the battle of Neville's Cross (also 1346). Most remarkable of all, in 1383 Bishop Henry Despenser of Norwich invades Flanders. He claims to be fighting a "crusade" against the French supporters of Pope Clement but instead he attacks the Flemish supporters of Pope Urban (whom the English also recognize). If it is too much to expect an aristocratic bishop to turn the other cheek, you would have thought at least he might obey the commandment "Thou shalt not kill."

The clergy as a whole are split into two sorts. The archbishops and bishops preside over the *secular clergy*—that is to say those priests and men in lesser orders who live in the world and administer to its needs. The *regular clergy* are, for most purposes, outside their jurisdiction, answering instead to the head of their house and ultimately to the head of their Order. Monks and canons withdraw from the world to live lives of quiet contemplation and prayer behind the closed doors of abbeys and priories. Their female equivalents—nuns and canonesses—do likewise. Friars go out into the world to preach, but their female counterparts (the Franciscan nuns, called "Poor Clares," and Dominican nuns) live in priories.

One question you are bound to ask, as you travel around medieval England, is this: if monks have withdrawn from the world to live lives of contemplation and prayer, how come you meet so many of them outside their cloisters, journeying around the country? The answer is monastic business. Abbots and priors need to attend meetings of

Types of Regular Clergy

Type	Orders	Notes
Monastic Orders	• Benedictines (also known as Black Monks, from the color of their habit) • Cluniacs • Cistercians (White Monks) • Carthusians	Monks follow the Rule of St. Benedict. They withdraw from the secular world, to contemplate and pray, and have no possessions of their own. The Benedictines are the oldest Order, and the most lax in their observance of the Rule. The Cistercians are much stricter, and the Carthusians stricter still, living in cloistered monastic cells.
Regular Canons	• Augustinian Canons (Austin Canons or Black Canons) • Premonstratensians (White Canons) • Gilbertines • Grandmontines	Like monks except that they follow the teachings of St. Augustine of Hippo. The Order of St. Gilbert of Sempringham is the only monastic order to be founded in England; it permits monks and nuns to live in double monasteries and worship in the same church.
Military Orders	• The Order of the Temple • The Hospital of St. John of Jerusalem (Hospitallers)	Orders of knights originally established to protect the pilgrim routes to the Holy Land. After the abolition of the Templars in 1308, only the Hospitallers have a significant presence in England.

| Mendicant Orders (friars) | • Dominicans (Blackfriars or Friars Preacher) • Franciscans (Greyfriars or Friars Minor) • Carmelites (White Friars) • Austin Friars • Friars of the Holy Cross (Crutched Friars) | Unlike monks, friars go out into the world, preaching the word of God to rich and poor alike. They have given up all their property and taken vows of chastity and abstinence, but otherwise they are free to roam where they will. |

their Order, and many abbots and a couple of priors are summoned to attend Parliament. Some traveling is undertaken by other monks to acquire things—including manuscripts to copy for the monastic-library—or to exchange news. But the vast bulk of monastic business is to oversee the abbey's estates. The monk in Chaucer's "Sea Captain's Tale" is allowed by his abbot to roam where he wants on the pretext of inspecting the monastic granges. Some monasteries have a great number of these, with vast estates all over the south of England. The great Benedictine houses of Glastonbury Abbey and Westminster Abbey have incomes well in excess of £2,000, and more than £3,000 in a good year. Most abbeys have an income of between £30 and £300.[15]

There is huge variety and range to the clergy in England. In addition to those mentioned above, there are hundreds of chaplains and priests in the seven hundred hospitals and chantries up and down the country. Add all these groups together and you begin to realize that "those who pray" are as rich and numerous as "those who fight." In total there are about 650 monasteries in 1348 (350 houses of monks, three hundred of regular canons). There are about two hundred friaries and 150 nunneries, making a total of one thousand religious houses. In 1348 these contain at least twenty thousand men and two thousand women. Add the hospitals—each with a complement of chaplains and other religious staff—and about ten thousand parish incumbents, plus an unknown number of religious hermits, private chaplains, chantry priests singing Masses for the souls of the dead, university theologians, as well as priests serving nuns, and you will see that there are at least thirty thousand full-time religious people in England. As you have to be eighteen to enter a monastery or to become a priest, this means that more than 2 percent of adult males in England are clergymen.

Those Who Work

You would have thought that the last of the three estates would be the most straightforward. "Those who work" equals "peasants." Not much call for hierarchy there, you might suppose. But you would be wrong. There are as many grades of wealth and status among the peasantry as there are among the aristocracy and the clergy combined. The status of a franklin or a yeoman who has a whole yardland (thirty acres) and his own plow team of eight oxen is far higher than that of a villein who is bound to serve his lord and has just one or two acres to his own use. If that franklin's daughter marries a younger son of a gentleman, his status is even higher. If his family provide the officers for the manor—the reeve (manorial overseer), for instance—his status is further enhanced. The idea of all the peasants pulling together as one, equal in rank and wealth, is a modern myth.

It is a moot point whether there actually is a group of people called "peasants." To a manorial lord there is such a group: it is not of great significance to him if one peasant is richer than another; they are all his tenants. However, the word "peasant" is not used at this period. Ask a "peasant" if he *is* one and he will probably just scratch his head and wonder what on earth you are talking about. A clerk will refer to him and his companions as *rustici* (countrymen), *nativi* (those born to servitude), or *villani* (villeins), but these peasants do not refer to one another as *rustici* and not all peasants are villeins. It is not what they have in common which gives them their identity but what sets them apart from one another. Uppermost in their minds are questions such as, Where are you from? How much land have you got? Do you have any practical crafts or skills? Can you play a musical instrument? Were you born out of wedlock? And most of all—more important than every other question of status—Are you a free man?

Freedom is the biggest single division in the peasantry (let us continue to use the word as a catchall for the sake of convenience). Those who are not free are villeins or bondmen. Villeins work the lord's land for him according to a set of customary expectations, normally three days' work per week. In addition they have to perform set tasks, such as plowing and harrowing a certain acreage of the lord's land, or collecting firewood or nuts for the lord from the manorial woods. In return for their service, they have the use of some land, for which they pay rent. At the beginning of the century, about 70 percent of all villeins have the use of between a quarter and a whole yardland; very few have the use of more.[16] On days when they are not working on the lord's land, or after they have finished work (about midafternoon), they can work on their own acres or tend to their gardens. But whatever they produce actually belongs—in law—to their lords, and he can take whatever he wants.

Usually lords demand nothing of their peasants' goods except a "heriot." This is the customary fine of a villein's best beast, or most valuable chattel, which his heirs must give up to the lord on the villein's death. But as one old abbot better versed in law than in diplomacy will tell you, legally his villeins "own nothing but their own bellies."[17] In fact, that abbot could rub even more salt into the wound of his tenants' servitude by reminding them that they have no right to leave his manor for more than a day. If he sells his land, he sells them and their families with it. Nor do they have recourse to any legal judgment but his. They have no right of trial before the royal justices, only in his manorial court. In some manors, the lord has the power of life and death over those found guilty.

There is worse. A lord has power over whom his villeins might marry. If a villein allows his daughter—who is, by implication, also unfree—to marry a man from another manor, then he must pay the lord a fine to compensate him for the loss of further generations of villeins. If a widow has not remarried within a few months of her first husband's death, and the lord's land is in danger of being neglected as a consequence, she will be ordered to choose a capable husband before the next court—normally within three weeks. If she does not, the bailiff or the reeve will select a suitable man for her. If the parties refuse to marry, they will be fined and, if they continue to refuse, imprisoned until they do consent. An arranged marriage, in which the parents choose the bride or bridegroom, is a blessing by comparison. It is not an exaggeration to say that there are aspects of a villein's life which you will find repugnant.

Villeins may escape from their servitude in one of two ways. One is to be made free by the lord. The other is to run away. If a man runs away to a town, and lives there for a year and a day, he is legally free. Of course he will forgo all his possessions in his original manor, and his nearest male relative will be fined.[18] If he is married then his wife and children will be turned out of the house and the family possessions confiscated—so married men do not often escape. If they try, their wives are likely to follow them and drag them home again. Also, it is worth remembering that a free man is not necessarily better off than his unfree cousins. Even if he has a craft or skill, he will not have the tools or money to start up in a trade. Most escapees have nothing to sell but their labor, and that is very cheap. In this way a town is regularly kept populated, mainly by younger sons seeking their fortune. As the poor men in the slums die off from malnutrition, injury, and disease, there is a regular stream of incoming young men ready to take their place, living in the cheap subdivided tenements while eking out a living by laboring in dangerous and unsavory occupations.

Just as there is a great difference between the villeins on the manor—between those who have more than thirty acres and those who have just one or two—there is a considerable range of wealth and status among the franklins and yeomen (freemen). At the high end are those who have acquired enough freehold land to sustain their families comfortably and to employ others to help them farm their acres. They also have several servants. But even within this group there is a degree of variation. At the very top there are some who have undertaken to rent the entire manor from the lord, farming the whole estate, court and all, as if they themselves were the lords. This is not that uncommon after the Great Plague, when lords are increasingly eager to offload the financial risk of managing their estates by renting them out lock, stock, and barrel for fixed rents.[19] The franklins who take on such an estate further blur the distinction between the gentry and the peasantry by marrying the daughters of esquires. A man who appoints his own bailiff, is attended by servants, has cousins among the gentry, and lords it over his fellow villagers in the manorial court hardly fits the usual image of a peasant.

The majority of freemen are not as well off as farmers of manors. Like villeins, most of them have less than a yardland in the common fields. Obviously they cannot farm all thirty acres at once—a third or so must be left fallow—so they have to earn a living from their remaining fifteen or twenty acres. In a good year this will leave them with a cash surplus; in a bad year they will struggle to get by. They may have other rights, such as the right to graze their livestock on the lord's common or to gather firewood in the wood, but the freeholder has a hard time of it when sequential harvests are bad. Those freeholders who have less than eight acres—about half of all free peasants—have the hardest time of all. In terrible years (like the Great Famine of 1315–17) they can see that the villeins are economically better off than they are. In such circumstances there is little to do but sell up to a wealthier, more secure franklin and start laboring.

For all these reasons, when you trot into a village on your palfrey, and see one villager's wife leaning over a wall talking to another, and think to yourself how harmonious everything seems to be, just reflect that there are many inequalities, tensions, and fears which you cannot see. The three or four families from which the local officers are most often drawn (the reeve, jurors, chief tithing-men, ale-tasters, constable, and hayward) may well be resented by those who have suffered most from their accusations in the manorial court. Some families consider other families beneath them on account of their villein status or because one of them is a servant. In most places the manorial lord will be held in a special position of esteem or hatred. The general philosophy—especially in the early part of the century—is that the harsher a lord is towards his tenants, the more he will be feared and respected, be he an abbot or a knight. And on the whole peasants *do* respect their lords. This is not surprising when you reflect that villeins in particular are dependent on their lords for their lands and their livelihoods, as well as customary feasts at harvesttime and Christmas. It is relatively rare for tenants to ransack and loot their lord's houses and granges. The idea expressed during the Peasants' Revolt of 1381—that all peasants should be freed from their manorial bonds—is a reflection of the changing circumstances after the Great Plague and not of a long tradition of widespread interclass bitterness.

Those Outside the Three Estates

You will already have realized many of the shortcomings of the "three estates" model. Bishops may take up arms and fight, and are manorial lords just like earls and barons. In some cases a rich peasant may be indistinguishable from a poor gentleman. But a bigger failing with the model lies in the fact that many people fall outside it altogether. For example, where are the merchants? As shown in chapter 1, about an eighth of the population lives in a town; so where do these people appear in the scheme of "the three estates"? They hardly count among "those who work," as their income does not support a lord. And what about everyone else? Where are the jugglers, the acrobats, and the jesters? What about the mariners, servants, and the emerging professions such as physicians and lawyers? Where do they fit into the three estates?

The people who fall outside the three estates are among the most interesting you will meet. Consider the servants. You might assume that a servant is the lowest ranking person of all, beneath even those who work. But as any servant will tell you, service has its reward, and the level of that reward depends on whom you serve and in what capacity. A royal sergeant-at-arms is a servant but, as a man-at-arms authorized to act as a king's enforcer, he commands a great deal of authority—more than the rich merchants whose merchandise he may be sent to impound. Similarly the man who acts as a lord's steward may be a manorial lord in his own right. A bailiff overseeing the running of a manor is similarly a lord's servant, but he has more authority than probably everyone else resident on the manor. A lord's son is often sent to learn how to behave by being placed in the service of another lord: he too is a servant, but not lowly in status, even though he receives no income. At the bottom end of the scale, a ten-year-old boy serving in the house of a hardworking villein or poor franklin has a very low status, lower than the other peasants. He might grow up to be a peasant farmer in his own right, but in the meantime he is the lowest of the low. His wages reflect this; boys and girls often receive nothing at all for their labor but board and lodging.

You can say similar things about merchants. At the top end of society there are some very wealthy merchants. Almost all the really rich ones—international traders with goods and property worth £1,000 or more—live in London. Their incomes, which roughly equate to a tenth of their wealth, put them on a par with wealthy knights. Approximately 14 percent of all London merchants fall into this category.[20] Many more have less than £50 worth of goods, and commensurately lower incomes. A significant number of them mix their trading of goods with renting-out of town houses in order to make a living. Lower down the economic ladder you have the various traders who can hardly be called merchants at all, on account of their relatively low incomes and the limited and specific nature of their work. Few of them earn as much as £5 per year. Those tailors, bakers, apothecaries, cordwainers, and butchers making £4 annually are doing well—much better than the average water carrier or laborer. At the bottom of the hierarchy are those who are not even freemen of the city and who have no right to carry on a trade within the walls. In the first half of the century, carters are lucky if they make £2 10s annually, and laborers if they make £2 (see chapter 4). And there are many people worse off than these men, who are at least employed.

The inequalities of wealth in a town, coupled with the domination of the manorial lords in the country, might make you yearn to escape the whole medieval hierarchy. If you do, you will not be alone. There are quite a few travelers on the road. There are the beggars who roam around the country, stopping in each place for a while, until they are moved on. Such men—and almost all of them are men—often have routes incorporating the houses of friendly hosts, with whom they will stay for a week or two each year. Lepers of course are forced into such a life, but, once their symptoms begin to show, they are made to feel so unwelcome that they tend to confine themselves to leper hospitals near towns. Much more readily received are the traveling performers: the tumblers and jugglers. Although most professional musicians are attached to great men's households and religious houses, you do come across wandering minstrels. It is not a bad life in the summer months: traveling around, playing a merry jig on a pipe or a rebec. You may decide to help with the harvest in the daytime, before keeping your fellow workers dancing in the evening. It certainly beats being one of the mass of men peddling some sort of service. Who would be a pardoner, selling documents purporting to guarantee the purchaser freedom from sins? Or a soothsayer, predicting doom? Or a hermit, living on the proceeds of alms given by passersby?

Women

Unlike men, women are not usually described by what they do but by their marital condition. Thus the medieval mind tends to categorize women as follows: maidens, wives, nuns, and widows. The status of a maiden or wife depends on that of the man who supports her. When she is a girl, this is her father or stepfather. On marrying, it is her husband. Once she has married, she becomes subject to his authority. She is unable to resist him sexually, to borrow money without his consent, or to dispose of any property—even to the point of being unable to make a will. Nuns depend on their nunnery in much the same way, being considered the brides of Christ. Only widows and aged spinsters can achieve a measure of independence, and even widows are often categorized according to the status of their last husband. This is the most fundamental aspect of women's lives. From birth until widowhood they are living under the control—nominally, at least—of someone else, in most cases a man.

From this it is only a small step to realize that women are constantly the victims of sexual prejudice. It is not that they are second-class citizens—class has got little to do with it; high-status females are just as highly respected as high-status males—it is that women are blamed for all the physical, intellectual, and moral weaknesses of society. It was a woman who first persuaded a man to take a bite from the forbidden fruit, with the result that all humanity was cast out of Paradise, and that is a difficult thing to live down. The fact that the Bible is "a text wherein we find that woman was the ruin of Mankind" (as Chaucer puts it) presents a fundamental platform upon which all manner of prejudices are founded (although Chaucer himself is remarkably free from these). According to a thirteenth-century work translated into English in the fourteenth century, women are smaller, meeker, more demure, more gentle, more supple, and more delicate, but they are also "more envious and more laughing and loving, and the malice of the soul is more in a woman than in a man." The author goes on to add that a woman "is of a feeble nature, tells more lies . . . and is slower in working and in moving than a man."[21] Clearly this author is not wholly unappreciative of female qualities, but his report of women is not exactly a glowing one.

Although you may find these sexual prejudices disturbing, it is difficult to see how things could easily change. This is not just because of the misogyny of society; it is also a matter of trust in the law and social norms. Men might act in the name of the law but that does not qualify them to change it, especially as it has been built up slowly, over many generations. Nor does the law help them understand the problem of legal prejudices against women. It is debatable as to how many people think there *is* a problem. Many women consider that this male-dominated society is simply the way things are, and the way that God intended the world to be, as a punishment on women. For if anyone looks anywhere for guidance in such matters, they look in the Bible, and Genesis is not the only book with a sexist slant. In addition, the intellectual developments of the thirteenth century—which increasingly form the basis of educated opinion in the fourteenth—have spread the Aristotelian dictum that women are basically "deformed men." A few educated women rail against this sexism but there is not much they can do about it except write witty antisexist polemics, to be shared with their friends and acquaintances.

The paralyzing factor in male–female relations at all levels of society is the inability to understand and control sexual desire. Medical knowledge, which is heavily based on the teachings of the third-century writer Galen, holds that women's wombs are "cold" and need constant warming by "hot" male sperm. In addition, if women do not regularly copulate, their "seed" (as Galen calls it) might coagulate and suffocate their wombs, thereby damaging their health. Therefore it is widely understood that women have a physical need to have sex regularly. Marriage is seen as an essential means of satiating both female and male lust through making each partner "indebted" to the other. By this reckoning, neither partner may deny the other repayment of the marital "debt." You therefore have a society in which men are led to believe that their wives are constantly aching to have sex as often as they can. At the same time the women are led to believe that they are the physical manifestations of lust and that their wombs will suffocate with excess seed unless they have sex regularly. For unmarried women this presents something of a problem. John Gaddesden—one of the leading medical lights at Oxford in the early part of the century—recommends women suffering from a superfluity of lust should find a man and marry him quickly. If this is not possible, they should travel, exercise frequently, and take medicines. If this regimen does not work, and the lust brings on a fainting fit, a woman should find a midwife who should lubricate her fingers with oil, insert then into her vagina, and "move them vigorously about."[22]

The results of this inadequate understanding of female sexuality, together with biblical, legal, and intellectual prejudices against women, are profound. Galen teaches that women must have an orgasm in order to conceive a child. That is all well and good for those women whose husbands will toil long and hard to help them conceive, but for those who come into contact with the mass of young men traveling around the country, it is dangerous. The implication is that if a man wants to seduce a woman, and rapes her so brutally that she derives no physical pleasure from the experience, she should not conceive. There is a specific statute making rape a crime, and it is taken seriously enough to be deemed one of the crimes which can only be dealt with by the king's justices (rather than in the local courts), but it is very difficult to apply. If the woman fails to conceive, and there is no other evidence that sex took place with the accused, it is unlikely that the perpetrator will be held to account: any trial would be just her word against his. On the other hand, if the woman *does* conceive, then she is deemed to have physically enjoyed the experience (according to Galen's teaching) and so legally no rape has taken place.

These difficulties are compounded by the social hierarchy of men. If the perpetrator of a rape is a high-status individual, it is very difficult for anyone to proceed against him. If a summoner tries to take action against a man of rank, he will incur the man's enmity as well as the embarrassment of accusing someone, on the dubious strength of a woman's slander. When a royal tax collector starts sexually molesting girls and young women on a systematic basis in 1381, his actions help trigger the Peasants' Revolt. Unlawful violence is practically the only form of revenge open to the outraged fathers.

The foregoing makes the woman's lot seem a particularly harsh one. However, there are some great advantages to being a woman. When the king issues writs to his sheriffs summoning an army, it is the men who have to risk their lives and fight, not the women. Despite this, high-status women are still entitled to all the benefits of being connected to "those who fight." They can inherit land in their own right, even when ownership entails providing military service.

High-status women also share the power of their husband's position and rank. Many widows are only too pleased for people to associate them with their late husbands—after all, how many dowager countesses want people to forget that they were once married to an earl? This can apply farther down the social spectrum. A villein's wife is a co-tenant of the manor along with her husband and valuable in her own right. Women in cities are able to carry on their husband's trade after his death. So a woman married to a tailor may become an independent tailor herself, or a practitioner of any one of more than a hundred trades—even an armorer or a merchant. Margaret Russell of Coventry is a prime example of an exceedingly wealthy provincial female trader. Just one of her ventures to Spain consists of goods worth £800. When women have this sort of capital, and are managing international trading ventures from Coventry, you can hardly look upon them as downtrodden. Nor should you forget that the second richest person in all of fourteenth-century England is a woman—Queen Isabella. The fact that a wife is legally subordinate to her husband is of relatively little consequence when she is socially superior to everyone else.

Another point to remember is that this discrimination against women is only legal, it is not personal. If a wife is spirited enough, she may do more than hold her own against her husband, as Chaucer's Wife of Bath will gladly relate. While a man may legally beat his wife, she may accuse him in a church court of cruelty, for beating her too much, and have the court force him to mend his ways.[23] But no man could take his wife to court for this—for husband beating—as no court will sympathize with a man so feeble that he cannot defend himself against his own wife. Similarly, if a man wants to take legal action against his wife for adultery, he has to admit he is a cuckold, and in so doing he may make himself appear ridiculous. If a husband and wife turn to crime—and many families do engage in criminal activity together—and if they commit a hanging offense, only the husband hangs. His wife simply has to plead that she was obeying her husband's orders. Through such technicalities, the apparent gross inequalities of the law appear more extreme on parchment than in the majority of people's daily lives. As the Wife of Bath puts it, "Any wife who knows what's what, can make her husband think that black is white, with her own maid in witness as support."

There are other advantages enjoyed by women too. A surprising number of townswomen are literate. Nunneries might be poor in their endowments but they are keen on their schools, and they educate as many girls as boys. Then there is old age. If a woman survives giving birth repeatedly there is every chance she will reach a greater age than her husband. Her respectability will have improved in comparison to his too. Men over the age of sixty are often seen as something of an embarrassment, no longer masculine, and unable to fulfill the dominant male role in society.[24] Women on the other hand are seen as having lost nothing in strength but having gained much in wisdom. Women do not have to enter tithings—the social control mechanism of the peasantry (see chapter 10). Another subtle advantage arises from the female role within the household. While it is true that women take on most of the routine work within the community—including washing clothes, tending the sick, and laying out the dead—the result is that they are far more aware of what is going on in the neighborhood. This also applies to their own households; through seeing with their own eyes what the servants have been up to, they have a far better idea of what is actually going on than their husbands. In many wealthy households the wife is the link between the staff and her husband, who might be elsewhere on business. She rules the household in her husband's absence and, when he returns, she tells him what needs doing and who must be disciplined, if she has not already seen to this herself. For these women it is hardly worth considering what the Bible says about females. Their own position is very much to their advantage, and if it requires occasional lip service to the odd snippet of biblical history to preserve the order of their home, then so be it.

As you can see, the lot of a woman in medieval England depends very much on her luck in the marriages stakes. Some husbands are absolutely devoted to their wives. This includes kings—Edward I, Edward III, and Henry IV, in particular, all deeply love their wives—as well as magnates and lesser men. In describing her married life, Christine de Pisan writes lovingly of her late husband, telling how, when he married her (when she was fifteen), he did not force her to make love with him on their wedding night, wanting her first to get used to his presence. Chaucer's own view is unequivocal: "What is better than wisdom? Woman. And what is better than a good woman? Nothing."

At the other extreme, a bad marriage can be fatal, literally, for the woman. That is why it is so cruel for a manorial bailiff to force a bond-woman to marry against her will. There is nothing she will be able to do to stop being bound to a man who will rape her and beat her, take and spend all her wealth, and force her into a life of repetitive drudgery, and then perhaps abandon her. On top of that, with every child she conceives she runs a small but significant risk of a painful death, roughly equating to a one in ten chance of dying over the course of having five children (see chapter 9). Her marriage vows include her oath to remain sexually faithful to her abusive husband—although he himself does not have to promise likewise—and if she leaves him she forfeits not only all her possessions but any dowry which would be rightfully hers should she outlive him. Given that some women find themselves in exactly this situation, it is not surprising to learn that there is a saint, St. Wylgeforte, to watch out for women who are plagued by bad husbands. You cannot help but have some sympathy for those women who have no one else to call on but St. Wylgeforte.

3

The Medieval Character

In the autumn of 1379 Sir John Arundel—younger brother of the earl of Arundel—rides up to a convent with a detachment of soldiers, planning to sail to Brittany. He sends for the prioress and asks for accommodation for himself and his men while they wait for the wind to change. The prioress is reluctant, fearing the number of armed youths with Arundel, but, since it is her duty to offer hospitality to wayfarers, including soldiers, she eventually agrees. Unfortunately, the wind does not change. To relieve the monotony the soldiers start drinking and flirting with some of the nuns. Unsurprisingly the nuns refuse their advances and lock themselves in their dormitory. Undeterred, the soldiers force their way in and rape them. This sets off a crime spree. They loot the nunnery. They enter a nearby church to steal the chalice and silverware, and they encounter a wedding party. They draw their swords; remove the newly married bride from her husband, family, and friends; and take it in turns to rape her too. Then, seeing that the wind is at last changing, they take this woman and as many of the nuns as they can out to their ship and set sail. A day or so later, a storm blows up from the east. The ship is swept off course and begins to take on water. Arundel gives the order for all the women to be thrown overboard, to lighten the load. Sixty women are hurled mercilessly into the turbulent sea as the ship heads on towards the coast of Ireland.[1]

This story is an extreme one, and it would be wrong to suggest it is a typical crime. Nevertheless it is believed in its entirety by the chronicler who writes it down, Thomas Walsingham, and that is the important point here. Medieval people believe that groups of young men do behave like this. Certainly young men can be extremely selfish and destructive, especially when armed, bored, drunk, and in a gang. As most of them travel with a sword, it is inevitable that there are undercurrents of fear and confrontation wherever they go. It is not sexism that prevents a woman from traveling between towns by herself, it is simply a sensible precaution. Add such exacerbating factors as geographical isolation and the relative lawlessness which prevails when there are few means of detecting a criminal's identity after the event, and you can see why medieval society is more fearful, guarded, and violent than that with which you are familiar.

Common men are conscripted to take part in the king's wars, and it is assumed that any man can—and will—fight. In many parts of the realm—especially on the south coast and the two Marches (those areas bordering Wales and Scotland)—men regularly have to defend their property from invaders. Also, the gangs roaming the countryside in the early part of the century force people in relatively safe areas to take up arms for the sake of self-preservation. As a result, many men practice archery and swordmanship as a means of self-defense, militarizing themselves in order to protect their property. A streak of violence runs through the whole population, attacker and defender alike.

This violence runs hand in hand with another dislikable aspect of the medieval character. People can be exceedingly cruel to one another. When you witness the punishments meted out to wrongdoers you begin to understand something of how the medieval mind works—how it seeks to expiate crime through the most hideous punishments, including hanging, disemboweling, and quartering. In the modern world we understand that the greater the severity of a crime, the longer the punishment should be. In the medieval world the worse the crime, the more extreme the *nature* of the punishment. Cruelty appears in day-to-day life too. People have few or no qualms about inflicting pain on animals and children. It is universally believed that beating dogs is the correct and best way to treat them, to get them to behave. Cockfighting is thought of as a children's game. Women as well as men love to watch bearbaiting and bullbaiting. These are not minority interests but hugely popular forms of entertainment. Anything that involves bloodshed is bound to draw a crowd.

Just as women married to brutal husbands can expect to suffer domestic violence, so too can children and servants. Children can expect to suffer as much from their mother's hands as from their father's. One educational tract, *How the Good Wife Taught Her Daughter*, states that "if your children are rebellious and do not bow, or if any of them misbehave, do not curse them, but take a smart rod and beat them in a row, till they cry mercy and be aware of their guilt."[2] Likewise "the good lady" in Chaucer's "Sea Captain's Tale" is described as having "a little girl for company, a pupil under her authority, quite young, and as yet subject to the rod." A dialogue book from the period states that "if ye have children, so chastise them with the rod and inform them with good manners [all] the time that they be young."[3] Some men maintain that a good father will beat his children at every opportunity, instilling in them a fear of breaking the law, whereas a lenient father is negligent of his duties. That children as young as seven can be hanged for theft perhaps goes some way to explaining these extreme measures (in the sense that violent discipline is part of a stiff moral education). But even so, boys are bound to grow up with an understanding that there is nothing wrong in a man exercising violence against children, servants, animals, and women. Give a gang of such boys swords at the age of seventeen or eighteen, and give them a lot to drink and put them under the command of a man like Sir John Arundel—and the result is a tragedy.

In such a violent environment it is important to know who your friends are, so great value is set upon loyalty. When lords fall out with each other, all their retainers and servants fall out with their opposite numbers too. In 1385 two men in the service of the king's half brother, Sir John Holland, have an argument with two esquires in the service of the earl of Stafford. Stafford's esquires murder Holland's men. Holland himself then takes up his dead servants' cause with Sir Ralph Stafford, the earl's eldest son. Unfortunately Sir Ralph stands resolutely by his father's servants. In the heat of the argument, Holland draws his sword and kills young Stafford, creating a state of war between the two houses.

Nor is this violent loyalty confined to secular lords. On one occasion in 1384, after the bishop of Exeter has refused to let the archbishop of Canterbury visit his diocese, three of his household esquires force the archbishop's messenger to eat the wax seal of the letter he is carrying.[4] Several members of the archbishop's household exact revenge by seizing one of the bishop's men and making him eat his own shoes. It is not exactly behavior appropriate for the servants of the highest-ranking clergy in the realm.

In any society as violent as this, it is vitally important to *belong*. Men from one town belong to that town in order to give them some protection when they venture to another. Men of one manor likewise belong to that place, for the sake of their security as well as their livelihood. Many men regard their membership of a town community as no less important than their nationality. When an untrustworthy trader (such as a fraudulent innkeeper) is made to forswear his trade and leave the city, he is not only losing his livelihood but also the companionship of those whom he could count on to protect him.

Sense of Humor

The passions of a violent society spill over into the sense of humor you will encounter. Yes, there is humor, lots of it, amid the violence and sexism. But whether you will find it funny is quite a different matter. For example, here is a medieval joke. One merchant asks another, "Are you married?" "I had three wives," the second merchant responds, "but all three hanged themselves from a tree in my garden." The first merchant retorts, "Pray, give me a cutting from this miraculous tree."

Sarcasm might be commonly referred to as the lowest form of wit in our own time, but in the fourteenth century it is just about the highest. It is arguably the only form which does not require the humiliation of a victim. One of the most famous humorous letters of the century is written by the young Edward II to Louis d'Evreux, in which he promises to send him a present of "some misshapen greyhounds from Wales, which can well catch a hare if they find it asleep, and running dogs which can follow at an amble, for well we know how you love lazy dogs."[5] Similarly, if you visit court in late 1328 you might be amused by Roger Mortimer's sarcastic reply to a letter from the earl of Lancaster, his avowed enemy. Having been accused of impoverishing the Crown, Mortimer denies everything vehemently and then adds, "But if any man knows how to make the king richer, he is most welcome at court."[6]

Practical jokes are perhaps the most common form of humor. Men and women are often amused when other people injure themselves. Take hocking, for example: at one level this is the Hocktide custom of capturing men and women and holding them prisoner and releasing them for a fee, in order to raise money for the parish. On Mondays men are captured by women, and vice versa on Tuesdays. But sometimes it gets out of hand. A group of lads lay a noose on the ground and wait for an unsuspecting passerby to step into it. Then they hoist him up, suddenly, by his ankles, often bashing his head on the ground in the process. Watch out at dusk, when it is difficult to see the rope against the mud of the street. Otherwise you will be kept hanging by one leg until you have paid a ransom. Those who see the spectacle will laugh heartily at your embarrassment.

In a violent society even the humor is violent. One day King Edward II is riding along the road behind one of his kitchen staff, called Morris, who falls off his horse. Something is wrong with Morris for he is unable to keep his balance and falls off again. Does the king ride up and offer him a helping hand? Or send a servant to inquire after the man's health? Nothing of the sort. Instead, he laughs and laughs and laughs. Wiping away a tear, he gives the man the equivalent of a year's salary as a present, not to help him get better but for making him laugh so much.[7] Sometimes such violent ribaldry is enshrined in annual games, such as the Haxey Hood game, which permits the man playing the Fool to kiss any girl or married woman he meets. At the end of the celebrations he will be cut down from the bough of a tree above a fire and burnt badly for his amatory indulgences.

There is a fine line between this brutal sense of humor and plain trickery, which is not so funny. You will be surprised how many people laugh at the idea of a man persuading a woman to sleep with him after promising to marry her, with his sole guarantee of good intentions being a ring made of wound rushes—which soon falls apart, like his promise of marriage. The idea of a young woman cuckolding her old husband with a handsome young man is one which constantly entertains and delights people. Chaucer uses it to brilliant effect in discussing the relations between men and women in his *Canterbury Tales*. Of course, in Chaucer's hands, even plain trickery can be hilariously funny. The end of "The Miller's Tale," where the carpenter cuts the rope holding his washtub in the rafters and falls to the floor, is slapstick at its very finest. But for every Chaucer there are ten thousand less-witty tricksters. In 1351 the mayor of London has to pass a bylaw prohibiting boys from playing practical jokes on the members of Parliament. Among other things, they had been running up behind them and stealing their hoods.

The Warrior's Love of Flowers

You might now be thinking that the medieval English character is composed of cruelty and violence. If so, you would not be far wrong—it has been formed through an intense awareness of both. But it is also composed of many other things. Just as a biographer only begins to understand his subject when he comes to terms with the contradictions and tensions within the character, so too you will only begin to understand the medieval mind when you begin to realize its contradictions. For example, the supreme masters of violence are those military commanders who can direct sudden and overwhelming force at their enemy. But when you begin to examine their true characters, these men are rarely brutal. Henry, duke of Lancaster, is one of the greatest military leaders of the century. He leads an Anglo-Gascon army to victory after victory in 1345. And yet what are his pastimes and pleasures? He likes all the usual things—hunting, feasting, and, by his own admission, seducing women, especially peasant girls—but he also loves the song of the nightingale and the scents of roses, musk, violets, and lily of the valley. The image of a great war leader closing his eyes and inhaling the aroma of flowers reminds us that some medieval lords are very far from being two-dimensional violent thugs. Henry even writes a book of spiritual devotion. There is poetry and sophistication in such men, intellectual awareness, human kindness, and generosity of spirit. And there is deep sincerity too. When the same duke swears an oath not to give up a siege until he has planted his banner on the walls of the castle, you can be sure that he intends to fulfill it. Not even a direct order from the king himself can persuade him to do otherwise. Perhaps one of the things which will amaze you most of all is how often a man in armor—a fighting machine—will resolutely stand by what he personally believes is virtuous. And how easily he can be moved to tears.

There is no more obvious contrast to the bawdy, insensitive humor and violence of the time than people's spirituality. To be modestly religious in the fourteenth century is to be fervent by modern standards—you will find the depth of religious feeling in daily life quite astonishing. Many people attend Mass every single day. Many give alms to the poor every day. Many will go on four or five pilgrimages a year, and some will visit more than a hundred different churches annually. You might think that this is all a show of religion, a demonstration of piety, in order to encourage the lower classes to believe their superiors are closer to God. But such a view would not only be extremely cynical, it would be wrong. Just as there is a violent streak running through the whole of society, so too there is a religious one. One of the greatest fighting heroes of the century is Sir Walter Manny, a personal friend of King Edward III and Queen Philippa. He is the sort of swashbuckling character who will throw himself at a horde of French knights with the conviction of an indomitable man; he has been known to rush out of a besieged town and attack a siege engine just because it is disturbing his dinner. And yet he is also the sort of man who establishes a great monastery—the London Charterhouse—and who buys enough land so that the poor of London have somewhere to bury their dead during the Great Plague. He might be a fighting machine, but when he removes his armor he is a man of sympathy and piety, and these virtues are as much a part of his character as his military prowess.

The key to understanding such men is the notion of respectability. If you want to flatter a man in any walk of life, tell him he is of noble bearing and behavior and deserving of respect. Men want to serve in important positions of office in towns and manors—it adds to their stature. Men want to be seen to be valued by the great men of the realm, especially the king. Most of all, men want to be honored and loved in death. It is no exaggeration to say that at some great funerals you will see more than ten thousand people in mourning. The greater the numbers at your funeral, the more loved, the more honored, and the more respected you must have been in life. Hence great men start rewarding paupers for attending their funerals. When Richard Gravesend, bishop of London, is buried in 1303, a total of 31,968 poor people attend the ceremony.[8] Such determination to appear dignified and respected is common to most men and women. Cursing or defaming someone is a serious offense, and the victim's pride may well cause the defamer to be hauled up in court. It is perhaps this very straightlaced respectability that explains why people find it so funny when a proud man has his hood stolen or gets hocked by his ankle and lifted into the air.

Education

To what extent is character a result of education? In the Middle Ages it is arguable that the answer is "not very much." Alternatively, you could turn the question around and say the opposite. The shortcomings of medieval education have a profound effect on the people.

In the towns and villages you will find the younger children being taught about the seven deadly sins once a week by the parish priest. Otherwise most forms of education are intended to do no more than equip boys and girls for the occupations for which they are destined. A knight's son will be sent off at the age of seven to serve in the household of another knight, often his maternal uncle. Great lords' sons and daughters are given their own private tutors. The children of an agricultural worker will be out in the fields at the age of seven. Craftsmen's sons likewise become apprentices at a young age, learning how to keep accounts—whether in a written form or on tally sticks—as well as the techniques of the trade. Those destined for the Church are sent off at seven to be tonsured, which entails the rather severe haircut which commences a career of worship. Education—like so many other aspects of medieval life—is a practical exercise.

There *are* formal schools in most towns but only for the minority. Cathedrals, Benedictine monasteries, nunneries, and friaries normally have schools attached to them. Others are associated with city churches, and it is from such establishments as these that the clerks and the clergy and the undergraduates of Oxford and Cambridge are drawn. The cost of a formal education can be as much as 10d per week per pupil—far too expensive for most parents. For villeins it is totally out of the question, as the parents would have to pay an additional fine to the lord of the manor for sending their child away. The minority who, at about the age of fourteen, do matriculate to one of the two universities can expect to study first the Trivium (grammar, rhetoric, and logic) and then the Quadrivium (arithmetic, music, astronomy, and geometry) for their liberal arts degree. But there are no more than a few hundred resident members of each university at any one time. Formal education is a rare privilege.

Given that only a small minority go to school, you will be mildly surprised by the number of people who are literate. You have probably been told at some time that only priests can read and write. That was true for England in about 1200: in those days the ability to read was legally synonymous with being a clergyman. But at that time manorial courts did not keep records, most bishops did not keep registers, and few great estates issued any documentation other than charters. Now in the fourteenth century things are very different. The proceedings of every manor court are recorded in detail, and so are the extent and customs of almost every manor. Every bishop keeps a register. Every great estate and major landowner employs a series of clerks. Every judge has his clerical staff, and so does every sheriff, escheator, and coroner. Most wealthy merchants keep accounts of some sort. By 1400 even churchwardens are recording their income and expenditure in account rolls.[9] All the professional men in a city—physicians, lawyers, scriveners, surgeons, and schoolmasters—can read and write, and maybe as many as 20 percent of other tradesmen are also literate. As for country areas, manorial clerks, parish clergy, and parish churchwardens form a literate core. When lists of the most reliable freeholders in a rural area are drawn up, literacy is often noted, revealing that many of them are literate.[10] Villeins do not feature in such lists, the majority being unable even to recognize their own name, let alone write it. Despite this you should reckon on a male literacy rate of 5 percent of the adult population in rural areas, and 20 percent in urban areas.[11] By the end of the century these are probably significant underestimates with regard to certain towns and cities.

Knowledge of the Wider World

Another myth often repeated in the modern world is that ordinary medieval people never travel more than five or six miles from their homes. As you will suspect from the masses pouring into towns on market days, this is not correct. It is true that most villeins do not travel more than a few miles from their manor, on account of their bond to their lord, but freemen can—and do—travel much farther afield.

Consider the position of a prosperous franklin who wishes to marry his six or seven sons and daughters to boys and girls of similar status. He will probably have to consider families outside his own parish. Nor will all the suitable families be in one single adjacent parish.

In this way, within a generation or two, one family is spread across a wide area. Each member of the family will end up visiting different market towns and passing on information about what is available in each place to his kinsmen. In one large village you may have three or four such families, and their pooled information about towns and political changes will be quite extensive. They will collectively know all the towns in every direction for a range of twenty or thirty miles. They will also know many of the most influential individuals. Thus a complex network is built up through kinship, friendship, and trade. Furthermore, when members of these families travel, they stay with their relations. Thus they keep in touch with their second and third cousins, thereby securing a mutually supportive network of contacts and places to stay.

Now consider the social responsibilities of the above franklin's family. Let us say one of his brothers is chosen to be the lord's manorial bailiff. That will entail him traveling between his manor and the steward of the lord's estates, who could be anywhere in the kingdom, traveling with his master. Perhaps the franklin has another brother, a friar, who travels between the towns and villages preaching. Or a mariner. Perhaps they have a cousin who acts as the township constable for a year. This will require him not only to travel around the manor and to the adjacent manors but also to attend the hundred court and the county court, which could be twenty or thirty miles away. If the mother of all these men was from a family which held a portion of a manor, they may well have kin among the esquires in a nobleman's household, traveling up and down the country. In this way information networks are extended far beyond the original manor.

As soon as you start to think of all the many different activities which entail travel, you realize that freemen regularly travel distances of ten or twenty miles or more. Freeholders of land worth more than forty shillings can vote for the county's parliamentary representative, and that entails a journey to the county town. The clergy of the diocese have to travel long distances for the ordination of priests or the trying of ecclesiastical cases. The royal justices and their clerks and servants move around the whole country, and, wherever they hold court, they draw in hundreds of local officers and accused men and women. Many people travel about the country on pilgrimages. Add those members of monasteries and noble households who have to oversee the running of distant estates, and you realize that travel is not just common, it is almost unavoidable.

A good example is the business of proving a will. Executors are required to swear their oath and prove the will in a particular ecclesiastical court. Thus they might have to travel to any one of several courts: the bishop's consistory court, an archdeaconry court, a special or "peculiar" court of a church official, or the court of the archbishop of Canterbury (at Lambeth). The lack of any public transport system is not an excuse for not attending. Nor is distance. When a man who lives on the border of Devon and Cornwall dies, leaving property in each county, the executor of his will has no option but to make a journey to Exeter and back, a round trip of about eighty miles, taking several days. If a man dies leaving property straddling the boundary between the dioceses of York and Lincoln, a journey to Lambeth will be necessary (a round trip of about three hundred miles). Official business forces men and women to travel, even if they would never do so for pleasure.

What do English people know about what is going on abroad? Here again practicalities come into play. When Edward III leads an army across France in 1346, the fifteen thousand men he takes with him are drawn from all parts of the kingdom. You can say the same thing for the armies sent to Gascony (the English kings' feudal lands in southwest France), or those summoned to fight in Scotland by all five of the fourteenth-century English kings. Those men from the south of England who march to Scotland visit many different towns, meeting many different men and women along the way, and hearing dozens of regional accents. No fewer than thirty thousand Englishmen cross the Channel to join in the siege of Calais in 1346–47, according to the official payroll. These men do not just find themselves whisked off to start fighting; many have to march two or three hundred miles from their homes just to get to the point of embarkation, bringing them into contact with many fellow soldiers from all over the realm and allowing them to see many places on the journey and spread whatever news and stories they have to tell.

Information about events overseas is carried in a variety of ways. First there are regular links between the English clergy and the pope. English clerks and messengers regularly travel all the way across

France to Avignon or Rome, coming into contact with people from all walks of life along the way, from innkeepers to monks and lords. A significant number of Englishmen go on long-distance pilgrimages to Santiago de Compostela, Rome, Cologne (the shrine of the Three Kings), and the Holy Land. These travelers similarly bring back their knowledge of the wider world. Thousands of Englishmen take part in the crusades in Prussia and Lithuania, or the crusade to Nicopolis; to do so they have to travel vast distances, meeting people from many different kingdoms. Then there are those letters sent to and from the king, containing news which is circulated around England by men coming and going from court. Messengers from France and Spain arrive regularly, partly on account of Edward II's wife being the daughter of the king of France and his cousin being the king of Castile. Edward III has much business with his kinsfolk in the Low Countries. Two of his sons marry Castilian princesses and one weds the daughter of the duke of Milan. Richard II marries a princess from Prague (Bohemia) and Henry IV's sisters are queens of Castile and Portugal. One of his daughters marries the king of Norway, Sweden, and Denmark in the early fifteenth century. England might be situated on an island, but it is far from being cut off.

Another means of obtaining international news is via sailors and traders. Mariners sailing from King's Lynn and Boston know their way around the shores of Sweden, Norway, Denmark, and the Baltic states. English merchants are permanently based in Copenhagen and Danzig (modern Gdansk); a few merchant adventurers have even made their way into Muscovy (as the Grand Duchy of Moscow is known). The duchy of Aquitaine is the inheritance of the king of England, and most of England's wine comes from Gascony, so sailors leaving Plymouth are familiar with the route down to Bordeaux. There are many and frequent sailings between the south coast of England and the Low Countries, especially to the great Flemish cloth-working cities of Bruges and Ghent, which import huge quantities of English wool. There are the German trading cities of the Hanseatic League, with which London merchants also do business. England might not be the most important trading nation in Christendom, but its economic links do reach from Ireland and Portugal to Constantinople and Moscow.

What does all this mean for the ordinary person? It depends on where he or she lives. Those in the towns and villages along the main roads between London and the major ports—especially Dover—are familiar with foreigners and merchants coming and going on a daily basis. But probably everyone in England knows someone who has fought in Scotland, Ireland, France, Spain, or on one of the Prussian crusades in eastern Europe. There can be no one who has not had direct access to the travelers' tales told by soldiers. So when Geoffrey Chaucer pipes up about a knight taking part in battles in Lithuania, Prussia, Russia, Portugal, and Turkey, most of his audience will be familiar with the names of these places and know how far they are from England, even if they have never seen a map. And when he starts talking about the Dartmouth sea captain who knows all the harbors between the Baltic and Cape Finisterre, and each inlet in Brittany and Spain, his audience understands; everyone has heard of the famous Sir John Hawley: pirate, merchant, and eighteen-times mayor of Dartmouth. Even Chaucer's references to Syria and Asia find a place in the medieval idea of the world. Henry IV—a man who has been to Jerusalem as well as to Vilnius, Königsberg, and Danzig—corresponds with the king of Abyssinia (modern Ethiopia).[12] Edward III entertains the son of the "king of India."[13] In 1400 the emperor of Constantinople visits England in person, bringing a group of Greek Orthodox priests from Byzantium. So it may be said that, while many villeins never travel far from their own manor, most people have some idea of what goes on beyond the seas, even if they have not left England in person.

Understanding what lies beyond the borders of Christendom is a completely different matter. No one in medieval England has ever been to China or India. World maps do mention the Chinese—they call them Seres on account of their wearing silk—but knowledge about Asia is so scanty that it can hardly be called knowledge at all. The ancient confusion of India and Ethiopia—which originated with Pliny the Elder in the first century AD—persists.[14] As a result of a forged twelfth-century letter, many people believe that there are in fact three Indias, fabulously wealthy countries ruled by a Christian prince (Prester John). India is accordingly considered synonymous with Asia, and, in its most extended form, is thought to cover half the globe. Such misunderstandings are not helped by the theories of monastic revisionists who do not themselves travel beyond the cloister and who suggest on the basis of theology that the eastern shore of India lies only a few days' sailing *westward* of Spain.

Although most people do know that the world is a globe, they do not think about the logical consequences of this—that one could sail to China *westward* from England, for example.[15] This will not be attempted until Columbus's voyages in the next century. People know that the landmass of Asia, Africa, and Europe is surrounded by a great ocean, but they understand that on the other side of this ocean—and thus on the other side of the world—there is a fourth continent, called the Antipodes, or *Terra Australis Incognita* ("the unknown southern land"). Men cannot go there because it is too hot. There live fantastic races like the Sciopods, who have only one large foot. When in need of relief from the heat, Sciopods lie on their backs and shelter in the shade of their feet. Alongside them in the Antipodes live more than a dozen fabulous races.[16] These include the Antipedes (people whose feet point backward), Amazons (women with a single breast), Cynocephales (men with the heads of dogs), Panoti (men with elephant trunks for ears), and Blemmyae (headless people whose faces are embedded in their chests).

Even knowledge of our own side of the Earth can be vague. Some of the fabulous races from the southern continent are confused with the inhabitants of far-off places like India and Ethiopia. Other domestic races are invented, such as the Ethiopian Troglodytes (swift-footed but dumb cave dwellers) and the Wife-Givers (men who encourage everyone who passes their way to sleep with their wives and daughters in the hope of securing presents). Some races in Asia are supposed to eat their parents, fattening them up in their twilight years before serving them up as a ritual feast. The widely believed authority John Mandeville states that on the East Asian island of Sandin, if a man is sick and the prognostication is not good, the remedy for his malady is for his family to suffocate him, and boil and roast his body, and then feed him in a festive dinner to all his friends and relatives.[17]

The problem is that not all such knowledge is wholly wrong. In East Asia there probably *are* cannibalistic communities. There *are* black people in Ethiopia (although they are not black from having been roasted by the sun, as the contemporary encyclopedias state). Geographical experts will tell you that there is a large island off the coast of India (which we know as Sri Lanka). Very good, you might think, until the same informant adds that Sri Lanka has two winters and two summers every year, and that dragons and elephants are common there. Elephants, yes, but dragons? Nor is this all: on the way home from Sri Lanka you will come across unicorns and phoenixes and any number of fabulous creatures. Perhaps the unicorn is a vague traveler's tale of the Indian rhinoceros? Perhaps the dragon is a vague memory of a man-eating saltwater crocodile? It is impossible to tell. Fourteenth-century Englishmen do know what elephants and crocodiles look like. Exeter Cathedral has a fine elephant carving on one of its misericords, and Henry III even kept an elephant at the Tower of London in the thirteenth century (it lived three years). As for crocodiles, Bartholomew the Englishman has written a description of one: "his bite is venomous, his teeth are horrible and shaped like a comb . . . if a crocodile finds a man by the edge of the water, he kills him if he can, then weeps over him, and finally swallows him." But it is fair to say that Englishmen know little for certain of the wider world. The only thing you can be sure of is that their understanding of what lies beyond Christendom is part fact and part fiction, and it might as well be all fiction considering no one can tell one part from the other.

Discerning Minds?

The lack of distinction between fact and fiction with regard to distant countries is understandable, but it should alert you to a wider failure to distinguish between the real and the fabulous. At times it seems that medieval people pride themselves on the *quantity* of their knowledge, not its quality or correctness. Well-educated and intelligent individuals are fully aware of the shortcomings of this attitude. Some have read the works of John of Salisbury, where it is noted that if three churches all claim to have the head of John the Baptist, at least two of them must be wrong. Chaucer similarly refers to many relics as "pigs' bones." And yet most people are not remotely bothered by such issues. Huge distances mean they do not have to deal with the problem of John the Baptist having three heads, and, by implication, the problem of the Church circulating untruths. For almost everyone, the principle of divine providence explains everything. Things are as they are because God has determined that that is the way they shall be—even to the point of John the Baptist having three heads.

For the man and woman in the medieval street, the real threat to providence is not rationalism but the work of the Devil. In some parts of the country flocks of crows are seen as the Devil's agents. In others, Celtic speakers are shunned as speakers of the Devil's words. Merely invoking the Devil's name is thought to turn milk sour or make fruit taste bad. Everywhere you go you will hear stories of when the Devil came to the parish or visited so-and-so's land or came into the church and drew the body of a recently deceased witch out of her grave. Interestingly, national disasters are not generally seen as the Devil's work but rather are portrayed as messages from God. When a terrible storm strikes the English army on Black Monday 1360, killing many men and horses with giant hailstones, it is interpreted as a divine intervention and a call to negotiate a peaceful settlement to the war. Similarly the Great Plague of 1348–49 is widely seen as a divine judgment on mankind's wickedness, in much the same way that God caused the Flood to wash away the sinfulness of Noah's world. The chronicler Thomas Walsingham even goes so far as to claim that the Peasants' Revolt is the work of God, divine punishment for Londoners' sinfulness. If you actually see the Essex and Kent peasants murdering indiscriminately, killing the archbishop of Canterbury, and assaulting the king's mother, you might disagree.

The word which best sums up the medieval attitude to the Devil, miracles, and everything in between is "superstition." People do not understand the laws of physics, the nature of matter, or even how the human body functions. Hence they do not see limitations on how the world operates. Their sense of normality is thus somewhat precarious. Anything can happen. In their minds, sorcery really does work, and all sorts of supernatural forces are suspected to have dreadful power. Astrology is used for everything from determining when to take medicine to when to take in the washing. Alchemy might well result in lead and iron being turned into gold. And as for the possibilities of witchcraft and magic, these are limited only by the onlooker's imagination; they have nothing to do with the witch's or magician's actual abilities.

At one end of the magical spectrum, the supernatural can be employed for day-to-day purposes. If you lose a valuable item and believe it to have been stolen, you might consult a magician or a witch. You are only likely to get into trouble if an innocent party is named as the culprit; then you or the magician may be accused of slander. Note that it is the slander, not the magic itself, which is unlawful; plain magic without heresy is normally tolerated. However, at the other end of the spectrum is heretical magic, and this is far more serious. In 1324 Dame Alice Kyteler, an Irish gentlewoman, and her companions are accused of renouncing Christ, making sacrifices of living chickens to demons, cursing their husbands, and creating unguents from the intestines of the chickens they had sacrificed, "with certain loathly worms and various herbs, and dead men's nails . . . and garments of children that died unbaptised, and many other detestable ingredients, boiled together over an oak-fire in the skull of a beheaded thief."[18] Although heretics are not normally burnt in fourteenth-century England—the practice only becomes a legally defined penalty in 1401—these accusations happen to be made in Ireland. The authorities take advantage of the opportunity to burn several of Dame Alice's accomplices alive.

Some aspects of this general credulousness are not considered heretical or superstitious at all, but are articles of religious faith, like John the Baptist's three heads. Consider the work of pardoners. People are mindful of their sins, for which they will be judged at the Day of Atonement. Hence they pay pardoners to grant them indulgences. A plenary indulgence—written on a scrap of vellum—clears away all your sinfulness; thus it is the most expensive. Less costly are the specific indulgences, clearing your conscience of a particular crime (say adultery), or the temporary indulgences, allowing you to forget about sins committed in a certain period of time (over the course of a month, for example). The whole strange business is one of blind faith and cynicism at the same time. You will be shocked by the immorality of pardoners selling indulgences cheaply when business is slow. Many people do regard the practice as wholly despicable, but many others believe that they can pay for forgiveness as well as pray for it. When you think about it, a pardoner selling the promise of spiritual salvation is not very different from a physician selling the promise of physical relief. Considering the standards of medieval medicine, the physician is far more likely to hurt you than the pardoner.

Perhaps the stranger aspect of this credulousness and superstition is the widespread belief in prophecy. The political prophecies of medieval England are an extraordinary phenomenon. For several centuries writers have produced mystical texts which purport to describe the political vicissitudes of the future. They take a number of forms: "Adam Davy's Five Dreams," written about 1308, is a sequence of mystical visions about Edward II, which contain a reference to him visiting Rome. The "Prophecy of the Six Kings," first written about 1313, tells the story of the six kings to follow King John and states that Edward III will reconquer all the lands held by his ancestors. The "Holy Oil of St. Thomas" explains the origins and mystical power of some oil brought to England by the duke of Brabant for the coronation of Edward II in 1308. These prophecies all have huge resonance. People believe them. And they have good reason, for they tend to come true, in some form or other. Edward II probably does go to "Rome" in a sense, when he goes to see the pope, at Avignon. Edward III does become a warrior who reclaims all his ancestral lands, defeats the Spanish in battle, and fights at the gates of Paris, as the "Prophecy of the Six Kings" predicts. Political prophecies thus have this self-fulfilling element, and people accordingly place trust in them. So when Henry IV becomes king, one of the first things he arranges is to be anointed with the Holy Oil of St. Thomas. The prophecy indicates that he will become a successful holy warrior.

There *are* rationalists and scientists in medieval society, but you will find their writings even more outlandish than the prophecies. The most extraordinary and famous example of this is a passage in the works of the great thirteenth-century scientist and philosopher Roger Bacon. In a text in which he tries to show how so many supposedly magical things are really quite normal, he writes:

Ships may be made to move without oars or rowers, so that large vessels might be driven on the sea or on a river by a single man, and more swiftly than if they were strongly manned. Chariots can be built which can move without any draught animal at incalculable speed . . . Flying machines might be made in the middle of which a man might sit, turning a certain mechanism whereby artfully built wings might beat the air, in the manner of a bird in flight. Another instrument could be made which, although small, will lift or lower weights of almost infinite greatness . . . Again, instruments might be made for walking in the sea, or in rivers, even to the very bottom, without bodily danger . . . And very many things of this sort might be made: bridges which cross rivers without pier or prop whatsoever, and unheard-of machines and engines.

It is not exactly what you expect of a Franciscan friar living in superstitious medieval England. We might even wonder whether some other time traveler has told Bacon about modern ships, cars, airplanes, cranes, diving suits, and suspension bridges. But think about this passage, as you pour scorn on the credulousness of the people. It is from the same belief that *anything* is possible that the greatest discoveries are made. "What others strive to see dimly and blindly, like bats in twilight, he gazes at in the full light of day, because he is a master of experiment," says Bacon, praising a contemporary.[19] The same could be said of Bacon himself: when anything is possible, experiment is essential. As for his flying machine and diving suit—if Leonardo da Vinci's drawings come to mind, it is not surprising. Roger Bacon's name appears in Leonardo's notebooks.

4

Basic Essentials

Walk into any of the churches and chapels up and down the country, and you will see that many of the walls are painted with scenes from the Bible. But it will take you a moment or two to realize they are biblical scenes, for the figures are not wearing clothing from the time of Christ. All of the people in every single one of these images of the Holy Land look as if they have just stepped out of medieval England. The Romans are dressed in medieval clothes. Christ and the disciples are similarly medieval in appearance. If there are pictures of boats or soldiers, then these too are medieval. There is simply no understanding of cultural development in medieval England, no understanding that people in different ages look and act differently, and no sense of Ancient Rome or Roman Palestine being culturally different. The irony of this for the visitor to the fourteenth century can hardly be missed, because it is precisely these cultural differences which you will find most striking—bewildering even.

This does not just apply to clothes. Languages, the date, working hours—almost everything about daily life in the fourteenth century is different from the modern world. Normally such cultural differences are given a low priority in traditional history books. But for this very reason it is necessary to describe a few of the most basic aspects of daily life. You need to know how to tell the time, when and where you may buy and sell goods, why some people pay tolls and others do not, and how to behave politely. Attention to these details should help you avoid being late for an engagement, placed in the town pillory, robbed, or regarded as just plain mad.

Languages

In the modern world, languages only change gradually. Pick up a book in your national tongue from a century before you were born and you will have little or no difficulty reading it, even if it sounds old-fashioned. Things are quite different in the fourteenth century. Whole sections of society are giving up speaking one language (French) and starting to speak another (English). This is extraordinary in itself; but even more surprisingly it is not those at the bottom of the social spectrum who are relinquishing their native language but those at the top. Although the aristocracy of England have been French speakers since the arrival of the Normans in 1066, and even though Robert of Gloucester noted as recently as the late thirteenth century that "unless a man knows French, people think little of him," linguistically everything changes over the course of the fourteenth century.

Why is this? The simple answer is that Robert of Gloucester's dictum—that only French speakers command respect—becomes obsolete. In 1300 it is true: if you cannot speak French, you cannot command much respect outside your local community. The king speaks French and so do his lords, knights, clerks, chaplains, and servants. All the official classes speak French. Very few high-ranking members of society are fluent in English. Nobody commissions any literature in English, and what little English verse is written almost entirely takes the form of protest poetry, directed against the clergy and nobility, or is religious in purpose. But by 1350 noblemen are increasingly having their sons taught English. The change is largely due to the nationalist outlook of King Edward III, who speaks English, expresses a pride in the language, and even has his own mottoes emblazoned in it. In 1362 he decrees that pleas in court can be made in the English language—before then you can only plead in French—and in so doing he publicly declares his support for English as the "tongue of the nation." In that same year his chancellor opens Parliament with a speech in English. By the end of the century, most aristocrats and prelates speak English as well as French. Edward III's own son has many books in English, including one of the earliest translations of the Bible, and his grandson, Edward of York, translates Gaston Phoebus's famous book on hunting into English. When Henry IV claims the throne in 1399, he does so in English, in Parliament, in front of all the lords and bishops. Later Henry writes to his chancellor (the archbishop of Canterbury) in English, and in 1409 he even writes his will in English. These two men, Edward III and Henry IV, do more than any other lords before them to make English the language of the official classes, reversing the disdain with which the court had viewed it for the previous three hundred years.

Of course, there are exceptions. You will come across a number of people even in the 1390s whose English is not fluent. A number of old-fashioned knights and ladies cannot be bothered to learn a new language, preferring to stick to their Anglo-French (which remains the dominant language at court). In Cornwall, the majority of the population do not speak English or French, maintaining their ancient Celtic tongue (Cornish). Obviously, if you stray over the border into the principality of Wales, you will come across communities where only Welsh is spoken. Even in England itself, the language is remarkable for the range and variety of its many accents and dialects. A man from Northumberland has great difficulty understanding a man from Devon. It is not unknown for some southern English speakers to mistake the language of their northern cousins for French, so strange do their accents sound when traveling to south-coast ports.

Geography and social class are not the only factors governing the choice of language. Very often you will find clerks writing in a different tongue than the one they speak. English itself is rarely written down. If you do give evidence in English in court after 1362, what you say will be translated and be written down in Latin.[1] Financial accounts similarly are written in the cod Latin of the Exchequer. Speaking in one language and writing in another sounds frighteningly complicated but in fact it does have some advantages. As Anglo-French is spoken by so many of the official classes, it acts as a standard means of communication across the whole country. Similarly French provides English administrators with an easy means to communicate with the men of Gascony. Latin has an even more valuable role, for it employs standardized spelling. There is no such thing as standardized spelling in French. Nor in English, which still employs two Saxon letters not in the modern alphabet: *yogh* (written as "ʒ" and pronounced "gh") and *thorn* (written as "þ" and pronounced "th"). Although few people habitually use Latin in conversation, it is very convenient to have a standardized means of communication which extends across the whole of Christendom, from the Canary Islands to Lithuania, and from Iceland to Jerusalem.

If you find yourself speaking English with the locals do not be surprised if their language gets a little rough around the edges. Just as fourteenth-century place names are direct descriptions of localities (for instance: "Shitbrook Street," "Pissing Alley"), so daily speech is equally straightforward and ribald. In telling his *Canterbury Tales*, Chaucer describes how one ardent lover pursued the married woman whom he fancied and "caught her by the cunt." At another point in the same work, Chaucer has his host declare to him, "Your shithouse rhyming isn't worth a turd." Daily language is direct and to the point. So if someone slaps you on the back in a hearty way and exclaims, "Your breeches and your very balls be blessed!" do not take it amiss. It is a compliment.

Dates

When does a new year begin? January 1? Not always. Although aristocrats do give one another New Year presents on January 1, medieval English people count the year of grace (the year of the Lord) as starting on Lady Day, March 25. Curious, you might think. But it gets "curiouser and curiouser." There are many ways of dating the beginning of the year, and several of them are in use simultaneously. In addition to January 1 and March 25 there is a third day on which to begin a new year, namely Michaelmas (September 29), which is used by the Exchequer. It is also adopted by the chronicler Adam Murimuth, whose work is widely copied, adopted, and adapted, complete with its odd dates.

Medieval dating systems become even more complicated for international travelers. The day on which New Year's Day gifts are exchanged in England for the historical year 1367 falls in 1366 in Florence and Venice, but in 1367 in the Italian port of Pisa, where the year begins on the *previous* March 25. If you sail from England on January 1, 1366, and land at Pisa in mid-February, there it will be 1367 already. Travel on to Venice, and arrive before the end of February, and you will be back in 1366. Leave after March 1 and Anno Domini will be

1367. Ride into Florence and you will be back in 1366 again. Return to your boat at Pisa on or after March 25 and it will be 1368. Sail on to Provence and you will find yourself back in 1367. Stop in Portugal or Castile on the return journey—where the date is still reckoned from the advent of the Romans—and it will be 1405. The Spanish Era (as the dating system beginning in 38 BC is called) is still in use in Portugal (until 1422) and Castile (until 1384).[2]

In reality, only a few English people actually use Anno Domini. Instead, most use a far more complicated system: the regnal year. This takes the form of the first/second/third year of the reign of the king. Under this system, the new year actually begins on the anniversary of the king's accession. The year AD 1388 might begin on March 25 but most English people will refer to that day as March 25 in "the eleventh year of King Richard II" (as Richard came to the throne on June 22, 1377). So far so good. The complications arise from the year being set on this secular cycle and the days of the year being set to an ecclesiastical one, based in part on a moveable feast (Easter). Hence March 23, 1388, is "the Monday before the feast of the Annunciation of the Blessed Virgin Mary in the eleventh year of the reign of King Richard II after the Conquest." Not exactly snappy. It is also a system prone to error. Replace "Annunciation" with "Assumption" and you get a totally different date in a different year (August 12, 1387). The fourteenth-century way of recording the date might sound poetic, but that is the only thing in its favor.

Measuring Time

Telling the time has its complications. These arise not so much from a split system as from the complexity of an old sun-based system giving way slowly to the "hour of the clock." Before Edward III introduces the first mechanical clocks to his palaces in the 1350s and 1360s, there are none in England—with the exception of an experimental one devised by an enterprising abbot of St. Albans, Richard of Wallingford. People tell the time by assessing the hour as a fraction of the day, starting at daybreak. As the day and night are split into equal halves regardless of the season, it follows that the daytime "hour" (a twelfth of the daylight) is longer in the summer and shorter in the winter.

Thus the way to work out the time in the fourteenth century is to assess the proportion of the sky which the sun has crossed. This can be done with a sundial or by looking at the angle of shadows cast, by a tall object. In the introduction to "The Sergeant-at-Law's Tale" Chaucer gives a good description of both methods. "Our host saw that the bright sun had traversed a quarter part, plus roughly half-an-hour, of the arc it covers from sunrise to sunset." A quarter of the twelve hours represented by the sun's arc is three hours after dawn; so, if you add the half hour mentioned, the time turns out to be between half-past nine and ten o'clock. Chaucer's narrator confirms this by noting that the length of each tree's shadow is equal to its height, implying the sun is at forty-five degrees in altitude, which he knows is the equivalent of about ten o'clock in April. Normally you would use a brass astrolabe for measuring the angle of the sun, if you know how. Most well-to-do people have one.[3]

The only mechanical clocks you will come across are large turret clocks built into the bell towers of aristocratic palaces and some of the major abbeys and cathedrals. By the end of the century there are clocks in the cathedrals of Salisbury and Wells, and in several royal palaces and castles, including Westminster, Windsor, Queenborough, and King's Langley. Chaucer refers to a clock in the abbey tower in his "Nun's Priest's Tale." Obviously clocks regulate the day in a wholly different way, measuring eighteen hours of daylight and six of nighttime in summer (not twelve and twelve). For this reason there are two sorts of time in use simultaneously: clock time and solar time. So it is necessary to specify "hour of the clock" (our "o'clock"), if that is what you mean, in order to differentiate between the two. Note that clocks do not *show* the time; they announce it by ringing a bell on the hour. Thus you will find people speak not only of "hours of the clock" but also of "hours of the bell."[4]

Even before clocks are invented, bells are an important means of telling the time in towns and cities. In London the great bell of St. Martin's le Grand is the one to listen out for. It is this bell which tells you when the markets are open, and when curfew starts. In a large city like London, where many bells are rung for a wide variety of reasons, knowing the sound each bell makes represents a third method of telling the time. Most people get up at daybreak. The first hour of their day is known as "prime." The third hour (about 9 a.m.) is called "terce"; the sixth hour (noon) is "sext"; the ninth hour of the day (midafternoon), "nones"; and so on. The bells ring across the town for "vespers" at the twelfth hour. As the bells can be heard all over town, it does not matter if they are a few minutes out this way or that, or whether they are using solar hours or hours "of the clock." Whoever rings the said bell sets the standard time for everyone else.

One time of day to which, as a traveler, you will need to pay particular attention is curfew. In London, when the bell of St. Martin's le Grand rings out at the end of the day, the gates to the city are closed and all the people return to their homes or inns. Within the city the watchmen begin their duty—six men patrolling each ward, more guarding the gates—and only men of good repute are permitted in the streets, and then only if they are carrying a lantern. All the taverns have to close their doors. All boats on the river have to be moored. Strangers found out after curfew are likely to be arrested as nightwalkers. For this reason, if you have not found yourself somewhere to stay by the time the curfew bell rings, your best bet is to leave the city straightaway and seek a place to stay outside the city walls, in the suburbs or at Southwark. Otherwise the watch will probably find you overnight accommodation in one of the city prisons. These are among the least savory places to spend any length of time, let alone a whole night.

Units of Measurement

Having seen that there is little or no standardization of language, spelling, date, or time, it will not come as a total surprise to hear that there are considerable variations in some of the units of measurement employed in fourteenth-century England. For example: a "plowland" is the amount of land which a plowteam of eight oxen can plow in a year—this results in a very different acreage in steeply sloping Devon to the same measurement in flat Norfolk. The acre itself is somewhat variable, reflecting its origin as the area which a team of oxen could plow in a day. Although Edward I tries to standardize the acre at 4,840 square yards (the "statute acre"), customary acres persist. The Cheshire acre is nearly twice the size of a statute acre, and the Yorkshire acre is considerably larger too. The Cumberland acre varies in size from place to place, from just over one to almost two statute acres.[5] The Cornish acre varies too but on a much grander scale, being anything from fifteen to three hundred statute acres.[6] As for distances, an Old French mile is about 1.25 statute miles, and many educated people in fourteenth-century England refer to distances in Old French miles.[7] This international standard is practically the only widespread measure of distance. Locally, miles of varying lengths are in use, such as the 2,428-yard mile in West Yorkshire (the modern mile of 1,760 yards will not be established until a statute of 1593).

There are considerable complexities attached to other measures. It is not so much that they vary as that they may be differently interpreted, according to what it is you are trying to measure. A foot in length is the same as your modern foot of 12 inches but if you are measuring cloth then you use the ell, normally 45 inches—but 27 inches if the cloth is Flemish. Probably the most complicated measures are those involving liquids. A gallon of wine is not the same volume as a gallon of ale. A standard hogshead contains 63 wine-gallons or 52.5 ale-gallons. Except that there is no such thing as a *standard* hogshead; there is a standard for wine, another for ale, and a third for beer (which is imported). If you are buying beer in London, a hogshead amounts to 54 ale-gallons; if you are buying ale, it amounts to 48.

This sounds complicated but it could be worse. Devon has its own peculiar weights and measures system, so any merchant doing business there needs to keep his wits about him. The Devon "rod" measures 18 feet, not 16.5, so an acre measures 5,760 square yards, not 4,840. There are 16.5 pounds to the stone (not 14), when measuring cheese or butter. The Devon pound weighs 18 ounces (not 16). A hundredweight is not 112 pounds as elsewhere in England but 120 pounds. There are 10 gallons in a Devon bushel, not the more usual 8. In a later century a traveler remarks that a man from the Midlands or the north of England "might travel through all the countries of Europe and not find practices more foreign to his own than those of Devon."[8]

Identity

At the start of the fourteenth century, it is not that unusual to come across people in rural England who have only one name. A villein called, say, Ilbert, who has always farmed the same clutch of acres across his lord's fields and has similarly spent all his life living in one cottage, Westcott, is unlikely to be addressed as anything other than Ilbert. A man of his lowly rank does not normally bear a hereditary surname. If he were called John, a much more common name, then the need to distinguish him from other Johns in the parish would doubtless arise, and the manorial clerk might describe him as "John of Westcott" or "John, Ilbert's son." But whichever appellation he is ascribed, it is simply a distinguishing feature, not a hereditary name. If John moves to Southcott he will soon become known as "John of Southcott." In 1300 only your official, wealthy, and political classes need to have hereditary surnames, so they can be identified outside their places of residence, or so testimony given on their authority can be repeated in future years. Hence all the franklins, esquires, and gentry you meet will have a hereditary identity. Villeins who do not travel far, or hold an office, have little need of one.

All this changes in the second and third quarters of the century. Partly as a result of downturns in the economy from the 1315–23 period, and especially after the Great Plague of 1348–49, villeins start moving around between manors much more often. The need to identify different people from many more places becomes apparent. Moreover, the concept of a consistent family name for everyone—not just the rich and well traveled—develops, so that by 1400 people expect that a man called "John of Westcott" or "John Ilbertson" will be called by the same name whether he is in Westcott or Westminster. Moreover, the idea of an unchanging family name means that even John's sons will be expected to carry the surname Ilbertson. By 1400 the idea of everyone having a hereditary surname has caught on.

Identity is much more than a name. It includes where you are from and, by implication, how far you are from those who will protect you. It includes status. In the case of a nobleman this obviously implies his title, or the name of his principal manor. A London freeman's company or guild may also form part of his identity. In other towns and cities, the very fact that a man is a freeman of the place is important: it implies that he has certain rights. An abbot similarly depends on his religious house for his identity; the abbot of Westminster is a far more important man than the abbot of Flaxley, for example. Then of course there is the heraldic aspect of identity, which distinguishes the lords, knights, and esquires from the rest of the community, including such merchants who are descended from heraldic families. These are not to be regarded lightly. Some knights value their coat of arms as highly as their family name and will enter into long and costly legal battles to prove their right to a particular design.

All these elements of identity come together in a seal. A seal is a matrix which creates an impression in soft wax, allowing a man or woman to authenticate a document. Most seals of the nobility contain either a coat of arms or a depiction of the lord in armor on horseback, bearing his arms on a shield. They normally have an inscription recording the lord's name and principal title or, if merely a knight, his principal manor. Secular lords' seals are round; so too are merchants' seals, which carry a design of a bird or some other emblem (if the merchant is not armigerous). Ecclesiastical seals are not round but a tall, symmetrical convex shape, as are noblewomen's seals. Normally a man keeps his seal about his person, or his secretary or chaplain will look after it. When he dies, the matrix of his seal will be broken. If it is lost, he will urge town criers to announce that documents sealed with it no longer carry his approval.

Seals are used to represent corporate identities too. Not only does an abbot have a personal seal, his abbey has a communal seal. Seals are used for cities and incorporated towns (those ruled by a mayor and corporation). A whole range of organizations have seals: merchant guilds and London companies, Oxford and Cambridge colleges, priories, collegiate churches, even some bridges. As with individuals' seals, these are marks of identity and authority: the medieval equivalent of a signature.

As for the seals of the kingdom, one of the king's two great seals is kept by the chancellor for sealing Chancery documents, and the other by the treasurer for sealing Exchequer documents. These huge seals, six inches across, are color coded: the Chancery uses red wax, the Exchequer green. The king's own letters are sealed with a much smaller personal seal, the privy seal. At least that is how things stand at the beginning of the century. In Edward III's reign the use of the privy seal is increasingly delegated to its keeper, who can deal with routine business as directed by the king. The king himself has a new "secret seal" or signet made to authenticate his personal letters and directions. This is kept by his secretary. By 1400 there are four royal seals in operation: the secret seal, privy seal, and two versions of the great seal.

Manners and Politeness

You might think that medieval society is dirty, violent, and uncouth. Maybe it is, but that does not mean it is without high standards of politeness. It is particularly important to behave in an appropriate manner in the company of the rich and powerful. Great lords can be very prickly, and any disrespect shown to them or members of their household is liable to lead to bitterness, enmity, and violent repercussions. Just look through the rolls of patent letters at the number of men who are forgiven for murder; and look at the thousands of gallows throughout the country, which are never empty for long. Manners maketh Man, they say. Certainly the lack of them can unmake a man.

The important thing is to remember the universal desire for respect. The modern idea of impressing your peers by showing an arrogant disregard towards your social superiors simply has no place in medieval England. When you come to the house of a social equal or superior, you are expected to leave your weapons with the gatekeeper or to hand them to your host. "He who comes to a house, look he bring nothing dangerous," as they say. Do not enter a man's hall without permission, whatever sort of man he be. In the case of a yeoman or a merchant, a servant will probably announce your arrival. With important lords, the chamberlain or the marshal of the hall, or one of his ushers, will take you to his lord or his lady. Take off your hat, cap, or hood and keep it off until you are told to put it back on. When you enter your host's chamber, if the man or woman is of an equal status, you will bow. If they are of higher status, you will kneel at least once (one knee, the right, all the way to the ground). If you are being led before the king, especially if you are not already familiar with him, you will kneel on entry to the chamber or hall, then progress to the middle of the room, stop, and kneel again. If the king wishes to speak to you, he will beckon you forward. When the chamberlain tells you to stop, do so and kneel again, three times. Wait until you are spoken to; do not address the king first. When you are requested to speak, always begin with a greeting, such as "God speed, my lord." Bow on each occasion you are requested to speak. Do not avert your eyes from the person of the king: you should look at him directly and honestly (as with everyone else of equal or higher social standing, unlike in later centuries). Never, ever, turn your back on a social superior. To do so is simply rude.

If you are invited to remain some time in the court of a great lord, you will end up spending a lot of time standing around. When this happens, do not sit down until the most important person present gives you permission to do so. This is not necessarily the lord; if the king or queen or any other superior is visiting the same house, and is present, then the social courtesies of rank are automatically due to the king or queen, not the man whose house it is. If a man who is superior in rank to you enters, move back and make room for him to stand nearer the lord or lady than you. When doing all this standing around, remember not to let your eyes wander around the room. Similarly don't scratch yourself or lean against a column or a wall. Do not pick your nose, teeth, or nails or spit indoors. Unless you are yourself of a high rank, or very familiar with the most socially elevated person present, be circumspect in your actions and gestures. Everything can be held against you as a mark of disrespect. And it is for the social superior to decide what is or is not disrespectful, not you.

There is no hard and fast line between behavior as a mark of respect and as a sign of general politeness; rather, one shades into the other. Consequently you need to know how to behave at table, especially when dining in the company of socially refined people. Forget all the myths you have heard about greedily gnawing large joints of beef and chicken and hurling the bones around the medieval hall. In no household is such behavior considered decent. There are strict rules of etiquette to be obeyed. You must wash your hands immediately before every meal. Cut your bread, do not break it. When offered a drink, wipe your mouth first before lifting the cup. Do not lean on the table. When the various courses are set before you, do not grab all the best bits and keep them for yourself but select them from the bowls one at a time. Do not pick them up and dip them in the salt—that is such poor behavior it will be considered disrespectful to the householder. Remember also the general marks of respect, such as not to speak with your mouth full or to talk to anyone when they are drinking. If you are offered a drink from the cup of a social superior, wipe your mouth, accept it, and then pass it back. Do not pass the cup on to another person; it is a sign of the lord's favor and meant only for you.[9]

For women there are other forms of politeness. It is not seemly for women to swear. Although the Wife of Bath does so, unless you are an independent widow, like her, you are likely to get into trouble for it, for it will bring shame on your husband or father. Young women should not toss their heads nor wriggle their shoulders, nor allow their hands to be touched by a man who is not of their family; and drunkenness in women outside the home is considered shocking. Similarly women should not attend public wrestling matches or enter into conversations with strangers, as they are likely to acquire a bad reputation. Women outside the home should normally be accompanied, walking arm in arm with either a male member of the family or a female companion.

Body language is often very differently interpreted by fourteenth-century people. Men and women cry when they are deeply saddened or grief stricken, of course; but you will also find people weeping for less emotional reasons. When a merchant or person in authority wishes to extort a financial due or a service you have promised, he may well weep on account of the distress it gives him to have to exact the full payment. Raising your arms to the sky is another element of body language that is subtly different: in the Middle Ages it is a sign of thanks to God, and thus connected with relief, not despair. Few people shake hands on greeting each other; rather, shaking hands is a demonstration of mutual agreement in front of witnesses.[10] Kissing between men needs a specific context: when men kiss in public it is a sign of peace, an acknowledgment of fealty or service, or a ceremonial act. It is not simply a greeting. Nor does it have any sexual connotations. A man publicly kissing a woman who is not of his family, however, *does* have sexual connotations, and so you should refrain from greeting an acquaintance of the opposite sex with a big kiss in public. Even a peck on the cheek will raise eyebrows.

Greeting People

Initial impressions count. If you are overfriendly or cold on first meeting somebody, you are likely to affect your relationship with that person in future. The best advice on this subject is to be found in a French-English dialogue book, which contains a number of phrases to be used on greeting people. For example:

When you go by the streets, and you meet anyone you know, or any-one of your acquaintance, be swift and ready to greet him or them first, if he or they be men of valour. Doff your hood for ladies and damoiselles; if they doff theirs, so set your own on again. In such man-ner may you salute them: 'Sire, God you keep!' That is the shortest that one may say to people in greeting. Or at other times:

'Sire, ye be welcome.'

'Yea, lady or damoiselle, ye be welcome.'

'Sire, God give you good day.'

'Dame, good day give you our Lord.'

'Fellow or friend, ye be welcome.'

'What do ye? How is it with you? Where have ye been so long?'

'I have been long out of the country.'

'In what country?'

'Sire, that should be overmuch for to tell; but if you please, anything that I may do, command it me as to him that gladly shall I do it.'

'Sire, gramercy of your courteous words and of your good will; God reward you!'[11]

Shopping

When the town bell rings prime, the shops start to open. If it is a mar-ket day, then the traders in the market too can start doing business.

Where you shop will, of course, depend on what it is you hope to buy. There is no point going to a market for armor or jewelry; you will need to find specialist shops in a city. Large cities and some towns have more than one market. A city market can become so crowded that several smaller, specialist marketplaces are necessary. In Stratford upon Avon, for example, there are separate markets every Thursday for corn, hay, livestock, poultry, and dairy products. London has a whole range of markets, from the daily poultry market at Leadenhall to the Friday horse market at Smithfield.

A town market is held primarily for the purpose of supplying goods to those who live in the town and its surrounding parishes. However, most markets also have a wholesale function, providing livestock for butchers, for example. In a coastal town, the daily catch of fish is sold in the fish market. Some of the catch is bought and consumed locally but most is transported inland to other towns by fish merchants for sale in those markets. There it is sold direct to the customer; there is no point in a fishmonger buying it to sell over the course of a whole week, it will not keep. Other sorts of market goods include items that are not required on a day-to-day basis. Furs of hares, rabbits, kids, foxes, cats, and squirrels (used as trimmings on the clothes of the well-to-do) are available in the market, but there is insufficient demand in most small towns for many shops to be dedicated to such commodities on a daily basis. Hence there are itinerant furriers, traveling between towns, arriving on their respective market days. The market also serves as a hardware shop. If you want a full picture of what is available, stand on the roadside and check what items are in the carts and wagons approaching the town. At Newark in 1328, for example, you will see the following being taken to market: grain (mainly wheat, barley, oats, and rye), salted meat and bacon, fresh meat, salmon, mackerel, lampreys, saltwater fish, stockfish, herrings, Aberdeen fish (cured salmon and herring), sheep, goats, pigs, fleeces, tanned hides, leather, furs, cloth of many descriptions, iron, steel, tin, woad, wine, sacks of wool, apples, pears, nuts, linen, canvas, timber, new carts, horses, mares, laths, wooden planks, hay, rushes (for hall floors), coverlets (for beds), glass, garlic, salt, faggots, coal, brushwood, nails, and horseshoes.[12]

This list of what you normally *can* buy in a market gives you a good idea of the things which you cannot. Hawkers might be selling pies as you walk around between the market stalls, but otherwise you will have to go to a cookshop to buy one. You might buy cloth in a market but you will need to go to a shop to have your clothes tailored. A cobbler will buy his leather in the market, and so it is to his shop you will go to buy shoes, not the market itself. Such shops are arranged in the vicinity of the marketplace, often fronting onto it. In Norwich the market is so busy that certain traders operate not in the marketplace itself but in the streets and alleys around it. The range of services available on a daily basis—including days when the market is not in operation—can be judged from the range of merchants resident in a town. In Colchester in 1301 you will find ten smiths, eight weavers, eight butchers, seven bakers, five carpenters, and thirteen mercers. The mercers all vie for the same trade—they all sell leatherware, such as gloves, belts, purses, and needle cases—but a few specialize in rarer commodities. One is also a cloth merchant, another sells verdigris and mercury for cosmetics and ointments.[13]

Towns which have weekly markets normally have an annual fair as well, usually held on a feast day between July and September (and always between May and November). Fairs are the great gatherings of medieval England. They usually last for three days, being held on the day before a specific saint's day, on the feast day itself, and on the following day. When a fair is in progress thousands of people flock to the town. Whereas markets present country people with a weekly chance to buy goods and commodities, fairs present them with a once-in-the-year opportunity to buy more exotic items. A fair is an opportunity for many townsmen to buy items in bulk from wholesalers; these will be stored in their warehouses for use in subsequent months. Dyers, for example, have difficulty obtaining some of the rarer colors; the hundred miles or so that these need to be transported from the nearest port prohibits their being taken to every market, but suppliers of dyestuffs turn up at fairs. Merchants importing exotic spices and rare fruit—such as oranges, lemons, figs, dates, and pomegranates—also attend fairs, especially those in or near a city.

Trade is regulated everywhere. Most major towns and cities normally have a "guild merchant" (sometimes spelled "gild merchant"): a trading organization which controls who can and who cannot trade freely in the market.[14] Such a body sets the duties payable by nonresidents selling goods in the market and charges a wide variety of fees, such as pontage (for maintenance of a bridge), stallage (the right to have a stall in a marketplace), and pavage (for maintenance of the road). In some cases they may ban the sale of certain goods by nonresidents altogether. The Leicester guild merchant has some strong rules forbidding anyone who is not a freeman of the town from selling cloth, wax, fish, or meat. The guild merchant may also impose restrictions on who can *buy* goods on nonmarket days, prohibiting all but their own freemen from buying wool, for example, or prohibiting butchers' wives from buying meat to sell again on the same day.[15]

There are reasons to be grateful for the supervision of trade. *Caveat emptor* (buyer beware) should be engraved in big letters over the entrance to every marketplace. You simply would not believe how many different tricks and deceptions are practiced on the unwary customer. Ask any clerk in the London Guildhall; he will tell you of cooking pots being made out of soft cheap metal and coated with brass and of loaves of bread baked with stones or pieces of iron inserted in them, to make them up to the legally required weight. If you visit the city you may well find out for yourself what tricks are employed. Items are arranged on stalls so as to conceal their defects. Wool is stretched before it is woven, to make it go farther (but then it shrinks terribly). Cloth is sometimes mixed with human hair. Shoes are made of substandard leather. Meat is sold even though it is putrid, wine even though it has turned sour, and bread when it has gone green and is considered to be in danger of killing the purchaser. Pepper is sold damp, making it swell, weigh more, and rot sooner. Short measures are a notorious problem, and from 1310 turners have to swear to make wooden measures of the appropriate size. Even oats can be falsely sold by a regrator. How come, you ask? Surely oats are oats? Not when a sack of rotten oats is sold with a few handfuls of good, fresh oats placed carefully in the top of the sack.[16]

Do not feel you have to accept being ripped off. Wherever you are shopping, you will find opportunities to have your grievances addressed. Guild merchants are acutely aware that their position is open to challenge from other markets and are thus keen to protect the good name of their own market and freemen. Lords of seigneurial boroughs are likewise very keen to make sure that nothing damages their income from tolls in their markets. Similarly the right to hold a fair conveys the right—and responsibility—to hold a court to try fraudulent traders. These are called "piepowder courts."

If you are the victim of malpractice, go straight to the authorities. At a fair, the perpetrator will be fined. In a town he will be pilloried, literally. The pillory is the wooden board which clasps the guilty man's head and hands and prevents him avoiding either his shame or the insults of the crowd—and anything else they might care to throw at him. A butcher selling bad meat can expect to be dragged through the streets of the town on a hurdle and then placed in the pillory with the rotten meat being burnt under him. Likewise a baker selling bad bread. A vintner caught selling foul wine is dragged to the pillory on a hurdle, forced to drink a draught of the offending liquor, and then set in the pillory, where the remainder of the liquid is poured over his head. The sweetness of the revenge makes up for the sourness of the wine.

Money

As you will have noticed, the currency is not a decimal system (one made up of multiples of ten). The basic unit is the pound (£1), which should be the equivalent of a pound in weight of silver. But there is no actual £1 coin. Nor are there any £1 notes. Instead there are small silver coins, of which the penny (1d) is by far the most common. Twelve pennies make a shilling (1s) and twenty shillings make £1.

Until 1344, the only coins in a merchant's purse are silver ones. A few big silver groats (4d) from the reign of Edward I are still in circulation, but otherwise you will only come across pennies, halfpennies and farthings (¼d). In 1344 Edward III mints a superb florin or double leopard (worth 6s) as well as a half florin or leopard (3s) and a quarter florin or helm (1s 6d). The purpose is to publicize his nation in the same way that the Florentine "florin"—used right across Europe—publicizes the international importance of the Italian city-state of Florence.[17] Sadly, you are extremely unlikely to see any of these coins: the gold in them is worth more than the face value of the coin and so they are almost all melted down immediately. But after several more attempts, Edward gets the size of coin right in the noble of 1351 (worth 6s 8d). This remains the pattern for the rest of the century. Henceforth he mints nobles, half nobles, and quarter nobles in gold. Groats, pennies, halfpennies, and farthings are minted in silver.

The value of a noble—6s 8d—at first seems an odd one. However, it is a particularly useful amount. There are two normal units of account in England. In addition to the pound there is the mark (13s 4d). One noble is exactly a third of £1 and half of a mark. Having one coin which equates to a substantial fraction of both units of account is a considerable advance on weighing out 160 or 240 little silver pennies for every mark or £1 of account.

If you take the purse hanging from the belt of any moderately wealthy townsman and inspect the coins you find inside, you will see how much variety there is in the design and size of medieval coinage. Coins last a long time. Even when their designs are worn and barely recognizable, the size of silver pennies means that they remain perfectly acceptable. Hence in the reign of Edward II the coinage predominantly consists of coins minted in the very long reigns of his father, Edward I, and grandfather Henry III. Slowly these become less numerous and Edward III's image takes over. By 1400, a handful of silver at random will mostly show the tumbling locks of Edward III in his heyday.

The range and variety of coin designs will amaze you. Between Edward I's great recoinage of 1279 and the deposition of Richard II (1399) there are about 160 varying sorts of penny struck—more than one per year. This is partly because, unlike in the modern world, there are several mints in operation at once. There are at least three royal mints, at Canterbury, Berwick-on-Tweed, and the Tower of London. There are also private mints, operated by the abbot of Bury St. Edmunds, the bishop of Durham, and the archbishop of York. Edward III opens an additional mint at Calais in 1351, and the abbot of Reading starts another mint on the king's behalf in the 1330s. Each of these mints has several moneyers who all mark their coins, and the mints at York and Durham change their marks when a new archbishop or bishop is elected. So, when a new king ascends the throne, or when a title (such as "king of France") is adopted or dropped by Edward III, a new batch of coins appears.

Prices

You will be pleased to know that prices are relatively static by comparison with modern inflationary standards. This is helped by long-standing legal provisions controlling the price of bread, wine, and ale. Expect to spend 3d on a gallon of average wine in 1305, and 1d on a gallon of second-best ale. The same prices apply a century later. In times of crisis, however, prices can go in all directions at once. Grain prices increase massively after successive harvest failures, while the cost of luxury items plummets. Conversely, in the year of the Great Plague (1348–49), there is so much food and livestock available that the economy enters a deflationary cycle. As the Leicester chronicler Henry Knighton points out, in 1349 you can buy a horse which was previously worth £2 for just half a mark (6s 8d)—a sixth of its original value. He also mentions that a cow is worth just 12d, whereas before the plague it was worth eight times as much.

In the modern world, the English are not accustomed to haggle.

This is something you will have to get used to: it is the principal means of establishing prices. The following is a contemporary example of how you may expect the system to work:

"Dame, what hold ye the ell of this cloth? Or what is worth the cloth whole? In short, so to speak, how much the ell?"

"Sire, I shall do you to reason; ye shall have it good and cheap."

"Yea, truly. Dame must me win. Take heed what I shall pay."

"Four shillings for the ell, if it please you."

"That were no wisdom. For so much would I have good scarlet."

"You are right, if ye may. But I have some which is not of the best which I would not give for seven shillings."

"I you believe well. But this is no such cloth, of so much money, that ye know well!"

"Sire, what is it worth?"

"Dame, it were worth to me well three shillings."

"That is evil-boden . . ."

"But say certainly how shall I have it without thing to leave?"

"I shall give it you at one word: ye shall pay five shillings, certainly if ye have them for so many ells, for I will abate no thing."

"Dame, then what shall avail long words?"[18]

Although there is modest inflation in the fourteenth century, it is impossible to give modern equivalents to the prices you will be charged. Any comparison is bound to be misleading. For example, in 1339, in Exeter, one hundred nails for constructing tables for the fish market cost 3d: about the same as the carpenters' wages for making those tables (2¾d per person per day, plus ale).[19] In the modern world, those nails would cost no more than £4; but nobody would give a day's work for so little, however much ale you gave them. A carpenter's daily wage at the time of writing is nearer £100—the wages have increased in price twenty-five times as much as the nails. Such disparities in long-term inflation are to be noted across most forms of produce and service. Henry IV has to pay 10s for a pound of saffron in 1391; today it is still picked by hand and has a retail price of £2,000 per kilogram (£909 per pound), an increase of 181,700 percent. In the same account Henry pays 5d per chicken (capon). If chickens had increased at the same rate as saffron they would cost nearly £38 each in the modern world. If they had increased as much as carpenters' wages, they would cost £154, thirty times as much as a plucked one actually costs at the time of writing.

The reason for stressing this point is to show that some things we take for granted are far more prized in medieval society than in the modern world. Food is far more valuable and expensive in the fourteenth century than in modern England. Labor on the other hand is relatively cheap. Land is dirt cheap (rents of 1d or 2d per acre for free tenants are common). But a chicken can cost more than a laborer's daily wage, and a pound of sugar costs more than twice as much. There is a different scale of need and demand underpinning these prices. Moreover, the relative demand for a service or commodity varies in different parts of the country. Food is much cheaper in rural areas than in the city. A pig normally costs 3s in the city but just 2s at a country market. Oats similarly cost half as much in the country as they do in a city. As a consequence of food being cheaper, everything else tends to be less expensive in the country too. Candles cost 2½d per pound in the city but only 1½d per pound in the country.[20] The laws of supply and demand operate on a far more localized pattern. Money has different values when the transportation of goods is so slow, difficult, and expensive.

Working and Wages

Earning an income in medieval England is not easy. Very few people start out in life as a villein and work their way up to a position of independent means. Those who make their fortunes in a trade, war, the Church, or the law tend to come from families which are at least reasonably well-off to begin with. Not even the semilegendary fourteenth-century mayor of London, Dick Whittington, can be said to have dragged himself out of the gutter. He did die an exceedingly wealthy man, it is true; but he was hardly poor at birth. His father was the Gloucestershire landowner Sir William Whittington.

What jobs are open to you and what do they pay? As you may have gathered, to enter any sort of worthwhile employment in a town requires you to become a freeman of the town by becoming a member of its guild merchant (or, in some towns, one of its craft-specific

guilds, such as the Carpenters' Guild or the Goldsmiths' Guild). Entry
to a guild is either by inheritance or by payment of an entry fine, often
£1 or £2. To become a member of a London guild (or livery company)
you might need to pay as much as £3. To become an apprentice similarly requires a sum to be paid to the master. Without the freedom of
a town and an apprenticeship in a trade or craft, laboring is practically
your only option.

Daily Wages of Hired Workers[21]

Worker	1301–10	1331–40	1361–70	1391–1400
Carpenter	2¾d	3d	4½d	4½d
Laborer	1½d	1¾d	3¼d	3¼d
Thatcher	2½d	3d	3½d	4¼d
Thatcher's mate	1d	1¼d	2d	2¼d
Mason	5d	5½d	6d	6d

Obviously there is some variation according to where and for
whom you work. There are also variations in payment according to
season. Masons chiseling away on the stones for Exeter Cathedral in
1306 are paid 1¼d per day in summer but 4½d in winter, because of
the shorter daylight hours. This is common for most sorts of building
and laboring work. Tilers in London in the 1340s can expect 5½d in
summer and 4½d in winter.[22] But even at a tiler's wage, you will find
it very difficult to save enough to pay a fine of £2 for entry to a guild
merchant. The low wages are rendered even lower by the fact that
food is extremely expensive. Laborers must expect at least two-thirds
of their wages to go on food and drink in the early part of the century.
You might be offered a choice: 1d with food or 2½d without. Casual
harvest workers especially experience this mixed form of payment, receiving wages (occasionally as much as 5d per day) plus as much food
as they can eat. However, as soon as the harvest is in, they are laid off.

Considering that no one should work on a Sunday, and considering
that there are between forty and fifty further "holy days" in the year,
which are also not working days, the most that your average mason
will earn over the course of the year is £7 1s 6d. This is a substantial

income, more than the vast majority of people earn. However, if he goes on to become a *master* mason, he stands to make much more. At Wallingford in 1365, the master mason is paid 4s. per week, and at Windsor Castle the master mason in charge of the grand rebuilding is paid 7s per week.[23] A master carpenter can earn similar amounts. This puts these masters into an earning bracket of £10 to £17, similar to highly educated lawyers and physicians. In this way you can work your way up to a high level of social respectability, even if you do not come from a landed family.

Service in someone else's household pays badly in comparison. Not even the royal household can be said to pay well. Although Edward II's chief officers do receive between 8 marks and £20 per year, and the next rank down—the king's sergeants—receive 7½d per day, plus food and clothes, the third rank are on just 4½d per day. Valets receive only 1½ per day, one meal in hall, and the right to share a bed with another man of the same rank.[24] And this is the best establishment in which to be a servant. Pages and grooms in other lords' households are lucky if they receive more than 1d a day. A live-in manservant in a yeoman's household might be paid as little as 4d per week. A live-in woman servant can expect little more than half this, about 2½ per week, and she is often paid annually, in arrears. The same goes for women and girls in laboring and harvest work: normally they are paid half the wages of their male counterparts.[25] When the ostentation of the wealthy is so great, and the wages of those who labor so low, it is not surprising that a great many people turn to crime.

5

What to Wear

Hollywood has given us the impression that medieval people dress in stereotypical uniforms. Kings wander around their palaces in ermine-trimmed robes, knights always wear armor, ladies flounce wistfully in long flowing gowns, and court jesters prance in red-and-yellow jangling jumpsuits. Similarly, the association of haute couture with glamorous modernity suggests that fashion in the modern sense cannot possibly have existed by 1400. These impressions are all wrong. The fourteenth century sees greater changes in clothing styles than any previous period of a hundred years. And men's fashion changes more than in any century since.

In 1300 clothes are straightforward and practical, appropriate to rank, adding distinction through color and fabric quality rather than cut and tailoring. Then about 1330 things begin to change. The essential difference lies in the way a sleeve is cut. The advent of tailored sleeves allows clothing to reflect the shape of the body. Clothes no longer just hang from the shoulders like tunics: they reveal the natural curves of men's and women's forms. As a result, there is greater differentiation in cut between male and female clothing. Around 1400 fashion reaches the pinnacle of design eccentricity, with trailing dresses, tunics cut so short that they allow men to show off their legs up to the hips, long-hanging sleeves, and ridiculously pointed shoes.

Despite this new figure-hugging sexiness, some important moral and social dimensions continue to limit what people may wear. At no level of society does clothing become a free-for-all. Women are never at liberty to show their naked legs or arms in public—the only female arms and legs you will see are those of washerwomen. Clothing remains a key means of preserving the social order. Prostitutes are tolerated in London as long as they wear the yellow hood of their trade and abide by the city regulations. To have prostitutes wearing normal clothes would be a threat to the respectability of the wives and daughters of the townsmen. Likewise lepers are expected to wear cloaks and bells; it forms part of the social contract under which they are tolerated. Friars and monks similarly are expected to wear the clothing appropriate to their status and order. Aristocrats wear expensive furs, lesser men and women cheaper furs, townswomen rabbit furs, and so on. In medieval society, what you wear denotes what you are.

In some respects your clothing also establishes who protects you and where your loyalties lie. The men who serve in lordly households are normally expected to wear the livery of that household: a sort of uniform which accords with the heraldic colors of the lord himself. Alternatively, a servant of a great lord might wear his lord's livery collar, notifying everyone that he has that lord's protection. This is a serious use of clothing: a symbolic threat. To attack a man who is wearing a great lord's livery is tantamount to attacking the lord himself. Conversely, if a man thus dressed starts attacking you, you had better beware. If his lord decides he will protect his man from the law—a practice known as "maintenance"—then the chances are that you will not see justice done. Men banded together wearing an identical livery are not above the law in theory, but in practice they are almost untouchable.

Obviously changes in fashion and the social functions of clothing are not wholly compatible. You cannot have a society in which clothing is both a conservative moral benchmark and yet changes with the season. Can you imagine the gossips of medieval London remarking on how the prostitutes are wearing their yellow hoods so much higher this year? No more so than you can imagine nuns wearing scarlet habits. As a result there is a fundamental tension between the agents of change and those who have a vested interest in the status quo. Hence the sumptuary laws are passed. These are restrictions preventing certain people from dressing to a standard above their station. In London, at the start of the century, it is the rule that

no common woman should go to market or out of her house with a hood furred with anything other than lambskin or rabbit fur, on pain of losing her hood to the sheriffs, with the exception of those ladies who wear furred capes . . . because shopgirls, wetnurses and other servants, and loose women bedizen themselves with hoods furred with ermine and minever, like ladies of quality.[1]

Sumptuary laws based on those of London are added to the statute books in 1337. From that year on, only those with an annual income of £100 per year are allowed to wear furs. This legislation is widely flouted, and plenty of merchants' and esquires' wives continue to wear their ermine and miniver with pride. So in 1363 the sumptuary laws are extended, on account of the "outrageous and excessive apparel of many people above their estate and degree, and to the great destruction of all the land."

Clothing Regulations Imposed by the Sumptuary Laws of 1363[2]

Status	What They May Wear
Lords with lands worth £1,000 annually, and their families	No restrictions
Knights with lands worth 400 marks (£266 13s 4d) annually, and their families	May dress at their will, except they may wear no weasel fur, ermine, or clothing of precious stones other than the jewels in women's hair
Knights with lands worth 200 marks (£133 6s 8d) annually, and their families	Fabric worth no more than 6 marks (£4) for the whole cloth; no cloth of gold, nor a cloak, mantle, or gown lined with pure miniver; sleeves of ermine or any material embroidered with precious stones; women may not wear ermine or weasel fur, or jewels except those worn in their hair
Esquires with land worth £200 per year and merchants with goods to the value of	Fabric worth no more than 5 marks (£3 6s 8d) for the whole cloth; they *may* wear cloth of silk and silver, or anything decorated with silver; women may wear

£1,000, and their families	miniver but not ermine or weasel fur, or jewels except those worn in their hair
Esquires, gentlemen with £100 per year and merchants with goods to the value of £500, and their families	Fabric worth no more than 4½ marks (£3) for the whole cloth; no cloth of gold, silk, or silver, no embroidery, no precious stones or fur
Yeomen and their families	Fabric worth no more than 40s (£2) for the whole cloth; no jewels, gold, silver, embroidery, enamelware, or silk; no fur except lamb, rabbit, cat, or fox; women not to wear a silk veil
Servants and their families	Fabric worth no more than 2 marks for the whole cloth; no gold, silver, embroidery, enamelware, or silk; women not to wear a veil worth more than 12d
Carters, plowmen, drivers of plows, oxherds, cowherds, swineherds, dairymaids, and everyone else working on the land who does not have 40s of goods	No cloth except blanket and russet at 12d per ell, belts of linen (rope)

Royalty

The sumptuary laws impose no restrictions on what the royal family can wear. The pressure on them is rather the opposite: to dress the part of majesty and thus to demonstrate their status through excessively rich clothing. For this reason, members of the royal family tend to be trailblazers for fashion. What they are wearing today, the nobility will be wearing in a few weeks' time, and the burghers of the provincial towns and cities will be wearing in the years to come, albeit in cheaper versions. Thus the king is at least partly responsible for the whole escalation in competitive fashion among the lower classes.

What do kings wear when not draped in ceremonial robes? Let us look at Edward III. In February 1333, aged twenty, you will find him at Berwick dressed in "an outfit of green velvet embroidered all over with pearls," or perhaps "an aketon [padded jacket] covered in vermilion velvet and embroidered with images of parrots and other decorations."[3] Two years later you might find him wearing "a coat and mantle of scarlet cloth garnished with silk fowl, trimmed with gold throughout, and decorated with birds on branches, the breasts of the birds being embroidered with two angels studded with pearls holding a golden crossbow crafted with gilt-silver and a string of pearls."[4] Edward is not one to hide his light under a bushel.

Edward II and Richard II are hardly less extravagant in their clothing. The queens of medieval England are similarly resplendent. Just as the kings set the standards for male extravagance, so the queens set the standard for the women. Queen Margaret (second wife of Edward I) and Queen Isabella (wife of Edward II) both maintain strong links with their native France. Surrounded by French servants, they are aware of the new fabrics and styles from Rheims and Paris. Queen Anne, wife of Richard II, similarly brings fashions from her native Bohemia. Queen Philippa retains contacts with her native Hainault, and in Edward III has the benefit of a husband who dotes on her and supplies her with almost as many precious items and jewel-encrusted clothes as he orders for himself and his friends. If you should come across a lady wearing "a hood made of brown scarlet studded with 154 stars of pearls and trimmed with gold, each star being crafted out of seven large pearls with an especially large one at the top of each star," or "a beaver-fur hat lined with velvet and adorned with white pearls and golden baboons," have no doubt: she is a queen.[5]

Aristocratic Men

As it is a common trait for men to ape their social superiors, it is instructive to begin by considering the clothing of the rich and powerful. Your average man-about-court in the first decade wears a suit of robes: three or four garments selected to complement one another. The most important is the tunic: a sleeved dress-like garment reaching down almost to the ankles. This is cut in such a way that there is normally no seam between the sleeves and the body. Front and back—including the sleeves—are each cut together from a single piece of material and sewn together. The result is that both the sleeves and body are loose, to allow the arms to enter easily. If the garment has separate, tight-fitting sleeves, these will be sewn up around the arm every time the garment is worn.[6] The body of the tunic remains loose; it hangs from the shoulders with as much grace as the wearer can give it. Sometimes it is worn with a belt but not always; a certain elegance lies in the folds in the rich fabric when it is allowed to hang loose. Normally a supertunic is worn draped over the top. This has short wide sleeves and is slightly shorter than the tunic itself, so the colors of the tunic may be seen. Contrasts are preferred; for example, a red tunic and green supertunic, or blue tunic and brown supertunic.

Most of the time you will add a third item, a hood, and a fourth, a mantle. The hood is made of soft fabric and hangs down the back when not pulled up to cover your head. The mantle will probably be square and made to hang around your shoulders (perhaps fastened across the front with a jeweled clasp). Alternatively it will be cut in a large circle, with a hole in the center for the head and two further holes for the arms. This long garment falls to the ground. Although its long sweeping folds make it look impressive, it is actually a little inconvenient, as it is very easy to trip over the hem. Convenience, you will soon realize, is not something to which aristocrats aspire. The more impractical the clothing, the higher the status of the wearer.

What should you be wearing beneath these robes? A linen shirt. The very best quality linen comes from Rheims; the second-best from Paris. Underwear on your lower half will consist of braies or "breeches"—not to be confused with the later outer garment of the same name. These also are made of linen and hang down the leg, sometimes being tied with small cords around the knees. The cord or belt of the braies at the waist will be threaded through the top of the garment, and the braies themselves will be drawn up and rolled around the cord, to stop it cutting uncomfortably into the skin. Braies at this period are very loose fitting: with long, flowing tunics and supertunics over the top, you do not need bottom-hugging linen.

From about 1330 you will notice variations appearing in the cut of the tunic. Men stop having their arms sewn into their sleeves and start using that great new invention: buttons.[7] Hurrah! You might not realize how much the humble button has changed the way both men and women dress. For the real advance comes in the applications of these buttons. Using them you can have a tunic or "cote" which opens at the front and which does not need to go over the head and hang like a cassock. Thus it can fit the body snugly, with all the social, sensual, and stylistic consequences of figure-hugging elegance.[8] Only the old, the fat, the prudish, and the clergy do not find this exciting. Hence the widespread disapproval among contemporary chroniclers.

Let us move into the 1350s. What should you wear at court to welcome the king of France, brought to England in 1357 after his capture the previous year? Your underwear will still consist of a linen shirt and braies, but now the braies will be cut short and tight, not unlike modern underpants, with a fastening cord at the top. Over your braies you will wear colored hose (leggings) of the finest wool, like modern tights. These are normally attached to the fastening cord of the braies—a bit like a modern women's garter belt. Over your shirt you will wear a tailored, mid-thigh-length cote. Alternatively you might go for a doublet (a padded version of the same). Both of these garments have tight-fitting buttoned sleeves and are buttoned up the front. They are normally in two colors: one half of, say, blue and the other of yellow. This is described as *"mi-parti"* or "parti-colored." If you are wearing just one color, or if it is cold, you will probably wear a contrasting surcote over the top, with a belt slung low. Alternatively you might just wear a buttoned cotehardie (a lavish doublet) over your shirt. Should you button up your newly tailored doublet only to find that close-fitting tailoring cruelly reveals a fat belly, do not forget that men also wear corsets at this time. While the traditional image of knights in armor is accurate and widely accepted, the equally representative image of knights wearing corsets and garter belts is perhaps less well known.

Of course, fashion never stands still, and never does it change more rapidly than in the mid-fourteenth century. As the disgruntled author of the *Brut* chronicle points out, people change the shapes and style of their clothing every year. He is not at all happy to have to remark on the tapets (trailing pieces of cloth), which courtiers have dangling from their sleeves and hoods, nor on the "dagges" of their clothing (where the edges of fabric are cut into points) nor on their lengthening of hoods. "The clothing of devils" he calls it, and blames the Hainaulters in Queen Philippa's entourage.[9] Nor is he alone in being horrified. In 1370 another writer remarks with shock that tunics have now grown so short that you can see the outlines of men's bottoms. By then, in order to be well dressed at court, you will wear a paltock: a form of doublet with a lining to which the tights or hose are tied directly. Alternatively you might wear a long gown. Both of these newfangled items of dress seem to originate in England and spread quickly to the Continent. You might wear a hood in a rakishly folded shape, tied in place by its "liripipe" (the extra-long tubular peak of the hood). To have it hanging down your back like a normal hood in 1360 is simply passé. The same goes for the circular mantle: no one puts their head through the central head hole anymore, but rather men try to wear the mantle rakishly, by putting their head through an armhole and gathering up the extensive folds over one shoulder.

The end of the century sees all this experimentation come to a riotous climax of fashionable excess. To be a nobleman in the 1390s means wearing long gowns and short gowns, and gowns of medium length, cotehardies, doublets, and paltocks. Most lavish of all are the full-length gowns occasionally called "houpelands": long, tailored garments with high waists, high collars (*really* high, up to the earlobes), and elaborate long sleeves with massive cuffs which hang down to the ground. In such a garment your foppish aristocrat can appear capable of tripping over his cuffs as well as the hem of his gown. At the other extreme you might prefer the "courtpiece" or *courtepie*, a very short doublet that not only reveals the wearer's bottom but hangs barely two inches lower than the belt around his hips, so he can show off the bulge in the front of his tights as well as the roundness of his buttocks.[10] Obviously there is a time and a place for such clothing: you would be unwise to stroll into Parliament wearing a courtpiece, for example, or to wear one to a funeral. But the end of the century marks the pinnacle in the sexualization of men's clothing. We have come a long way since the reign of Edward I, when lords still wear tunics which hang from the shoulders like a pair of velvet curtains.

The development of men's shoe styles is almost as radical and extreme as their clothing. In 1300 there is no real difference between left and right shoes. They might be decorated in gold, stitched very tightly so the seams are nigh on invisible, but still one shape is cut to fit both feet. Over the course of the century cordwainers—men who make the best shoes from soft Cordovan leather—begin to distinguish between left and right. The really striking development, however, is the length of the toes. In 1300 your average nobleman wears shoes which would look expensive but not outlandish: the toe is a neat little point, nothing remarkable. In the 1330s the toe begins to grow. And grow. On both sides of the Channel noblemen seem to be in competition to wear the longest shoes. Whatever the cause of this trend (length of feet and manhood?) by 1350 the artificial lengthening of the toes is well under way—six inches long, seven, eight—with the points being partly stuffed with wool to make them semi-rigid. By the reign of Richard II some lords can barely walk without tripping over their own shoes. Although older men still wear normal-length shoes under their long robes, the younger men with very short paltocks push the boundaries of style ridiculously far. The longest style of all—the twenty-inch Crackow, an imported fashion from Bohemia—is so long that its tips have to be tied to the garter. Walking upstairs in them is almost impossible.

With all the radical changes in dress and footwear, it is something of a surprise to reflect that there is very little variation in men's hairstyles over the century. The king sets the trend, of course, but you will not notice a significant difference between the hair of Edward I and that of his son, Edward II, or even that of Edward III before the age of fifty. All three men have their hair parted in the center, kept in place by a crown or circlet, so the long locks tumble down the sides of the face to chin level. In later life, Edward III wears his hair longer, to shoulder length. Even Richard II and Henry IV do not have hairstyles very different to their predecessors—at least, not until Henry goes bald. Richard has his hair cut very slightly shorter, so it hangs down thickly over the ears and is slightly longer at the back.

All of these kings with the sole exception of Richard are noticeably bearded. Their beards may be short and bushy like Edward II's, or long and flowing like Edward III's in old age, or short and forked like those of the Black Prince and Henry IV. Whatever the chosen style, most secular lords wear a beard. By contrast, clergymen never do. They are shaved and tonsured (the hair cut from the top of their head) every two weeks.[11] Shaving is thus considered slightly inappropriate for a nobleman and, by implication, for a king. Richard II, who hardly has any beard at all and barely a wisp of moustache, is quite an alarming figure in some men's eyes, because his boyishly clean face contrasts so much with that expected in a king.[12] The suspicion with which he is viewed by his people for most of his reign is a telling sign of how important it is to look the part in medieval society.

Aristocratic Women

Just as it is important for clothes to reflect social rank, so too it is important that they reflect sexual differences. But how do you distinguish between male and female dress when it just hangs loosely from the shoulders? Men and women are wearing similar forms of tunics in 1300. There are differences in the neckline and the length of skirt, but the main difference lies in the way the head is presented. For the first three decades of the century, attention is focused not on your hips or breasts, nor on your arms or legs, but on your hair and face. It is not going too far to say that before 1330, in matters of clothing, men and women differ more from the shoulders up than the chest down.

By the end of the century the similarities in styles of clothing have almost entirely disappeared. Men's clothing has become sexually more revealing whereas women's skirts are still long and hanging. Certain rules remain unchallenged. Women may not expose their arms or legs without being deemed to have acted lewdly. Nor should an unmarried girl wear a headdress: the wimple is the preserve of the married woman. Nevertheless, this is the century during which men and women start to wear radically different clothing from each other. In the modern world, in which female clothing is more often designed to attract the attention of the opposite sex, the radical sexualization of men's clothing is doubly surprising. It is not women's skirt lengths which change with the times but those of men. No wonder monastic chroniclers feel obliged to pass comment: they blame the men for displaying very short skirts and well-packed hose, and they blame the women for being delighted by what they see.

Ladies wishing to cause a stir at an event in 1300 might wear a long-sleeved tunic, with a chemise or fine linen shift underneath. The sleeves to this will be sewn up after you have put it on, to bring the material close to your arms. Over this you will probably wear a sideless gown of a contrasting color; this is like a full-length surcote but with large cut-away gaps instead of sleeves (hence "sideless"). Sometimes the sides are laced up with gold threads with tassels on the ends. The sideless gown is nearly always of a contrasting color: if your tunic is red, a blue floor-length gown is most appropriate. Over the whole ensemble you might consider wearing a mantle: perhaps a gold-lined one of violet cloth, woven with vermilion and blue patterns, cut long enough to trail behind you. Alternatively you might opt for an even longer, loose-sleeved, fur-lined *peliçon:* this is a cope of rich fabric which has such a long train that a servant is required to carry it for you.

By the middle of the century, the sideless gown is beginning to look dated. All that cloth trailing from your *peliçon* looks similarly old-fashioned and impractical. Besides, it has become fashionable for women to show off their necks (low necklines start to appear about 1325) and even their bare shoulders. Tailored sleeves and buttons mean that from the 1330s you no longer have to be sewn into your clothes but can wear long gowns and buttoned cotehardies like the men. You will still wear a long shift as your prime undergarment, so your skirts remain ground length. Your sexiness is, however, enhanced by having your tunic or cotehardie cut very close around your breasts, waist, and hips, to show off your figure. Some women exaggerate their buttocks with bustles made of foxtails.[13] Alternatively, you might accentuate your waist with a corset. If you go for the figure-hugging style, golden and jewel-studded belts are slung low around your hips. At the same time, your mantle should be draped at a lower level than before and fastened with a golden cord or braid just above the breasts, allowing you to show off your bare shoulders.

By 1400 the best dresses to be seen at court have very little in common with those of 1300. They are cut from similar fabrics—mainly imported from Flanders and France—but the styles are wholly different. Long full and flowing skirts of bright purple and red, often with designs of heraldic symbols embroidered into them, are trimmed with gold brocade and jewels. Over this you might wear a short bodice of a contrasting color, with a corset underneath accentuating your hour-glass shape, and with a matching fur-trimmed hip-length courtpiece on top, cut so that the fur rides up along the edges of the courtpiece and over your breasts and to the points of your shoulders. Gold and jeweled buttons complete the picture of an exquisite damsel. Of course, this glamorous style does not suit all sizes and shapes; there are plenty of women who would be appalled at the prospect of being clothed in the latest corset-restricted and hourglass-shaped dresses. But by the end of the century it is almost only the old, the fat, and the religious who still wear the long hanging tunics of 1300.

Nothing about the medieval female "look" would be complete without the headdress. Nor is it possible to describe the headdress without referring to hairstyles. At the start of the century, perhaps the most popular aristocratic style of coiffure is the ramshorn. The long hair (all noblewomen wear their hair long) is parted in the center; each side is woven into a single long plait; this is then wound round and round into a sort of bun or ramshorn over the ear and fastened in place with hairpins. If you are married you will wear a circlet, hood, hat, or veil on the top of the head and fasten your wimple on either side. In 1300, with your tunic reaching to the ground, and your sleeves so long they reach to your knuckles, your face and your fingers are often the only parts of your entire body which can be seen.

In the reign of Edward III everything changes. The most striking development is the practice of taking the two plaits of hair and running them up and down over your temples to form columns of plaited hair, framing your face. Often the columns of plaited hair are carefully enmeshed in golden gauze, which is the way Queen Philippa likes her hair done in the 1360s. Her exact contemporary, the countess of Warwick, has her hair similarly dressed; but rather than stiff golden columns of hair framing her face she has the two plaited columns woven into one on top of her head and then encased in a gold-lattice frame. The result is a striking arch of golden hair all around her face. These are lavish hairstyles, which take hours to set in place. Most noblewomen are happy with simply long plaits of hair, or a variation on the ramshorn style, and their circlet, coronet, or hat and a wimple (if they are married). Richard II's wife, Anne of Bohemia, favors a single long plait down her back. Unmarried girls tend to adorn themselves with jewels in their hair—often artificial flowers made of gold and precious stones—or fur-trimmed hoods. It is highly unusual for noblewomen to appear in public with their long hair loose and free-flowing. Even if just tucked up under a coif, it will be concealed. In the previous century, and in the next one, it is common for women to wear their hair loose, but fourteenth-century noblewomen tend to do this only in the privacy of their solar chambers. Long, loose hair is generally considered seductive and so, like naked arms and legs, concealed to avoid impropriety. Only wild and wanton women dare to leave their hair undressed and loose in public.

Noblewomen's shoes at the start of the century, like their clothes, are more or less comparable to men's. But as male and female modes of fashion become more diverse, so too do their shoes. Women's tunics become more like skirts and gowns but still remain long, so there is very little ostentation of footwear. Certainly there is never any call for women to wear exceptionally long shoes; they are merely an inch or so in the point. Women thus avoid the ridiculous ostentation of the Crackow.

Townsmen and Townswomen

Many of the changes in aristocratic dress are mirrored in the clothes of townsmen and townswomen—those most acutely aware of the signs of their social standing. At the start of the century the streets are full of men wearing tunics which reach down below the knee, with hose and a hood. The principal differences between their garments and those of noblemen are the length (merchants' tunics are generally cut shorter than lordly ones) and the quality of the cloth. Much the same can be said for townswomen's clothes in 1300: the well-dressed merchant's wife will have her long-sleeved tunic and sideless gown, like her noble contemporary, but the fabric will be of an inferior quality. So will the furs around the cuffs and the hood. Of course, a wimple is de rigueur when outside the house for a married woman.

By the end of the century, shopkeepers, traders, and craftsmen are wearing colored hose and thigh-length cotes and doublets. Perhaps they might add a felt or beaver-fur hat, if they can afford it. Alternatively they may still have a hood. Your rich merchant is showing off as best he can with the whole houpeland and high-collar ensemble, long cuffs and all, although using a less expensive material and not having cuffs as long as a lord's. If anyone in town is wearing a rakishly folded hood, it will be him. But the length of the toes of his shoes will not be excessive, even if he is wearing a short doublet and hose. As an alternate to cordwainers' shoes he may well wear boots made from ordinary tanned leather or calfskin. In the latter part of the century townsmen sometimes avoid actual shoes, preferring to have leather soles sewn onto the foot section of their hose, so that their "shoes" are the same color as their leggings.

The fur-trimmed velvet jacket, so favored by aristocratic women in the 1390s, represents a style which most townswomen can only dream of. Instead they wear plain kirtles—ground-length tunics, with tailored narrow sleeves—over their linen smocks or chemises, without a surcote over the top except when the weather demands an extra layer. The Wife of Bath wears a long scarlet gown with laced scarlet stockings, new soft shoes, "a riding skirt round her enormous hips," a wimple under her chin, a hat, and spurs. Dressed like this she does not represent the richest sort of townswoman—as she herself admits, she weaves her own cloth—but she certainly dresses to look the equal of anyone of her own class.

The laborers will be shirtless, wearing just braies, a hood, and a simple tunic—this being pulled in with a woollen or rope belt. Some hitch up the bottom hem of the tunic and tuck it into the belt to make it easier to work. Hardly any changes in their clothing are to be noticed over the century. Otherwise, only the clergy are wearing clothing similar to their predecessors in 1300. Friars, priests, and senior members of the churches and cathedrals all wear traditional tunics or cassocks, often black, off-white, and brown in color, befitting their Order and station. Franciscan friars wear grey cassocks; Dominican friars wear black. Their reluctance to adopt the new fashions is not because they do not pay any attention to clothing; the retention of the traditional, unsexy shape of the clothes is every bit as important to them as the latest fashion is to a wealthy merchant. Friars never wear socks. Not wearing something is also a way of making a fashion statement.

Countrymen and Women

You could be forgiven for thinking that the changes in dress after 1300 only affect urban social climbers and have no significant effect on the clothes of the peasantry. In the early part of the century, you would be right. Wandering along a rural lane in 1340 you will see that there is practically no difference from the clothing worn in 1300. But when everyone wears nearly the same thing it is deemed all the more important to include a little distinctive item of clothing, especially among the better-off peasants. Countrymen do not wear the parti-colored clothing of nobles and wealthier townsmen; they do not wear pointed shoes or any unnecessary and expensive items. Nevertheless, as you watch the tenants of a manor going about their business, you will notice that no two men are wearing exactly the same form of apparel.

Take a manor in Lincolnshire in 1340, for example. Over here is a better-off villein driving a team of oxen. He wears a reddish-brown tunic which reaches just below his knees, slit a few inches up the sides. On his head is a matching reddish-brown hood, with a short pointed tip (or liripipe). He wears a good-quality leather belt, a woollen light-brown supertunic, and calf-length leather boots. He holds a long whip and scowls back at the plowman who is following, supposedly guiding the plowshare. The plowman has a reddish-brown hood too but this hangs down his back. On his head he is wearing a smart felt hat with a high front brim. He also wears an undyed buttonless tunic that hangs down to his knee, with a belt, blue-grey hose, thick gloves, and laced calf-length boots. Elsewhere in the field another villein is scattering the grain that he carries in the folded-up front of his apron. Birds swooping down to pick up the grain are picked off by a boy with a sling; he wears a short russet tunic with a linen belt, with his long hood pushed back, the liripipe hanging down well below his waist. Similar tunics of dyed cloth are worn by the lord's servants back at the manor house but without the hood. In the kitchens some of the cooks have stripped to their braies. With the heat of the great fires and their work environment, they have no need to look their best, only to do their work.[14]

If you step forward in time to see these men's grandsons in the last decades of the century, you will see brighter colors (especially red and blue cloths) and styles that have been adapted from the tunics of 1300–1340. The man driving the team of oxen now wears a leather cap and a sleeveless tabard over a long-sleeved tunic, which is short, just thigh length. As he lifts his whip arm, the edge of his tunic reveals hose which are more like trousers, held up with a rope belt. The plowman to whom he turns and scowls is wearing a buttoned short jerkin with the sleeves rolled up over his forearms and his shirtsleeves similarly rolled up. He is still wearing an old felt hat, bashed over the years, not wholly unlike that worn by his grandfather so many years before. The boy with the sling is still bare legged but he now wears a short cote with a leather belt. The servants in the lord's manor house are much better dressed than their predecessors: in clean linen shirts and quilted doublets, hose, folded hoods or hats, with knives hanging from their belts.[15] Of course, the kitchen servants are still half naked, sweltering in the heat of the kitchens. As in all ages, progress does not affect everyone equally.

The women in the country have one important thing in common with the five-times-married Wife of Bath: they make their own clothes. They might not all spin their own wool and weave their own cloth, but most do. No one knits—knitting has yet to be invented—so some heavy-duty fabrics need to be woven to keep these country-women and their families warm in winter. Once these have been made, they need to be dyed. Then they need to be turned into clothes. Once you realize that a countrywoman's role includes these spinning, weaving, dyeing, and dressmaking tasks, as well as cooking, cleaning, milking, nursing, and helping with the harvest (among other things), your admiration for her will increase immeasurably.

The clothes worn in the country are practical and plain, made of coarse woollen cloth collectively described as russet—mainly grey, green, murrey (dark brown), brown, reddish brown, and undyed. In the early part of the century a farm woman wears a full-length tunic over her linen smock, with a linen headdress and wimple all in one. She wears linen "clouts"—a female form of braies—when nature forces her to do so. Sometimes she will wear a hood instead of a head-dress and stride about the farmyard with the lower part of her sleeves rolled up. Unseemly it may appear to some, but most women's work is done in the company of other women, in the barns or in the home. If working outdoors she may well wear a thick woollen mantle and hat, as well as the wimple. The plainness and the homely nature of coun-trywomen's dress brings us to the other end of the spectrum from the courtpiece- and Crackow-wearing male popinjays about court.

Accessories

For most people, clothes are just one element of how they present themselves. Urban and aristocratic women might use perfume, in which a few city merchants specialize. Musk, ambergris, cloves, nut-meg, and cardamom are used to sweeten the smell of the body. Olive oil is used to help keep beautiful hair supple. Pastes made from the ashes of vine stems, boiled for half a day in vinegar, are used to make white hair blond again. As for makeup, the perfumers' shops may also sell whitening cosmetics, small round mirrors, combs, scissors, tweezers, and pitch. The tweezers are for young women to pluck their eyebrows. The pitch is for manual removal of unwanted or unsightly hair. Quicklime is also used for this purpose, but, as you can imagine, you need to be very careful as it is easy to burn yourself and end up looking more unsightly than before you started.[16]

Most people carry a knife which they use for daily tasks as well as cutting their food. If you visit a market or a town you will have a purse suspended from your belt. This might be a simple leather pouch drawn together with a cord or it may be a hinged, metal-framed purse, with sides of velvet or wool covered in silk. Pockets are only just coming into use in the 1330s, so purses are commonly associated with the need to carry coins.[17] Beware that it is very easy for someone in a crowd—a "cutpurse"—to slice the cords by which your purse is suspended from your belt. You probably will not even notice it happening.

Most people of significant social standing also wear jewelry. This might take the form of a livery collar for men, as well as gold rings, badges, and clasps. Women too might wear livery necklaces as a demonstration of their political loyalties. But jewelry goes far further than political symbolism. Gemstones are widely held to have magical and medicinal properties. In the Book of Revelation, the foundations of the New Jerusalem are "garnished with all manner of precious stones, namely jasper, sapphire, chalcedony, emerald, sardonyx, sardius, chrysolyte, beryl, topaz, chrysoprasus, jacinth, and amethyst." Thus it is no surprise to see men wearing gemstones in their rings and brooches as much as women. Rubies are the most prized of all. Sapphires come next, and then diamonds, emeralds, and balas rubies (paler, rose-red rubies). Rubies protect the wearer from poison, and emeralds protect against sickness and madness. Diamonds protect people from bad dreams and help the wearer achieve wisdom.

To get a glimpse of the richness of jewelry at the top end of society, take a look at Henry of Lancaster's goldsmiths account for the year

The Wheel of Fortune is a common metaphor in medieval England. Fortune herself turns a great wheel on which kings, clergymen, burghers, and peasants all find themselves lifted up to great heights only to fall soon after their moment of glory.

Knowledge of the world beyond Christendom is very vague. This early-fifteenth-century image shows Alexander the Great receiving a present of white elephants.

All women of quality have long hair; but they are expected to conceal it in public, not to have it wantonly flowing loose. Here a maidservant is plaiting her mistress's hair into two long plaits, and winding each plait into a ramshorn hairstyle.

Married women, when in public, are expected to wear a wimple. This garment covers the hair, sides of the head, neck, and chin.

Most women are expected to work hard, and not just within the home. At harvesttime they labor alongside their menfolk, to bring in the lord's harvest as well as their own.

Women married to violent men have tough lives. As long as he does not actually kill or maim her, it is lawful for a man to beat his wife as often and as hard as he likes.

On the other hand, the law is biased so heavily in favor of men that it does not recognize that a woman can beat her husband. Thus she can do so with legal impunity.

Women of rank like to hunt, but moral codes still apply. This lady might look carefree, but her hair is carefully dressed in a ramshorn style and her arms are not actually bare: she is wearing a pale, long-sleeved tunic.

Noblemen's clothing in the early fourteenth century. Note the long, flowing robes, the loose sleeves, and the sensible footwear.

Noblemen's clothing in the late fourteenth century. By 1395 there is great variation in men's dress. Note the very short tunic with tight hose and long, pointed shoes. Men's clothing changes more in this century than in any other.

Noblewomen's clothing in the early fourteenth century. The queen wears a red undertunic, a grey supertunic, and a long cloak or mantle. Like men's attire of this date, it is loose and simply hangs from the shoulders.

Noblewomen's clothing at the end of the fourteenth century. Tunics are still ground length, but the supertunic is now a figure-hugging, short, fur-trimmed garment, like a modern jacket. Tunics also become more closely fitted to the upper body and arms, like modern dresses.

Peasants' clothing in the early fourteenth century. Tunics and supertunics are shorter and more practical than the flowing robes of their social superiors, but the principle of cutting clothes that hang from the shoulders is the same.

Laborers' clothing at the end of the fourteenth century. Here builders are wearing tailored cotes with buttons, or doublets, and more substantial hose.

Women's clothing in the early fourteenth century. The long kirtles hang from the shoulders and reach to the ground. Sleeves are kept close to the wrist with laces.

In 1400 working women are still wearing long-sleeved kirtles much like their grandmothers, although they may be closer fitting. Only the noblewoman at the loom is wearing a modern tailored gown of more than one fabric.

The braies this boy is wearing are like those commonly worn by men in the early fourteenth century. They are loose, tied at the knee, and then drawn up and rolled around the waistband.

Images of extreme cruelty provide an opportunity to study men's underwear. This late-fourteenth-century picture of the Templars' burning shows how braies are now much shorter and tighter, to allow men to wear tight hose and very short tunics over the top.

1397–98. This includes thirty individual payments, including: mending his balas ruby brooch, buying a balas ruby ring, silver for several dagger sheaths, a chain for a medicinal stone to protect him against poisons, a silver chain for a hunting dog, silver to cover the scabbard of his sword, several dozen silver livery collars to be given to his retainers, gilt-silver collars for him to wear himself, pendants, jeweled belts, "seven hundred and ten golden suns with which to decorate one black velvet hanseline [an extremely short paltock] and for making the same" (at a cost of £15 9s 10d), "sixteen gilt-silver lilies for decorating one kettle-hat" (a kind of helmet), and so on. This does not even touch on the actual gems. Over the next page and a half we see listed the jewels he buys during this year. There is a golden figure of St. John the Baptist as a present for the king, a golden hind with pearls for the queen, golden tablets and brooches for other members of the royal family, a couple of golden rings with diamonds, a gold ring with a ruby, four gold rings with sapphires, dozens of other gold rings, and nine brooches for his closest (male) companions.[18] As you can see, clothing is just the foundation for a noble appearance. On top of the right cut, you must also sparkle.

Nightwear

There is no special nighttime attire in medieval England. You should wear what is appropriate, depending on where you are and how private your accommodation. Women should either remain in the chemise they have worn during the day or replace it with a similar clean garment for bed, together with the ubiquitous nightcap (which everybody wears). Only when sleeping with a lover should you be naked. Men have more leeway, as male nudity is less taboo. Thus you might keep a shirt on at night, but equally you might choose to wear nothing but a nightcap, even when sharing a bed at a hospital or an inn.[19] Chaucer refers to himself sleeping naked when in his own bed in *The Book of the Duchess*. However, men who have a sense of decency keep their braies on when staying away from home.[20] Monks are always expected to sleep clothed in their dormitories—they are expected even to have baths in their braies.[21] And in some circumstances it is particularly important not to get caught with your braies down. When

Edward Balliol, king of Scotland, is attacked in the night in September 1332, he only survives by riding away, bareback, in his nightshirt, all the way to Carlisle.[22] Even worse, when the English knight Robert Herle is attacked at night in 1356, he and his men are found naked.[23] You cannot put up much of a fight against armed soldiers in the nude.

Swords and Armor

This is not a book about medieval combat, so this is not the place to discuss arms and armor. Besides, you would be crazy to think you could engage a fourteenth-century man in combat and have a chance of surviving. Most of them are much stronger than you. From the age of six or seven the knights have been taught how to fight, first with a wooden sword, then with the genuine article. Many of them are proficient jousters by the age of sixteen. You will not be able to compete. Nor will you be able to compete with the longbow. Most northern lads learn how to shoot a bow from the age of seven; by the time they are sixteen they are able to pull the weight of the most lethal killing machine of the Middle Ages. As for guns, the few cannon that are to be found are all in the royal armories. These are not articles which you can buy.

Cost is another reason why you can forget about wearing armor. Even at the start of the century you will need a helmet, iron breastplate, full-length hauberk of chain mail, leggings of chain mail, and ailettes (plates protecting the shoulders) as well as a lance, sword, axe, dagger, and shield. Beneath all this you will need a quilted jacket (aketon) and other padding. You can probably buy all of this for £5 or £6. But armor rapidly develops in both form and price. By the 1320s you will need to have greaves (for your shins) and knee coverings, curved ailettes, elbow protectors, gauntlets, and plates of armor covering the arms. As soon as you start to invest in good-quality plate armor, the cost escalates. By 1350 you will need reticulated gauntlets and foot armor, greaves, thigh pieces, plate armor for the arms, a backplate as well as a breastplate, a gorger to protect your throat, and protection for the back of your neck. By 1390 your average knight will be carrying in excess of eighty pounds of armor when he rides into battle. If you do the same, it is unlikely you will have the strength to lift your sword and fight for an hour or two, even if you do have some skill with a blade.

The cost of a suit of armor is prohibitive. A breastplate and back-plate can easily set you back £3, a shield 18s, and a helmet £2. When you add up the total cost, you will have little change from £20. And then of course you will need to buy a warhorse, plus armor for the horse, and the wages of the boys to tend it, a dozen lances, a better sword—not to mention the costs of the man whom you will need to employ to dress you in your armor . . . And at the end of the day, all this expense is going towards a set of steel "clothes" which are decidedly uncomfortable and which someone is simply going to bash with a sharp implement. Attractive though the joust might look, you would be wise to leave it to the knights.

Having said this, you need to remember that, under the provisions of the Statute of Winchester (1285), every man between the ages of fifteen and sixty must have arms of some sort, for the purpose of keeping the peace. Those with goods worth 20 marks or more, or £10 income from land, must have an iron breastplate, a hauberk (chain-mail shirt), a sword, and a knife. Those with £5 income from land must have a quilted jacket, breastplate, sword, and knife. Even the poorest men must keep some weapons: a sword and knife and a bow and arrows, or—for those who live within forests—a crossbow and bolts.

It is a good idea to invest in a sword. Not only will this allow you to abide by the provisions of the statute, it is reasonable for you to arm yourself, if only to deter the arm-chancing robber from attacking. The swords which peasants use are cheap—you can buy a blade in some places for as little as 6d—but if you are sensible you will wear a weapon that looks as if its owner knows how to use it. A serviceable blade with a leather-bound hilt can be bought for 1s to 2s; a good scabbard and belt will be 1s more. Learn how to wield a blade and you should be relatively safe on the road, especially if you are traveling in company. Bear in mind that there are strict rules about when you may wear a sword. After 1319 you may not wear a sword in London unless you are a knight; you must leave your weapon with your host. The same goes for other towns and cities later in the century. You cannot wear a sword in church, nor in Parliament. If you visit another man's house or castle, you should unbuckle your weapon and leave it with the gatekeeper. Although you may read in "The Reeve's Tale" of students merrily riding along with their swords at their sides, when they get back to their hall of residence in Cambridge they will take off the said weapons. It might all seem slightly bizarre—that you can wear deadly weapons in Trumpington but not in Cambridge—but it all goes to show that, while medieval society might appear brutal and frightening, it is not unsophisticated in its brutality and fear.

6

Traveling

Imagine that you are in London and you need to go to Chester. How do you set about it? You might think that you have just two options: riding a horse or taking a ship all around the coast. But when you begin to consider the practicalities, it is not quite that simple. If you have enough money to pay your way by road, you will need protection. If you decide to take a ship you run the risks of wreck and attack, especially in the Irish Sea, where Scottish pirates like Thomas Dun are at large in the reign of Edward II. Long-distance travel is something to be carefully planned. Although many peasants do travel all the way across the country when sent to fight in the Scottish or French wars, no one is going to bother them, especially traveling together in a band, armed with longbows and swords—not for the sake of a few pence anyway. You, on the other hand, sauntering along, whistling an outlandish tune, with enough silver in your purse to attract every scoundrel who saw you at the last inn, are a walking liability.

Your first problem is to establish exactly which route to take. In the modern world, you would look at a map. That is not an option here. There are very few maps of the country and those which do exist are not to scale. Nor are they intended to help travelers. Medieval maps are a means of recording knowledge in a spatial framework—they are reference works for use in libraries, not for consultation on the open road. The best map, the so-called Gough Map, does include roads and towns, but being so large (it is about the size of a door) and made of stiff vellum, it does not lend itself to being folded up and put in a traveler's pouch. Whoever made it probably drew it up as a reference work to be kept in the office of some great household, probably the royal palace at Westminster.[1]

As a result of the shortage of maps, you will have no option but to ask for directions. But how does a Londoner know his way to Chester if he has never been there? The key to navigating is to start off in the right direction. As Chester is in Cheshire, a county in the northwest, it makes sense to set out along the highway which leads northwest. It is not the actual points of the compass which serve as your guide (the compass has yet to be adopted in northern Europe, although it is used in the Mediterranean).[2] Rather it is the itinerary—the series of towns between you and the country of your destination—which will guide you. A dialogue book gives the following example:

> "Good people; I go to [insert name of town]. At which gate shall I go out? And at which hand shall I take my way?"
>
> "On the right hand, when ye come to a bridge, so go there over; ye shall find a little way on the left hand which shall bring you in a country where you shall see upon a church two high steeples. From thence shall ye have but four miles unto your lodging. There shall ye be well eased for your money."[3]

So, if you ask a well-informed Londoner how to get to Cheshire, he will tell you to head out by Aldersgate; go across Smithfield; take the road north towards Islington, Finchley, and Barnet; and from Barnet take the road to St. Albans. Beyond that he probably does not know the way, but when you arrive in St. Albans you can ask again, and then be directed on to Towcester and Daventry, and so on, all the way to Cheshire.

What is amazing is that, even without a compass or map, some people can think spatially about huge areas of the country. Yes, they have certain other techniques: the stars are an important means of navigating, the position of the sun too. But these are of limited use when it comes to maneuvering an army quickly against another army twenty miles away, in the hope of ending up in a strategically better position. Imagine you fall in with the five Lords Appellant in December 1387. Your army is attempting to trap the king's favorite, Robert de Vere, who is heading southeast along Watling Street, towards London, with a force of about four thousand men. You are approaching from Northampton, marching to intercept him around the Warwickshire/Oxfordshire border. De Vere hears of your approach and changes course. He heads directly due south, through Oxfordshire. How do you set about trapping him? Without a map, how do you even know *where* you can trap him, or how long it will take you to get there? The answer lies in a knowledge of the rivers and the places where they can be crossed. In this instance, a large part of your army sweeps around behind de Vere's force and chases him southward. Another part of your army goes ahead on a forced march, day and night, aiming for the two key bridges over the River Thames in Oxfordshire (New Bridge and Radcot Bridge). In this way de Vere and his men are trapped between the bulk of the army behind them and the small expeditionary force holding the two bridges ahead of them. All this seems an obvious strategy when you look at a detailed map of the area. But when you stand in North Oxfordshire, looking at the hills around you, and try to work out exactly which way to send your men to cut off de Vere's advance on the Thames, it is very far from straightforward.

It goes without saying that it is unlikely you will lead an army around medieval England yourself, but the principles underlying such generalship are of use in normal day-to-day navigation. If you know the countries through which the major rivers flow, and where those rivers can be crossed, you are well on your way to picturing a region in outline. Some people think of their countries not as a series of roads and towns but as a series of rivers and valleys. If you are in a strange part of the country, or abroad, following the major rivers is one of the most efficient means of long-distance navigation possible. Not only does a major river lead you in a consistent direction, it will also bring you to a trading town, for goods are normally transported by water. There you can find people who have experience of long-distance trading networks. Where there are no rivers, in sparsely populated regions, you might use local guides, paying one each day to take you on to the next town and the next guide. Navigation is thus a mixture of local knowledge; awareness of which town lies in which country; determining the points of the compass by the appearance of the sun and the stars; and familiarity with the rivers, river crossings, hills, and moors.

Roads

In the modern world we have different roads for different purposes—motorways for long-distance travel and lanes for access to fields.

Medieval England is similar. There are the great highways of the Fosse Way, Ermine Street, Watling Street, and Icknield Way—Roman roads which have remained in use throughout the Saxon and Norman centuries. At the other end of the scale are the unmarked rights of way across open land: routes marked only by the occasional stone cross, with nothing otherwise to reveal the existence of a road at all.

The highway structure of the kingdom—that is to say the network of roads connecting the towns—is based on the network of Roman roads reaching westward to Exeter and northward to the border of Scotland. This amounts to about ten thousand miles of roads. The Gough Map shows about three thousand miles of main roads in use in 1360; close examination reveals that about 40 percent of these are of Roman origin.[4] These were almost all constructed before the end of the second century, and so it is not surprising to know that their condition varies. In some places the stones are still in place, deeply rutted where cartwheels have worn away the surface. In other places the stones have been taken away to build something else. Sometimes you find interruptions in the road due to subsidence or a large fallen tree. Even an important road like the Fosse Way can be blocked from time to time. Thus not all Roman roads are now as straight as they once were. In fact, not all Roman roads are still *where* they once were. Where the stones of an old road are at angles and uneven, they may present more of an obstacle than a surface, and in such cases the medieval road tends to run along smoother ground nearby. Also, a large number of towns are off the Roman network. Plymouth, for instance, has no Roman foundation and thus is nowhere near a Roman road. The same goes for every town in Cornwall—the farthest west the Romans built was Exeter. One can say the same for the rich town of Coventry, the university town of Oxford, and most of the towns established on new sites by Edward I. So, although the road system is based on that built by the Romans, do not imagine that this means there are smooth flagstone-covered straight roads emanating from each town in all directions.

The highway network is supplemented by the local networks: the streets and alleys of towns, the lanes between enclosed fields, and the wide paths and drove ways (for driving sheep) across the open fields and common land. In addition there are lanes between manors, lanes connecting farmsteads to the centers of the villages, roads connecting hamlets to the local churches, cartways, portways (highways between markets and ports), and monastic roads (connecting monks' churches with their estates). Some of these will be along old Roman roads but most will be medieval constructions—if there is any construction to speak of. A number of old lych ways and packhorse routes are merely tracks and paths across high moorland. The sheer diversity of roads precludes a neat, collective description.

On the whole, the main highways are kept in good repair. They have to be, for the king regularly travels along them. True, he does not travel around the whole kingdom; no fourteenth-century reigning king visits Cornwall or Devon, for example.[5] But on the whole any roads found blocked or in a bad state of repair result in a speedy royal writ being dispatched to the manorial lord in charge of their maintenance. Thus kings and lords are able to maintain relatively high speeds. In January 1300 the sixty-year-old Edward I and his whole court are able to trot along at a regular nineteen miles per day, even though there are only nine hours of daylight and at least two of those hours are spent eating. In September 1336 a youthful Edward III, unencumbered by his household, rides to York at an average speed of fifty-five miles per day.[6] This would not be possible if the highways were in such a state that he has to worry about his valuable horses stumbling.

Other roads, however, are not so well maintained. Constantly you will hear in manorial courts how so-and-so has let the road outside his house become impassable, blocking it with timber, broken carts, and rubbish. Sometimes too you will find that the offending blockage is the overflow of a latrine pit after heavy rain, which has left feces, sticks, and farmyard debris all over the road. When hillside paths collapse, the packhorse drivers and other travelers simply find a way around the treacherous part and make a new path. The same applies to the drove ways; because these are not Roman roads but medieval rights of way, with no actual marks as to where the road is, the drivers simply move the "road" to the left or right when one part becomes unusable. The most treacherous roads are the lanes and highways connecting manors and small towns. Sometimes the local residents see the opportunity to get some clay cheaply by digging it out of the road. In good weather this makes the road surface uneven, necessitating a detour. In wet weather it creates deep puddles. One notorious spot is the road between Egham and Staines. In bad weather it will look as if you are heading into a series of flooded stretches of road; there is nothing to warn you that the water is between eight and twelve feet deep. In 1386 a man drowns in one of them. The abbot of Chertsey, who is responsible for keeping the road in good repair, has the audacity to claim the man's goods, on account of the death occurring on his land.[7]

Bridges

We take bridges for granted. Almost always, when a modern road meets a river, there is a bridge to help us across. Riding through medieval England you will soon realize that good stone bridges are relatively scarce. If you are riding along a highway between two prosperous and reasonably close market towns, or a highway connecting a county town with London, the chances are that you will have a pleasant jaunt over a smoothly paved stone structure with sharply pointed arches and fine triangular cutwaters projecting on either side. However, if you are traveling off the highway, most of the time you will find your trackway simply disappears into the mud and flow of the river. Occasionally pedestrians might benefit from stepping-stones or a clapper bridge (in the West Country), but more often than not you will get wet.

The great age of stone bridge building begins in the reign of King John (1199–1216). London's great bridge dates from then. The other great stone bridges—such as those at Exeter and Rochester—are later thirteenth-century constructions. Before that, river crossings were either fords or wooden bridges. Even now, in the fourteenth century, many significant rivers have wooden bridges, in various states of repair. Some are so rickety you would be well advised not to risk crossing them but to ride through the original ford, which usually remains to the side. In very hilly and highland regions there tend to be very few bridges. As the land is that much poorer, the absentee manorial lords are inclined to see little reason repeatedly to rebuild a wooden structure which is incapable of withstanding the fast-flowing torrents that pour down in winter. For this reason, if you travel into the Lake District or the skirts of Dartmoor, you will find that a good bridge is as rare as a well-maintained road. Westmorland has twelve stone bridges by 1400.[8] That equates to one bridge for every forty-one thousand acres in the county.

The construction of stone bridges might put you in mind of the huge number of parish churches which are being rebuilt, extended, or refashioned in this century. The two are not unconnected. Just as founding a chantry or rebuilding a church is seen as a pious use of money, so too is the building of a stone bridge. It is something done for other people and thus is exactly that form of long-lasting conspicuous charity from which fourteenth-century men and women derive such pride. Hence the building of bridges is heavily dependent on the increasing wealth of the merchant classes. Like the upkeep of the parish church, the maintenance of a bridge is considered a pious act; the responsibilities of a patron do not end on completion. Hence most stone bridges are kept in good shape. This is helped in many cases by the local bishop granting a plenary indulgence to all those who contribute towards the repair of the structure. In this way a large number of people can be conscripted through religion to serve the community: the person who originally endows the bridge is immortalized and those who contribute to the upkeep are forgiven their sins. In keeping with these religious connotations, it is wholly fitting that most great bridges—and many smaller ones—have chapels built on them.

Tolls

Before moving away from the subject of bridges, there is one very obvious and decidedly nonreligious way of keeping it in good repair: levy a toll on those who cross it.

Imagine you are a merchant. You will have to pay to cross a bridge into town. You will have to pay extra for any cart you are bringing with you, according to what is inside the cart. If there is no bridge you will have to pay a toll for the ferry instead. Then you may have to pay to enter the town by a certain gate. Once in the town you will have to pay for the market stall (stallage) and for storing your goods (lastage). If you are at a port you may have to pay wharfage and cranage too. You may have to pay extra to the guild merchant for the right to sell certain specific commodities. And all this is on top of the customs and pannage (toll on imported cloth) you pay when importing goods into the country in the first place.

Nothing which can be priced is given away freely. Even if you are not a merchant but riding about for private purposes you may have to pay murage (a toll to ensure the defensibility of the town walls) and pavage (a toll to pay for the paving of the streets). A toll to cross a bridge (pontage) is thus just one of several dozen sorts of toll. Moreover, as you are a stranger, these tolls will fall disproportionately heavily on you. Towns which manage to acquire a charter tend also to pay for the freedom from tolls at the same time. If the lord granting the charter is just a minor lord, this will not extend very far. But if he is a great lord it may extend to all the other towns in his authority. If he is the king, then the freedom from paying tolls will apply to all the other towns which hold a royal charter. So a freeman of the city of York, for example, does not have to pay a toll when entering another royal borough charging murage and pavage to all those entering. This freedom from tolls applies so widely that the shortfall has to be made up by those who *are* liable, and that includes strangers, like you.

How much are these tolls? They vary from place to place. You should expect to pay 2d for a ferry from Westminster to London. Taking a cart into London will set you back 1d. Taking a *full* cart out of London will cost you another 1d, or more, depending on what you are carrying. In 1356 there is a drive to raise money to repair the city roads, and so every visitor arriving at each of the seven gates is required to pay 1d. Each packhorse you have with you will cost an extra farthing (¼d). In this way, traveling between towns with a couple of servants and a few horses can be an expensive business. The freedom from paying royal tolls—available to freemen of royal boroughs—is thus a significant advantage.

Road Transport

The principal reason why you might think twice about traveling by road is the danger of attack. The Statute of Winchester requires all manorial lords to clear the ground on both sides of the highway for a distance of two hundred feet. This includes clearing all the trees as well as the undergrowth, excepting only the great oaks, which are so valuable for the construction of buildings and ships. This clearance is not always effectively maintained, and people do still get robbed by highwaymen. In some cases, a lord might pay for armed guards to patrol a stretch of road, when many travelers are coming to an important fair within his lordship, for example. But this is rare. Normally you will have no protection other than your fellow travelers. It is often a good idea to meet up at an inn with others taking the same road as you.

Before setting out you will need to acquire a horse, unless you are determined to walk, like the most zealous pilgrims. Horses come in a wide range of shapes and sizes. It is commonly said that "a good horse should have fifteen properties and conditions, namely: three of a man, three of a woman, three of a fox, three of a hare and three of an ass: like a man, he should be bold, proud and hardy; like a woman, he should be fair breasted, fair of hair, and easy to lie upon; like a fox, he should have a fair tail, short ears and go with a good trot; like a hare he should have a great eye, a dry head and run well; and like an ass, he should have a big chin, a flat leg, and a good hoof."[9]

The largest horses, and by far the most expensive, are warhorses, known as "destriers." These can cost up to £40—in exceptional cases they might change hands for even larger sums, up to £80.[10] Obviously, such animals are only for wealthy lords. Most of the warhorses which are lost or killed in Edward III's campaign of 1338–40 in the Low Countries are worth between £10 and £20.[11] This is still more than you should expect to pay for a riding mount. A good courser—for hunting—will cost you up to £10. You will be looking for a good palfrey or riding horse, nearer the £4 or £5 mark. Animals worth less than this—rouncies, hobbies, nags, and hackneys—are usually only good for shorter distances or carrying baggage. Packhorses and sumpter horses are normally in the 5s to 10s category; cart horses are a little more. Note that blind horses are usually worth only about half their usual price. In case you are wondering why there are so many blind horses, it is because they have been stolen, and blinding a horse is one way to prevent it from finding its way back home or recognizing its true master.

Having acquired your mount, you will need a number of other items. Expect to pay up to 5s for a good saddle. A halter and its accoutrements will be an extra 6d to 12d. As for spurs: the rowel type are in vogue (spinning spiked wheels on a small axle behind your heel); these will cost about 2s. If you cannot afford rowels, a plain metal prick buckled to your shoes will do (6d). In bad weather you will need a protective leather or waxed overmantle. Few women ride sidesaddle (the practice is introduced by the ladies of Anne of Bohemia's entourage, after Anne's marriage to Richard II in 1382), so to preserve decorum a riding skirt is essential. Some people travel with many more objects, for instance a knife, a spoon, a bowl, a lantern, candles, a comb, a horse brush, shoemakers' thread (strong enough to sew the saddle back together after it has burst its stuffing), a bodkin, and a leather flask (for ale to drink on the road). Those on long journeys go even further and load up a packhorse with their own bedding, a cushion, a pillow, sheets of muslin or ordinary linen, and woollen blankets. Finally, do not forget your medal showing St. Christopher, the patron saint of travelers. Given the pits in the roads and the outlaws in the woods, you might need it.[12]

As you would expect, the more you take with you, the slower your progress. It will take time to pack up all this bedding. It takes time to lead a few packhorses along even the best highway. Thus, when it comes to traveling at speed, less is definitely more. Most travelers in no particular rush to get to their destination will cover perhaps three miles per hour. There is a limit to how many hours each day you want to remain in the saddle, so most people set themselves a target destination and attempt to go no farther. A journey of fifteen miles a day is quite respectable for most people, especially if they are older, fatter, or accompanied by a large household. A king traveling at twenty miles a day with his court is practically dragging them along; ten miles per day is more usual. It is rare for people traveling alone to cover more than thirty miles a day in summer, or more than twenty in winter.[13]

Higher speeds are possible. A messenger who is fit and has a good horse can cover much greater distances. If he is a royal messenger, with an important message to pass on and enough money to hire extra horses on the way, he can achieve considerable speeds. The long-distance record for summer is held by the man who rides with news of the death of Edward I, at Burgh on Sands, at about nones (roughly 3 p.m.) on July 7, 1307, and delivers the same news to Prince Edward—now Edward II—in London on or before July 11.[14] This amounts to a distance of at least 310 miles, covered at a rate of about 80 miles per day. In autumn a fast rate is represented by the urgent message sent from Berkeley to Lincoln via Nottingham on September 21, 1327. The messenger covers the distance of about 150 miles in two or three days, arriving during the night of the twenty-third.[15] An autumn speed of sixty miles per day is thus possible, or even a little more if the roads are dry and the messenger has moonlight to help him. As for winter, news that Richard II has died is brought to Henry IV by a valet from Pontefract (178 miles) in February 1400. This takes between three and four days, including one change of horses, and equates to about fifty miles per day.[16] These are exceptional cases. Not even royal messengers normally travel at these speeds. Most messengers cover between twenty and thirty miles per day (depending on the season). Their horses are their own, not the king's, and so wearing them out on royal errands is the last thing they want to do.[17]

If your horse does fall ill, you will need to pay for veterinary care. Many farriers will be able to advise you on the best treatments for your ailing steed. Fat might be applied to the legs and hooves, as might honey and butter. In some cases, plasters and pills can be obtained for sick horses.[18] Dry accommodation, food, and rest is the best palliative for most animals. When valuable horses are hurt in tournaments they may well receive surgical care, such as dressings for their wounds. In January 1397 Henry of Lancaster buys various medicines to help a horse of his called "Lyard Gylder," which he has to leave in Calais. He also pays for medicines for another horse of his which he has brought over from France. The two vet's bills in this case come to 3s 7d. A third horse of his, called "Sorrell Blackwell" falls ill soon afterwards and requires 5s worth of medicine. When his destriers fall sick, the vet's bills go much higher. One for food and medicine for "several destriers and coursers" hits £6.[19] Traveling is not a cheap business, especially if you are a lord with many servants and many horses.

If you do not fancy riding, what other options are there? For a start you will probably rule out carts. Carts are two-wheeled vehicles, drawn by horses, for transporting *things*, not people, and normally quite specific things at that. A dung cart is for transporting dung, a hay cart is for hay and bushels of grain. If a cart is used for moving coal, it will probably have no other purpose. Animals are moved on the hoof, and most other market produce is shifted on packhorses. Even the largest vehicles—four-wheeled wagons—are generally only used by great households for transporting the lord's equipment: his armor or large purchases of tuns of wine. Wagons are sometimes also used for bulk transport to and from a fair. These cumbersome contraptions, pulled by six, seven, or eight horses, rarely carry people other than the driver. They are simply too slow, being even slower than a large team of packhorses, and unable to cover more than twelve miles a day.[20]

A similar thing can be said for coaches. In the early decades of the century it is unlikely that there are more than a dozen coaches in the kingdom. Only female members of the royal family or elderly noble-women are likely to travel by coach. Even at the end of the century they are very expensive vehicles, costing hundreds of pounds and sometimes as much as a thousand.[21] Four six-spoke, six-foot-high wheels are linked by axles directly under the body of the coach and heavily greased (they do not have any suspension). The chassis is made from huge painted oak beams. Above this is a wooden-framed, barrel-shaped roof, covered in brightly painted cloth or leather. Along the sides are brightly painted architectural carvings, making the whole thing resemble a palace on wheels. Inside are seats, beds, cushions, tapestries, and rugs. The windows have silken curtains and leather external drapes. There are even hooks for the ladies' songbird cages and perches for their hunting birds.

Such mobile palaces are certainly the only way of traveling around the country with any certainty of staying dry, but they are very rarely seen on the road. They are not just costly to buy, they are hugely expensive to run. They are heavy and require a team of four or five horses (normally tethered all in one line) to pull them. The horses require feeding and grooming, the axles require constant greasing, the harness requires maintenance (keeping the long leather reins supple, for instance), and every jolt in the road threatens the stability of the vehicle. Just making strong-enough spoked wheels, complete with iron tires, is costly; wheelwrights of this caliber are not as commonly found as they will be in later centuries. Usually you can count on a bill of three shillings or more for repairs to the coach and its wheels after every long journey. Add the cost of oats for the horses and the wages of men tending them, and the wages of the men-at-arms safeguarding anyone so wealthy as to be seen traveling in a coach, and you can see why this mode of transport can set you back hundreds of pounds every year, far more than most barons and merchants can afford.

The last option, the litter, is the one preferred by aristocrats when they are unable to ride any longer or, in the case of women, when pregnant. Two long poles carrying the seat are supported by two horses, one before and one after.[22] The seat itself has a round, wooden-vaulted canopy, like a small version of a coach. Such litters are not without problems of stability, and thus they are not entirely comfortable. If the road is uneven the leading horse might stumble and, with the weight of both litter and occupant, might collapse. Even if it stays upright you might find the litter rocking from side to side as the horse proceeds, making the occupant travel sick. Towards the end of his life, the duke of Burgundy has the road from Brussels to Halle leveled by workmen advancing in front of his horse-drawn litter with spades and pickaxes so he can travel along it in greater comfort.[23]

Water Transport

There is a romantic notion that the sea is timeless, never changing, crashing on the shingle beaches of this world relentlessly. Global warming is just beginning perhaps to alert us to some of the short-comings of this view, but even so we tend to think in terms of the sea being something which was *once* timeless. The truth is that the sea has always been changing, and so have the rivers. Water levels rise and fall; estuaries, rivers, and harbors silt up; and coastal erosion wears away at cliff faces. Sands shift on the seabed, making some navigable paths along estuaries trickier. Shoals of fish move, drawing fishermen farther from the shore. And the coastal defenses and harbor walls of ports crumble under the pressure of high tides and spring storms. The constant crashing of waves on the beach is practically the only thing about the sea which does not change.

All the foregoing are the results of natural phenomena. If you add social and political factors, the sea is even more subject to change. The dangers of being lost at sea diminish rapidly with the improvement of mathematical tables and astrolabes, which can be used for measuring the angles of stars as well as the sun, for the purposes of navigation. In 1300 many people find the idea of being out of sight of land psycho-logically disturbing: the sailors themselves do not like it, preferring to follow the coasts. Thus the Irish Sea is not for the fainthearted. Nor is the voyage around Portugal to the Mediterranean, especially when there is a risk of being caught in a storm and swept right out into the

Atlantic. But by 1400 astrolabes are common and many people know how to use them. Chaucer writes a treatise for his son on how to use one. Compasses are still not yet in general use—Chaucer's Sea Captain knows his way by his knowledge of the moon, tides, and currents—but with solar and lunar tables and astrolabes, mariners can sail across the open sea with greater confidence.

On the political front, just think how much safer it is to go to sea in peacetime, when you can be more confident that the crew of that Castilian vessel on the horizon will not return to a hero's welcome if they board your vessel, cut the throats of everyone they find, and fling your corpses overboard. Naval victories—like the destruction of almost the entire French fleet at Sluys in 1340 and the crushing of the Castilian fleet off the coast at Winchelsea in 1350—are hugely significant, for they mark safer trading and easier journeying for everyone.

Although it is often said that hostilities between England and France break out in 1340, in reality the two sides have been engaging in piratical activity for many years. The Flemish pirate John Crabb, for instance, goes from his native Flanders to help the Scots—allies of the French and Flemings—in their war against England in about 1319. His manner of fighting as a mercenary is what frightens people. If you take part in a pitched battle on land, and it looks as if your side is about to lose, you can run away. At sea you cannot. Often those who are not killed in the battle are murdered afterwards and thrown overboard. When you realize that Scots, French, and Flemish pirates are picking off unprotected merchant vessels, you can see that traveling by sea is not necessarily safer than traveling by land. So it is a cause of great relief and celebration when John Crabb is captured in 1332 by Sir Walter Manny. Of course, French people are equally terrified of men like the great English pirate-merchant Sir John Hawley. But France is not an island, whereas Great Britain is. Certain things have to come to England by sea—the annual wine fleet from Bordeaux, for example—and you can be certain that if such consignments are not well defended, they and their crew will never see the shores of Britain.

SHIPS

At the start of the century the two main sorts of ship you will see in English waters are hulks and cogs. Both varieties are clinker-built: a method in which the strakes (the joined planks of wood which reach from one end of the hull to the other) all overlap. Both have a single large square sail hanging from a yardarm on a central mast. The main difference is that the overlapping strakes of a hulk project out of the water both fore and aft. This gives it a very spacious, curvaceous, buoyant look. The strakes of a cog are fixed to straight stem and stern posts, giving it a more directional, pointed shape and a more pronounced keel. The two varieties also differ in the way they are steered. Cogs, having a straight stern post, normally have a stern rudder in the center. Hulks, being curvaceous, have nothing rigid and vertical on which to fix a stern rudder, so they continue to be steered by side rudders (very long oars).[24]

In the middle decades of the century, Genoese ships from the Mediterranean start to appear in British waters. These are large vessels, called "carracks," and sometimes they carry more than one mast, allowing use of lateen sails (irregularly shaped sails in line with the ship, not across it like the square sails hanging from the yardarm). These enhance the ship's maneuverability. The vessels' greater size is due to the way they are constructed: they are carvel-built rather than clinker-built. In a carvel-built ship the strakes are laid flush against each other and nailed or pegged directly onto the frame of the hull. This uses much less oak or beech and is cheaper and much lighter. Thus the ship is also faster and more maneuverable. Similar principles are used to construct large galleys (up to 130 feet long), which use both sail power and banks of oars. Obviously the latter permit a greater degree of control and maneuverability than any vessel which relies entirely on the wind, and so they are very sought after for naval defense. Northern European shipbuilders are skeptical at first; they stick with their clinker construction until the second decade of the fifteenth century.[25] But the lesson in Mediterranean shipwrighting techniques encourages them to rethink and experiment further, altering existing forms to make larger and faster clinker-built vessels.

The results of English shipwrights' rethinking—or, rather, the rethinking of their political masters who have seen the power of these Genoese ships—are largely to be seen in the changing sizes of ships. Hulks are built larger for long voyages. Very large ships cannot be steered by a side rudder, as any rudder which is long enough to do the job is unwieldy. So central rudders suspended from the stern are developed for hulks. Some have a second mast to aid their steering.[26] Cogs also become bigger, reaching nearly 130 feet in the cases of a few royal warships. In addition, the basic constructional difference between a hulk and a cog begins to break down. By 1400 some ships have the strakes out of the water at one end, like a hulk, and a stem post at the other, like a cog. Some ships have more than one sail on the mainmast, adding a small topsail or "bonnet." Shipwrights start to produce better cabins, making the sterncastle on the cog in particular into a raised deck, with a large cabin beneath. The forecastle of a cog shrinks as the bow becomes more streamlined. The larger cogs are given more pronounced keels, allowing them to use their stern rudders more effectively.

Let us say you are at the port of Boston (Lincolnshire) in the 1370s, looking out across the quay. All sorts of ships are bobbing about in the harbor. Cogs of varying shapes and sizes: large cogs and small ones, some with masts very far forward in the boat, others with masts set back. If you look at the boats drawn up out of the water for caulking at the nearby shipwrights' workshop, you will see that some have pronounced keels and some are shallow draught. The keel type are stronger and heavier for the open seas; the shallow draught are versatile vessels for inshore transport and rivers. There is the odd moored hulk, waiting to take a large consignment of goods across to Sweden and Denmark. Maybe there is a large Genoese galley or carrack in the harbor, about to take a load of wool over to Flanders or down to the Mediterranean.

A typical merchant's cog is moored in front of you. It belongs to a man called Richard Toty, who uses it for shipping wine around the coast. It is about eighty-feet long and about twenty-seven feet in the beam. It has a keel and incorporates some flush-laid strakes in the carvel style, although it is predominantly clinker-built. The shipwrights have used small nails and iron bolts as well as treenails (wooden pegs) to hold it together. It has a narrow bow and elegant lines, with a spacious "castle," or upper deck, at the stern. Here is the tiller, which controls the stern rudder. There is no forecastle. Nor is there a deck as such; there is a low planked area inside the hull where the wine barrels are stored, open to the sky in port but covered with canvas when out at sea. The only cabin space is under the raised deck at the stern. Four anchors and a rowboat with oars are stored in the hull of the vessel.[27]

This is not the sort of ship in which you will make a very long voyage. There is insufficient space for more than a handful of passengers, let alone enough shelter. But if you do cadge a lift across the Channel or down to Bordeaux or Spain to buy wine with Richard Toty, then you can be reasonably confident you will arrive at your destination. The big square sail is not unwieldy, and although it works best when the wind is blowing you in exactly the right direction, it does not prevent the ship from sailing into the wind. Toty has sufficient experience to take the bottom corner of the sail and lash it to a forward point on the side of the ship, or even the prow, and tack into the wind.[28] Of course, this puts great sideways stress on the rigging, so "shrouds" are necessary to secure the mainmast laterally, as well as the strong "stays," which support the mast longitudinally. But these ships are up to the task. Cogs are the mainstay of England's international trade.

LIFE AT SEA

It is a very hard life, taking a cog along the sea-lanes down to Bordeaux or Spain, and an even harder one crossing over the Baltic to Scandinavia. Food does not keep well, no one washes, no one shaves. It is almost impossible to keep anything dry in a storm, and you can expect to be wet and miserable most of the time. The cabins stink of urine, feces, and vomit, not to mention the smell of rat urine. They also tend to get unbearably hot in summer. Not only will you have to bear in mind the water in the hold, there is very little to stop more water getting in from the waves breaking over the sides of the vessel. You may also be woken by the constant noise of the waves. In high seas the timbers grind against one another, as if the ship is trying to wrench itself apart. If you are stuck on such a vessel for several weeks, then nerves and tempers wear thin. Men get rowdy, get drunk, and fights often break out. When that happens, you might find the old draconian sea-laws of Richard I applied. If one man murders another on board, the penalty is to tie him to the corpse and fling him into the sea. If a man so much as punches another, he can expect to be tied up with a rope and dunked three times in the sea. Bear this in mind when you feel like giving the ship's mate a belt around the ear for laughing at you for being seasick.

Then there is the weather. If your ship is becalmed, or driven off course, you may find yourself with insufficient food and fresh water. Normally ships only carry provisions for the immediate journey, so an unexpected extension to the voyage can prove fatal. Shipwreck is the greatest fear (besides piracy). There is always a chance that you will set out to sea just as a storm is brewing beyond the horizon. Storms can be deadly for sailors and their passengers: scattering fleets, capsizing and flooding ships, driving boats onto rocks, or just dragging them out into uncharted waters. Ships' captains often keep an axe on board, to cut down the mast if a storm looks like wrenching the vessel apart. And ships certainly do get pulled to pieces at sea. They tend only to last twenty years or so anyway, for the caulking wears out, the tree-nails and strakes rot, and iron nails rust. Sailing at night is particularly hazardous. There are very few lighthouses; St. Catherine's Lighthouse on the Isle of Wight, built in 1328, is one of only a handful lit nightly as acts of charity.

A voyage across the Channel should take no more than a few hours—certainly less than a day—but there are instances of it taking three, four, or even more days. On one occasion King John of France spends eleven days at sea trying to cross the Channel, and the even more unfortunate Sir Hervé de Léon spends fifteen days sailing between Southampton and Harfleur.[29] Most travelers make an offering of 4d at a favorite saint's shrine before sailing.

Let us suppose you are back in Boston again, planning to sail to Poland. Such a journey will take about three weeks. A small cog is therefore not going to be suitable; you want a larger ship, probably a twin-masted hulk, in excess of one hundred feet long, to take you and your servants. As you cross the quay you will see the barrels, crates, and cages waiting to be loaded onto the vessel by crane. Cross the gangplank and step aboard: this large ship has a specially built deck. It has wooden animal cages where chickens are kept alive for the journey and stones where the cook maintains his fires. Above you is the rigging, the shrouds, the stays, and the sails. Lashed on deck you might find the spare timbers carried to effect repairs at sea. Going down the stairs you will see the piles of spare rope and canvas. Canvas stretches beyond repair after a while, or rots and tears. New ropes are regularly needed for mooring, and the rigging is replaced twice yearly. Down here, too, are the berths for the passengers. It is dark. A small candle is all you have to see by as you suddenly shift from bright sunlight and the calls of gulls to the stinking darkness below deck.

Of course it does make a difference how wealthy you are. If you are a duke's son, setting out on a voyage such as this, then you have your own paneled cabin, newly constructed for you, with a hanging bed, portable altar, perch for your favorite falcon, and hooks for hanging lamps.[30] The hulk in which you sail may even have a stable below deck for your horses. Your cooks will have the use of tiled hearths and clay ovens while on board. Your sacks of almonds—which will be crushed to make milk for cooking on the journey—can be stacked in the hold, along with all the herbs and spices you may wish to take with you. Barrels of live lobsters, eels, and crabs stand on deck, along with casks of ale and wine, cages for your laying hens, and even a cow for fresh milk, and, in due course, a feast. Salted fish and sacks of fruit will be loaded on board. You can spend your days looking out to sea, hunting for sea birds with your falcon, or playing dice with your companions, or practicing swordsmanship. Or drinking large amounts of wine and listening to your minstrels play. Once a week you will put in to land for fresh water. In such a fashion it is possible to travel by sea to somewhere very distant in relative comfort.

Even the most magnificent lord has to face the fact that living in such close proximity to so many people hampers one's lifestyle. A Dominican friar who once traveled to Jerusalem explains it thus.[31] When you go to bed, you will have beside you a small urinal. This is made of terra-cotta, not glass (which is liable to break). As most people want to sleep below deck—especially in bad weather—it tends to be very crowded. It is also very dark, so the chances are that the urinal into which you are expected to urinate and vomit will be overturned by dawn. This is a good reason to sleep in a hammock.

In the morning, when you get up, and your bowels begin to move, you will join the queues at the bow head, where there are two seats, one projecting out on each side of the prow. Delaying too long on the precarious seat over the water is a bad idea, as the queue behind may be quite long and you are in one of the most vulnerable positions it is possible to be. On a galley in the Mediterranean, where most people sleep on deck, you have to climb over all the people to reach the seats at the prow during the night. If there is no moonlight, you will be in almost total darkness. The chances of actually making your way back to your berth are small. If you fall overboard while using one of these facilities, it will be the last mistake you ever make. You will have been, literally, "dying for the toilet."

As a result of these problems, our Dominican friend tells us, some people actually climb onto the edge of the ship—what you would call the gunwales—and, as the ship plunges along in the darkness, they feel their way to the prow and the seats of mercy. Such desperation! But when a storm strikes, there is very little you can do. You will either have to squat down in a quiet corner below deck—where everyone is crammed together, on account of the bad weather—or risk being swept away by a wave. Now you can begin to understand why it smells so bad below deck. Every storm has seen men and women emptying their stomachs, souls, and bowels down here in darkness and in fear.

7

Where to Stay

If you travel long distances you will need to find accommodation. It normally follows that how you spend the night depends on where you find yourself at dusk. This is not necessarily something within your control. If the heavens open and the road turns into a quagmire, you may find that you are forced to seek shelter in the nearest cottage. Similarly, if you learn from fellow travelers that the road ahead is beset with thieves, you may choose to wait at an inn until people have gathered in sufficient numbers for you all to brave the highway together. Even if you do reach your intended town or village before nightfall, you may arrive too late to find yourself a bed, especially if it is market day or there is a fair in the vicinity. If the king's court or a nobleman's retinue is about to arrive at the same town, you will have even greater problems finding accommodation.

Nevertheless, people in medieval England do understand the difficulties faced by travelers, and you will find many prepared to share their lodgings and victuals with you. Even the mean miller in Chaucer's "Reeve's Tale" is prepared to offer two disreputable students a bed for the night. Hospitality is considered a work of charity, and listening to a stranger's news over a mug of ale and a plate of bread and cheese is one of the most pleasant and rewarding forms of charity there is. However, you do need to remember that not all people are equal; social rank plays an important role. If you are a lord, you will be entertained almost wherever you go (barring only the houses and castles of your political enemies). If you are a peasant, and if you knock on the door of a bishop's palace, the chances are that you will be shooed away. At best you will be told to come back in the morning when the leftovers from the bishop's kitchens are handed out to the poor.

The warm welcome generally extended to travelers comes with some unwritten rules. Firstly, you must respect the property of your host. Secondly, your host is legally responsible for you during your stay. Therefore at a monastery, manor house, or inn you will be expected to surrender your sword and any other weapons you are carrying. When staying at a private home, it is simply courteous to offer your sword to the master of the house. Thirdly, if you die in someone else's house, the goods with you automatically become his property. The last rule is to avoid outstaying your welcome. As the old saying goes, after three days, two things begin to smell: fish and uninvited guests.

Inns

Inns are perhaps the most obvious places to seek accommodation, but that does not mean they are all welcoming, homely establishments. They are businesses built on necessity—the very opposite of luxury hotels. The number of visitors to a town is never dependent on the number of inns; rather the opposite is true. If you have an offer of a bed in a private house, you would be well advised to take it.

The harsh practicalities of running an inn are reflected in the personages and figures of those who choose to make their living in the trade. Innkeepers are often stout, no-nonsense men, built like bears and familiar with the tricks of thieves, peddlers, beggars, and ruffians. If a traveler loses all his money in a game of dice, his pleas of poverty will fall on deaf ears when the time comes for him to pay his bill. The landlord will turn him out without his possessions, his horse, and even without his clothes if there is no other way of making good the loss. Likewise, if a traveler causes trouble at an inn, he is thrown out onto the dark streets, to be found either by a cutpurse, cutthroat, or the town watch. And, as if a rowdy clientele is not enough, an innkeeper also has to deal with the local authorities who regulate the trade. They expect him to comply with the fair prices set for food and to take responsibility for his inebriated and sometimes violent guests. It is not an easy way of making a living.

Finding a bed at an inn is not always straightforward. It is up to you to convince an innkeeper that it is worth his while accommodating you. In some towns, the bylaws require innkeepers to offer every visitor a bed, whether they arrive on foot or on horseback. The very need for such bylaws is a reminder that landlords often refuse people accommodation. If you arrive on horseback, especially if you have sent a servant on ahead to make inquiries on your behalf, you will have no difficulty obtaining a place to stay, if there is space. If you arrive on foot, a landlord can get around the bylaw by claiming that you are a vagrant. If you look as if you are poor, and might not be able to pay your bill, the chances are that you will not be offered a bed. As many landlords are fond of pointing out, inns do not exist for the sake of charity. If you want charity, go to a monastery.

Let us say you are riding into town on a late summer's evening, weary after spending eight hours in the saddle. Your servant has arranged for you to stay at an inn called the Angel. You see the handsome stone structure from some distance, with a wide street frontage and an arch in the middle of the building. The image of an angel is painted on a board which hangs above. As you ride beneath the arch, note the heavy wooden door which separates the inn from the street. Such security is necessary if the innkeeper wishes to continue to attract the wealthiest clientele.

Now you find yourself in a courtyard, which is not paved or cobbled but simply flattened earth—you come across mud in even the best establishments. On either side of you are wings of accommodation, two-storey timber-framed buildings with steep shingle-covered roofs. These have doorways on the upper floor, reached by external staircases and galleries, as well as on the ground floor. In the courtyard you dismount; one of the stable boys will take charge of your horses, leading them to the stable yard at the rear, where they will be fed and watered. Alternatively, if there is no boy present, tether your horses at the post in the courtyard before making your way through to the hall to find the landlord or his wife. "Dame, God be here!" you might say, entering the hall and seeing the innkeeper's wife, wearing a leather apron and serving some guests at the long trestle table.

"Fellow, ye be welcome."
"May I have a bed here within? May I here be lodged?"
"Yea, well and cleanly, all, were ye twelve, all on horseback."
"Nay, but we two. Is there to eat here within?"
"Yea, enough, God be thanked!"

"Bring it to us. Give hay to the horses, and straw them well; see they be watered. Dame what owe we? We shall reckon tomorrow and shall pay also that ye shall be pleased. Now, bring us to sleep; we be merry."

"Jeanette! Light the candle and lead them there above in the solar, and bear them hot water to wash their feet, and cover them with cushions, and see the table be well set."[1]

The hall where you find yourself having this conversation is very high, open to the roof beams, with a hearth set on flagstones in the center. The trestle table where the other guests are eating runs down one side. Smoke rises and exits through a louver in the roof. Here of an evening you and your servant can sit with other travelers while ale, pottage, bread, and cheese are served. In most towns, innkeepers are prevented from serving food and drink to anyone other than a guest, so the hall tends to be a gathering place for people on the move. Here traveling plans and partnerships are formed and thirsts assuaged late into the night.

If this picture of gathering around a fire in a hall with a crowd of fellow travelers exchanging tales and drinking ale seems like a pleasant way to pass the evening, be warned: there are more than a few less-romantic aspects to staying at an inn. The hall itself is often characteristically aromatic on account of the amount of moldy food, stale drink, mud, horse dung (trodden in from the street), and the urine of talbots (guard dogs) mixed in the rushes which cover the hall floor. While the best inns will see such noisome rushes quickly removed and replaced with fresh ones, intermingled with lavender, rose petals, and herbs, the worst will replace them infrequently, without the petals or herbs. In the evenings the only light apart from the fire comes from candles made of tallow (animal fat) or rushlights (rushes dipped in fat and supported on metal stands). As methods of lighting, these are poor. They also reek. If the toilet facilities are close at hand, that will not help the smell. The usual toilet is a barrel and seat, emptied every morning by some poor servant who has to carry it to the town's equivalent of Shitbrook. If there is a cesspit situated not far from the hall, it is inevitable that smells will waft up from time to time.

If the smell and poor lighting in the hall come under the heading unsanitary, the sleeping facilities are likely to be labeled unsavory. If you are lucky you will be lodged in a chamber adjacent to the hall.

If not, you will have to go outside and climb the wooden staircase to your bedchamber. There you will find several beds, sometimes a dozen or more. Each bed may accommodate two, three, or even more men. Women will be expected to share the same quarters, although females hardly ever stay at an inn by themselves. Married couples have the advantage that they pay double for a bed, so if you are with your spouse you can expect the landlord to ask a single man to vacate a bed to make room for the two of you.

The beds themselves are made of wooden frames strung with rope. A straw mattress, encased in a hemp or canvas cover, is placed on top of this. In a good inn, you will probably have a second mattress on top of this first one. In the best establishments, with just one or two beds per chamber, you may also find a chest for personal possessions and a pitcher of water and a brass basin for washing hands, faces, and feet. Should you or your companion in the bed feel the urge to get up in the night, you will need to make a short walk in the darkness. Hence the sound of travelers stumbling along the gallery or down the stairs is not uncommon. Down below, the talbots are easily disturbed. It is not unusual to wake up in the middle of the night to the barking of dogs, the snoring of travelers in your chamber, and the unmistakable sounds of someone urinating or drunkenly vomiting from the stairs or gallery down into the yard.

Another unsavory fact about staying at an inn is the cost. A bed for the night will set you back about ½d to 1d, plus 1½d to 2½d for a meal (more if with meat and more again if with wine). In addition, it is most important to have your horse fed and looked after; you can expect to spend between 1½d (in summer) and 3½d (in winter) on stabling and fodder per animal. Of course you will also have to pay for a bed (¼d) and board (1d) for your servant too. At a fine, stone-built city inn with a good reputation, the bill will be higher. In some cases you may have to pay a total bill of 1s 6d for a single night's accommodation for yourself, a servant, and three horses. And do not forget that, if you have been well served, your landlord will expect a tip as you leave. This applies to everywhere you spend the night—including the houses of wealthy and private citizens. As Chaucer puts it in "The Sea Captain's Tale," the welcome guest will "not forget to tip the meanest page in the whole house" and give to "his host and all the servants in the place some gift that is appropriate to their standing."[2]

Town Houses

The poorest town dwellers are not people with whom you are likely to stay. As you have already seen (in chapter 1), their lowly single-storey dwellings are smoky, filthy, crowded, and damp. A wealthy merchant's house, on the other hand, has all the spaciousness of an inn with many more comforts besides.

The layouts of merchants' houses vary hugely. But take the substantial house built by the tallow-chandler Richard Willysdon in Thames Street, London, in 1384. Looking at the front you see a line of shops, which Willysdon lets out to traders. These form the ground floor of a three-storey timber-framed structure leaning out over the street. The ground floor is twelve feet high, the first floor ten feet, and the second seven feet. In the center of the building is an entrance arch with a gate, leading from Thames Street into the courtyard. If you go through this you will find yourself in a large entrance court, with storage buildings on your left and a high, long hall on your right. A short flight of stone steps leads up to this hall. Directly ahead of you are several timber-framed buildings where you will find the parlor, the chapel, and bedchambers.

Turn to your right and enter the hall. This is a room designed to impress you and every other visitor whom Willysdon receives. Its size and height will strike you—forty feet long by twenty-four feet wide, and between thirty feet and forty feet high. Its architectural wooden roof adds grace to the spacious and airy interior. The painted wall hangings and the colorful cushions on the benches along the walls add vibrancy. The stone floor gives the hall a sense of solidity; beneath it there is a vaulted undercroft where goods are stored. The shutters are open, and through them you can see that the windows are glazed with thick greenish glass, which is opaque but allows light in and keeps the cold out. There is a fire on the central hearth, smoke from which is rising in the sunlight towards the roof.

Turn around and explore this house further. You entered by means of a "screens passage"—a covered passageway enclosed behind a screen, which prevents the hall door opening directly to the cold. If you go back into this passage and go through the door directly opposite, you will find yourself in the buttery, where ale, wine, and all other "wet" things are kept. The next door off the passage leads to the pantry, where bread and all "dry" things are kept (including spices, tablecloths, and other linen). At the end of the passage, beyond these rooms and tucked in behind the tenanted shops, is the kitchen: a large square room open to the roof beams, with wide fireplaces.

Walk back into the hall and go to the far end. Here you will see the merchant's table. On one side is his aumbry, where he displays his finest pewter and silverware: silver spoons, flagons, mazers (silver-bound drinking vessels), and hanaps (two-handled drinking cups). In the end wall these is a door leading through to the south-facing parlor or solar, where Willysdon and his family spend much of their day. Upstairs from this are the main bedchambers for the family and guests, with views across the garden and down to the river. Willysdon even has his own private wharf. The rent he pays for this valuable piece of land is £12 per annum.[3]

The sort of items you will find in merchants' houses are as varied as the houses themselves. If you stroll through the private quarters of Willysdon's house and those of his neighbors you will see feather beds in the bedchambers, painted wooden altarpieces in the chapels, gilt-silver crucifixes, seals, Bibles, and even the odd vellum-bound book of romance or history. You will find the swords and breastplates which good citizens are expected to carry, chests of clothes, and utensils for washing your hands (such as basins and ewers). You will see large quantities of linen for the bedchambers and many varieties of tableware, from pewter plates to bronze flagons and enameled gilt-silver covered goblets. Furniture is relatively scarce, but in the parlors you will see benches, chests, candlesticks, and painted wallhangings; and in the bedchambers you will find a surprisingly varied range of beds—from large, comfortable feather beds to low, narrow truckle beds for children and servants. The personalities of these men and women are to be noted in the objects which hint at their creativity: an astrolabe for measuring the stars, for instance, or a musical instrument such as a harp, tambourine, or flute. Most interesting of all are the prized, luxurious possessions. In 1383 in the house of William Harecourt, a trader of Boston, you will find a gentleman's falcon and a couple of other hawks. In 1337 in the house of Hugh le Bever, a taverner of London, you will see a rare cup made out of a coconut.[4]

Two Merchants' Household Inventories

Household Goods of Hugh le Bever of London, 1337[5]

Item	Value
One mattress	4s
Six blankets and one serge	13s 6d
One green tapet [carpet bedcover]	2s
One torn coverlet with shields of sendal [a fine silk]	4s
Seven linen sheets	5s
One tablecloth	2s
Three tablecloths	18d
Three feather beds	8s
Five cushions	6d
Three brass pots	2s
One brass pot	6s
Two pairs of brass pots	2s 6d
One broken brass pot	2s 6d
One latten candlestick, a plate, and a small brass plate	2s
One grate	3d
Two andirons	18d
Two basins with one washing vessel	5s
One iron herce [a frame supporting candles]	12d
One tripod [for lighting]	2d
One iron headpiece	2d
One iron spit	3d
One frying pan	1d
One funnel	1d
One small canvas bag	1d
Seven savenaps [table napkins]	5d
One old linen sheet	1d
Two pillows	3d
One cap	1d
One counter	4s
Two coffers [chests]	8d
Two curtains	8d

Two remnants of cloth	1d
Six chests	10s 10d
One folding table	12d
Two chairs	8d
One aumbry	6d
Two "anceres" [tubs?]	2s
Six casks of wine	£4
One mazer	6s
One cup made out of a coconut with a silver foot and cover of silver	£1 10s
Six silver spoons	6s
Firewood	3s

Household Goods of William Harecourt of
Boston, Lincolnshire, 1383[6]

Item	Value
Eight mazers bound with gilt-silver	£5
Three silver cups with lids	£4
Six plates of silver	£2 10s
Two beds	£1 6s 8d
Four more beds of worsted	£3
Eight blankets and six quilts	£2
Eight pairs of sheets	£2
Ten more pairs of sheets	£2
Four pairs of worsted curtains and two half-tester beds	£1 6s 8d
Three brass pots	40s
Eight more brass pots	13s 4d
Three great brass pans	10s
Five small pans	10s
Three basins and three water jugs	13s 4d
One great basin	6s 8d
Thirty pewter vessels	£1
Four pewter bottles, six quart pots, two gallon pots, and four pint pots of pewter	10s

One backplate for a fireplace, four andirons, two spits, an iron candlestick	£1
A great leaden pan and five small leads	£2 10s
Two great arks [wooden coffers]	£1
Five small arks	16s
Three tables and three pairs of trestles	3s
Three dossers [ornamental cloths behind a chair], six bankers [embroidered covering for a bench or chair], and eighteen cushions	£1 10s
Three feather beds	15s
A screen	6s 8d
Two hawks and a "gentle" falcon	£10

Monasteries and Other Religious Establishments

If you travel any distance, then at some point you will stay overnight in a religious house. Whether this be an abbey, priory, or hospital, they all offer hospitality as part of their Christian duty. It is particularly important for monks and nuns to do so on account of the exhortation in the Rule of St. Benedict: "Let all guests that come be received like Christ, for He will say: I was a stranger and you took me in." However, it has to be said that this is a duty more eagerly observed by some monks than others. Those near remote ferry crossings see far too many travelers and pilgrims—more than they can afford to keep. Birkenhead Priory has an inn specifically for coping with the travelers hoping to stay a night before catching the morning ferry across the Mersey.[7]

The sort of accommodation you can expect to find at a monastery depends upon your social standing as well as the wealth of the establishment. Noblemen and higher clergy are normally invited to share the abbot's lodgings. It is unlikely that you will be allowed into the cloister or permitted to see much of the monastery apart from the nave of the church, the outer courtyard, and your place of accommodation. Even a place in the guesthouse should not be taken for granted. At the busier monasteries, only those arriving on horseback or carried in a litter will be offered a place here; anyone arriving on foot is likely to be directed to the dormitory above the stables to share the accommodation of pilgrims, monastic laborers, and the itinerant poor.

The guesthouse of a reasonably prosperous monastery generally consists of a plastered, aisled hall of two or three bays open to the roof and heated by a central hearth. Some are larger: the hall of the guesthouse at Kirkstall has five bays, with a central hearth and chambers for the most important guests. There is normally little in the way of decoration, the purpose of the building being the fulfillment of a spiritual duty rather than the comfort of visitors. If there is a kitchen adjacent, it will be supervised by two of the brethren of the monastery; if not (as in most small priories), food will be fetched for you from a serving hatch in the outer wall of the monks' kitchen and brought to the guesthouse to be served on cloth-covered trestle tables by the monastery's servants. After dusk the windows are shuttered and tallow candles lit to supplement the light of the fire. If the building is of stone it is possible that cresset lamps will be lit. These are scooped-out stones protruding from the wall, filled with oil and containing a burning wick. As for sleeping arrangements, you will need to make yourself as comfortable as possible on one of the straw mattresses. At least you can be grateful that the straw inside them is replaced every year.[8]

It is with regard to sanitation that monastic guesthouses come into their own. Many monasteries have efficient systems of providing water for washing, drinking, and cooking. Many also have highly developed drainage systems, even having the facility to flush drains. Generally a monastic house takes water from a spring into a stone or lead-lined conduit and transfers it along stone drains or through lead pipes underground (sometimes controlled by brass taps) to the various parts of the monastery. The drains taking water away are lined and covered with flagstones. They run beneath all the latrines, including those of the monks' dormitory and the guesthouse. With regard to the latter, these are very "public" conveniences. The usual sort of arrangement is three or four wooden seats in a row—sometimes more—with no partitions between them. Sitting down and chatting with your fellow traveler while trying to pass a meat-diet-engorged stool is something you might have difficulty getting used to.

One form of religious house exists largely for the purpose of entertaining travelers. This is the hospital. You may associate hospitals with sickness and medicine—and some are exclusively concerned with ill people, especially lepers—but many are for the provision of hospitality (hence the name). In particular, those which are called Maison Dieu or Domus Dei—"God's House"—fall into this category. Normally they take the form of a hall, with beds placed around it, their head ends against the walls. There is always a chapel where you will be expected to say prayers on arrival and to attend Mass before you leave. Sometimes the hall is exceptionally long; that of the Newarke hospital at Leicester is seventeen bays—about two hundred feet—in length. This is run for the benefit of one hundred poor and infirm people, attended by a warden, four chaplains, and ten women.[9] Obviously it is a very large establishment, and it caters for itinerant poor as well as the long-term sick, who are permanently resident. The small Maison Dieu at Ospringe is perhaps more typical of the sort of hospital at which you might stay. Situated on the main road from London to Canterbury, it is expressly for the benefit of pilgrims and lepers. It is run by a master, three brethren, and two clerks. As you may gather from the idea of lepers and travelers staying together and sharing the same bed linen, their priority is not the comfort of the guests. A large hospital might have its own kitchen and refectory in which one of the brethren will read a lesson aloud during the meal. If not, rye bread and a thin vegetable soup or pottage is likely to be your repast. Unless you have a particular craving for straw mattresses with torn sheets, rye bread, watery ale, and a pungent leper in the next bed, it is worth considering staying elsewhere.

Castles and Fortified Manor Houses

Often modern historians declare that the great age of castle building is over by 1300. If you stand in front of Windsor Castle in the 1350s, or Bodiam Castle in the 1380s, and watch the dozens of carts and wagons carrying stones and timbers daily across the muddy approach roads, you might disagree. Castles and fortified manor houses continue to be built and rebuilt on a massive scale. One reason for this is security. Dozens of new licenses to crenellate are issued by the king, especially in the reign of Richard II, when there are renewed fears of invasion from both France and Scotland. But there is another reason for all the rebuilding. Older castles are increasingly proving to be uncomfortable, with their small chambers and gloomy halls. All over the country you will find noblemen rebuilding their homes in pursuit of greater luxury. The earl of Devon almost entirely rebuilds his castle at Okehampton. The earl of March rebuilds his family seat at Wigmore and develops Ludlow Castle on a truly palatial scale. The earl of Warwick rebuilds Warwick Castle in a similarly extravagant fashion, with a new great hall, new gatehouse, and two of the finest residential towers in the kingdom (Guy's Tower and Caesar's Tower). Lord Neville rebuilds his castles at Bamburgh and Raby. Lord Berkeley rebuilds most of the domestic ranges at Berkeley Castle. John of Gaunt rebuilds the domestic ranges within his great castles at Kenilworth and Hertford. His younger brothers, Edmund and Thomas, rebuild Fotheringay Castle and Caldicott Castle, respectively. Most of all, their father, Edward III, repairs or extends a huge number of royal castles. He also builds the last completely new royal castle at Queenborough, at a cost of £25,000. His works at Windsor Castle, where he rebuilds practically everything within the outer walls, cost more than £50,000, making it the most expensive building project in medieval England. If the fourteenth century is not the great age of castle building, then it is certainly the great age of castle *rebuilding*.

Where new fortified residences are constructed, they are designed to overawe and entertain, as well as to defend. The dozen most important new castles from the late fourteenth century are all well-defended buildings, with high towers, drawbridges, and portcullises.[10] But they are all symbolic of lordly power as well. Life within them is comfortable, with large halls, well-lit solars, substantial kitchens and bakehouses, and enough chambers to allow every visiting esquire to have a room of his own. If anything distinguishes these new castles from their twelfth- and thirteenth-century predecessors, it is the number of chambers they have. By 1350 noblemen have shifted their priorities from communal defense to incorporate individual privacy. Bodiam Castle, for example, has more than thirty rooms which can be used as private bedchambers.

When you come to a castle or fortified manor house and have crossed the drawbridge, you will catch sight of the courtyard. This is typically square in a fourteenth-century residence, with the white-washed walls and glazed windows of the hall, solar, and chapel facing it. If the lord is in residence, liveried servants will be scampering about, carrying food from the storerooms to the kitchen, fetching water from the well to fill the dozens of pots for heating bathwater, and carrying firewood to stack inside the hall. A groom will proceed to show you around: this door leads through to the ale-cellar, this door to the general kitchen, this door to the meat stores, that door over there to the chapel, and this set of stone steps to a staff dormitory above the storerooms. If you look up you will see the hall and solar are roofed with lead. Above the whole building flies the armorial banner of the lord.

As in every other medieval building, the center of life is the hall. Noble halls vary in size primarily according to the function of the building as a whole—more so than to the status of the lord. The hall of the earl of Devon's castle at Okehampton, which is little more than an administrative center and a hunting retreat, is forty-four feet long, twenty-four feet wide and about forty feet high—the usual size for the hall of a manor house or a rich merchant's town house. That of a wealthy knight's country seat may be far larger. Sir John Pulteney's great hall at Penshurst (a fortified manor house) is sixty-two feet long, thirty-nine feet wide, and no less than sixty feet high. The chief castles or fortified manor houses of the nobility have halls on a similar scale, with exposed wooden roof beams of architectural complexity, albeit darkened with smoke.[11] For example: the earl of Huntingdon's hall at Dartington is sixty feet long, thirty-eight feet wide, and forty-eight feet high.[12] The floors of such halls are often covered with patterned tiles. In the middle is a fire raised on flagstones. All the interior walls are plastered and painted, either with red lines imitating courses of stonework or more elaborate designs, such as heraldry, moons, and stars, or bees, butterflies, and flowers. At the upper end of the hall, raised on a dais, are the lord's table, his chair, and several benches. Projecting out above the principal seat in the center is a rich canopy, known as a baldaquin, the red silk of which hangs down like a curtain behind the seat.

Items at Dartington Hall, Devon, in the Lord's Absence, 1400[13]

One bed of silk embroidered with bulls and divers other arms with three curtains of tartarin [a rich Eastern silk fabric imported from Tartary] covered with gold foil with bulls, with two rugs of tapestry with bulls, and eight cushions of silk embroidered with bulls

One bed with a baldaquin embroidered with the arms of England and Hainault, with three curtains of red sendal

One bed of red tartarin embroidered with letters with a curtain of red tartarin belonging to the same bed

Nineteen white Arras tapestries showing parrots

Fourteen rugs of red tapestry with the arms of the late earl of Huntingdon and of the lady his wife, and with the wheat-ear livery badge of the same earl

Twelve rugs of blue tapestry with the arms of the late earl of Huntingdon

Two long cushions of red cloth of gold

Two long cushions of red velvet and eight short cushions of the same cloth

Eight short cushions of red cloth of gold and twelve cushions of white cloth of gold

Four long white cushions of white damask cloth embroidered with M's with golden crowns and two short cushions of the same material

Two long cushions of green damask cloth

One cushion of black damask cloth

Three golden Arras rugs

One long cushion of old damask

One hanging tapestry for the hall

Four green rugs of tapestry

Seven rugs of white worsted embroidered with black ragged staves

Three curtains [for a bed] with one valance of white tartarin of the same ragged staves design

One bed with a baldaquin with three curtains of red tartarin

Eleven old rugs of white and blue linsey-woolsey

One bed with a green baldaquin and three curtains of green
tartarin

Eight carpets

One old bed with a torn baldaquin and three curtains of blue
tartarin

One other old Norfolk bed with three curtains of card [a form of
linen]

An old bed of red embroidered worsted with three matching
curtains

An old bed of red worsted embroidered with oak leaves, with three
curtains of tartarin and seven worsted rugs to match

One dosser and two costers [sidehangings] with the same oak-
leaves pattern

One cover for a silk bed of red and white

One missal, one antiphonal with a psalter contained within it and
one gradual

Altar coverings, vestments, surplices, and curtains in the chapel

Eight tablecloths, six hand towels, and five other cloths for the
table

Two silver bowls and a silver washbasin

One silver pot and one covered salt of silver

Three silver cups, one with a cover of gilt-silver

Six silver spoons, six silver plates, and four silver saucers

Five chests bound with iron

In the kitchen, four great standard pots of bronze

Five smaller pots of bronze

Six small bronze pots

Five very small bronze pots

Two great cooking vessels

Two small cooking vessels

Four great ladles of copper

Four small ladles of bronze

Four frying pans

Three great iron griddles, and one old iron griddle

Six iron rakes

Five great mortars

156 tin plates

Before each meal the serving lads put up trestle tables along each side of the hall. They bring brightly glazed green and gold ceramic wine jugs and ale flagons to set out in readiness. Others place candles on the spikes protruding from the walls, and light the candles on the chandeliers. These are iron or silver hoops, about six feet in diameter, raised on pulleys. On the lord's table, a plain white linen tablecloth is placed, reaching to the floor. Then a second cloth with a colored strip down the center is placed over it; this is the sanap, on which the choicest dishes will be placed for the delectation of the lord and his guests. Brightly colored cushions are placed on the benches on the dais. Good-quality wax candles are impaled on the spikes of the three-legged candlesticks on the lord's table, along with other precious luxuries, such as his gilt-silver saltcellar and enameled gilt-silver drinking cups.

What will impress you about life in a castle is not so much the gold and silver but the scale of everything. A man who drinks out of an enameled gilt-silver cup is rich, but a man whose *steward* drinks out of such a cup is powerful. Most barons have about forty-five men in their household. The earl of Devon has 135 in 1384, the bishop of Ely eighty-three.[14] John of Gaunt—the richest Englishman of the century (excluding the kings)—has 115, but this does not include a further 150 armed retainers contracted to serve him whenever he wants them. Edward II has about 450 to 500 men in his household in 1318.[15] Edward III has considerably more than eight hundred in the period 1344–47, during much of which time he is fighting abroad.[16] In the more peaceful 1360s he has between 350 and 450. The largest household of all in peacetime is not that of a king. It is that of Thomas, earl of Lancaster, cousin to Edward II, who at the start of the century has no fewer than 708 men. Imagine traveling along the highways of northern England with that small army buzzing around: people come out of their houses just to see him pass by.

As you wander around the castle, you may be surprised to see that there are hardly any females present. Of the 135 people in the earl of Devon's household, only three are women. This is normal—even in those households which are headed by a woman.[17] A washerwoman might be employed (cleaning clothes is strictly a woman's job in medieval England) but she will not live within the household. The only resident females will be the lord's wife and daughters and their personal companions. Kitchen staff, grooms, valets, pantlers, butlers, even the dishwashers—all of these positions are filled by men and boys. If the men choose to marry, then they must leave the lord's household and set up their own.

The Royal Household in 1392–93[18]

Office or Rank	Number
Officers (a steward, chamberlain, controller of the household, keeper of the wardrobe, cofferer, keeper of the privy seal, secretary, almoner, physician, surgeon, and dean of the royal chapel)	11
Chamber knights	8
Clerks	25
Sergeants-at-arms	3
Sergeants of offices	17
Esquires	101
Huntsmen	10
Valets of the chamber	20
Valets of the stables	89
Other valets (including messengers)	80
Grooms	53
Carters	14
Cleaners	2
Total	433

When processing into the hall, say, before a great feast, the marshal of the hall will direct a couple of grooms to make sure that everyone enters and is seated according to their status. Even the lower ranks—the gentlemen, valets and grooms of the household, and lesser servants—are seated hierarchically. The most senior officers sit next to the dais, on the right-hand side of the lord. This table is called the "reward." Opposite is the "second mess." At this more privileged end of the hall are seated important men, such as the lord's chief retainers, his chaplain and steward, and any other important guests. Farther down are the chief household servants: the almoner, the keeper of the wardrobe, the clerk of the kitchen, the receivers of the lords' manors, the marshal of the stables, the cofferer, and the lord's secretary. Farther down still are the more menial members of the household: the gardener, the slaughterer, the baker, the brewer, the candle-maker, the farrier, the blacksmith, the poulterer, messengers, and other servants (although some households have a separate hall for these men).

In winter, when it is dark outside after the evening meal, the candle-light hardly allows you to see the full length of the hall. The servants faces appear rosy cheeked as they sit at the long tables, talking and laughing—your own servant among them. When the hall is full of people, it becomes warm quickly, on account of the movement and clamor of many bodies and voices. The mood is also warmer. Monastries might have better drains, inns might be geographically convenient to city centers, private houses are certainly the most comfortable to sleep in—but you are unlikely to find better entertainment and conversation than around a nobleman's fireside. Many lords like to have verse romances read to them by the fire of an evening. Otherwise it is conversation, storytelling, and wit which will keep you amused, or dancing if it is a special occasion. Most great lords maintain their own minstrels, who play during and after supper. Traveling musicians regularly stay at manor houses, paying for their lodging and food with their music and hoping for a bonus if they perform well. Late into the night, the senior household servants sit on benches around the fire in the hall, talking, ordering the boys to fetch firewood while playing dice or chess in the light of the fat-dripping candles of the chandeliers.

If you are considered of sufficient rank to be allocated a chamber, you and your servant will be led to a room in a solar wing or castle tower. The staircase will be steep and dark, normally spiraling clockwise upwards (a traditional layout, originally to prevent right-handed attackers from using their swords). The servant leading you will no doubt carry a lantern or lamp in order to light your way. In the chamber itself he will light the candle affixed to the bed frame. The window will be shuttered from inside. A small fire might be burning in a fireplace in the wall. In the dim light you might also be able to make out a chest for linen, a doorway leading to the garderobe, a low bed for your servant, and a cupboard in the wall for small possessions.

The bed in an aristocratic residence is distinguished by the enclosing curtains and feather mattress.[19] Linen sheets, feather pillows, woollen blankets, and a bright bedspread make you feel comfortable (until the bedbugs bite). A rail on which to hang your clothing is attached to the bed or to a bracket on the wall. There too is a rail or perch where you may set your favorite falcon, feeding it choice cuttings of meat supplied from the kitchens. In case you are wondering about the candle affixed to the frame of the bed, the idea is that this is either left burning through the night or extinguished before you go to sleep. Some men feel it is acceptable to put this candle out by throwing their tunic over it.[20] As you might realize, this is unwise.

You may have been led to believe that the latrines in a castle are very smelly. This is not necessarily the case. The new latrine blocks are highly refined. The boards of the garderobe seat are covered with green cloth and the opening plugged with a cushion, to prevent any odors or drafts.[21] In some castles there is a long drop beneath the seat—the ordure falling down the side of the castle mound into the ditch. In other places it drops down a chute into a strategically positioned barrel, which will be emptied by the castle gongfermor (latrine pit cleaner). Most advanced of all are the close-stools invented for members of the aristocracy at the end of the century. These are made of iron with removable brass basins beneath velvet-covered seats.[22] Wherever you go, a neat pile of wool or linen will be provided for you to "wipe your nether end."[23] Some great lords insist on cotton but it is not always available. A basin and jug of water will be ready for you to wash your hands when you have finished.

Much more could be said about staying in a lordly residence but space prevents it. There is perhaps just one other important thing to say. If you arrive when the lord is not in residence, you will have a very different experience. If you are of sufficient rank you may still be given accommodation in a chamber, but the hall will be cold. No saucerers will be stirring pots over the great fires in the kitchens, no boys will be turning joints of meat on spits, no liveried grooms bustling around the courtyard with firewood and water for the ewers. Most castles are almost empty when the lord is not in residence, and this applies also to royal residences when the constable is away. Just a castellan and three or four valets are present, together with a couple of menial servants. The vast hall will be cold and dark, the fine linen absent, the chandeliers unlit, and the aumbry bare. There is normally no need for large numbers of men to garrison an empty castle. Unless it is situated in a particularly dangerous area, it is unlikely to be attacked. The fact that a medieval building is fortified is enough to deter most robbers from attempting to enter it.

Peasant Houses

There are as many different sorts of peasant houses as there are peasant families, and there are huge variations across the regions. But perhaps you are wondering about staying in the house of a moderately prosperous Midlands yeoman, with thirty acres to his name. His house is likely to be a wooden structure of three bays (about forty-five feet by fifteen or so) built on a stone foundation plinth. The hall extends to two bays; the third bay at one end is a storeroom at ground-floor level and the family bedchamber above, reached by a ladder. Normally the frame of the house is made up of two curved oak timbers (crucks), joined by a heavy ridge pole across the top of the house, with oak or elm purlins forming the frame of the walls. The whole structure has a slightly warped look since it is built with unseasoned timbers that twist into their own shape as they harden over the first few years. The walls themselves are made of ash struts encased in cob. The roof is framed with ash struts across oak beams and thatched with osiers, or rye or wheat straw. A few slates or tiles cover the parts likely to be affected by sparks from the fire. One problem with this organic design is that, while it holds heat well, it attracts vermin which burrow into the walls and roof of the house.

You enter by way of an oak door set on iron hinges. This fits into a frame which is strong enough to warrant the door having a lock. Immediately inside is the hall, which is quite dark, being lit only by a central fire and shuttered unglazed windows which are small enough to keep the heat in and the winter weather out. The furniture includes a chair, a pair of benches, several chests, and little else. The walls are not painted but might be plastered. Looking up, you will see that the beams and upper parts of the room are blackened with smoke. Some of the householder's possessions are hung on the walls or suspended from the beams: some tools, joints of salted meat kept over the winter, tubs, tripods, hoops, and buckets. The floor is strewn with rushes and herbs. Beneath the rushes is bare earth which is swept with a broom of clustered twigs when the rushes are replaced.

The fire rests in a clay-lined pit in the center of the hall and is kept alight day and night from late autumn through to spring. If it is used for cooking it may be kept alight all year round—although cooking tends to be done outside in summer. Utensils, such as a spit or grid-irons, are stored here beside the hearth. Here too is a brass cauldron in which much of the food is boiled. Pans of riveted copper plates, a mortar and pestle and bakestones (for oatcakes) are hung on the wall or kept in a chest. Some peasants even keep their grain and vegetables in wooden chests in the hall.

Once your host has made you welcome he will offer you a bench beside the fire so you may warm yourself as the family bustles about, preparing for the meal. You will not be expected to assist in any way—you are an honored guest. The householder or his servant (most yeomen have a servant or two) will set up the table board on a couple of trestles and arrange its furnishings of wooden bowls, ceramic jugs, and drinking vessels. If he thinks highly of his social position, then he will have invested in a couple of silver spoons. The tablecloth is linen or canvas and hangs down to the floor. The householder sits at the head of the table. He takes charge of cutting the bread and meat—if there is any—and distributing it. The rest of the family sit at the table beside you on the benches. A boy, carrying a ewer, ensures that everyone has the opportunity to wash their hands thoroughly before the meal.

After supper the householder will have his children sent to bed in the family bedchamber and spend the evening talking with you beside the fire. You see his face in the small golden glow of a tallow candle. Even in this poor light you may find his wife darning or stitching clothes for the family, squinting at her needlework. When the time comes to go to bed, you and your servant will be offered a made-up bed in the bedchamber upstairs. This is a mattress, stuffed with straw or oats, placed on wooden planks, and covered with linen sheets, woollen blankets, and a pillow, together with a bedspread. In Chaucer's "Reeve's Tale," the two students staying overnight are given a made-up bed to share in the bedchamber; there too sleep the miller and his wife (who share a bed), their daughter (who has her own berth), and their baby (in a cot). At night the room is totally dark—no candle is left burning through the night in a peasant's house. If you should need to answer a call of nature, you will have to get up, feel your way to the door, descend the ladder, and go outside: you will not find a chamber pot.[24]

Household Goods of Robert Oldham of Cuxham, Oxfordshire, c.1350[25]

Item	Value
Three brass pots	2s each
Two pans and a tripod for cooking	1s
Hoops for wooden vessels	1s
Two metal ewers	6d each
One basin and ewer	8d
Another basin and ewer	2s 8d
Canvas cloth	9d
A tapet	3d
A tapet with sheets	3s 4d
A tapet with two sheets and four blankets	5s 4d
A tablecloth	2s 6d
A towel	6d
Two cloths	8d
A coffer	2s
Two stools	8d
One bench	1½d

Most peasant houses are sparsely furnished, like those of their social superiors. In Robert Oldham's house the only items of furniture mentioned are a chest, two stools, and a bench. The appraiser has apparently regarded the value of his bed and table as nil. But Robert's clothes are valued at 34s, setting him far above most peasants. The poorest villeins live in cottages which are little more than hovels. They consist of a single room of one bay only, perhaps just thirteen feet square. The roof is of thatch or turf, which leaks after a few years if not repaired. In winter it is quite likely that you will have to step over a puddle of water which has collected in the rut worn in the doorway. The door itself swivels on a stone at its base and is tied to the frame of the house at the top; therefore it does not swing easily. There is no lock, only a latch. The shutters are hinged with pieces of hide on their upper edge and propped open at the bottom with a stick. The floor is bare earth, covered with straw. The whole house is damp. It is smoky: "full sooty was her bower," as Chaucer would say. The arrangement of the shutters means that the house is often dark, even in the daytime. Eating facilities might include a trestle table, an earthenware jug, wooden bowls, a bench, and a stool. The sleeping area is tucked behind a wattle screen along one side of the room: a bed made of three planks, a mattress of dried heather or fern, a single sheet, and an old blanket on top. Other possessions might include a brass cooking pot, an old cauldron, a basket, and a tub outside for storing water brought back from the well. It might be someone's home but "homely" is not a word you would use to describe it.

8

What to Eat and Drink

The modern traveler, coming from an age of good food guides and supermarkets, is liable to forget that people in medieval England still starve to death. Bad years for wheat are 1315–17 (the Great Famine), 1321–23, 1331–32, 1350–52, 1363–64, 1367–68, 1369–71, and 1390–91.[1] And these are just the bad years for *wheat*; there are just as many paltry harvests for all the other cereal crops, and when any one of them fails, people suffer. If a season's storms leave all the crops under water and rotting in the fields, and the cattle, sheep, and pigs drown in the swollen rivers and mud, and catch waterborne diseases, there is simply nothing for the poor man and his family to eat except the fruit from the trees (if there is any) and the preserved remains of last year's harvest. When two years' crops fail in succession, families die. The undernourished children perish first, susceptible to diseases in their weakened state, but it is not long before the adults follow. Men and women will eat anything—herbs, grass, drawk and darnel (forms of weed), vetches, acorns, and even bark—in their efforts to stay alive. They turn to crime—stealing food and livestock wherever they can.[2] Sometimes the king and his council try to relieve the situation but there is little they can do except lower the duties on imported grain. This has no effect outside the major towns, for the rural peasantry cannot physically transport themselves to buy the grain. Even if they could make the journey they could not afford to pay the inflated prices being charged.

The pangs of starvation are felt just as severely by those caught in a siege. When you find yourself in a castle or town, with overwhelming force beyond the gates, you may well have to decide between two terrible fates: surrender and death by hanging on the one hand, or resistance and the likelihood of a slow death through starvation on the other. Those who choose the latter may suffer the most unimaginable tortures from lack of food. If you visit Calais in the summer of 1347, you will see just how bad things can get. At the outset of the siege, in September 1346, the French captain of the town expels most of the women, the children, the old, and the unfit, so there are only able-bodied men left. Over the next eleven months those men use up all their supplies. They eat every animal in the town: every dog, cat, and horse. By July they are catching rats and eating those. When they finally give in (on August 4, 1347) it is because, as the captain states in a letter to the French king, they have nothing left to eat but one another, and they would rather die on the battlefield than consume the flesh of their friends and relatives.

Calais is an extreme case, and this chapter is predominantly concerned with tastier things than rats, horses, and dogs. Nevertheless, the extremes are worth bearing in mind as you peruse the metaphorical menus of medieval England. A number of your favorite foods will not be available. There are no potatoes or tomatoes; these come from lands yet to be discovered. For the same reason there are no turkeys: your Christmas dish instead—if you can afford it—is likely to be a swan, a goose, beef, ham, or bacon.[3] You will search the markets in vain for carrots, which have yet to be developed from their inedible purple wild variety. Rice is imported only in small amounts, and pasta—although regularly made in Italy and Sicily—has yet to make an appearance in England. Like all true travelers you have no option but to eat the local food, and in many cases you will find that the only alternative is hunger. If an unchanging diet of boiled bacon, rye bread, and peas does not appeal, then consider yourself lucky not to be stuck in a house in which the bacon has gone rancid, the flour has been eaten by rats, and the peas have become damp and rotted.

Rhythms of Food

The modern convention of three square meals per day does not apply in medieval England. Here you will eat just two. With the exception of a few high-status, self-indulgent individuals, people do not normally have breakfast. A householder might take some bread and cheese on rising, especially if he is planning to ride a long distance or be very active, but on the whole he will eat nothing until dinner. This, the main meal of the day, usually takes place between ten and eleven o'clock in the morning, depending on the season. It is followed by supper, a more modest affair, in the late afternoon—between four and five o'clock. Although the medieval diet does not come close to our ideas of healthy eating—for example, boiling cabbage until all the vitamin C has been destroyed—in one sense it has merit, for it delivers the greatest boost of energy in the late morning, when people still have most of the day to work off the calories.

Another important gastronomic rhythm arises from the strict rules about eating meat. The Church forbids the consumption of animals on Wednesdays, Fridays, and Saturdays, and throughout Lent and Advent. This equates to just over half the year. In Lent even the eating of eggs is forbidden. As this applies to the whole of society, even the king, no host or patron will break the rule in your presence. Anyone who eats meat on a nonmeat day is liable to find himself or herself hauled up before the church courts. It is a sin and will play upon a man's or woman's conscience until he or she is relieved by confession, an indulgence, or a penance imposed by the courts.

The third layer of dietary rhythms is simply that of seasonal availability. Fruit is fresher in autumn, and at harvesttime all sorts of things become plentiful, from white bread to pies and flans. Meat is also more plentiful in late autumn. The expense of feeding animals through the winter months means that many are slaughtered at Martinmas (November 11). Some are roasted and eaten straightaway; others are salted for consumption during the winter. Obviously garden produce is seasonal; in fact, vegetables are arguably the most seasonal products of all, as there is little monetary value in them and thus no long-distance trade. As for fish, more fresh varieties are available in summer, when the seas are not so rough and the merchants coming from the coastal towns have longer daylight hours to transport their cargoes to the inland markets. In winter, market fish is mainly salted or dried. Even the form in which things are cooked varies with the seasons. A great deal of cooking takes place out of doors in summer. This is partly because of the weather and partly because keeping a large fire burning on the hearth of a small house tends to make it unbearably hot. Communal cooking of roast meat is common in late summer and autumn; in winter food is older and more often boiled.

For all these reasons, a request for your favorite food when you fancy it—especially if it is a meat product—can only rarely be satisfied. Times of day, days of the week, and seasons of the year all matter much more than they do in the modern world.

Peasant Households

As noted in chapter 2, there are rich peasants and poor peasants, and it goes without saying that married yeomen with thirty acres have a better diet than poor single laborers with no land or garden. It also goes without saying that hungry travelers are not welcome in a place where food is scarce. But let us say you find yourself sitting down at a yeoman's table, like that in the three-bay house described in the last chapter.

There could be several sorts of bread in front of you. At the start of the century, dark rye bread is common, as is bread made from wheat and rye mixed together, known as maslin.[4] It is unlikely that before 1350 you will be offered fine white bread in a yeoman's house, but on special days—considering you are a guest—it might happen, if your host keeps a portion of his land sufficiently enriched with dung for growing wheat. On other days you might find bread made from barley (especially in the western counties), or oats, or a mixture of oats and wheat. You might be offered oatcakes as well as bread (especially in the north). If these do not tempt you, consider eating "horse-bread." This is made from a sort of flour of ground peas, bran, and beans—if contemporaries look at you strangely, it is because it is not meant for human consumption. But in some places you might be expected to eat the brown wholegrain bread known as "tourt." When this gets old, it is cut into slices and used for trenchers or plates. After use, the trenchers are given to the pigs to eat, soaked in the juices of the meal. Nothing is wasted in a peasant's household. Even the plates are edible.

As you will gather, bread is an important part of the medieval peasant's diet. Accordingly, its price is controlled by law (the Assize of Bread). The *buying* of bread, however, is a typically urban activity. Your rural yeoman is more likely to make his own. He or his wife will take their grain to the manorial mill (normally a watermill but just possibly an early wooden windmill), where the miller will grind it and take a small proportion in payment (normally a sixteenth or a twenty-fourth). If the yeoman has a stone or a clay oven in one of his outhouses, he and his wife might bake the bread themselves. Otherwise they will take their ground grain to the village baker for baking. The end product might be kept up to a week in the home, although when it is that old it is usually used only for trenchers and animal feed.

If there is any rival to bread as the staple food of the English peasantry, it is pottage. There are thick and thin pottages, from thick white porridge made with oats, and runny green pottage made with peas, to white porray made with leeks. Your host will expect your eyes to light up when he sets before you a bowl of a pottage containing peas, herbs, some bacon, and white beans. The most basic ingredients are meat stock, chopped herbs, oats, and salt, but beyond that almost anything can go in. Breadcrumbs are often used as a thickener. If you take a wooden spoon and start digging around, you are likely to find onions and garlic and other garden produce, such as cabbage. The peas might either be the small green sort with which you are familiar, or they may be a white variety. In poor peasants' houses, large grey peas are used. As with everything else which is green, or greenish, these are boiled thoroughly prior to eating. There is a widespread understanding that green vegetables—cabbages in particular—are not good for you, and potentially harmful if raw.

It is likely that the vegetables served in a peasant's house all come from his own garden. If you look around it you will see that there are few ornamental shrubs or flowering plants (except lavender and sweet-smelling roses), and the only trees are productive fruit trees. There is no lawn; the garden has no recreational element in its design. Instead there are rows of herbs and vegetables. If the peasant wants to eat turnips or to feed them to his animals, he needs to grow them himself. More to the point, if he wants a safeguard in case of a complete harvest failure, growing turnips is a good insurance policy. Gardens thus fulfill a twofold function: sustenance and taste. The fields are essential for his cereal crops, and the manorial pastures and downlands are important for grazing his animals, but the greatest variety in his diet comes from his garden. How proud he is of his onions, garlic, peas, leeks, chibols (spring onions), cabbages, beans, parsley, and sage. If there are well-kept fruit trees in the orchard, then no doubt his family eats well—and not just in autumn, for fruit can be preserved for a long time, both naturally and in preserves and pickles. Everyone keeps apples but look for pears, cherries, plums, grapes, walnuts, and damsons. Gooseberries, strawberries, and mulberries are also occasionally cultivated. Blackberries and sloes are so commonly found in the wild that there is no need to grow them.

What about meat, you ask? What about dairy products? Where do these figure in the peasant's diet? After all, that meat stock in the best pottage has to come from somewhere, as does the bacon. True—but do not forget that that meaty broth was in honor of a guest. And meat stock can be made to last a very long time, with the bones being boiled and reboiled. The fact is that many peasants, especially villeins, do not have many opportunities to eat meat. As the poet William Langland puts it, describing the diet of Piers Plowman,

> I have no money to buy pullets,
> Nor geese nor pigs but two green cheeses
> A few curds and cream, and a cake of oats
> And two loaves of beans and bran to bake for my children
> And yet I say by my soul, I have no salt bacon
> Nor eggs, by Christ, to make collops;
> But I have parsley, leeks and many cabbages
> And a cow and a calf, and a carthorse,
> To draw dung to my field while the drought lasts
> And by this livelihood might we live to Lammastide
> By when I hope to have my harvest in my croft
> So I may serve a dinner to my heart's delight.
> Then all the poor people fetched peascods,
> Beans and baked apples they brought in their laps,
> Chibols and chervil and ripe cherries many
> And proferred Piers this present to appease Hunger.[5]

Meat is the food of the rich and is in demand not only by the rich but by all those yeomen and townsmen who would like to be seen living *like* the rich. It is thus a status symbol, and it follows that those at the bottom of the social ladder eat much less of it than those at the top. Nor is it easy for those at the bottom to make up for this disadvantage by catching wild animals. Hunting of game is rarely permitted, being reserved for the lord of the manor. There are some exceptions:

wildfowl are plentiful in some areas—estuaries, for example—and they can be caught in large weighted nets or killed with slings. Hares are available to trappers, as are coneys (rabbits), these having bred rapidly in the wild since their introduction to England in the twelfth century. Even though these count as game—and are often caught unlawfully—a manorial court will normally impose only a small fine for poaching them. Even those taking hares from the royal forests will not be severely punished. If you do catch some hares, here is how your host might cook them:

> Take hares and flay them; pick the bones clean; hew them into pieces and put them into a pot with the blood, and seeth them. Then put them into cold water. Put the broth with other good stock, almond milk and parboiled minced onions. Let it boil on the fire. Add powder of cloves, cinnamon and mace, and a little vinegar. Take the well-washed flesh, and the bones, and set them all to boil in the broth, and then serve.[6]

There is another reason why peasants do not often eat meat or only eat wild birds and hares. Living animals have many more uses than dead ones. Cows, sheep, and goats provide milk, which, although it does not last long, can be made into cheeses, which can be kept for months. Piers Plowman would be a fool to slaughter either his cow or his calf. Sheep and goats provide wool—essential for warm clothing—so you will not find lamb or kid on a peasant's table (although you will find roast or stewed mutton, especially in November). Chickens, ducks, and geese are far more valuable for the hundreds of eggs they can produce than the one or two meals which their flesh will provide. Of course, when a chicken has ceased to lay, there is no better place for her than a cooking pot but it is worth waiting until she is old. Oxen, the largest and most valuable of all animals, are vital for pulling the plow—essential for the production of cereal crops. (The special rigid collar which one day will enable large horses to take their place has yet to be developed.) In addition, by carefully slicing the upper legs of cattle and controlling the flow, sufficient blood can be obtained without killing the animal to make blood pudding. Mixed with oats, salt, and herbs, and then boiled, it is a rich source of protein and a tasty variation in winter to pottage or cheese.

You would have thought that fish would provide a welcome, non-meat source of protein for the peasantry. Welcome it is indeed, but it does not figure greatly in most rural families' diets. For those living inland, there are obvious problems of obtaining fresh fish—transportation adding greatly to the cost. But there is another, underlying reason. The Church's prohibition of meat consumption on certain days helps to create a strong demand for fish among the nobility, gentry, and clergy. For this reason fish is expensive. Manors where the peasants are allowed to fish for themselves (like Alrewas in Staffordshire), are the exception, not the rule.[7] Normally the common man is not allowed to fish on the lakes, ponds, and rivers near his home—such rights belong to the lord of the manor. If you are hired to go fishing, your catch will go directly to the lord's table. Even if the bailiff quietly allows you to keep a fresh trout, you might well sell it. Your peasant host will certainly have no difficulty choosing between two days' wages and eating a status symbol. Members of the royal family send fish as presents to one another. The duke of York regularly sends pike, sea bream, tench, and salmon to his cousin, King Henry IV. When the royal family set such a high value on fish, what hope does a commoner have? Pickled and salted herrings are the peasant's usual fish dinner, with salt fish (normally a white fish, like cod) and stockfish (dried cod) the next most common. These are available throughout the year from town markets. Eels may also be bought, either in sticks of twenty or in pies and pasties, being plentiful in medium-sized rivers and relatively inexpensive.

What is in that painted and glazed ceramic jug on the yeoman's table? The answer is almost certainly ale: that is to say, a drink made from malted barley or oats without any hops in it (the inclusion of hops being the difference between ale and beer). Ale is so important in the medieval diet that its price, like that of bread, is governed by statute law. Four gallons of ale should be sold for 1d when the price of barley is 2s per quarter. The very best ale—which can be sold for as much as 2d per gallon—is made in Kent. But do not expect to find Kentish ale throughout the country: it does not keep. Without hops it goes sour very quickly. When alewives have brewed a new vat, they set about selling it straightaway, putting a bushel on a pole above the door of the house to advertise its availability. In peasant families, the brewing is done on a regular basis by the women of the household, and when the ale begins to turn sour, it is flavored with herbs and honey or caudled with egg yolks. If spices are available, the sourness might be concealed with ground pepper, galingale (blue ginger), cinnamon, and other exotica, purchased from the local market. In this way, ale is turned into a sort of mulled drink.

Lifting your wooden mug or mazer and taking a swig, you will find that the ale in a peasant household tastes a little sweet. It is also weak. As most prosperous peasants have an aversion to drinking water—which is liable to convey dirt and disease into their bodies—they drink ale exclusively. Only the single laborer and widow, living alone in their one-room cottages, drink water (rainwater is preferred, collected in a cistern in the yard). Married men expect their wives to brew ale as one of their household duties. Cow's milk is considered suitable only for cooking and for old women and children. Thus the ale cannot be too strong, otherwise the yeoman's judgment would wobble under the effect of drinking strong alcohol all day every day. In some areas of the country cider and perry (cider made from pears) are drunk instead of ale, especially in the western counties. The cider *can* be strong. It is also quite cheap—half the price of second-best ale, at ½d per gallon. The same can be said of the honey-based drinks, mead and metheglin (the latter being flavored with herbs), which also are to be found in the west and south of the country: extra strength at half the price. Although your English peasant will never have encountered spirits and probably very little wine, drunkenness is by no means unknown. If a yeoman's wife is good enough to brew full-strength ale or cider and let him drink eight pints of it in rapid succession, the result is quick, predictable, and not peculiar to the fourteenth century.

Towns and Cities

When you sit down to dinner in a town house, your expectations will probably be governed by what you see around you. If you are in a small wooden building, dining in a small, poorly lit hall, and being attended by your host's wife, then your fare will probably be less tasty than the yeoman's meal described above. If your host is an important merchant, on the other hand, and you are being entertained in the well-lit hall of a large house, with several fine pieces of silverware and smart white linen tablecloths on display, and with a whole pile of trenchers stacked up in front of you (one for each course), then you can expect food far richer and more varied than the peasant could ever dream of offering. You might drink red wine and eat beef, lamb, or kid in sauces prepared by the merchant's own cook, and taste wafers and sweetmeats afterwards, as would a lord.

In all probability your diet in a town will fall somewhere between the two extremes of peasant and lord, so let us here just consider what it is about food in towns and cities which is different from the country. For the countryman living three or four miles from a town, it is not just the cost of buying things which is restrictive, it is the time taken in getting to the market itself. Whereas the rural yeoman will try to cover all his needs in one trip, the merchant, shopkeeper, or laborer living in a town has no problems nipping to the bakery, or to the fishmongers' market stalls, or sending a servant. Consequently the townsman—and especially the city dweller—has far less control over his food supply than his country cousins. If he needs bread, he buys a loaf directly from the baker; he does not normally go to the miller with his own grain unless he lives in a very small town and has a few strips of land in the open fields just beyond the walls. Similarly, his garden cannot provide all the fruit and vegetables he needs (except in the cases of a few prosperous merchants, who have substantial town gardens). Most people have to go to the market for garden produce.

As a result of this dependence on the market, food is both better and worse in a town than in the country. There are specialist cooks, who will prepare meat pies and pasties and sell them in the street, either from their cookshops or by wandering around with their wares. Meat is brought into town to be sold, and as there is no particular reason to farm an animal once it has arrived, townsmen are readier to buy and eat young ones, especially lambs and kids, which are less chewy and better tasting. More and more white bread is eaten in the towns and cities over the course of the century. Old men and women in the 1390s will tell you how their grandfathers who grew up in the country used to eat nothing but rye bread, vegetables, and the odd bit of boiled pork; but now they eat lamb and beef and regularly enjoy the luxury of white bread. Nor do they go without fruit. Apples are plentiful in the markets, as are plums and cherries (in season). More exotic fruit, such as oranges, figs, and pomegranates, are imported in

small quantities, although you will only find such luxury items at a fair
or in the market of a major city.

Victuallers' Prices, London, 1363[8]

Item	Price	Item	Price
Best goose	6d	A woodcock	3d
Best suckling pig	8d	A partridge	5d
Best capon	6d	A pheasant	2d
A hen	4d	Leg of roast mutton	2½d
Best rabbit	4d	Baked capon in pastry	7d
A teal	2½d	Roast goose	7d
A mallard	5d	Best carcass of mutton	24d
Four larks	1d	Best loin of beef	5d
A snipe	1½d	Best leg of pork	3d

Herein lies the advantage of the town. If you have sufficient money
you do not need to grow things for yourself; you can just buy what
you need. Moreover, in the larger markets you can obtain many things
which are unavailable anywhere else. If you want to buy sugar, wine,
almonds, dates, aniseed, licorice, sweetmeats, nutmeg, cinnamon,
pepper, coriander, currants, raisins, figs, cloves, ginger, salt, rice, trea-
cle—you name it—the market is the place to go. All these things are
available in London in 1390. The list above is from one single account
of Henry of Lancaster, drawn up by his officers as they prepare for
a sea voyage.[9] The key issue is cost. One pound of licorice is only 1d
but a pound of green ginger costs 2s, a pound of cloves more than 4s,
and a pound of saffron 10s. A pound of orange conserve ("citronade")
costs 3s, as much as a skilled laborer earns in nine days. Can you imagine working for nine days for one pound of orange marmalade, or
that it should cost a third as much as saffron *by weight*? Small wonder
that the poor skip breakfast.

Not all spices are prohibitively expensive. In town you will discover that the better-off—and that includes the master craftsmen
and prosperous officials, lawyers, and physicians as well as the

merchants—have a range of spices in their cupboards, which they often keep locked away. Pepper is one of the most popular, costing 20d to 22d per pound. Nutmeg may be obtained for 18d per pound. A cheaper way of buying spices is to opt for a mixture made up by the spicerer. These are sorts of curry powder: powder forte (strong) which contains ginger, pepper, and mace; and powder douce (mild, also known as powder blanche), which contains ginger, cinnamon, nutmeg, and possibly sugar and cloves. Talking of sugar, you will be amazed by the number of forms in which it comes. At the spice shop you will find an array of unrefined brown loaves weighing several pounds each and delicate cakes of refined sugar ("caffetin," 18d per pound in 1390), red and white flat sugars (cheaper, 12d per pound), Cyprus sugar (cheaper still, at 8d per pound), and then all the derivatives: pot sugar, sugar water, sugar syrup, rose sugar, violet sugar, and barley sugar. The level of refining makes the difference between the cheapest sugars and the most expensive. Interestingly they are all used as spices (not as sweeteners) in sauces to accompany meat and fish dishes, especially those using vinegar, or in fruit pottages.

Although the foregoing makes the town sound appetizing, remember that town dwellers face at least two distinct food-related threats. The first arises from their lack of control of the food supply. If there is no grain, then there is no bread. If the price of grains escalates, and the town authorities try to insist on the prices established by the Assize of Bread, then the bakers are liable to go on strike. Without bread, the town quickly grinds to a halt and disorder breaks out. The second problem arises from having so many middlemen in the food chain. How can the town authorities police the sale of foodstuffs? It is very difficult. When a wild pig is seen dead in a street, and then suddenly disappears, people do not know whether it has been cleared up or cooked. Often they are right to suspect it has been disposed of in their take-away pies. London records are full of cases where a dead pig has been decomposing in the town ditch for a week or so and then ends up being scavenged by a pie-maker. Sometimes medieval people take recycling too far.

A major difference between dining in the country and in a town is the access to different sorts of drink, especially wine. Even a small barrel from a vintner costs between 8s and 10s. This is beyond the reach of a modest yeoman's income. However, proprietors of urban

taverns buy wine in bulk and sell by the cup. In this way, at a cost of a
½d or 1d, many people can afford to drink a small amount of wine. Of
course the cost varies, depending on how sweet the wine is and where
it comes from. Most red wine drunk in England is from Gascony, the
area around Bordeaux (although it is not yet called claret).[10] This sells
for between 3d and 4d per gallon to bulk purchasers—more if being
purchased by the cup. Twice as expensive is Rhenish wine, from the
Rhine, costing between 6d and 8d a gallon wholesale. The wines of
Rochelle and Spain—such as Lepe, a strong Spanish white wine, or
Osey, another Spanish white—are comparable in price to that of Bordeaux. Sweet wines from Greece, Crete, and Cyprus sometimes called
Romonye and Malvesey (or Malmesey) are about the same price.
Cheapest of all is English wine, which is only ever white and normally
half the price of Gascon wine. It is scarce, however. Most wine pro-
duction in England is carried out by the nobility and clergy for their
own use. It rarely appears in taverns.

As taverns generally sell wine, not ale, they tend to be quite upmar-
ket establishments. Given their numbers—there are 354 of them in
London in 1309—it is not surprising that they vary in quality.[11] Their
wine similarly varies. Establishments which sell poor wine tend to
attract the rougher sort and are regularly closed down by the authorities. But there are some reputable establishments. An example of the
latter will have mazers of silver-edged wood and clean linen cloths on
the tables. It will serve professional people, such as clerks, merchants,
officials, and the gentry. The taverner, mindful of the importance of
a good reputation, will very probably show you the door with po-
lite firmness at closing time (he is responsible for your actions after
curfew). The wine itself is stored in a cellar, in its casks, and carried
through to you at your table. In case you have any concerns about
what you are drinking, ask to see the barrel. The taverner should keep
his cellar door open at all times during opening hours and allow you
to check the marks on the barrels. In London, prices are fixed by the
authorities, so if you think you have been sold cheap wine in place of
the best Rhenish vintages, you should be able to check and take the
matter further. If guilty, the taverner will probably back down, knowing that if he is caught misselling his wine, he is liable to be fined or
closed down, as well as being drawn to the stocks and having his own
supply of wine poured over his head.

If you do happen to wander past the stocks and see a chap with his head and clothes soaked in liquor, the chances are that he is—or was until recently—an alehouse keeper. On the whole these establishments sell no wine, only ale and sometimes cider and mead. They also sell simple food, such as bread and cheese, and perhaps cheap meat pies. Dark and smelling of stale ale, with rushes strewn across the floor, they can be rowdy establishments, full of adventurers' tales and bawdy song. Unlike inns (whose main purpose is to provide accommodation to wealthy travelers) they exist to provide entertainment, and consequently are a resort of every sort of interesting character, from carters and wagoners to builders, carpenters, bakers, pilgrims, mummers, cutpurses, prostitutes, fishwives, gongfermors, low-lifers, and roustabouts.

Noble Households

When it comes to good food, the nobleman's table is the place to be. The very best cuisine, and the greatest variety, is served directly to the lord himself at dinner. Long after the grooms and valets have consumed their rations and left the hall, the nobleman will continue eating with his companions, seeing more courses placed before him. The same is the case at supper, even though that is a smaller, less ostentatious meal. At breakfast, the trestle tables will not even be set up for the servants. They have work to do, and there is a belief that too much food makes the worker indolent. Thus the nobleman's hall represents a spectrum of food quality and quantity, from relatively small amounts of basic pottage at the lower end of the hall to the most expensive dishes and lavish use of color and spices at the top table.

Food and drink in a lord's residence is based on a series of rules and regulations far more complicated than seasonal availability and economic necessity. In addition to the nonmeat rules set by the Church, late-fourteenth-century aristocratic households are expected to follow legislation restricting the quantities of food. From 1363 even a lord is limited by law to five dishes at any meal: this being part of the aging Edward III's attempts to control extravagance. By this same legislation, gentlemen are allowed only three dishes and grooms two. Of these two, one may be of meat or fish. Although this law is not always followed to the letter, it nevertheless gives you an idea of the level of protocol to expect. Do you rank as high as a gentleman? If you do, you can expect to be seated alongside the gentlemen of the household and fed accordingly.

Let us suppose you have been assigned a place at the top table, along the bench to the right of the nobleman—a position of high honor. Before actually taking your seat, you will have to wash your hands. One servant, the ewerer, will pour the water; it is caught in a bowl beneath your hands by another servant. There is no soap but a third servant will hand you a towel. Then grace is said by the lord's chaplain, and the first course is brought in and placed before the lord. He will take a trencher and start to help himself from the dishes laid before him. Once he has had a chance to try them, they are passed around.

The first course normally consists of boiled and baked meats in sauces, perhaps ground meat in a spiced wine sauce, or meat balls in aspic. An example of a daily first course of five dishes served to a lord is brawn with mustard, a meat pottage (containing beef or mutton, wine, herbs, and spices), another meat pottage containing chicken or boiled pork, stewed pheasant or swan, and a meat fritter (normally made with the entrails of animals). "Leche Lombard" is a popular first-course dish, consisting of pork, eggs, pepper, cloves, currants, dates, and sugar all boiled together in a bladder—like haggis—then sliced and served with a rich sauce. Another is "mortrews": chicken and pork with breadcrumbs, powder forte, sugar, saffron, and salt. Perhaps you would prefer boiled venison with almond milk, onions, rice flour, and wine, colored with alkanet (a dark-red root) and seasoned with powder douce?

The food is actually prepared in "messes" of two or four portions, which are then shared at the table. Several dishes might be set before you. Do not feel you must empty a mess entirely onto your trencher; you are expected to leave a good proportion of it. Leftovers—including the trenchers—will be given to the poor after the meal. Besides, with five different meat dishes to choose from, you could quite easily stuff yourself sideways in just the first few minutes of the first course. Resist the temptation to do this: dinner will go on for about two hours. There will be three courses, each consisting of several dishes from which you should pick tasty morsels, and each course will be separated by a small, intervening course. As you can see, food in a nobleman's household is not just about sustenance, it is a matter of honor.

After the first course of boiled and stewed meats in piquant sauces, there will be a short interlude for the serving of fruit, nuts, a "subtlety," or intervening course. This is not always something to be eaten; sometimes it is just to be looked at, especially during a great feast. Perhaps you will see the real "four-and-twenty blackbirds baked in a pie." Bird lovers need not worry: the pie is baked first and allowed to cool. The birds are placed inside alive afterward, so when the pie is opened they do begin to sing—and fly out and swoop around the hall.

The second course consists of roast flesh. This is where the lord shows off, with exotic meats delicately carved. There will be meaty pottages and meats in aspic as well as a selection of roast venison, fawn, kid, baby rabbit (a coney under one year old), bustard, stork, crane, peacock, heron, partridge, woodcock, plover, egret, larks . . . This list could go on much longer. As the boys will tell you, every one of these animals has to be carved in its own particular way. A mallard is not carved but "unbraced." To cut up a hen is to "spoil" it. Herons are "dismembered," coneys "unlaced," and so on. If you are young enough to be serving in a lord's household, you will need to learn all these terms and how to wield a pair of carving knives (there are no forks). When the marshal of the hall directs you to "sauce that capon," "break that deer," or "display that crane" you need to know which are the tastiest morsels for presentation to the lord. This is not easy, especially with almost no light in winter except that shed by a rushlight and the kitchen fires.

Remember when picking out the tasty morsels during the second course to save some room for the third. The smallest, most delicate animals are normally served at this point, such as roast curlew, sparrows, and martinets (a kind of swallow). Alongside these you might be served baked quinces, damsons in wine, apples and pears with sugar or syrup, fruit compotes, or a fruit pottage. The upper-class English are just as fond of their fruit as their underlings. Plums, damsons, cherries, and grapes are served before dinner, to whet the appetite. Pears, nuts, strawberries, whinberries, apples, and mixtures of fruit tend to be served afterwards, as the season allows. Spiced baked apples and pears are popular, especially in winter. At the end, there will be a cheese course, if you still have room. With a drink of hippocras—a spiced red wine—and wafers, the meal is finally over. Your trenchers and the uneaten remains are cleared away by the servants and boys, who then either surreptitiously eat the lord's leftovers themselves or pass them to the almoner for division among the poor who may already be arriving at the manor gatehouse.

The above menu is only for meat days. For the other 194 or 195 days of the year (Advent, Lent, and every Wednesday, Friday, and Saturday) the diet switches to fish. Does the food at the top table become modest and humble, reflecting the religious nature of this custom? Not a bit! On a fish day you might be served a first course of lampreys baked in vinegar, pepper, ginger, and cinnamon; minnows or eels in a pie; baked herrings with sugar; pike in "galantyne" (a very popular sauce made with cinnamon, galingale, ginger, salt, breadcrumbs, vinegar, and stock); or poached mulwell or gurnard. After that lot you will move up the fish ladder to taste more highly prized varieties. Options for the second course include conger eel, doree and salmon in syrup; or roasted turbot, halibut, sea bass, mullet, trout, bream, sole, eels, and lampreys. Henry IV has been known to spend as much as 7s on a single turbot.[12] In the 1330s you will often find pike and bream on the menu in the royal household, these being specifically purchased by Edward III for special occasions.[13] It is possible that towards the end of the century you will be offered a carp, although the taste for it is really something which belongs to the next century.[14]

By the time you get to the third course, you will have realized that the religious prohibition against eating meat is seen as no obstacle to culinary excess by the majority of England's nobility and gentry. For it is at this point that the really special fish are served. Sturgeon comes top of the list: a *fresh* sturgeon is a rarity—normally it will be barreled and pickled, to preserve it—but if you can get hold of one, you can expect to pay in the region of 35s.[15] Like salmon, bream, tench, and pike, it is deemed suitable to be given as a present from an earl or duke to a king. Salmon in rich sauces is the very favorite food of one of the great fighting heroes of the century, namely Henry, first duke of Lancaster. Accompanying dishes might include sea bream, perch in aspic, fried herring, and seafood (especially whelks, mussels, and shrimps). But even this list hardly does justice to the enormous range of the cooks. It is not so much that many fish have been left off this list—one could add whiting, plaice, ling, loach, luce, flounder, had-dock, swordfish, dace, dogfish, hake, and perhaps two dozen other varieties—but that there is wide scope for including animals which you would never expect to eat. Whales are technically the property of the king, but generally they are eaten by everyone in the vicinity when they are beached. Seals, porpoises, dolphins, barnacle geese, puffins, and beavers are all classed as fish as their lives begin in the sea or in a river. Hence they are eaten gleefully, even on nonmeat days. Me-dieval knowledge of the fish *at sea* might be limited—the chronicler Thomas Walsingham believes that dolphins can fly over the sails of ships—but once landed, and brought to the kitchen, they are perfectly understood. You only need to hear the terms of carving—"sauce that plaice," "barb that lobster," "splat that pike," "culpon that trout," "tranche that sturgeon"—to know that these men are no amateurs.[16]

You are wondering, no doubt, how an aristocrat manages to come by all this fish. After all, once out of water, they quickly go bad, and the means of transporting them from the sea to the kitchen are slow. No one can carry a barrel of sturgeon faster than twenty miles per day, nor a barrel of herrings for that matter. Besides, the nets of seagoing fishing vessels are relatively small and not very strong, and constantly in need of repair. In answer, no part of the country is more than sev-enty miles from the sea, and the vast majority is within forty miles. Some of the most active ports are situated inland on great rivers, like Gloucester, on the River Severn. Fish can be transported live, in barrels, and this is certainly the means of carrying oysters, mussels, whelks, lobsters, and crab, which are consumed in large quantities by the rich during Lent. Eels too are transported live in barrels from the rivers in which they are caught, and pike can be kept in vats for use when and where required. Most rivers have weirs and fishtraps on them, allowing roach, tench, dace, and bream simply to be lifted out of the river and dispatched in baskets, amid layers of wet straw. Fish-traps are also placed in estuaries, allowing thornback ray, gurnard, sea bream, salmon, grey mullet, herring, mackerel, plaice, and other sea fish to be caught without a net having to be cast or a boat launched. Lords with estates far inland maintain fishponds. The customs of a manor normally protect all freshwater fish for the lord, and he will ei-ther maintain his own fishermen to reap the benefit or hire occasional workers to do the fishing. So with all the rivers to draw on, and almost all the country within two days' ride of a port, those who can afford it have access to a very wide variety of fresh fish. If you then add the pickled, salted, smoked, and dried varieties—for example, kippers, salt cod, and shrimps and mussels pickled in brine—there is no shortage of river fish and seafood for the noble household.

Accompanying all this meat and fish is an array of vegetables and herbs. Lords, just like everyone else, cultivate as much garden produce as they can on their own land. But vegetables are not served independently; rather they are used in the sauces accompanying meat and fish. Cookery books include fruit sauces to go with many of the meat and fish dishes, such as applemoy (made out of apples) and verjuice (a sour grape juice used in cooking). Many vegetables and homegrown ingredients are necessary for the lord's meat pottages and the more basic pottages which are fed to the less-important servants and the messengers and servants from other households visiting on business. Kitchen staff are employed chopping and cooking leeks, onions, herbs, colewort, cabbages, garlic, peas, parsley, and beans for the big pottages, feeding as many as a hundred men. For the lord's dishes, cauliflower, peascods, borage, fennel, hyssop, and perhaps even parsnips and celery are used.

With regard to bread, the lord himself and his favored guests will be given slices of the best freshly baked white bread, made with wheat, called *"pain demain."* So precious is this that the flour to make it is sometimes kept in a locked chest. The important officers and gentlemen of the household probably eat "wastel," the next best wheat bread, costing ½d per loaf. Third-best is "cocket," a round white loaf. And as you go down the hall, the quality of the bread goes down too. Brown rye bread may be eaten by those at the lowest end of the hall, and certainly by the stable boys who only get to eat in the hall at Christmas and on other feast days. If those at the bottom of the hall do eat cocket, it will be three or four days old.

The range of wines available in a nobleman's cellar is far greater than you can buy in any tavern. It is normally illegal for a taverner to sell Rhenish wine alongside Gascon or Spanish wine. But it is not illegal for a lord to keep a good stock of both. Edward III's order for wine for the royal household in 1363–64 amounts to ten pipes of sweet wine (a pipe being 105 gallons), twelve pipes of Rhenish wine, and 1,600 pipes of Gascon wine—a total of 170,310 gallons.[17] Not all of this is drunk by the king and his companions; quite a lot is given out to friends and retainers (a gallon a day to Geoffrey Chaucer, for example). But a lord's household is never short of wine.

The butler in a nobleman's residence has to deal with just as much ale as wine. The servants and staff all require drink, and only the important officers are allowed wine. Each man has an allowance of a gallon of ale a day, but that is purely a nominal quantity. There is no flagon assigned to one man which he drains over the course of twenty-four hours. There is a clear distinction as to who may drink the best ale and who is drinking second and third best. Normally ale is brewed in the household's own brewery from malted barley and is kept until it is all used up or has gone off. But a butler might buy ale from local alewives, if the stocks are running low or if his master has arrived unexpectedly at a manor house before his brewing staff have managed to make enough for the whole household.

Monasteries

The provision of food and drink in a monastic establishment is just as complicated as that in a nobleman's household. Although the monks are all equal in the eyes of God, they are far from equal in their own eyes. The abbot gets the best food, and also gets to share the lordly fare provided in his house to the monastery's noble guests, who stay with him in his lodging. Certain monastic officers, such as the almoner, sacrist, infirmarer, and chamberlain, have rights to better fish and more exotic fruit than the other monks. Those monasteries which have lay brothers provide them with their own refectory, kitchen, and diet. Guests staying in the monastic guesthouse may be given a different diet altogether.

On one level you could describe the monastic household as a lordly one, with the abbot or prior as the lord. That would be superficial for many reasons. First, the man in charge has been elected to his position by the other monks, and so his relationship with his fellows is wholly different to that between a lord and his servants. Also the monastic refectory is a restricted area; only monks may eat there.[18] Important guests eat with the abbot in his lodging, less important guests in the guesthouse or at the beggars' gate. But most of all it is the extraordinary customs about eating meat which have developed over the centuries which make dining in a monastery unique. Like everyone else, monks do not eat any flesh on Wednesdays, Fridays, and Saturdays, nor in Advent or Lent. In addition, they are not supposed to eat the meat of four-legged animals at all, according to the Rule of St. Benedict. However, St. Benedict lived a long time ago—in the sixth century—and over the subsequent eight hundred years, monks all over Christendom have found ways to circumvent the Rule. These monks mostly come from well-off families, and so were stuffed with the best and richest meats from the day they could sit up at their father's table. Then they entered the Church and were completely deprived of meat. The result is that many of them simply crave it. And the Rule states only that they should not eat meat in the *refectory* . . . Consequently, many monasteries have built a second dining room, called the "misericord" (place of mercy) where meat eating can take place. Also, although eating quadrupeds is banned, there is nothing in the Rule specifically against eating offal, which is removed from an animal prior to roasting it. Realizing that all this is not wholly within the spirit of the Rule, but realizing also that he cannot stand in the way of progress, Benedict XII (pope from 1334–42) suggests a compromise.[19] As long as at least half of the monks eat in the refectory, the remainder can head off to the misericord and gorge themselves on whatever meat they choose, provided it is not a Wednesday, Friday, or Saturday, or a day in Advent or Lent. Those who remain in the refectory must refrain from eating the flesh of quadrupeds but may eat fowl and can include meaty ingredients—such as liver and other offal—in the cooking. On the nonmeat days everyone must eat together in the refectory and observe the nonmeat rules.

Each member of a religious community has an allocation of a gallon of ale each day—although the officers are allowed more, if they want it. This is no hardship: monasteries brew very fine ale indeed. When offered for sale it regularly fetches 1½d per gallon or even 2d. A few monasteries also have their own vineyards and make their own wine, but the majority import the wines of Gascony, like most large households. Wine is drunk only on saints' days, when the meal is more of a feast. Fortunately for the monks there are sixty or seventy of these in the year.

As with a noble establishment, not everyone in a monastery has breakfast. Only the abbot and the principal officers are likely to be allowed to sit down and eat bread and cheese in the morning. The others must content themselves with Mass, in line with the old saying, "The sacrament is a good breakfast."[20] For most monks, lay brethren, and guests, the first meal of the day is dinner. In the refectory, it starts with a pottage. Thereafter, depending on whether it is a fish day or not, you may be served "umbles" (sheep entrails cooked in ale with breadcrumbs and spices, often served in winter), "charlet" (chopped meat, eggs, and milk), "dowcet" (a custard dish, containing milk, cream, eggs, sugar, and currants), or a rich cheese flan. Somehow the Benedictine monks at Westminster manage to justify eating bacon—even though it is most certainly the meat of a quadruped—and so bacon and eggs ("bacon collops" as it is called) is served in the refectory as a treat just before Lent.[21]

When the misericord is functioning, the monks display a huge appetite for meat. Pope Benedict's compromise means that a monk may only eat in the misericord for a maximum of eighty-six days per year. Hence he looks forward to his turn, especially if it follows a long period of abstinence, such as Lent. The first course at dinner is almost always beef. The second course normally consists of more beef plus three further roasted meats, veal, mutton, pork, or goose. Lamb is eaten in late spring, boiled pork in winter; at other times of year, mutton is served. At supper, only one meat course may be served. Thus most monks eat about four hundred meat dishes per year. You might agree that that is hardly following a Rule which dictates that he should not eat the flesh of quadrupeds at all.

Many species of fish appear in a monastic diet. Every day the refectory sees fried, poached, baked, and roast fish served at dinner. Note that it is only at dinner that monks eat fish: at suppertime they eat shellfish, such as cockles and whelks. About half the intake is preserved sea fish, whether salted, smoked, dried, or pickled; but as monasteries often have the tithes of parishes, or are institutional lords of manors in their own right, they can expect to be sent freshwater fish on a regular basis. Some of the largest fishponds in the country are owned by monasteries—Gracious Pond (Surrey), constructed by the abbot of Chertsey in 1308, extends to over thirty-five acres and the ponds at Frensham (also Surrey) extend to over a hundred acres. Thus you will often find dace, roach, and bream served in the refectory, or that old favorite, pike in galantyne sauce. The abbot might eat more expensive seawater fish: turbot, gurnard, thornback ray, sole, conger eel, and salmon. It depends whether he is eating privately in his quarters with a guest or with the brethren in the refectory.

One last thing. There is an old traveling minstrels' trick which you might want to keep up your sleeve. How guests are treated in a monastery is the decision of the almoner. If he treats you badly, or serves you the most miserly portions of food, or if you get given "a vile and hard bed," go to the abbot and praise him to the skies for the generosity of his house, and emphasize the large amount of money which the almoner must have laid out on your behalf.

> My lord, I thank you and your worthy convent for the great cheer I have had here, and of the great cost I have taken of you; for your good liberal monk, your almoner, served me yester evening at my supper worthily, with many divers costly messes of fish, and I drank passing good wine. And now I am going he has given me a new pair of boots, and a good pair of new knives, and a new belt.[22]

The abbot will have little choice but to take such thanks at face value and bask in the fictitious glory. But have no doubt: the almoner will have a lot of explaining to do later.

9

Health and Hygiene

If you are ever asked whether you would rather live in a past century, you would be wise to consider the problem of ill health before answering. How much better to live at a time in which, when you fall sick, you go to a doctor or a surgeon and get well again. It has to be said: the prime reason to avoid medieval England is not the violence, the bad humor, the poor roads, the inequality of the class system, the approach to religion and heresy, or the extreme sexism. It is the sickness.

In almost every respect fourteenth-century life is unhealthy compared to our own. True, there are no exhaust fumes in the streets to pollute your lungs, and no tobacco smoke for that matter either; but there are open fires in many houses and the exposure to smoke for so much of the year causes lung diseases of a similar nature. There may be no fish-killing chemicals accidentally released by pharmaceutical companies into the rivers, but there are all sorts of other things which get into the water supply, from overflowing cesspits to dead animals. Children do not suffer from allergic reactions caused by dust in wall-to-wall carpeting or the excessive use of cleaning fluids, but you can hardly say that that is a good thing when nearly half of them do not live to adulthood. Very simply, if you do fall ill, or are seriously injured, you are going to suffer far more in medieval England than in the modern world.

Ideas of Illness

Why might you fall ill? There are, of course, many reasons. Not least is the likelihood that you will be struck by a blade, an arrow, a staff, or even a cannonball. The violence inherent in society, coupled with a near-complete disregard for what we think of as health and safety, mean that serious injuries are very common. In addition, even where such injuries are not fatal, poor knowledge of medicine and hygiene means that blood poisoning often leads to death or the amputation of a limb. There is very little understanding of how diseases spread or how the body functions. Hospital staff often put seriously ill people in one bed together, even when they are suffering from infectious illnesses. Germ theory is unknown. The circulation of the blood is a complete mystery. If you are found in a comatose state in 1300, no one will check your pulse to see whether you are still alive; instead they will place a bowl of water on your chest, to see if you are still breathing.[1] Medieval life might be unhealthy, but some medieval medical concepts are unhealthier still. Before long you will think of medieval medicine as a bizarre mixture of arcane ritual, cult religion, domestic invention, and a freakshow.

The most common cause of illness is, according to most opinions, divine judgment. As God makes all things happen, so too all afflictions must ultimately come from God. Some people argue that, because God is a caring deity, ill health and suffering must also have an origin in divine care. From this proceeds the widespread understanding that disease and physical suffering are the means by which God purifies the soul. Diseases are seen as tempering fires in which an individual's belief in God's mercy is put to the test. It is thus obvious why people are just as ready to seek religious cures for their illnesses as they are medical ones. Even if a physician is successful in curing them, such success will only have been obtained through God's grace. The altars of churches are regularly strewn with little wax models of arms and legs, votive offerings made by sufferers so that God might relieve them of their ailments. Or at least permit a physician or a surgeon to act as a conduit for divine healing. Without the religious remedy in place, no one has a hope of being cured medically.

Other ideas about the origins of disease are bound up with astrology. When the king of France asks the faculty of medicine at the University of Paris to explain the causes of the Great Plague of 1348–49, the worthy professors report that the pestilence is due to

> an important conjunction of the three higher planets in the sign of
> Aquarius, which, with other conjunctions and eclipses, is the cause of

the pernicious corruption of the surrounding air, as well as a sign of mortality, famine and other catastrophes.

As they go on to explain:

The conjunction of Saturn and Jupiter brings about the death of peoples and the depopulation of kingdoms . . . The conjunction of Mars and Jupiter causes great pestilence in the air.[2]

Such planetary alignments are thought to lead to local miasmas: concentrations of fetid air and noxious vapors. These miasmas are then blown on the wind and enter men's and women's bodies through the pores of their skin. Once inside they disrupt the balance of the "humors" (the substances believed to control the body's functions), and people fall sick.

The alignments of the planets and stars have significance for the health of individuals as well as communities. Letting blood at some stages of the lunar cycle can be beneficial; at other times it is deemed harmful. Specialists use astrology to determine when a particular patient might recover, based on the positions of the planets at the time he fell ill. Even having sex during some lunar and planetary conjunctions is thought to be harmful, regardless of whether the intercourse takes place within marriage, adulterously, or with a prostitute. Some medical men, clinging to older medical writings, say that the movements of particular planets control the functioning of certain organs: Mercury controls the brain, Jupiter the liver, and so on. The business of diagnosis is thus much more complicated than merely ascribing all illnesses to divine causes.

Complicated such systems might be, sophisticated even, but the resultant gamut of medical knowledge is far from adequate. Consider the medical practice of John Mirfield, a priest and adviser at St. Bartholomew's Hospital, London, at the end of the century. He advises his fellow physicians that, if they wish to know whether a patient might survive or not, they should follow this procedure:

Take the name of the patient, the name of the messenger sent to summon you, and the name of the day upon which the messenger first came to you; join all their letters together, and if an even number result, the patient will not escape; if the number be odd, he will re-cover.[3]

Such numerological practices are not peculiar to Mirfield: variant methods include the Sphere of Apuleis, wherein one assigns a numerical value to each letter of a name and subtracts thirty from the total to determine whether the patient will live or die. Considering that the standardized spelling of names has yet to be introduced, this is extraordinary: a practice of introducing sufficient random variables so that the whole matter is one of chance, or, as Mirfield would rather have it, divine providence. Other diagnostic advice of Mirfield's includes this:

> Take the herb cinquefoil and, while collecting it, say a paternoster on behalf of the patient. Then boil it in a new jar with some of the water which the patient is destined to drink; if the water be red in colour after this boiling, then the patient will die.[4]

One is tempted to be cynical. In fact, in this case, one cannot help but be cynical. Following the first procedure, 50 percent of his patients are doomed. Following the second, perhaps all of them. Given such diagnostic skills, the absence of physicians across much of England is not wholly unfortunate.

These ideas about causes of illness and diagnosis might be astonishing but they reveal an important point. Medieval people are not ignorant, in the sense of having no knowledge. It is simply that their knowledge is very different from our own. They probably have as much medical "knowledge" as we do, only it is based on astrology, herbology, religion, a little direct experience, philosophy, fundamental misconceptions about how the body works, a lot of hearsay, and a large measure of desperation. When you extend this form of understanding to the physicians and surgeons, and combine it with the ability to charge fees, you realize that medical practitioners have colossal amounts of information at their disposal and a wealth of experience. Unfortunately not much of it will help you in your sickness, and some of it is seriously dangerous, if not lethal.

Medicine as taught in the leading Christian universities is heavily influenced by the teachings of two men from the ancient world,

Galen and Hippocrates. Whether your aspiring Bachelor of Medicine chooses to study at an English university or goes abroad to one of the great continental ones (for example, Paris, Salerno, or Bologna) he will be led to believe that the entire universe is made up of four basic elements: fire, water, earth, and air. He will be taught that these are mirrored in the four basic humors of the body: choler (or yellow bile), phlegm, black bile, and blood. The ideal is to keep these four humors in balance. However, as a result of illnesses, miasmas, and old age, it is inevitable that these humors will eventually go awry and you will grow sick. When there is too much choler, or yellow bile, you grow "choleric" in temperament. Too much phlegm makes you "phleg-matic." Too much black bile leads to "melancholia," and too much blood makes you "sanguine."

All very straightforward, you might think, even if somewhat mis-conceived. However, "straightforward" it certainly is not. One of the reasons why humoral theory continues to hold such sway is because it is so involved and complex. Its numerical harmony (the four ele-ments, the four humors, etc.) allows for endless refinement and in-vented complexity. If two men are identically injured—let us say, with a sword cut to the lower arm—a physician will treat them differently according to whether they are sanguine in temperament or melan-cholic.[5] Alternatively, if two men are sick with the same disease they may receive wholly different treatments due to variations in the ap-pearance of their urine. The physician will ask each man for a sample and judge it according to its color, scent, and cloudiness.

> Urine which is milky on the surface, dark at the bottom and clear in the middle is a sign of dropsy. But ruddy urine in a dropsical patient is a sign of death . . . urine which is red, like blood, is a sign of fever caused by too much blood; blood should be let immediately when the moon is passing through the sign of Gemini. Green urine, coming after red, is a sign of inflammation, a mortal sickness . . . saffron-coloured urine with thick, smelly and frothy substance is a sign of jaundice.[6]

A physician may also inspect the feces and the blood of the patient. Some physical diagnoses require the physician to taste the patient's blood. You might find it alarming to think that your doctor will not actually need to see you in person but might make a diagnosis based on the position of the stars, the color and smell of your urine, and the taste of your blood.

Dirtiness and Cleanliness

How do you define cleanliness? Most people, when asked this question, tend to define it in terms of personal experience. They know when their kitchen work surface is clean because everything which makes it dirty has been cleared off and it has been wiped down with detergent. What they are thus defining is the completion of a cleaning process, not a state of cleanliness itself. Medieval people do much the same thing, only using different processes. To regard a medieval kitchen as "dirty" because it has not been wiped down with modern detergent is to apply our own standards inappropriately. It is like someone from the distant future telling us our kitchens are dirty because we have not wiped them down with some superdetergent invented in the twenty-third century.

Cleanliness operates on several levels. For us, the most important is probably that of eradicating certain germs. Germ theory has, however, only been around since the late nineteenth century, so medieval people are a long way off understanding what germs are, let alone how they spread. Instead, complementing the idea that illness is a consequence of God's direction and care for the soul, they have a sense of spiritual cleanliness. This includes a theoretical range of smells which are, literally, heavenly. When saints die there is supposed to be a smell like the breaking open of many perfume bottles: the odor of sanctity.[7] For most people this form of cleanliness, this saintly sweetness, is far more important than whether they have washed behind their ears or not. If a man is spiritually clean, and without sin, he is far less likely to have to go through the purifying fires of illness and seek redemption through God's mercy. He will smell sweet to those around him. He will be without the stench of sin. In the modern world we have no equivalent to this form of cleanliness. Instead we have antibacterial wipes.

Once you start to break up notions of cleanliness in this way, you begin to realize that there are many varieties of cleanliness. Domestic cleanliness, culinary cleanliness, public sanitation, and personal hygiene can be added to spiritual cleanliness. All of them are of great importance, even if some of them are very difficult to control—especially public sanitation. When you hear modern people idly refer to the Middle Ages as dirty, spare a thought for the fourteenth-century housewife working hard, with her sleeves rolled up above her elbows, sweeping the hall floor clean, wiping down the tabletop, scrubbing her clothes and those of her husband and children, rinsing the cutlery, and scouring the pots and pans. Picture her looking up with concern as a rain cloud approaches just after she has laid the sheets out on the grass to dry. Of course there are some houses which are not so well attended, but foul-smelling homes have connotations of sinfulness, corruption, and decay. No one wants that sort of label; rather, they want the opposite: cleanliness and respectability. In a community in which everyone knows everyone else, the cleanliness of your home may be more than just a matter of common decency. It may be an important aspect of your personal identity.

The relationship between cleanliness, identity, pride, and respectability requires individuals to pay attention to their personal appearance as well. Areas of attention include the face, teeth, hands, body, fingernails, beard, and hair. Can you imagine a nobleman turning up at court, unwashed, in dirty clothes, not caring about what the king or his peers think of him? And can you imagine the king choosing a man to be his ambassador whom he cannot trust to keep himself clean? An ambassador who stinks will bring disgrace on the whole kingdom. In real life, men and women represent one another: dependants, relations, allies, and friends. Their appearance reflects the status and dignity of their social network and the esteem in which they and their friends are held. If you smell like the fetid air of a miasma, people will shun you like the plague and regard you as immoral, sinful, and perhaps mad. If you smell less savory than the common man, how can you hold your head up high in aristocratic society? If you wish to be reckoned important, and capable of mixing with your social superiors, you will do all you can to avoid smelling of the dunghill in the yard and endeavor to smell as sweet as the lavender scattered among the fresh rushes in your hall floor.

It is one thing to speak of the ideal of cleanliness and quite another to achieve it. Methods vary according to wealth and social class. At the bottom end of the scale, those who work with noxious materials are aware of the need to bathe themselves daily and so make use of rivers. London gongfermors end their working day with a dip in the Thames.[8] Babies, wrapped in linen swaddling—ideally sweetened with rose petals ground with salt—are regularly given baths.[9] People who do not spend their days up to their necks in excrement have baths less regularly; it is simply too labor-intensive and time-consuming to heat enough pots of water to fill a bathtub. But they do wash parts of themselves frequently. In the morning the first thing self-respecting men and women do is wash their hands and face: those parts of the body which show.[10] This will normally be done in a basin of water. Monasteries usually have a stone lavabo or communal fountain and washing basins for monks to wash their faces and hands, complete with a towel cupboard nearby. In addition, *every* meal sees a washing of hands, both before and after, and this applies across all sectors of society: lords and ladies, all the servants eating in the hall, monks, merchants, and people eating at an inn. Thus most people wash their hands at least five times a day. Those who undertake long journeys are usually expected to wash their feet afterwards, in a foot basin. Monks bathe their feet weekly, and many self-respecting people do likewise. As for full baths, Cluniac monks have two a year, Benedictine monks four, and only the rich have more than this. Nevertheless, the regular washing of hands, feet, and faces means people are not all as filthy as you might imagine.[11]

For the aristocracy, and those rich merchants and their wives who ape the aristocratic lifestyle, taking a bath is a luxury as well as a means of washing the whole body. Bathing is, after all, a royal habit. In the previous century, King John used to have a bath every three weeks. Henry IV, on the eve of his coronation, establishes the Order of the Bath, drawing attention to the noble ritual of bathing—purifying oneself both physically and spiritually—before becoming a knight. King Edward I has running water in his bathroom, controlled by gilt bronze taps. Edward III builds several bathrooms in his palaces, some of which have *hot* running water as well as cold.[12] In such bathrooms, which are usually tiled, the lord has his wooden bathtub. This is lined with cloth. The tub is filled from the taps (in the case of the king) or pots of hot water. Rose petals, spices, herbs, and other fragrant things are added. Normally the whole bath will have a silken canopy, to keep away drafts, and the bath itself may be covered, to retain heat. The lord is given a large sponge to sit on, and his servants sponge his body down with warm rosewater.[13] In some cases, the larger baths are for sharing. Two men, or a man and his wife, might share a bath. They might share some refreshments at the same time and listen to musicians play, while enjoying the warm fragrant water together. At such moments, life is sweet.

Luxurious bathing, especially when it involves members of the opposite sex, has undertones of licentiousness. Thus you need to be careful when going to public baths or stews. Of course you will find plenty of hot water and steam at the stews in Southwark—they specialize in steam baths—but the Flemish women who run them may offer to do much more than scrub your back. All the cleaning of bodies and clothes is done by women, so naked rich men being bathed by semiclad unmarried poor women is bound to result in a degree of temptation, on both sides. Especially considering that prostitution is tacitly permitted in most towns and cities. Needless to say, this sort of bathing spreads diseases rather than prevents them.

Given that public bathing establishments are more for pleasure than purity, how does the common man, woman, and child stop building up their own miasma within their clothes? Again, one has to stress that some people do stink. Older, less able people who cannot bathe themselves in a river, or wash themselves in a basin, are dependent on their caregivers, and, if they live alone, they might not wash at all. The single peasant who has just the one shirt and tunic to his name will see washing his clothes as part of the same process as washing himself. Given that men do not normally wash anything except dishes, this might be quite infrequent. At the start of the century, villeins only rarely wash their bodies, being almost wholly preoccupied with the cleanliness of their hands and faces and their internal, or spiritual cleanliness.[14] For them, an unwashed smell indicates virility. An occasional clean shirt and regular delousing by their womenfolk is the extent of their toilet. But the growing sensitivity of men and women to others' smells—especially in towns—is revealed by the regular use of perfumes towards the end of the fourteenth century, especially musk, civet, lavender, and rosewater; one ends up "smelling of roses," literally. In summer, bathing in rivers is common; it is relaxing at the end of a long day to go down to the river with the rest of the manorial workers. It also relieves you of the irritation of insects living on your unwashed skin. The leading English physician John Gaddesden particularly recommends having a bath in salty or sulphurous water as a cure for such parasites. He believes it cleans the pores in which the lice breed.[15]

When lice and bedbugs are an irritating part of everyday life, and when you are at the same time trying to minimize your body odor, nothing is as important as fresh, clean linen. Gaddesden himself recommends frequent changes of clothes. In winter, when few people wish to bathe in a river or even strip off the upper body to wash under the arms in a basin, fresh linen is the most common form of cleaning. The linen soaks up the sweat. The body may then be scented, and once more you are presentable in public.

Yes, you say, all very well; but how clean is the linen? And how clean are your other clothes? After all, is not urine used in the fulling of cloth? The answer to that is yes, to a point: the practice of using urine continues until 1376.[16] But fulling is only a means of processing wool. The cloth is dyed and washed before it is worn, and the washing involves soap. There are several varieties available. The best is Castile soap, available in cakes. This is made in Spain with Mediterranean potash, which is saltier, and thus harder and less caustic, than the northern European soft soaps. It costs about 4d a cake.[17] Cheaper white, grey, and black varieties for cleaning cloth are made in England. They come in liquid form, cost about 13s 4d a barrel in the 1380s, and are decanted into bowls for use. The washerwomen, leaning over their washtubs and washboards, or trampling clothes in a stream, tend to have their legs stained grey from the black soap. Obviously you cannot use black soap on white linen, so the more expensive white soap is necessary. Such soaps are powerful. You could not use the liquid soaps on your hands without damaging your skin—one glance at a washerwoman's blistered hands, arms, and legs will put you off. These soaps are also widely available: Henry of Lancaster replenishes his soap supplies when he goes on crusade to Prussia in 1391. In some towns it is possible to hire washboards and washtubs: Henry does so when visiting Calais in 1396.[18] If you have sufficient money, you can appear clean wherever you go.

Attitudes to hair are more complicated. Men expect their womenfolk to comb their hair for them, often beside a window, allowing them to see any lice and to remove them. However, excessive combing of hair among men is frowned upon. Moralists write diatribes against the practice, castigating the Danes, who are supposed to be so vain that they comb their hair every day and have a bath every week. Women too come in for censure, largely because their personal grooming is seen as a display of vanity. Ignore such moralists: most people appreciate cleanliness. Besides, as women are not permitted to wear their hair down in public, it must either be styled or covered. Hence it is important for women to comb their hair so it may be dressed. Both sexes do wash their hair: brass basins are employed for this purpose. A mixture of spices is used, such as cinnamon, licorice, and cumin, rather than an irritating soap.[19]

Similar mixtures of spices are used for the teeth. In "The Miller's Tale," Chaucer's characters chew cardamom and licorice. Aniseed, cumin, and fennel are sometimes recommended to women.[20] The purpose is not to keep the teeth free from disease so much as to make the breath smell fresh. Clean-smelling breath is most important. Bad breath, it is believed, carries disease. The breath of menstruating women can make a wound go bad, and so can the breath of a physician who has recently had sex with a menstruating woman (or so the Nottinghamshire surgeon John of Arderne will tell you, apparently from personal experience). Similarly it is believed that the breath of lepers can give you leprosy; hence they are segregated from society. This means that almost all dental care is about smell, not about preserving the teeth. For this reason, the whole subject of dental care might make you squirm. Grinding grain between millstones means small particles of stone get into the bread, and the attrition of the teeth can be severe. The increasing availability of sugars means that dental caries is actually worse in the fourteenth century than it was in Anglo-Saxon times. Depending on where you are in the country, by the time they die adults will have lost between an eighth and a fifth of their teeth.[21] Physicians will tell you that toothache is due to tiny worms eating into the enamel. Remedies include using myrrh and opium. If you cannot afford these, "take a candle of mutton fat, mingled with seed of sea holly, and burn this candle as close as possible to the tooth, holding a basin of cold water beneath. The worms [which are gnawing the tooth] will fall into the water."[22] Alternatively go to a tooth drawer, who will yank out the tooth for you. Then, like John Gaddesden himself, you may replace your own teeth with false ones.

Diseases

The differences between medieval and modern personal hygiene account for relatively little physical suffering. Far more serious are such factors as inadequate diet, poor sanitation (particularly the proximity to feces and rotting meat), parasites, and shared living space. No matter how often you wash your body, simply being around other people is going to lead to the spread of illnesses, as it does in modern times. Even withdrawing from the world and residing in a monastery might not save you. In fact it might make things worse because monks eat, pray, sing, sleep, and work very near to one another. The average life expectancy for monks entering the urban monasteries at Westminster and Canterbury is about five years less than those living outside a monastery.[23] Being a monk in or near a town might actually shorten your life, despite the good sanitation and the much better diet.

PLAGUE

You have no idea what destruction a disease can wreak upon society. When you see people consumed from within, as if they are being eaten alive by some invisible creature—when you look at the faces of mothers and fathers staring at their feverish blood-vomiting infants, lying in their own beds, in the very places where they parted with a kiss the previous evening, then you might get an inkling. When you are there in 1348, and have been relieved of any complacent assumptions that *anyone* will survive this hideous calamity, and have come face-to-face with the very real prospect that it will annihilate the whole of humanity, and that God has deserted mankind, then you will start to realize how destructive the plague is.

The Great Plague—the term "Black Death" is not invented until the nineteenth century—is one of the most horrific events in human history, comparable only with those traumas which people have inflicted on one another in modern times. Arriving at the eastern end of the Mediterranean in 1347; spreading along the sea-lanes to France, southern Spain, and Italy; and making its way up across the Continent to England by August 1348, it shakes society in every conceivable respect. It destroys large portions of the population and leaves parts of the country completely empty of people. It starkly reveals the limits of both professional and amateur medical assistance. No doctor of medicine can help the victims; no one can attend the dying with any feeling but revulsion and despair. It reveals the inadequacy of a concept of society based on the "three estates." Frankly, if "those who pray" cannot protect the population, and "those who fight" simply run away, why should "those who work" feed them? Similarly, the plague forces men to reappraise the fundamental relationship between themselves and God. This horrific disease does not just affect the sinful; it kills the innocent too. If this is the work of God, then He is indiscriminate in his judgments.

According to the papal physician Guy de Chauliac, the first two months of an outbreak see it at its most virulent, with a continuous fever and spitting of blood. This will kill you within three days, sometimes within hours. This phase of the infection passes and a second, less virulent stage takes over. This too is marked by continuous fever but it also gives rise to the boils and black buboes of bubonic plague in the groin and armpits. Catching the disease in this phase will kill you within five days.[24] For those affected in the first waves of the plague, death can occur overnight. Some people go to bed and never wake up. These are the lucky ones. If you feel something is wrong, and you are beginning to feel feverish, lift up your arm and start tapping around in your armpit: if something makes you wince, prepare for your final hours of life.

The often-quoted figure of one-third dead—"a third of all the people in the world" as the contemporary chronicler Froissart declares—may lead you to believe that two-thirds of the population survive the disease. This is misleading. If you catch it you will very probably die of it. Those who survive are predominantly those who do not catch it, having some natural or genetic defense against the infection, or just being plain lucky. When it gets into a monastery, normally half the monks die, if not more. At Peterborough in Northamptonshire, thirty-two of the sixty-four monks perish. At Henwood in Warwickshire, only three nuns are left out of the original fifteen. Scare stories spread—of how in some towns tens of thousands of people are dying, and how in Bristol nine-tenths of the population are already dead. There is utter panic. No one can tell really how many people are dying up and down the country. In London two hundred are buried every day. Those clerks who compile episcopal registers have the best measure of the scale of the mortality: they at least can see how many clergymen are dying. In the dioceses of York and Lincoln, 40 percent of all the beneficed clergy die in 1348–49, some of them infected while administering to their dying parishioners. In the far southwest and Herefordshire, the figure is higher, almost 50 percent. The peasantry fare little better: half the population of a manor dying is not unusual. Fifty-five percent of the tenants of twenty-two manors belonging to Glastonbury Abbey die; 43 percent of tenants on three manors in Essex; 39 percent of those holding land from the bishop of Winchester.[25] To put these figures in proportion, remember that less than 6 percent of the adult male population of the United Kingdom perish over the whole four years of the First World War, and the overall mortality figure is just 1.55 percent.[26]

Guy de Chauliac's advice to those wishing to avoid infection is as follows: "Go quickly, go far, and return slowly." It is good advice but most cannot follow it. Among those who can—the gentry and esquires—the death rate is a little lower, at 27 percent. But even if you survive the 1348–49 outbreak, you are not safe. The Great Plague is just the first of several waves of plague that sweep across Europe. Miss it in England in 1348–49 and you can catch it later in 1361–62, 1368–69, 1375 (with various minor outbreaks in subsequent years) and 1390–91. The 1361–62 and 1390–91 outbreaks are particularly distressing, as they kill many children. Twenty-three percent of all young heirs of estates die in the 1361–62 plague.[27] Overall, the death rate from the second visitation probably kills about 15 percent of the population, and the third, in 1369, about 10 percent. Although the mortality rate is thus in decline, the population continues to shrink further with each outbreak. By 1400 about half of all those born over the previous seventy years have died of plague.

The deaths in 1348–49 are so numerous that the statistics are much easier to talk about than the individual tragedies. Looked at from the safe distance of the twenty-first century, one can see its beneficial effects—how the Great Plague cauterizes feudalism, frees up capital, and allows society to develop in a more democratic way. But a visit to the time reminds you, with a sharp shock, of both the reality and the scale of the suffering. If anything, it proves the value of virtual history—of understanding historical events as lived experiences, as opposed to impersonal facts. Imagine a disease were to wipe out 40 percent of the modern population of the UK—more than 25 million people. Now imagine a historian in the future discussing the *benefits* of your death and the deaths of your partner, your children, and your friends . . . You would want to cry out, or hang your head in despair, that historians could blithely comment on the benefits of such suffering. There is no shadow of a doubt that every one of these people you see in 1348—whether they will die or survive—deserves your compassion. When you see women dragging their parents' and children's corpses into ditches, weeping and screaming—when you listen to a man who has buried all five of his sons with his own hands, and, in his distress, he tells you that there was no divine service when he did so, and that the death bell did not sound—you know that these people have entered a chasm of grief beyond description.[28] In the fields lie dead and rotting sheep, five thousand in one field alone, according to Henry Knighton. As you look around and see ravens flying through deserted streets, and half-wild dogs and pigs eating the corpses abandoned on the edge of a village, you will see something which no historian will ever see. The doors of houses left blackly open, thus to remain as night comes and day dawns, until someone enters and finds the cold body of the owner. The passing bells are banned by the church, the traditional laments thrown away. Even prayer fades into a mere whisper of horror.

Beyond this, although one could say a great deal, there is little which needs to be said. What you will see is just too shocking.

LEPROSY

Put plague in a category of its own as a cataclysm beyond human understanding but do not regard it as the only horrific disease. Before 1348 leprosy is the most terrifying illness which people can imagine. Leprosy is known to us as Hansen's disease but in the fourteenth century it can include all manner of skin ailments, including eczema, psoriasis, and lupus. Basically if you have a skin disease which results in long-term disfiguration you need to cover it up for as long as possible. If it is seen, and if it is judged by other people to be *possibly* leprous, then in line with the decree of the Third Lateran Council (of 1179) you will be shunned by society, forced to wear a covering cloak and to ring a bell wherever you go, and be regarded as one of the living dead.

Your leprous breath will be considered to be of a similar quality as the miasma around a cesspit, and likely to lead to leprosy in others, so no one will tolerate your presence. Perhaps some people will pity you in your ailing condition and look upon your situation charitably. Many will not, seeing your affliction as divine judgment on you for your sinful life and your suffering as nothing more than an opportunity to atone for your sins, and thereby purify your soul, before you die.

Leprosy is not uncommon in 1300. If you catch it you will find that it progresses very slowly through your body, removing first the sensations in your hands and feet, and later paralyzing your extremities, leaving them badly ulcerated. After a few years your fingers and toes will melt off. You will probably bleed from your palms. Your body hair and eyelashes will fall out. You might suffer from claw-foot or claw-hand. Men will see their penises putrefy. At some point the bridge of your nose will collapse and you will be left with a smelly liquid constantly running from the gaping wound where your nose was. The ulcers in your larynx will grow and give your voice a coarse, croaking quality. You will probably lose some teeth, your eyeballs may become ulcerated, and your skin will be marked with large nodules. Ultimately you will be wholly deformed, stinking, repulsive, and blind. That is why it is called the "living death." That is why people are absolutely terrified of it. And that is why, if you catch it, very few people will dare to come near you.

The good news is that leprosy is on the wane. By 1400 there are very few lepers in leper hospitals, and increasingly the beds are being occupied by tuberculous patients and, in a number of cases, even travelers. When Edward III throws the lepers out of London in 1346, a number of hospitals are set up for them. There is one in Kent Street, Southwark, another between Mile End and Stratford Bow, another at Kingsland (between Shoreditch and Stoke Newington), and another at Knightsbridge. All around the rest of the country leper hospitals are set up on the roads out of towns. Therein, it is supposed, the lepers are fornicating furiously, in line with their supposedly sinful natures, and so most lepers do not actually go to these places until forced to do so. Wearing the cloak and the bell is a preferable alternative. Most communities want nothing to do with those poor souls who suffer from the disease. Given how important it is to an individual to belong somewhere, to throw him or her out of the community is no small thing. You can understand why the London baker John Mayn repeatedly refuses to leave the city when ordered to do so by the mayor in 1372. That order to abjure the city amounts to his loss of income, possessions, home, protectors, friends, and family. And who is to say he really has leprosy? Perhaps it is just some eczematous skin on his hands and arms, an occupational hazard of medieval baking.[29]

TUBERCULOSIS

As leprosy declines, tuberculosis is on the rise. It is a case of out of the frying pan and into the fire. Tuberculosis is an infectious disease which comes in many shapes and sizes, and none of them are pleasant. One common version is scrofula, or the King's Evil, which is a tuberculous infection of the lymph nodes in the neck. If you catch it, you can expect your neck to swell up until it resembles that of a pig.

The particularly interesting thing about this disease is that it has a supposed cure. The person of the king has the power to alleviate the suffering, or so it is thought, by touching the sufferer or, rather, by touching a coin passed to the unfortunate person. Thousands of people queue up to benefit in this way. Edward I undertakes touching up to two thousand individuals each year. Edward III touches about four hundred individuals every year in the 1330s and 1340s, giving each one 1d, only ending the practice in 1344.[30] From that date onward he prefers to have all those pennies melted down underneath the Neith Cross (a reliquary holding a piece of the True Cross), which then can be fashioned into cramp rings for the cure of epilepsy. Later monarchs revive the touching for scrofula: it is a good way to demonstrate their divine right.

Although you can get tuberculosis from drinking infected cows' milk—many children get it this way, with fatal results—most adults are infected by human-to-human contact. This does not require them to touch or even be in the same room as one another. Aerial transmission of the bacillus can take place as a result of talking, coughing, spitting, sneezing, breathing, or just singing. Once the droplets containing the bacilli have dried out, they can rest in the dust of the house or the parish church (an important place for spreading disease) and remain infectious for up to eight weeks. Once in the body, the bacillus remains dormant until the body's resistance fails, but further bacilli may be spat or breathed out, spreading the disease further. Of course, medieval people do not know this. They just see the results. If you catch pulmonary tuberculosis you will find you are affected by an increasingly frequent and violent cough. After a short while your sputum will be flecked with blood. In addition you may experience fatigue, anorexia, weight loss, lethargy, anxiety, chills, muscular aches, irregular periods, sweating, and fever; ultimately you will die. Given that hundreds of men and women suffering from this infectious disease are brought before the king each year, it is a wonder that the royal family survives.

As you may imagine from these sources of infection, tuberculosis is a particularly urban problem. This is another reason why living with monks in a dormitory is a dangerous thing to do. Once one monk is infected, the whole dormitory goes down. Sufferers need to be taken to a hospital—or a monastic infirmary, in the case of monks—to be given good food and fresh water and allowed to rest. Keeping up your strength is about the only effective remedy, unless you include the psychosomatic value of going to see the king. Other remedies have a certain antiquarian charm but you would not want to undergo them. John Mirfield's handbook for physicians at St. Bartholomew's Hospital recommends that women's milk should be used as a cure, and that it should be sucked directly from the breast. However, before any tuberculous men rush off to St. Bartholomew's, they should note that Mirfield adds that if no lactating women are available, then asses' or goats' milk should be used, and this too should be taken directly from the udder. In addition, the patient should take a medicinal bath. For this the physician's assistant should "take blind puppies, remove the viscera and cut off the extremities, then boil them in water, and bathe the patient in this water four hours after he has eaten." While he is in this bath, he needs to keep his head entirely covered and his chest completely wrapped in the skin of a small goat, as a preservation against a sudden chill.

OTHER DISEASES

There are myriad other diseases in medieval England which you may end up catching. Many of them will cease to exist before the advent of the modern world. Several ailments described by the chronicler Henry

Knighton do not correspond with anything known to modern medical science. Similarly there are afflictions such as "styche" and "ipydyme" which have no modern equivalent.[31] Some diseases have simply become less common: malaria is endemic in marshy areas, such as Romney Marsh in Kent and the Fens of Lincolnshire and Norfolk. On the other hand, fourteenth-century England is free from a number of diseases which affect us in later centuries: you will not find cholera or syphilis.[32] In some cases this is due to barriers of travel. In others, it is because our vulnerability to specific infections alters with our living conditions. Diseases change as they circulate around the pool of humanity. Rodent carriers of diseases are replaced by different rodents carrying different diseases. Certain illnesses which are initially lethal grow progressively less dangerous as the decades go by. The entire medical landscape is slightly different—the diseases being as changeable as the remedies.

Childbirth is an exception. The problems of babies presenting themselves the wrong way up, or with umbilical cords wrapped around their necks, or developing within mothers whose pelvises are too small to give birth to them, are timeless. What alters is the level of medical help available. There are no forceps in fourteenth-century England. There is no vacuum extraction. A Cesarean birth is a last resort, as it is always fatal for the mother. In fact, giving birth is often fatal, whether or not it ends with a Cesarean: 2 percent of all confinements result in the mother's death.[33] That statistic—one in fifty—does not sound a high proportion, but most married women give birth more than once, and many loyal wives do so more than a dozen times. Every single pregnancy is thus like a game of Russian roulette, played with a fifty-barrel gun. A dozen children is like firing that fifty-barrel gun a dozen times. Twenty-two percent of women will not survive that number of pregnancies. Often it is not the birth itself which is fatal but the blood loss afterwards. As for the babies, a much greater proportion do not survive the ordeal. The exact rate is unknown but more than 10 percent are stillborn. Of those who do survive the birth, and live long enough to be baptized, one in six will be dead before their first birthday.[34]

Typhoid fever is another exception to the strangeness of the medical landscape. Whenever you have armies on the move, you have a wide variety of enteric diseases moving with them. The idea that a siege is always weighted in favor of the besieging force fails on this point: any army attacking a castle has to remain in the same place for a long time, and, as a result of poor sanitation, they tend to suffer very heavy casualties to typhoid, or "camp fever" as it is sometimes known. The same goes for dysentery. Even royalty may suffer when in the field. For all his glory at the battles of Poitiers and at Nájera, Prince Edward (the Black Prince) suffers from dysentery in the course of his long, wasting disease.[35] A later warrior king, Henry V, will die from it.

A third exception is poisons. Although ergotism—poisoning from rotting rye bread—is rare in England (it is not documented here before the eighteenth century) there are other natural and man-made poisons.[36] The occupational hazards of working in a mine, such as lung diseases and ankylostomiasis (an infestation of parasite worms), are well known. Gongfermors are particularly at risk. Sometimes they die from the fumes in the cesspits; sometimes they die from the diseases suppurating in the pools of rotting excrement and urine. When you think that a city latrine pit may contain a thousand gallons of sewage to be cleared—at a cost of 6s 8d—you can appreciate that the danger is ever present.[37] Add in the public health issue of the cleanliness of the water supply, and you can see that even having a wash after work may lead to illness. Pipes might be made of wood—elm or oak—but often they are made of lead, as in the case of Exeter's urban water supply. The lead poisoning is not so acute that it leads to widespread nervous disorders but over the course of a lifetime of drinking lead-polluted water you can expect to see the early stage symptoms: constipation, muscular weakness, blue gums, and, discolored skin. Those workers who specialize in making lead pipes (plumbers) and laying lead roofs can expect a heavy dose of lead poisoning over the course of their career, possibly ending in nervous disorders, tremors, paralysis, and blindness.

Although they have to cope with the basic problem of crop failure, the English manage to avoid many nutrition-related diseases. Scurvy is prevented in the diets of the rich by eating plenty of cultivated and preserved fruit. It is prevented in the diets of the poor by the reliance on cabbages and root vegetables, and the storage of apples and pears through the year. Pellagra is not a problem in England, as there is no reliance on corn. Rickets—a disease in which children's bones do not harden and are bent with muscle use, resulting in bowlegs and curved arms—is rare, for vitamin D deficiency is offset naturally as a result of sunlight acting on the skin, and children spend much of their time out of doors. So, as long as you can get enough to eat, and can avoid all the various lethal infections, the dangers of childbirth, lead poisoning, and the extreme violence, you should live a long time.

All you have to worry about are the doctors.

Medical Practitioners

As you will realize from humoral theory and the astrological basis for miasma theory noted above, medicine and religion are uneasy bedfellows. If you add the popular magic applied by ordinary people in desperate situations, you can see that it is difficult for the Church to stop people straying from religious faith and veering into the occult in search of medical relief. Besides, if the Church allows astrological means to explain a plague, why not use the same means to predict when the next plague will be? That logic leads to fortune-telling and sorcery. Thus the Church increasingly denounces medicine. As a result of the Fourth Lateran Council (1215), the Church forbids priests of the rank of subdeacon or above from engaging in any activity likely to draw blood. They are forbidden to cut into the skin, and anatomy is regarded as unholy (the Church refuses to permit Christians to dissect corpses until the late fifteenth century). The division leads to the growing separation of the professions of physic (medicine) and surgery.

PHYSICIANS

If you feel ill you will need to seek out a physician or doctor of medicine. (The term "doctor" does not become interchangeable with "physician" until the end of the seventeenth century.) This is not a straightforward matter: qualified physicians are rare. There are probably fewer than a hundred medical degree holders in the whole of England, and only the very largest cities and towns have a medical doctor in residence. Moreover, many of these highly qualified men are contracted to serve a particular household, for instance a monastery or a great lord. Their capacity for doing extra work is relatively limited. No matter how far a physician is from his lord, if the lord needs him he must attend when summoned. Because his fees are so high, he rarely refuses. When Queen Isabella is dying in 1358 she sends a horse for her physician, Master Lawrence, to come to her immediately at Hertford Castle. When her health worsens, she sends for him again, even though he is at Canterbury, seventy miles away.[38] As her situation is desperate, she also summons other physicians from London, twenty-one miles away. Even if you are a queen at death's door you may have to wait a day or more for a qualified physician to come to you.

An alternative is to go to hospital. If you are admitted your clothes will be taken from you and you will be put to bed with one or two other people in a well-lit hall. Fires are lit here in winter. The floor is swept regularly and washed down every day with water. The plaster walls are redecorated every year. The linen sheets are washed regularly, perhaps even as often as twice per week. Mutton is provided three times per week, being considered a good aid to recovery. You will also be given the usual pottages and a gallon of ale each day. Medicinal baths are regularly employed. Women have their hair washed once a week; men's beards are trimmed weekly too. All in all, the standard of care may be considered very high.[39]

The physician serving in a small town or a hospital is unlikely to be a university man. Most rely on brief manuals which direct the course of the diagnostic process. These include details of planets' movements and eclipses of the sun and moon. They also include advice about phlebotomy (letting blood) and all twenty-four varieties of urine, as well as numerological methods of establishing whether you are likely to die or not. The physician will need to know when your illness started, so he can establish where the sun and moon were at the time, as well as the planet governing the health of the afflicted organ. Using these details, he will prepare a series of concoctions for you. First there is the preparative, to help your body to cope with the trauma it is about to experience. Then there is the purgative, to rid it of corrupt matter, either through vomiting, defecation, or urination. Then there is the remedy. Alternatively the physician may open a vein and let your blood. From his diagrams he will work out exactly which vein to cut in order to bleed you appropriately. This has as much to do with the moon and stars as with your symptoms. When the moon is in Leo, he should avoid incisions of the nerves and the back. When it is in

Aries, he should avoid cutting veins in the head. When it is in Scorpio, he should avoid slicing into your testicles, anus, and bladder.[40] If he is uncertain, or in holy orders, he will leave all this to a surgeon. After the ordeal is over, you should expect him to advise a final restorative process: good food, lots of rest, and fortifying drinks, to restore the balance of the humors.

The purgative bit is awful enough. If given orally, this might be made of linseed fried in fat or mallow leaves in ale. Alternatively, an enema containing mallows, honey, salt, and soap may be squirted up your anus with the use of a pig's bladder. Needless to say, no one likes being bled. However, it is the remedial part of the process which will worry you most of all. The remedy for a bladder stone, as prescribed by a well-respected physician like John Gaddesden, includes dung beetles and crickets and requires you to "cut off their heads and fry them in oil." His recipe for diseases of the spleen is not dissimilar, incorporating "the heads of seven fat bats." Less highly qualified physicians might have even more imaginative and repulsive treatments. A treatment for jaundice reads: "Seethe wormwood in water and wash the sick man in it three times, and give him to drink ivory shaven in water." If you suffer from quinsy (an abscess in the throat following untreated tonsillitis), the following remedy might be prescribed:

> Take a fat cat, flay it well, and draw out the guts. Take the grease of a
> hedgehog, the fat of a bear, resins, fenugreek, sage, honeysuckle gum
> and virgin wax, and crumble this and stuff the cat with it. Then roast
> the cat and gather the dripping, and anoint the sufferer with it.[41]

Not all medical recipes are animal-based concoctions. There are some which have respectably stood the test of time. You will hear physicians like Gaddesden and Nicholas Tyngewick recommend a truss for hernia and scarlet cloth for smallpox. The latter is a method which reputedly cures one of Edward II's half brothers and may be a mark of some genuine medical intuition (infrared light is now known to prevent smallpox scars). Although no physician can cure gout, it is well known that its symptoms can be alleviated through the administration of colchicum. Likewise the medicinal properties of some herbs are widely known. Camomile oil is used effectively for earache.[42] Pomegranates are correctly used for digestive ailments. The problem with such medicines is obtaining them. In 1327, when Lord Berkeley is ill at Berkeley Castle, he has to send servants to Hereford (forty-five miles away) and Winchester (eighty miles) to buy pomegranates. The journeys take several days—and the fruit, at 2s to 3s each, are certainly not cheap.[43]

SURGEONS

Surgeons are more commonly found than physicians. They vary in skill and experience from barbers (later called "barber-surgeons") to highly experienced medical professionals as skilled as the best physicians. The royal household ordinances allow for there to be a royal surgeon as well as a royal physician, and these officers are known for carrying out effective operations.[44] Their numbers generally are on the rise. Fewer than fifteen barbers are admitted as freemen of the city of York in the first half of the century but more than sixty are admitted in the second half.[45] Thus you should have no difficulty in finding a barber or surgeon to help you in any sizable town. Just look for the sign of a bandaged bloodied arm. Or, until 1307, the unsanitized version—a bowl of blood in a surgeon's shop window.

As the name "barber" suggests (from the Latin *barba*, "a beard"), the principal service performed by local practitioners is that of shaving and trimming beards. However, the number of men willing to let someone come close to their throats with a sharp knife is insufficient to support many barbers. They diversify into other routine knife-related practices, such as letting blood (to maintain good health). The more surgical barbers and more specialized surgeons also undertake staunching blood flow, cauterizing wounds, opening the skull to deal with maladies of the brain, dealing with cataracts, setting broken bones, removing teeth, sewing up cut flesh, and lancing boils. Some might even consider cutting into the body to remove bladder stones—although most surgeons, if they complete this operation successfully, will kill the patient. High-status surgeons attending noblemen might also embalm their erstwhile employers, cutting open the body to remove soft parts and replacing these with herbs and spices.

The standard of surgery you might receive far outweighs that of medical advice. Obviously if a young man has an arrow sticking out of his face, no complicated lunar diagnosis is necessary. The arrow must be removed, the arrowhead drawn out, the wound dressed and sewn up, and prayers said to prevent blood poisoning. The only doubt is how best to remove the arrowhead; if it is in a leg, and not lodged in a bone, it is normally better to drive it all the way through the flesh with one strong blow than try to pull it out. For those who can afford them, good anesthetics are available. The leading surgeon John of Arderne, writing about 1370, suggests henbane, mandragora, hemlock, black and white poppies (opium), or henbane in alcohol, so the patient sleeps and that "he shall not feel whatsoever is done to him."

John of Arderne stands out as the foremost surgeon of the century. This is partly because of his use of anesthetics, partly because of his concentration on cleanliness following the completion of his operations, and partly because of his very wide range of medical as well as surgical skills. He lives and practices in Newark, Nottinghamshire, but his books are widely copied and distributed by the end of the century. Among his most significant achievements is his rediscovery and perfection of an ancient Arabic method of curing anal fistula, a nasty affliction following abscesses in the colon which particularly affects men who have spent too long riding in wet saddles (according to Arderne). This is an advance on the medical knowledge of Gaddesden, who writes that anal fistula is incurable. Arderne also specializes in operating on other diseases of the colon and rectum. In his use of clean sponges to stem hemorrhage and his reluctance to keep changing dressings (which introduce further infections) he pioneers a new and successful approach to advanced surgery. He also has a positive attitude to treatment: not only must a surgeon have clean hands and be skillful, he must also have the ability to make his patient laugh. This is not easy when the patient in question is bent double and the surgeon is sewing up three large abscesses in the side of his rectum.

Arderne is not alone in being able to undertake advanced operations. Eye surgeons are to be found who can successfully couch cataracts, a very difficult operation. Some surgeons set themselves up as specialists in bones and do nothing but set broken limbs. Nevertheless, even Arderne has some beliefs which you will consider strange. Like all other surgeons he believes in using the "zodiac man," a diagram linking each part of the body to a sign of the zodiac, and inferring from this when the best time to operate might be. Similarly, he believes in the virtues of bloodletting. All surgeons regard the letting of blood as prophylactic, and it is consequently one of the mainstays of their income. They perform the act usually by making an incision in the basilic vein (on the inside of the forearm, just below the elbow), and allowing the blood to run into a bowl. Alternatively, if the patient is old or weak, they might apply hot glass bowls to cut skin, drawing the blood out by means of the vacuum created by the glass as it cools. Another form of bloodletting is the application of leeches, either to suck out blood or to eat away the corrupt matter around a wound. Needless to say, all these processes are likely to do you far more harm than good. If you are unfortunate, and die from the blood loss (occasionally an inexperienced physician cuts an artery rather than a vein), it is unlikely there will be any repercussions. There is a widespread tolerance of death by medical misadventure.

10

The Law

Everywhere you go in medieval England you will see disturbing signs of the rigid and frequent application of the law. Beside crossroads you will see gallows, the bedraggled bodies of naked thieves swinging heavily on creaking ropes. On city gates you will see the putrefying heads of traitors. In town pillories you will see fraudulent traders. In the villages you will find men and women in the stocks. Every county town has its gaol, normally in the castle. On every road in the kingdom you are likely to find someone heading to a court of some sort. Justice is very visible in medieval England.

Given this, it is somewhat surprising to recall that *there are no policemen*. As every modern schoolchild is told, the earliest police force is the Bow Street Runners, established in London by Henry Fielding in the eighteenth century. But if this is so, who arrests all these men and women? Who detects the culprits? Who provides the links in the chain between criminal activity and the gallows?

Local Justice

In order to understand how justice is enacted in the fourteenth century, we must remind ourselves how people actually live. The key aspects to bear in mind are that everyone *belongs* somewhere, and that people live *communally*. Whether they live in the town or country, whether they are free or unfree, villeins and freemen alike are known in their home town. People worship in church together. They work in the fields together. They attend the manorial courts together. Even times of celebration and relaxation are spent in one another's company. As a result, people generally know who their neighbors are, whether they are of good character or not, and where they might have been when a crime took place.[1] Those who do not live in such a community are vagabonds, vagrants, and strangers: on the very edge of the law, and normally presumed to be outside it.

The actual processes by which society polices itself are ancient, dating back to Saxon times. The basic element is "frankpledge." Every male villein between the ages of twelve and sixty must be a member of a group called a "tithing." Each member of a tithing must swear at the age of twelve to observe and uphold the law. Placing his hand on a Bible, the initiate states, "I will be a lawful man and bear loyalty to our lord the king and his heirs, and to my lord and his heirs, and I will be justiciable to my chief tithing-man, so help me God and the saints."[2] In theory, each tithing consists of ten men, but, as you will see, in reality it tends to be all those living in a hamlet or in the same street of a village. So if there are fifteen men in a hamlet, that tithing might consist of all fifteen. If one man breaks the law, all the others are responsible for reporting his actions and delivering the culprit to the constable of the township. If they do not, they are fined heavily. The leading man in the tithing, the chief tithing-man (or "capital pledge" as he is often known), is expected to make sure that his tithing is full and complete and to report the same at the manorial court and again at the hundred court. Above all else, he is responsible for ensuring that all the men in his tithing observe the law. Hence his position is one of the most important in the community.

If a crime is discovered, the person making the discovery is expected to raise the alarm: the "hue and cry" as it is called. The actual sound varies from place to place, but it is a distinctive, alarming noise, and from it people can tell whether it relates to the finding of a dead body or evidence of a burglary.[3] All those in the vicinity—not just the members of that particular tithing—are expected to come in from the fields or get up from their beds to view the scene of the crime and to pursue the criminal. If he is caught, he is handed over to the constable of the township. Whether or not he is apprehended, the crime is reported at the next hundred court. As a result of the news being circulated at this assembly, all the nearby tithings are informed of the crime and made aware that there is a likelihood that a criminal is hiding out in their locality. The sheriff or his deputy (the under-sheriff) may be informed straightaway if the crime is deemed serious enough

Units of Secular Administration

Unit of Administration	Chief Law-Enforcement Officer	Description
County	The Sheriff	The largest unit of administration. There are thirty-nine ancient counties in England, ranging in size from Rutland (142 square miles) to Yorkshire (5,961 square miles). In addition, there are four "county boroughs," which are administered like counties: London (except it has two sheriffs, not one), Bristol (a county from 1373), York (from 1396), and Newcastle (from 1400).
Hundred	Bailiff of the hundred	Called "wapentake" in the north. A subdivision of a county, containing a number of townships. There are 628 hundreds in total, 270 of which are in the king's lordship. Devon, a large county, has thirty-five. A smaller county like Bedfordshire has nine. Huntingdonshire has four. Rutland has five (one of them being called a "soke"). The bailiff of a royal hundred answers to the sheriff of the county. Bailiffs of private hundreds normally answer to their lord.

Township	Constable	A subdivision of a hundred, often coterminous with a manor or a series of adjacent manors, containing a number of tithings. The constable reports the crimes within the township to the hundred bailiff at the hundred court.
Incorporated borough	Mayor and bailiffs	Deals with bylaws and infringements of the common law according to the rights established in its royal charter.
Manor or seigneurial borough	Steward of the lord and the bailiff or reeve	The manor is a unit of land tenure rather than law enforcement. However, manorial courts do deal with local customs, disputes between customary tenants, and infringements of the lord's rights. Some incorporate courts leet, which also deal with criminal cases.
Tithing	Chief tithing-man or capital pledge	The smallest unit of law enforcement. A group of about ten male villeins who live close to one another within a manor, all of whom are responsible for one another's good behavior. The chief tithing-man answers to the manorial court and liaises with the constable of the township.

to warrant calling out the *posse comitatus:* a group of armed men who will pursue the criminal until he is caught. In such cases, a criminal evading arrest may be beheaded on sight—provided the coroner is present and provided the wanted man has not reached the sanctuary of a church. Alternatively, if the thief apprehended is a woman, she may be taken to a river and forcibly drowned for resisting arrest. This ancient system of law and order is codified at the end of the thirteenth century by Edward I in various statutes, most notably in the Statute of Winchester (1285). This stipulates that, if a robbery is committed, the criminal must be pursued from town to town. It also orders that city and town gates are closed at sundown and opened again at sunrise, and that there are to be watches in every settlement. The number of men who must keep watch in each place varies: there must be six watchmen for every gate in a city, twelve watchmen in every other borough, and either six or four men to watch in every town (according to its population). London, a special case, has six watchmen in each of its twenty-five wards and a further six on each gate: nearly two hundred watchmen. Every stranger who lodges in a region becomes the responsibility of his host. Every person found out of doors at night is liable to be arrested. The intention is that every effort is made by members of a community to keep the king's peace.

THE SHERIFF AND THE COUNTY COURT

The sheriff is the king's chief officer in a county. He receives the king's writs—about 120 of them every month in an average-size county—and carries out the king's orders. These might be to summon a jury to try a particular case or to arrest someone. They might require him to send an indicted man or woman to the royal courts, or to make an inquiry into damage and report back to the king, or to hold an election to send two representatives to Parliament. In times of war the sheriff might be ordered to gather men to fight in Scotland or France. The sheriff is also expected to make arrangements to feed such fighting men—not an easy business when he is ordered to gather two thousand archers. He thus has heavy financial responsibilities and has to account for them at the Exchequer. He is also expected to maintain the country gaol and to build wooden cages in the castle yard when the prisons are full.

As you can see, a huge amount of power is vested in the sheriff. He may arrest you, imprison you, and send you in chains to London. Few people will be able to stop him if he chooses to extort money from you or decides to torture you. Ironically, the one thing he cannot do is try you for a serious crime. Apart from matters of small consequence, such as debts or brawling, the only time a sheriff can legally act as a judge himself is when he catches someone trying to evade the law—for instance a man who tries to escape from gaol (whom he may behead), or a thief caught red-handed (whom he may also behead, or drown in the case of a woman). Even in these cases he may only proceed to justice if the coroner is present. In this sense, the sheriff and his bailiffs, combined with the constables of the townships and the chief tithing-men, are the equivalent of a police force. Just as modern policemen do not actually try the criminals they catch, so too the sheriffs, bailiffs, constables, and chief tithing-men have to leave all the serious cases to judges sent out from London or local justices of the peace.

The sheriff is obliged to hold several courts, most notably the county court, which is held every four or six weeks. Much of the business dealt with is routine: the swearing-in of officers, the announcement of royal proclamations, and the ordering of inquiries into trespasses. The county court also acts as a small claims court: men may sue one another for sums of up to £2. It undertakes preliminary hearings of Crown pleas, referring these where necessary to the royal courts. And it serves as the court at which men are declared outlaws. If a criminal is at large, he is summoned to the county court. If he fails to appear four times, he is declared an outlaw on the fifth occasion. Thereafter he may be beheaded on sight.

The county court also may proceed to justice through a "trial by battle." If you are the victim of a serious crime (like rape, serious wounding, or arson) and you appear in court personally, you can "appeal" your assailant of the crime. You or your representative may then fight the accused—or his representative—to determine his guilt or innocence. You might be surprised to hear that this also applies to disputes concerning land. Several monasteries have cause to thank men who triumphantly represent them in cases concerning their rights.

HUNDRED COURTS AND THE SHERIFF'S TOURN

Each hundred holds a court every three weeks. The bailiff empanels a jury of twelve freemen to hear all the presentments. Many cases are the consequences of fights. If a man draws blood, this needs to be reported at the hundred court. Other ordinary business includes relatively minor trespasses such as fraud, disputes over small debts, and thefts of household goods and animals. Punishments are almost always fines, varying from place to place. As a rule of thumb, expect to pay between 6d and a shilling for starting a fight, 2s or more for drawing blood (although note that most towns have higher fines for this), and 6d for unnecessarily raising the hue and cry. Of course, if anyone has been caught grievously wounding someone, or killing them, or raping a woman, he will be arrested, to await a special hundred court: the sheriff's "tourn."

The important thing to remember about hundred courts is that they cross jurisdictions. Manorial business can be dealt with in a manorial court, so if a villein allows a stream across his land to get clogged with detritus, causing a flood, the manorial officers can force him to unblock it. However, if the flood damages property on the *next* manor, or blocks the king's highway, the case needs to move up the scale, to the hundred court. Similarly, while tithings are adequate means of controlling villeins, freemen are outside the frankpledge system. The hundred court is where freemen's misdemeanors need to be reported and where cases of their debts and the fights they have caused can be dealt with. So, if a freeman has stolen your cattle, or has failed to repay a debt and has sufficient animals to cover the sum, you can expect to see the hundred bailiff arresting him, or leading his cattle away, until the matter is settled.

Twice a year, normally at Easter and Michaelmas, the sheriff's tourn comes to the hundred. The purpose of the sheriff's appearance in these enlarged hundred courts is to receive those indictments which need to be presented to the royal judges and to make sure all indicted felons are taken into custody. Massive fines—£10 or even more—might be levied on tithings when their members are found not to have reported the misdoings of one of their members. It does not take a brilliant legal mind to see that the modern idea that villeins all stick together like a band of brothers against the dominant lords of manors is not universally true. Those men and women swinging on the gallows might be arrested by the sheriff and his bailiffs but only after they have been reported by their fellow tithing-men. More often than not, the chief tithing-man and the village constable will make the arrest, to avoid the tithing being fined heavily at a sheriff's tourn for failing to do so.

Now you can see how there come to be so many people brought to justice in the days before police forces. If you; a stranger in this country, are seen in a village at the same time as a burglary is discovered, and the hue and cry is raised, you might be arrested by the local people. You will then be handed over as a suspected felon to the local tithing-man and constable who will personally take you back to your home village and hand you over to the local constable there. In your case this is going to be a little difficult, so the constable will simply lock you in the village prison or stocks (the means of trapping people by their legs) until he can present you at a tourn or take you to the county town, where the sheriff's gaol is situated.[4] There you will remain, in the pit or cellar set aside for felons, or in the wooden cages outside that serve as temporary cells, unless you can obtain bail. The next time the royal judges come to the county, a jury will try you and either hang you or let you go, depending on what they hear of your reputation. You may have to wait months in prison before that day of "justice" arrives. This also applies to women, who are not given any special treatment or protection. One woman accused of stealing a lady's jewels is locked up in Guildford Gaol "with all the other thieves of the county" for forty-seven weeks before a jury finds her innocent of all charges.[5]

A surprisingly large number of indicted men choose to accuse other people of crimes, or of complicity in their own crime. This system is known as "approving." When a condemned man is brought out of his wooden cell or the common pit, and dragged before the judges who are going to try him, he accuses his enemies by way of "appeal." He is then taken off to be hanged. Notwithstanding his death, writs go out to empanel juries to try those he has accused. It is a shocking system. If you are a criminal and you know you are going to die, then why not accuse your enemies of complicity in your crimes when you face the judges? If your enemies are found guilty, they too will hang. Similarly, if you are going to die anyway, and your gaoler promises you that he will treat you better in your last days if you appeal one of *his* enemies, then what have you got to lose?[6] At Salisbury in the first decade of the century, one Roger Prye is arrested on suspicion of larceny. He confesses before the coroner, so he knows he is going to hang. But, having done so, he then turns approver and appeals Henry the Baker and Eve his wife of receiving him after he stole fourteen bushels of the abbot of Glastonbury's wheat. Prye is then hanged, but Henry and Eve are dragged in and charged with sheltering him. They plead not guilty, and a jury from the area is empaneled to try them. Fortunately, the jury considers them not guilty, so they are let go.[7] You can see how important it is to be considered of good character in your hometown. If your enemies accuse you, often it will only be your good reputation which saves you from the gallows.

MISCARRIAGES OF JUSTICE

Local justice is designed to find somebody guilty; it does not necessarily follow that that somebody is the person responsible for the crime in question. If you begin to look at those who are indicted of serious crimes, it soon becomes apparent that many of them are strangers. In some places as many as 30 percent of all suspected murderers and thieves are described as vagrants.[8] How guilty all these men are is a moot point; many of them have probably been accused simply because the people who live in a village are cautious of strangers, and fearful of them, and thus very quick to point the finger at them when a crime is committed. There is a lot of false justice in the country. Just as some men are wrongly accused, others are wrongly acquitted. You even have a few cases in which murderers can be arrested and get off scot-free, having killed an innocent man to prove their own innocence. This sounds completely daft, but it happens. If one man is accused of a murder, and pleads not guilty but appeals an "accomplice" of involvement, he may end up fighting a judicial combat—trial by battle—with him to determine his guilt. If he defeats his opponent, he is deemed to be guiltless of the original offense and may go free.

Bad justice sometimes arises from those who administer the law. There are 628 hundreds in medieval England; but only 270 of them are in royal lordship. That leaves 358 in lords' hands.[9] Many of these private hundreds allow the sheriff and his bailiffs access to their courts,

so the sheriff can hold his tourns in the same way as he would in a
royal hundred. But some lords of private hundreds have the right to
refuse the sheriff access. It is not quite accurate to say that in such
places the king's writ does not run, but it is the lord of the hundred
who receives those writs, not the sheriff, and it is the lord who takes
responsibility for enacting the king's orders. Such lords hold their own
courts, hold their own equivalent of tourns, and sometimes even appoint their own coroners. They often have the right to hang felons as
well. The bailiff of such a hundred can hang those whom he chooses
at will, provided the coroner is present. It is very unlikely that anyone
will stop him.

There are very few checks or balances in this system. Hence there
is a great deal of blatant corruption. The sheriffs and those acting
under their authority can easily abuse the system. It is by no means
unknown for a sheriff to let an approver appeal a dozen of his enemies
of involvement in some crime or other, and, having hanged him, to
extort a sum of money from each of the dozen accused people, to secure their bail.[10] They pay, of course, to avoid long stays in the county
gaol. Thus the sheriff does very nicely out of what is, in every respect,
an injustice.

There are worse cases. Torture is supposed to be against the law in
England, and so it is—apart from a brief period in 1311, when Edward
II acquiesces to the pope's request to torture the Knights Templar.
But the law means little to a powerful sheriff. In 1366 the sheriff of
Yorkshire, Thomas Musgrave, is accused of malicious arrest, wrong-
ful imprisonment, extortion, and the entrapment of an innocent man
through employment of a packed jury. What he is up to is an old
game played by sheriffs for centuries. He has seized one of his enemy's
servants, tortured the man until he is almost dead, and forced him
to confess to a series of felonies. He has then forced him to turn approver, appealing his master of complicity in all his crimes, allowing
the sheriff to proceed legally against the master, his enemy.[11] This is
hardly justice. Nor is it justice when a woman who is accused of murder has to hide from the law for fear of her gaoler. One poor woman
hides when summoned because the sheriff's clerk in charge of Newcastle Gaol where she will be imprisoned has promised to rape her and
pull out all her teeth when he has got her in his power.[12] One cannot
help but sympathize with women in such a position. If they are caught

evading arrest, they may find themselves being outlawed in the county court. If they submit to the law, the indignities forced upon them might be greater than the crimes they have supposedly committed. Nor is it just women who are vulnerable to such humiliations. Sheriffs have been known to have men stripped naked and tied to a post in a miserable gaol pit and left there for days, freezing, in their own urine and excrement, in order to extort payments from them.

And so it goes down the social line. Beneath sheriffs, bailiffs of hundreds abuse their powers in similar ways, waking people up in the middle of the night and carrying away their goods and chattels if they refuse to pay bribes. Some bailiffs make themselves wealthy by ordering townships to have a jury empaneled and then charging the township for organizing that empanelment. They then make even more money by accepting bribes from those who do not wish to serve. Constables of townships might do the same—even tithing-men accept bribes from their fellows for not reporting crimes or reporting false ones. Arguably the most corrupt of all the officers involved in local justice are those who act as gaolers. You can tell that things are fundamentally wrong when a statute has to be passed (in 1330) to stop gaolers refusing to accept certain prisoners. It seems they are refusing to imprison criminals who are not rich enough to bribe them.

Justice is a relative concept in all ages. The fourteenth century is no exception.

MANOR AND BOROUGH COURTS

The manorial court is not always held in a manor house but often meets out of doors, by a specific tree, if the weather allows. The abbot of St. Albans holds his court "under the ash tree in the middle court-yard of the abbey." At Moulsham (Essex) the court is held outside the manor house, under the boughs of the Court Oak.[13] In bad weather, however, it might be adjourned to a manorial hall or barn.

The court's purpose is the safe and efficient running of the manor. Thus you will find all the villeins in attendance (including all the chief tithing-men and all those belonging to their tithings) and a few of the freemen.[14] Cases include simple managerial aspects, such as cattle and pigs straying; infringements of the lord's land and rights, ownership of land; or responsibilities for maintaining paths, lanes, and hedges.

Any trespasses and nuisances which fall wholly within the bounds of the manor, such as wrongly appropriated cattle, poaching, and blocked streams, are settled here. If a villein has extended his land by turning unused or "waste" ground into farmland (known as "assarting") he will pay an agreed sum for the right to farm the new land and a rent will be settled. Disturbances of a minor nature concerning the villeins will also be dealt with; these may include fistfights and cases of slander. Heriots are paid (if a tenant has died), and a whole welter of small fines are payable, from women brewing poor ale to the fine of "leyrwite": a charge for adultery among men and fornication among unmarried women.

"What?" you ask. "The manorial lord has a right to administer the behavior of his villeins too?" Although these are moral crimes, and thus punishable in the church courts, the fines levied on the villeins by those courts can be considered fines against the lord (as the villein's property is technically that of his lord). Take the case of John Monk, for example. He is a villein on a manor held by the abbot of Ramsey in the reign of Edward II. John is rather keen on Sarah, the wife of Simon Hewen. In fact, he cannot keep his hands off her. So ardent are they in their lovemaking that John has been fined and admonished several times already by the church courts for adultery. Nevertheless they carry on shamelessly. The abbot's steward, in despair, eventually commits John to the stocks until he agrees to desist and pays the massive fine of one mark in compensation to the lord.[15]

Where a lord of a manor holds his land by a charter which states he has the right of "infangenthef," the manorial court has another, darker dimension. Infangenthef is the right to hang a thief caught red-handed on the manor. Sometimes it is accompanied by "outfangenthef": the right to hang the thief even if he or she is apprehended elsewhere.[16] In this context, "red-handed" includes being in possession of stolen chattels. Lords of these manors, like lords of hundreds, are supposed to wait until the coroner has arrived before hanging the culprit, but very often they—or, rather, their bailiffs—do not bother. In 1313 a man of Bodmin wakes to find that one of his horses has been stolen in the night. The next morning he sees his horse in Bodmin marketplace, in the possession of a man called Robert. He raises the hue and cry, and both men are arrested and ordered to appear in court. The lord of the manor, the prior of Bodmin, who has the right of infangenthef, orders a court leet (a jurisdictional manorial court) to sit straightaway, and when Robert confesses, he is hanged without more ado. Although the prior should rightly have summoned the coroner, Robert's fate is sealed by his having the horse in his possession.[17] Coroners do not stop men being hanged; they simply make sure the value of any chattels or fines which should go to the king are not appropriated by the lord.

The right of infangenthef in some manors leads to thresholds for hanging men and women being set locally. The abbot of Crowland will hang you for stealing sixteen eggs, worth about 2d to 3d, whereas other lords will not hang you for far worse crimes.[18] In Sowerby, Yorkshire, in 1313 there is a man called Roger son of Amabel who twenty years ago burgled a house and stole oatmeal, salt, and loaves. Although he was indicted at the hundred court at the time, and was bailed, he has never actually been acquitted. Moreover, he still has in his possession the chattels of his brother, John, who was hanged eighteen years ago for stealing six sheep and five quarters of oats. These should have been surrendered to the king on John's execution. Although Roger is thus guilty of two capital offenses—theft and receiving the goods of a criminal—he is not hanged but declared a common thief and fined 2s.[19]

In London, there is no messing about. The city itself has the rights of infangenthef and outfangenthef, and its mayor has permanent judicial authority, so it has the necessary powers to deal speedily with all wrongdoers. On February 2, 1337, John le Whyte of Cambridge is presented by the sheriffs to the mayor and aldermen. He is accused of breaking into the shop of a mercer at night and stealing gold and silver rings, pearls, linen thread, and bracelets to the value of £5. Found guilty by a jury he is ordered to be hanged immediately at Tyburn. On May 19 this same year, Desiderata de Toryntone is accused of stealing thirty dishes and twenty-four saltcellars of silver, worth £40, from Lady Alice de Lisle, when she was staying at the bishop of Salisbury's house in Fleet Street. Fourteen of the dishes and twelve of the saltcellars have been found in her keeping. She too is dragged off to be hanged at Tyburn straightaway.[20] This brutally efficient system of punishment is how the dream of finding wealth in London ends for so many young men and women who have come in from the country. You might think that Gilbert son of Gilbert of Stapleford, Wiltshire, is a lucky boy to have been placed apprentice to a London spicemonger,

Geoffrey Adrian, in 1341. His father has taken considerable effort on his son's behalf and can be sure that the lad is on the path to prosperity. But on June 17 of that year, young Gilbert is found with £40 of his master's money in his pockets. Poor Gilbert is taken by his outraged master before the mayor and aldermen that same day. He confesses his deed. Within a few hours of his giving in to temptation, he is dead. Despite all his father's efforts to give him a good start in life, his corpse is twisting on a rope at Tyburn.

Most chartered towns by 1350 have sets of local bylaws or "ordinances." These govern the behavior of traders as well as visitors. Every set includes articles concerning the baking of bread and the brewing of ale, the use of weights and measures, and the penalties for shedding blood in a fight. More interesting are the differences between the various regulations. In London, for instance, it is forbidden to play dice while wearing a mask (as a result of a bylaw of 1343). In 1359 the mayor of London forbids begging within the city. Able-bodied beggars are to be placed within the stocks on Cornhill for half a day the first time they are caught and a whole day the second time. The third time, they are imprisoned for forty days. The fourth time they are banned from the city forever.

The sets of ordinances drawn up for the towns in the marcher lordship of Glamorgan around 1330 (based on those for Hereford) include some interesting clauses. Cows may not be milked in the High Street. No one shall play at dice or bowls within the town (penalty 12d). Butchers may not throw the heads and feet of animals into the High Street or any other lane within the town walls. No one shall cast dung or any other filth into the streets or the town ditch, or within forty feet of the town gates, or near any part of the walls. No taverner may open his tavern after ten p.m., or nine p.m. in the case of an alewife. To this last regulation, one is tempted to ask, "Why the difference?" But your curiosity about the various closing times of drinking establishments run by men and women will probably be overcome when reading this ordinance: "If any woman be found guilty by six men of scolding or railing any townsman or his wife, or any of their neighbors, then she is to be brought at the first fault to the cucking stool [a seat with ankle fastenings, pivoted on a pole, like a seesaw] there to sit one hour, at the second fault two hours. And at the third fault to let slip" with the result that the woman is dropped into deep water.[21]

Borough Ordinances of Worcester (selection)[22]

Article	Penalty
9. Bakers should not be fined for any failing in their craft but should be punished according to the Assize of Bread. Also in summer bakers should buy no grain in the market before 11 of the bell, and in winter before 12 of the bell. Nor shall they resell any grain coming at the market. Their bread is to be weighed and tested for quality every Saturday.	20s
10. Bakers should not receive any grain in their houses on Saturdays (market days) until 11 of the bell	6s 8d
11. Ale must be sold to the citizens of the borough, and that the price is to be three gallons of small ale for 1d. The two ale tasters are to be citizens and "sad and discreet persons" to see that the ale be good and set.	6s 8d
13. Strangers may not buy barley, malt, or any other grain in the market until the corn brewers and maltsters of the borough have made their purchases. This is to be done by 11 of the bell in summer and by 12 of the bell in winter.	6s 8d
14. If any man's wife becomes indebted, and sells any victuals or goods, she is to answer at court as an independent woman, and any legal action against her is not to name her husband.	
15. The beaters are to be ready with their horses and equipment to bring water to every citizen, when called to do so by any man or child when any peril of fire is within the city.	40d
19. No horses are to be left standing in the marketplace on market days.	1d
20. Every man is to keep the road in front of his tenement clean.	40d

Article	Penalty

21. Bawds, scolds, and chiders, and resetters of
servants and children [those who harbor them
after they have run away from home] who are
found guilty in the borough court are to be
punished by the bailiffs at their discretion.

22. Five pageants are to be held yearly by the craft   40s
guilds, to do worship to God and to the city.

23. There should be peace between the citizens and
the gentlemen of the shire. No gentleman's
livery is to be given to or received by any citizen.

24. The entrails of butchered beasts and pails of blood   12d
are not to be carried away by day but only by night.
No pail of blood should be left uncleansed for a day
and night, whether in winter or summer.

25. Five fire hooks [to pull down burning materials]
shall be stationed in three parts of the city.

26. No timber chimneys are allowed in the city, nor   6s 8d for
thatched houses. All timber chimneys are to be   each six
rebuilt in stone and all thatched roofs are to   months it
be tiled.   is not done

30. No man may play tennis or *jeu de paume*
within the guildhall.   40d

32. Every citizen within the city shall keep a weapon   20s
and be ready and willing to support the bailiffs
in keeping the king's peace.

33. No citizen may give or receive a lord's livery in the   40s
city, nor may he gather in an unlawful assembly,
nor may he go armed. Also no citizen shall harbour
"pillagers, robbers, despoilers, oppressors of people,
manslayers, felons, outlaws, ravishers of women,
unlawful hunters of forests, parks and warrens,
other miss-doers," or anyone else accused of
such offences yet to be tried.

	Article	Penalty
34.	If a man starts a fight within the city, or draws his sword or dagger, he is to lose the weapon. If he draws blood he is to be fined, and, if he cannot pay, he is to be imprisoned. This does not affect the right of a householder to correct his servant or apprentice within the law.	6s 8d
38.	No citizen shall be put in the common prison but in one of the chambers of the guildhall, unless he be imprisoned for a man's death or a heinous crime, or a debt exceeding £10.	
40.	No citizen may rebuke the bailiffs or reprove the aldermen, chamberlain, or recorder.	20s
44.	The election of citizens to represent the city in parliament shall be made openly, by freeholders with 40s per year, in the guildhall, "by the most voice" [note: no secret ballot].	
45.	No citizen may sue another citizen of this city in another court outside the city, except over the ownership of land.	
49.	All those laborers who would be hired within the city should stand daily by Grace Cross on the day of work, in summer at 5 of the bell, and in winter at 6 of the bell.	
51.	No saddler, butcher, baker, or glover, nor any other person, may cast entrails, "filth of beasts' dung," or dust over Severn Bridge. Also no one may shave flesh, skins, or hides but above the bridge, between the watering place at St. Clements Gate and the said Severn Bridge. And they may wash nothing here except beneath the bridge, and on the far side of the Severn, or beneath the Slip.	6s 8d
54.	The quay, slips, and the pavement of the Great Slip shall be overseen and repaired regularly.	

Article	Penalty

55. The bailiffs must attend to the repair of the walls
and gates of the city.

56. No man may cast "dung or harlotry" at the Slip,   40d
nor upon the quay. And no man may have pigs
roaming at large, to the annoyance of his neighbors;
he must put them away when warned by a bailiff
to do so.

57. The tilers of the town may not compel strangers
who are tilers to serve them. Nor may they have
their own parliament. Every tiler must mark his
tiles with his own mark.

68. No man may sell ale from his house unless he   6s 8d
puts up a sign at his door.

69. No butcher may work in the city as a cook.   13s 4d

73. All the crafts within the city which have   40s
pageants—for the worship of God and the profit
of the city—and all the crafts that contribute to
these, and to the lighting of torches and tapers
used by the said crafts, shall continue to enjoy their
customs as before. All master craftsmen and
journeymen coming to the city must also join one
of these crafts after being resident in the city for a
fortnight. Every craft holding a pageant shall
provide a lamp every year, to be borne before the
bailiffs of the city on the vigil of the Nativity of St.
John the Baptist, at the common watch of the city;
and the wardens of the said craft and all their
members shall wait upon the bailiffs at this time,
dressed in their finest clothes.

75. No baker shall bake horsebread or keep a hostelry.   6s 8d

76. No person may keep a hostelry unless he has a   6s 8d
sign above his door.

Royal Justice

What is the law of the land? Where does it come from? How does anyone know what the letter of the law is? After all, there are relatively few law books to be found, especially outside London, and those there are tend to be old and out of date. While obviously it is a crime for anyone to injure another person physically without reason, or to damage or remove his property, how far can one go in defending oneself? The case of John de Burgh illustrates the problems. John is a five-year-old London boy. One Monday evening in April 1324 he is playing in the house of Richard and Emma de Latthere, his parents' neighbors. He takes a fancy to a ball of wool belonging to Emma and hides it under his cap. Emma discovers what he has done and chastises him with her right hand on the left side of his face. Such chastisement is perfectly in order, especially in her own home; Emma has done nothing wrong. However, the blow causes some other, unseen damage—probably a hemorrhage in the brain—and the lad dies the next day.[23] Should Emma face charges? Terrified that she will be accused of murder, she flees, thus compounding her guilt and, by implication, her reputation for involvement in the "crime." Does she deserve to be hanged, though, when chastisement of this nature is positively encouraged by society, to teach children a sense of right and wrong?

The law of England is basically a compendium of the old laws of the Saxons which have been repeatedly revised and rewritten by the royal judges (or justices) since the Conquest. These same royal judges go out to the county towns and hold trials in those places. It is thus called "the common law" because it is commonly applied to everyone in the kingdom and takes precedence over local customary laws and ordinances. This shows why it is important for local officials to wait for an experienced royal judge to arrive to try their prisoners. Where sheriffs take the law into their own hands, they run the risk of committing a crime themselves.

The common law can only remain relevant if it is adapted to suit changing circumstances. Increasingly it falls to Parliament to initiate changes in outdated laws and introduce new ones. A Member of Parliament who wants the law changed in some way—be he a nobleman, a prelate, one of the seventy-four representatives of the shires, or a representative of a borough (normally there are about 165 to 185 of these)—must present a petition to the king in Parliament. Some of these petitions will be dismissed by the lords and prelates appointed to consider them, but some form the basis of new legislation.

Many of our most basic laws are written over the course of the fourteenth century. Many are clarifications by Parliament of old customs, such as benefit of clergy, and sanctuary. Some Acts of Parliament, it has to be said, are completely ignored by the people: the repeated attempts to establish a single, universal system of weights and measures is a good example. But a few Acts are of vital importance. For example, there are officially two races—the English and the Normans—until this law of "Englishry" is repealed in 1340. The Act of 1362 which enables people to plead in court in English is a similar milestone in the history of the nation. Some important Acts are still in force in the modern world. The main clauses of the Treason Act of 1351, by which Edward III establishes exactly what constitutes "high treason," are still on the statute books. One can say the same for Acts forbidding men to come to Parliament armed, and the Act of 1383 forbidding maintenance (where lords protect their criminal retainers). Also still in force in the modern world are an Act of 1331 making it illegal to arrest someone contrary to the terms of the Magna Carta, and an Act of 1381 making it treasonable to begin a riot (passed in the wake of the Peasants' Revolt). Interestingly, an Act of 1354 is also still in force, making it illegal for a man to be deprived of his lands or property, or executed, without first having had the chance to answer the accusations against him in court. Sadly, recourse to this particular law is normally made posthumously, when an heir is trying to clear his executed father's name and reclaim his inheritance.

Parliament has another important function besides establishing and confirming new laws: it is the highest court in the land. If a lord is to be tried for a crime, the trial takes place before his peers, in Parliament. Similarly, trials for high treason take place in Parliament. Some of the most dramatic moments of the century are thus to be witnessed at Westminster. On November 26, 1330, the traitor Roger Mortimer, first earl of March, stands bound and gagged before his peers as he is condemned to death for fourteen specified and many unspecified crimes. The process of the trial is that his crimes are "notorious" and known to all. There is no need for anyone to produce any evidence: he is guilty. He is drawn from the Tower of London to the gallows at Tyburn on a hurdle three days later, stripped, and hanged. If you visit Tyburn at any point over the subsequent two days, you can see his naked body turning in the breeze.

Lord Mortimer is lucky in some respects. The full penalty for treason is to be drawn to the gallows on a hurdle or an oxhide, then to be stripped and hanged until nearly dead, then cut down, disemboweled and emasculated, and finally to be quartered. In the fourteenth century the full penalty is very rarely carried out. Most men who are deemed traitors by Edward II are either killed in battle, beheaded, or hanged like common thieves. In 1305 the Scots patriot and outlaw Sir William Wallace undergoes the full drawing, hanging, disemboweling, and quartering, by order of Edward I. In 1317 the dignified Welsh nobleman Llywelyn Bren is similarly hanged and disemboweled by Hugh, Lord Despenser. His illegal death is avenged in 1326 when Despenser himself suffers the same fate, by order of Lord Mortimer. Despenser is drawn to the place of execution behind four horses, hanged on a gallows fifty feet high, then cut down and eviscerated and emasculated while still alive. His entrails are thrown into a fire. Only then is he decapitated and quartered. By 1400, this gruesome punishment has received an extra tweak for those guilty of the highest treason. The disemboweling takes place *prior* to hanging. In 1399, having been found guilty of witnessing the murder of the king's uncle at Calais, John Hall is sentenced to be

> drawn from Tower Hill to Tyburn Elms, and there disembowelled, and his entrails burnt in front of him, and then hanged, beheaded and quartered, and his head sent to Calais.[24]

In case you are wondering whether the disembowelment kills him before he is hanged, the answer is no. The executioner ties up his most important tubes so he can live long enough to witness his entrails being burnt.[25] And when he is quartered, he really is *quartered:* it is not just a case of chopping off limbs. After his head is cut off, his torso is hacked into four pieces, each with a limb attached. If you go onto London Bridge you can see a stake set up with the quarter of him which was the right-hand side of his chest, rib cage, lung, shoulder, and right arm.[26]

ROYAL JUDGES

There are three central royal courts: the Court of the Exchequer, the Court of the King's Bench, and the Court of Common Pleas. The Court of the Exchequer hears cases concerning financial arrangements with the Crown. The Court of the King's Bench hears criminal cases and appeals from lesser courts. The Court of Common Pleas is also a court of appeal, but its predominant business is to hear those personal cases in which people are trying to sue each other over debt, theft, fraud, unlawful distrains, and similar offenses.

Most people will never see one of these courts. Their enormous importance lies in the fact that the judges from the King's Bench and the Court of Common Pleas head out to each county, usually twice a year, to try all the serious cases referred to them from the sheriffs' tourns and the county courts. These men are thus the principal agents of royal justice in the kingdom.

The commissions under which they try felons and trespassers vary. Every seven years there is supposed to be a commission of general "eyre," which means the judges must try all unsettled cases. It is a great event when the judges come to town—up to two thousand people attend the 1313–14 Kent sessions.[27] More regularly the king issues a commission of *"oyer et terminer"*—to "hear and determine"— all the cases awaiting a verdict in a county. A special form of this commission from 1305 is named "trailbaston." Another form of commission is that of "assize": judges travel through the counties on six circuits, trying all the criminals they encounter. Lastly there is the commission of "gaol delivery." As the name suggests, the purpose of this commission is simply to empty the gaols. In the early part of the century, when the judges of the King's Bench travel with the king, they hear the cases of all those in the gaols wherever they stop. Those awaiting trial in the sheriff's lockup suddenly find the judges are coming. They are asked how they wish to acquit themselves. If they plead "not guilty," the case is heard and a jury is asked to determine the guilt or innocence of the accused. If the jury says they are innocent, they go free. If the jury says they are guilty, they are punished. Over and over again one may see life and death situations come to a dramatic resolution, resulting in either an outpouring of relief or screams of despair as a woman realizes her husband has been found guilty and sees him dragged off to be hanged at the gallows outside the castle.

As the gaols are filled with thieves and murderers, the sentence passed on these men is usually simply that of hanging. Overall, about a third of all the accused men are executed, the remainder being released. There are few other punishments. It is not unknown for a man to be given life imprisonment: Hugh le Bever of London (whose goods are described in chapter 7) is sent to prison for killing his wife, Alice, "there to remain in penance until he should be dead." But a sentence of life imprisonment like this is very rare. Occasionally, if a woman is convicted of petty treason (the killing of her husband, lord, or employer), she might be burnt alive, but this too is rare. Witches and heretics are generally hanged in England, not burnt. The punishment of burning alive for heresy is not properly introduced until the parliament of 1401. The customary laws in some ancient boroughs demand the loss of a limb for certain crimes. Attacking an alderman of London, for example, can result in the hand which drew the sword or dagger being cut off.[28] According to the Charter of the Forest (issued about 1217), poachers should not have their hands cut off, as in the days of King John, but loss of limb is still meted out on their animals. Thus a poacher who escapes with a fine will still see his dog lose a paw. If a horse kills its master, then it should be confiscated as a "deodand" and sold, its value being payable to the Crown. Even a ship can be deemed guilty of murder and confiscated as a deodand, the proceeds of its sale being given to the king to be distributed as alms. Extraordinary though this practice seems, it is at least slightly more rational than the system which prevails in France, where donkeys, pigs, and cows are often tried and hanged for murder, if they happen to kill a child. In 1349 a cow is solemnly burnt at the stake for just such a crime.[29]

COMMISSIONS OF THE PEACE

Commissioners or Keepers of the Peace are the forerunners of what we know in the modern world as Justices of the Peace. (Technically they are only justices when they have the power to judge cases.) In 1307 and 1308 Keepers of the Peace are empowered to arrest people on suspicion of felony, and in 1316, in Kent, they are empowered to judge the cases of those they have arrested, so the gaols can be cleared.[30] Although they are appointed by the king, these keepers of the peace are local men. This raises a serious question: should you have local justices? If you do not allow local people to hang felons on a regular basis, the felons get out of control. If you *do*, corruption is unavoidable. Many innocent people will be killed without recourse to the common law.

The gradual breakdown of law and order decides the issue. The last general eyres are commissioned by Roger Mortimer and Queen Isabella in 1328–30. Trailbastons fade out similarly in the following decade. Attempts are made to bolster the authority of the keepers of the peace, but with varying levels of success. Finally, in 1361, Edward III establishes the office of Justice of the Peace. It is stated that JPs are to be "three or four of the most worthy in the county, with some learned in law." They have the legal powers to restrain peace breakers and rioters, to punish them according to their offenses, to arrest men and women on suspicion of breaking the peace and to imprison them, to ensure suitable sums of money are secured to guarantee the good behavior of suspected persons in future and to try people for their felonies and trespasses in accordance with writs of *oyer et terminer*. This act of 1361 is another of those still partly in force in the modern world.

After 1361 the magistrates' powers increase steadily. In 1368 they are given supervision of the laws preventing workers from overcharging for their labor. In 1383 they are empowered to arrest vagabonds and vagrants, or to bind them over for large sums of money to ensure their good behavior. They also acquire the responsibility for stamping out the practice of maintenance. In 1388 the numbers of JPs in each county are increased, and it is enacted that they be paid 4s for each day of their sessions. With a payment level twelve times the average working wage and the powers to arrest, imprison, judge, fine, and hang people, the local magistrate becomes a very important person indeed.

Organized Crime

A large sum of money—£4,000 in gold, to be precise—is due to be transferred from London to the king at Leicester, a distance of ninety miles. How many men to do you think will be guarding it? Fifty? A hundred? Two hundred? You might be surprised to hear that this

massive treasure is to be guarded by just five archers.[31] Your thoughts
on this might not differ greatly from those of many criminals in England at the time. However good those five archers are at their job,
entrusting such a huge sum to so few men over such a long distance
is simply asking for trouble. It is no coincidence that tales of Robin
Hood enter popular culture at this time. There are rich pickings to be
had from waylaying those with money, and those who can organize
a gang to carry out a series of killings and robberies stand in a very
good position to obtain considerable sums.

Roughly a third of all organized criminal gangs in England are
composed of family units.[32] Obviously the majority of these are in-
formal collaborations. Husbands and wives often work together on
the wrong side of the law, and so do brothers. Sometimes even sisters
get involved. The Waraunt family of Salle, Norfolk, includes three
sisters, one brother, and another male relative, John Waraunt. Two
of the sisters and the brother are accused of receiving stolen goods in
1321; they escape punishment, as does another sister in the same year.
John, however, is found guilty of stealing clothes and household goods
worth eight shillings from a fellow townsman. He is hanged. In 1325
the four remaining members of the Waraunt family are back behind
bars. A specific instruction is issued to their gaoler that they should be
treated harshly. They all survive, and they also survive the appeal of
an approver in February 1326 that they have stolen a quantity of cloth.
Two of the sisters are again accused of theft in August 1326. They remain at large, thieving where they can.[33]

Families like the Waraunts are obviously a nuisance to their neighbors but, in relation to some gangs, they are relatively harmless. Far
more serious are the armed criminals who use force against their
victims. You really do not want to run into the likes of the Worcestershire gang leader Malcolm Musard, who in 1304 attacks a rectory with
a group of archers, having been paid to terrorize the new incumbent
by the aggrieved old one. Nor do you want to come up against John
Fitzwalter, an Essex gang leader, who twice besieges Colchester and
holds the entire town for ransom.[34]

How are these gangs able to remain at large? The answer will
probably shock you. And yet it will probably not surprise you. The
perpetrators very often have links with the richest and most powerful elements of society. A number of them are knights and members

of the gentry or even the nobility. The earl of Devon threatens to murder a Justice of the Peace as he rides through the county. It is not unknown for a knight to draw his sword in court and hold it against a judge's throat.[35] Even the most prominent judges are affected by threats and bribes. Sir John Inge, a justice of the Court of Common Pleas, admits taking bribes. Sir Richard Willoughby is accused of "selling the laws like cattle" and fined £1,000. In 1350 no less a figure than Sir William Thorp, Chief Justice of the King's Bench, is imprisoned for accepting bribes.

A good example of what the judges are up against is the Folville gang. At the time of his death (in 1310), John Folville, lord of the manors of Ashby Folville (Leicestershire) and Teigh (Rutland) has seven sons: John, Eustace, Laurence, Richard, Robert, Thomas, and Walter. The eldest, John, inherits Ashby Folville and remains within the law. The others do not. The most dangerous, Eustace Folville, inherits Teigh and joins with two of his brothers and the Zouche brothers (Ralph, Roger, and Ivo) in forming a gang to waylay their long-standing enemy, Roger Bellers. Bellers is an important man: a baron of the Exchequer, he is protected by none other than the king's favorite, Hugh, Lord Despenser. Nevertheless, on January 19, 1326, on the road between Melton Mowbray and Leicester, they murder him. They drive a long knife down past his collarbone and into his heart.

The guilty men flee the country. In their absence they are declared outlaws. But they are in luck, because in September 1326, Roger Mortimer and Queen Isabella invade England and put an end to Hugh Despenser. All proceedings against the Folvilles are quashed, and they are pardoned. Free to return to England, and believing they have political protectors of their own, they embark on a series of robberies in Lincolnshire. In 1327 they grow bolder, roaming the highways with a larger gang of confederates, looking for victims to threaten, rape, and incarcerate for ransom. Over the next couple of years Eustace is personally accused of at least four murders, a rape, and three robberies, and these figures are almost certainly an underestimate of his crimes. But the net closes in around them once more, and, in late 1328, they are forced to rehabilitate themselves by joining Mortimer's army in putting down the rebellion of the earl of Lancaster. They all secure pardons again. But while under Mortimer's protection they loot the people of Leicester to the tune of £200 worth of goods.

Attempts in 1330 to arrest the Folville gang are ineffective. Their position in Leicestershire is unassailable. The eldest Folville brother, John, the only one who has taken no part in any crime, has by this stage been appointed a Keeper of the Peace. He may well be supplying his brothers with information. Sir Robert Colville tries to arrest Eustace at Teigh, but is beaten back and later accused of an illegal attack. Roger de Wensley is hired to track down both the Folvilles and the other notorious gang in the region, the Coterel gang (led by James Coterel), but when he finds the Coterels he simply joins them.

In 1331 the Folvilles are hired by a canon of Sempringham Priory and the cellarer of Haverholm Abbey. These clergymen, who have previously sheltered the gang from the law, pay them £20 to destroy a water mill belonging to a rival. Soon the mill is a smoking ruin. The Folvilles' next crime is on a far more ambitious scale. They join forces with several other criminal gangs, including the Coterel gang; the Bradburn gang; the Savage Company (led by Roger Savage, a friend of James Coterel); Sir Robert Tuchet, former constable of Melbourne Castle; and Sir Robert de Vere, constable of Rockingham Castle. The plan is to kidnap a rich royal judge, Sir Richard Willoughby (the same judge who will later be accused of "selling the laws like cattle"). They seize him on January 14, 1332, while he is carrying out an *oyer et terminer* commission in the region. They rob him of £100 of his goods and ransom him for the colossal sum of 1,300 marks (£866 13s 4d).

Such extraordinary, reckless banditry cannot go unchecked, and it is with the Folville and Coterel gangs in mind that the most stringent of all the trailbaston commissions is issued in 1332. In charge are the three most important judges in the kingdom: Geoffrey le Scrope (Chief Justice of the King's Bench), William de Herle (Chief Justice of the Common Pleas) and John Stonor (the previous Chief Justice of the Common Pleas). Despite this show of strength from the government, they fail to bring the key criminals to justice. James Coterel and Roger Savage retreat into the wilderness of High Peak forest in Derbyshire. Orders are issued to arrest no fewer than two hundred adherents of the Folville and Coterel gangs. Only a quarter appear before the judges, and virtually all of them are acquitted by local juries, composed of men too scared to convict them.

In the late 1330s the Folvilles and the Coterels find ways to assimilate themselves back into society. A large number of them join

Edward III's military expedition to the Low Countries in 1338. After this, Eustace gives up crime. In an extraordinary turn of fortune he is knighted and dies peacefully in 1347, having served on the Crécy campaign the previous year. Leadership of the gang passes to Richard Folville, rector of Teigh. He and his fellow criminals meet their end in 1340, when their archenemy, Sir Robert Colville, finally catches up with them. Colville pursues them to Teigh, where they seek sanctuary in the church. After ten years of trying to arrest them, Colville has no intention of giving them any hope whatsoever, and he attacks. There is a bitter shootout; the Folvilles send volleys of arrows flying from the church windows but they are unable to resist Colville. They are dragged outside, one by one, and beheaded for resisting arrest.[36]

Ecclesiastical Courts

After reading about Richard Folville, you might well ask what right a clergyman has to lecture you on matters of law. Such opinions are shared by a number of people. How come bishops and archdeacons can enforce the law on moral behavior? Some high-ranking clergymen even publicly acknowledge their own illegitimate children.[37] Nevertheless, no discussion of the law would be complete without reference to the church courts. One particular aspect—the benefit of clergy—means that you, as a literate person, should never have to face the death penalty for a felony.

There are various sorts of church courts in England. The most important are the consistory courts, with jurisdiction over the whole diocese, and the archdeaconry courts. Many sorts of cases can be brought. Where one person wishes to take action against another in a moral issue—for example, slander or wife beating—and both individuals live within the same archdeaconry, then it is to the archdeaconry court they will go. It is not a cheap business, however. To raise a suit costs 3d. The libel (the document requiring the defendant to turn up and defend himself or herself) 2s 1d. The examination costs a further 1s. Securing a sentence could cost 7s 8d in the diocese of Canterbury so you will only find this sort of action being taken in the most extreme circumstances.[38]

Just as important are indictments for moral offenses reported to the church courts. These include defamation of character, drunkenness, swearing, trading on a Sunday (especially butchers and barbers), not attending church on a Sunday, heresy, perjury, false alms taking, eating meat on a nonmeat day, attacks on clergymen, failure to pay tithes, usury, ill treatment of wives, divorce (on grounds of consanguinity or nonconsummation), and legal cases against clergymen. By far the largest category of cases are those concerned with sexual offenses. Between a third and two-thirds of all moral disputes arise from sexual behavior, mostly fornication, bigamy, and adultery but also including prostitution, bastardy, homosexuality, and incest. These are all dealt with in the consistorial court. In such cases, the bishop's commissary may order the offending parties to be fined, to be whipped, to carry candles in procession in the church on a Sunday, to make offerings at the altar before everyone else in the church, or to stand in a white sheet at the door of the church on three successive Sundays, confessing his or her crime. Failure to attend court results in suspension (so one cannot enter a church until making good with the court) and, in the worst cases, excommunication.

Just as any nobleman has the right to be tried by his peers in Parliament, so too any clergyman has the right to be judged by the church courts. The right is called "the benefit of clergy," and it is vigorously upheld in an Act of 1315. The "benefit" element is obvious: even if found guilty of a felony by Convocation (the highest church court, the ecclesiastical equivalent of Parliament), a clergyman will not face the death penalty. Interestingly, the test for whether you are a clergyman is very low: can you read a passage from the Bible? If you are accused of a felony, and find yourself in court, you should claim benefit of clergy and read the text you are given. In theory you will be tried again by the church courts—even if already found guilty by the king's courts—but normally the clergyman who takes responsibility for you will simply let you go.

Sanctuary

For those who are guilty of a serious felony, and in fear of retribution, there exists one last resort. If you can get to a church before you are arrested, you can claim sanctuary. With the slamming of that consecrated oak door behind you, you are safe—in theory—for up to forty days. Sanctuary is confirmed by your confession, while in the said church, to a witness. Those pursuing you at that point must place a guard over the door to prevent you escaping—and they can be fined if you escape. According to the Act of 1315, anyone claiming sanctuary cannot be forced from the church by hunger—the guards should feed you. Furthermore, you may freely leave the church to urinate and defecate outside. The coroner should turn up within the forty days and confiscate your goods. He will then assign you a sea port from which you will abjure the realm. You will make your way to it along the king's highway, bareheaded and barefoot, and take the next ship leaving the kingdom.

That is, at least, how sanctuary should operate. In reality, you will be lucky to reach exile, especially if you are a murderer. Sometimes the community is "unable" to persuade the coroner to attend and will stop feeding you after forty days. Sometimes they will not feed you at all. When a thief is set to abjure the realm, a large crowd normally gathers to pursue him on the highway, making his life a misery as far as they wish. Personal circumstances often complicate the exercising of the right. On one occasion a man charged with the murder of a priest escapes from the custody of the priest's servants and seeks sanctuary in a church. As the man is a fugitive from justice—the priest's servants were trying to arrest him when he fled—he is denied the right to abjure the realm. After forty days he is given the choice of starving to death in the church or giving himself up. He chooses the latter—and is promptly hanged.[39] In 1320 Isabella de Bury kills the parish clerk of Allhallows on the Wall, London, and takes refuge in the same church. The bishop of London himself sends word that the Church refuses to shelter such a woman, and she is dragged out and hanged.[40]

Finally, it is worth noting that the right of sanctuary is often ignored. As the case of Richard Folville shows, a priest taking shelter in his own church can hardly claim sanctuary when he is a notorious criminal. When Chief Justice Tresilian is found hiding in sanctuary at Westminster Abbey during the Merciless Parliament, he is not allowed to abjure the realm but is dragged out by the king's uncle and hanged. Many people during the Peasants' Revolt take sanctuary in churches: large numbers are forcibly removed and beheaded as if they are fugitives from justice, regardless of the law. Everything depends on the level of feeling against the culprit. A Breton, taken in by a much-loved old widow in London, murders her in her bed and steals her goods. When caught, he flees to sanctuary. It is a brief respite. As soon as the coroner has assigned him a port, the murderer sets out on the road. But the widow's grief-stricken friends wait for him and stone him to death.[41] In medieval England, popular justice is no more forgiving than the royal judges and the hangman's noose.

This fourteenth-century view of the world shows East at the top, Jerusalem in the center, the Red Sea top right (in red), and England bottom left (also in red). Also labeled are Damascus, Babylon, the tower of Babel, Rome, Paris, fourteen English towns, various places mentioned in romances about Alexander the Great (Macedonia, Alexandria, and Persepolis), and regions inhabited by fabulous races, such as the cyclops and troglodytes.

This map is at least forty years old by 1300 but it demonstrates the importance of rivers in picturing the country. The position of Canterbury—southwest of London—should warn you not to use it for navigational purposes.

Coaches can cost up to a thousand pounds and are only used by royal women and countesses. Note the five horses all in a line: this is usual practice for pulling heavy wagons and coaches. Note also the pet squirrel on the arm of the lady at the front

Early-fourteenth-century cogs have stem posts and stern posts with rudders. Typically they have single masts and one large sail. Ships like this are the mainstay of the merchant fleet, as well as the basis of the navy in wartime.

Late-fourteenth-century cogs incorporate elements of the designs of hulks and Genoese carracks, and are larger—up to 120 feet long in a few cases.

Not every royal dinner is a feast. Here the king is dining with his closest advisers. Note the baldaquin above him, the aumbry with his silver vessels, and his minstrels.

This scene depicts a dais during a royal feast. The king is flanked by his advisers. Servants kneel before him when presenting dishes. To his right is the "reward," the table for the principal officers. Behind him stands the marshal, with his staff of office.

Hanging people is often a production-line process. Several clergymen are on hand, each gallows supports up to a dozen people, and crowds look on, often including the kin of the condemned. It is a slow, ignominious death.

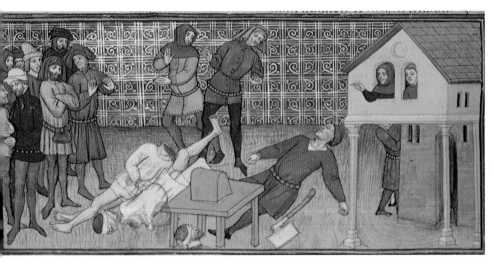

Medieval men see beheading as preferable to hanging. Royal family members are often granted beheading as a favor. Here the executioner, having performed his duty, has been struck with a fit.

The village stocks serve as both a form of lockup for serious offenders and a humiliating punishment for less serious crimes. Presumably this married woman and the monk fall into the latter category.

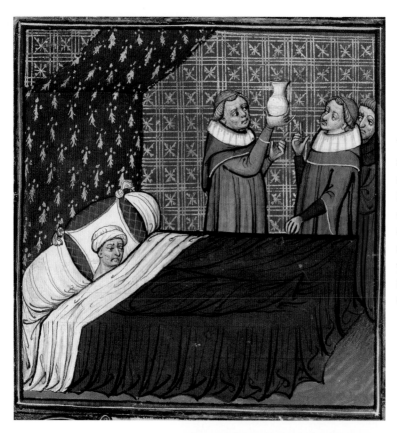

Your physician might not actually examine you. Instead he will diagnose your condition from an inspection of your urine and the constellations of the stars.

Physicians administering medicine with a spoon. This scene is comparable with modern life. What is on that spoon, however, is almost certainly not.

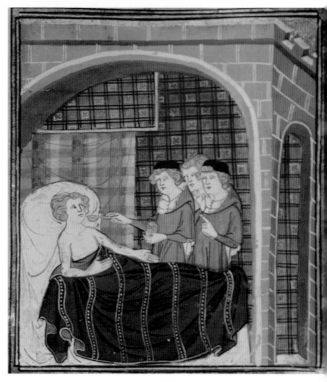

Plague-stricken clergymen being blessed by a priest. Men and women in religious communities such as abbeys are especially vulnerable to infectious diseases.

After plague, leprosy is the most feared disease: "the living death," as it is known. This leper carries a bell to warn people of his presence.

John of Arderne, the great surgeon, performing a fistula operation. Surgeons should be able to make their patients laugh, he says. Not easy, in this situation.

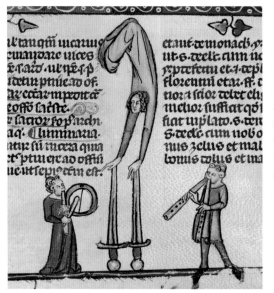

Acrobats and dancers often accompany minstrels around the country. Here a woman performs to the accompaniment of pipes and a fife and drum.

The carol of love. Caroling is group song and dance, not just to do with Christmas. People join hands and dance in a circle, singing the chorus.

Bearbaiting is just one of many cruel sports that people enjoy. Here the bear has grabbed one dog but another has bitten its ear.

I I

What to Do

It is a challenge, when confronted by the extreme adversities of life, to remember that fourteenth-century England has a strong element of joy running through it. It is a calamitous century, no doubt about it, but people cope. Indeed, they are exuberant about life, whether it be caroling and dancing that gives them pleasure, or fighting jousts and hunting with hawks. Lords and kings have their jesters and minstrels to tell them jokes and stories and to play music, dance, and sing. Laughter is an integral part of daily life. When no one can bear to tell the king of France about the defeat of his navy at Sluys in 1340, it is his jester who breaks the news to him, exclaiming, "How brave the Frenchmen are, throwing themselves into the sea, unlike those cowardly English, who cling to their ships." Edward II is thoroughly entertained in 1313 by Bernard the Fool and fifty-four nude dancers.[1] You might speculate as to what this says about Edward II, but there can be few people whose curiosity is not aroused by such an event, whatever era they come from.

Music and Dancing

Listen.

It is very quiet.

Out on the open road, you can hear nothing but the wind in the trees, the streams trickling, occasional calls of voices, and birdsong. The French knight of La Tour Landry, wandering in a garden, remarks on the wild birds singing in their different languages, "full of mirth and joy."[2] The poet William Langland, lying by the side of a brook, leaning over to look in the water, remarks that the ripples in the stream *sound* so sweetly.

Indoors, there is practically no noise but the crackle of the fire, the thud as a wooden vessel is set down heavily on the stone floor, the clatter as a pewter plate is dropped. People speak to one another and sometimes sing to themselves. The loudest noises you will ever hear are thunder, trumpets being sounded; bells ringing across a city; the rumble of warhorses' hooves (in a cavalry charge, for example, or during a tournament); and very, very occasionally, the sound of a cannon being fired. But, apart from musical instruments and bells, these loud noises are unusual. Sitting at a table in the great hall of a castle, the loudest noises will be the chatter from the lower tables.

As a result of this comparative quiet, people listen differently. They hear with greater clarity. When a dog barks, they can recognize whose dog it is. They are more sensitive to voices. And, above all else, they listen intently to music.

Medieval people love music. It is—along with a love of good food, good jokes, and good stories—one of those aspects of life which unites everyone, from the most powerful nobleman to the most miserable villein. Even monks have been known to enjoy minstrelsy, especially the plucked notes of the harp. Music is part of the largesse of a great lord, offered to all those in his hall. Without it, his hospitality is considered inferior. Musicians are highly valued. In February 1312 Edward II makes a gift of forty marks (£26 13s 4d) to his herald-cum-minstrel, "King Robert," and his fellow performers at a feast.[3] In 1335 Edward III cheerfully gives fifty marks (£33 6s 8d) to another herald-cum-minstrel, Master Andrew Claroncel, and his companions, for "making their minstrelsy" for the king and his companions at court.[4] These are huge sums for a few hours of entertainment. Roger Bennyng and his minstrels receive only twenty marks (£13 6s 8d) when performing for the king and queen at King's Langley in July 1341, but that is certainly not a sum to be sniffed at.[5] Nor is the personal payment of just half a mark (6s 8d) to Hanekino in return for playing his fiddle in front of the king before the statue of the Virgin at Christchurch, Canterbury, in 1369.[6] Most people have to work for at least three weeks to earn as much.

The instruments played by these musicians vary and are constantly evolving. There is no one pattern for a harp, or a trumpet, or even a fiddle. No two instruments are exactly the same, being handmade and thus rather of a type than an exact design. The numbers of strings on

a harp may vary, so too may the length of a trumpet. The arrangements of instruments in a band vary considerably too. Those depicted
on the Exeter Cathedral minstrels' gallery (built about 1350) include
a set of bagpipes, a recorder, a fiddle, a harp, a trumpet (without any
valves), a portable organ, a tambourine, and three other instruments
which you might not immediately recognize: a gittern, a citole, and a
shawm.

As music is one of the few ways of making a loud noise, it has
other purposes besides delighting audiences. "High" minstrelsy is
the description of loud instrumentation—using trumpets, sackbuts,
bagpipes, clarions, shawms, and nakers—while "low" minstrelsy is the
more melodic variety. The cooperation between heralds and trumpeters is obvious; many heralds are in charge of troupes of musicians, for
making loud, proclamatory sounds. Lords when traveling or setting
out for war take minstrels who are experienced in high minstrelsy.
Edward III's household in France in 1345–47 includes a department
of minstrels, with five trumpeters, a citoler, five pipers, one tabor
player, two clarion players, a nakerer, and a fiddler.[7] Henry IV, as earl
of Derby, sets out on his journey across Europe in 1392 with two
trumpeters, three pipers, and a nakerer.[8] Town "waits" or bands of
watchmen also use musical instruments, in case they need to sound
the alarm. As brass trumpets and clarions are very expensive, and thus
rare outside noblemen's households, shawms are the next best thing,
carried by those guarding city gates. If no shawm is available, a good
old hunting horn is used.

As for "low" music, the more melodic variety, where might you
hear it? The answer is, almost anywhere. You will always hear musicians at a nobleman's feast—no fewer than 175 of them are employed
at the knighting of the prince of Wales (the future Edward II) in
May 1306. But you will also hear shepherds playing their flutes and
whistles in the hills. Nicholas, the Cambridge student in Chaucer's
"Miller's Tale," plays a psaltery. Absolon in "The Reeve's Tale," plays
the bagpipes, and so does the "Miller," who tells "The Miller's Tale."
The esquire serving the narrator of "The Knight's Tale" plays the
flute. Wander across the Lincolnshire manor of Sir Geoffrey Luttrell
in 1340 and you might see a peasant playing bagpipes while a female
acrobat dances before him. You might see other peasants there playing a hurdy-gurdy, nakers, bagpipes, bells, and even a portable organ.

Fourteenth-Century Musical Instruments
(excluding those still in common use)

Name	Description
Gittern	A small round-backed instrument, like a lute, but without a neck (its neck being merely an extension of its teardrop-shaped body). It has four or five pairs of strings and is plucked with a quill plectrum.
Citole	A stringed instrument peculiar to the thirteenth and fourteenth centuries. It has a holly-leaf-shaped body, a short neck, a flat back, and three or four pairs of strings which are plucked with the fingers.
Shawm	A long wooden pipe with a double reed at the top (like a modern bassoon) and a bell shape at the bottom. It resembles the main pipe in a set of bagpipes but is much larger.
Nakers	Metal drums, like kettledrums, played in pairs suspended from the waist or, in much larger versions, set on the ground.
Tabor	A handheld drum which includes skins stretched across a frame (often played in conjunction with a pipe or whistle).
Rebec	A fiddle with three strings, played with a bow.
Psaltery	A metal-stringed medieval harp in a square box, plucked with a quill.
Clarion	A curved trumpet.
Sackbut	An extended and curved trumpet, like a trombone.
Crumhorn	A curved shawm with a mouthpiece over the reed, allowing it to be used by men on horseback (otherwise they would break the reed with every jolt).
Hurdy-gurdy	A stringed instrument played by the rotation of a hand-driven wheel passing over the strings (often played in conjunction with bagpipes).

Come the time when ale is brewed at the church house—a scotale as it is called—then all the working instruments in the village will be put to good use for the enjoyment of all.

Where there is music, there is dancing. As minstrelsy includes acrobats and jugglers, often dancers and musicians will travel together, as a troupe. Sometimes their performances are extraordinary: doing a handstand on the points of two swords while being accompanied by a man playing two recorders at once is a trick you ought to see.[9] Acrobats doing tumbling acts to the beating of a drum, or young women dancing the erotic dance of Salome are hardly less eye-catching. Alternatively, the spectacle of a dancing bear or a performing dog might be built into a musical act. At a local event, like a scotale, you are likely to find the common folk taking to their feet. Most amateur dancing takes the form of "caroling" in which everyone holds hands or links arms in a big circle and skips to the left or right around the leader, who stands in the middle singing the verses of the song. Everyone taking part in the dance then sings the chorus. Unlike modern carols, which tend to be exclusively religious, many medieval ones are bawdy songs, and some are downright lascivious. As caroling sometimes takes place in a churchyard (dancing outdoors is as common as indoors), a number of priests are offended. Some will wag a finger at you and remind you of the story told by William of Malmesbury—how, on a Christmas night, twelve dancers went caroling around the church and persuaded the priest's daughter to join them. The priest forbade the dancers from dancing and swore that, if they did not desist, he would see to it that they would carry on dancing for the next twelve months. And so it occurred: his curse worked, their hands became inseparably joined, and they could not stop dancing. When the priest's son ran out to try to save his sister, he seized her hand and her arm broke off like a rotten stick.[10]

Pay no attention to William of Malmesbury or finger-wagging priests. Everyone dances. Everyone sings. In the churches and monasteries the clergy sing Mass. English descants (three-part polyphony) and motets are written in the last decades of the century. By 1400 England is on the brink of becoming the preeminent musical kingdom in Christendom. Even the royal family write and play music (the recorder and the harp). In his youth, Henry IV and his first wife, Mary de Bohun, sing and play music together. Chaucer writes of how

Henry's mother, Lady Lancaster, used to "dance so comely, carol and sing so sweetly . . . that never has Heaven seen so blissful a treasure." Even his Wife of Bath declares that "I could dance to a small harp, and sing like any nightingale, when I had downed a draught of mellow wine." Similarly Chaucer says of the carpenter's newly wedded wife in "The Miller's Tale" that her voice is "as brisk and clear as any swallow perching on a barn." At the start of William Langland's *Piers Plowman,* a whole crowd of people come over the hill making music. Everyone sings and dances. In a century of plague, war and suffering, you have to.

Plays

Traveling from town to town you are likely at some point to come across a performance of a play. The most common sorts are the miracle plays and mystery plays which are performed on feast days in the larger towns. The sequences of plays performed at York, Chester, and Wakefield are very famous, but you will also find mystery plays put on at Coventry, Newcastle, Norwich, Northampton, Brome (in Suffolk), Bath, Beverley, Bristol, Canterbury, Ipswich, Leicester, Worcester, Lincoln, London (at Clerkenwell), and Exeter.[11] Worcester's five plays or pageants are enshrined in the town ordinances (see chapter 10).

The York mystery plays are held on the movable feast of Corpus Christi (the Thursday after Trinity Sunday). Each of the city guilds (otherwise known as "mysteries"—hence the name) takes responsibility for putting on one play. The Guild of Goldsmiths stages the "Coming of the Three Kings" and the Guild of Shipwrights performs the "Building of the Ark." How apt, you might think, until you realize that the "Death of Christ" is performed by the Guild of Butchers. Each play is staged on a two-storey wagon, with a stage on the upper floor and the changing room and props area below. These wagons are pulled between the twelve watching places around the city. So all you have to do is turn up at one of these places and see each play brought to you, over the course of several days.

Just as people in the modern world rush to see a star performer, so medieval people flock to see a familiar religious play. In medieval drama it is God, or Jesus, or the martyred saints who are the stars.

Members of the audience can become passionately involved. Watch
the fascination on their faces as they see Christ suffering, in agony, giving his life on the cross *for them*. When the crowd watches Eve tempt-
ing Adam with an apple in the Garden of Eden, they see the Fall of
Man for themselves. Similarly, the reenactment of Noah and the Flood
symbolizes the destruction of evil people and their desire to escape
damnation. They can see with their own eyes a representation of what
might happen to them if they do not repent of their sins. In a century
which has seen God smite nearly half the population with plague,
these scenes have huge resonance.

Another variety of religious play you might come across is the morality play. As performed by clerks, in Latin, these have a long history,
dating back centuries. In English they are only just beginning to take
off. The great morality plays, such as *The Somonynge of Everyman*, will
not be written until the fifteenth century. Nevertheless, if you come
across a drama which takes the form of a battle between the vices and
the virtues, then you are probably watching an early morality play.
Characters will include the likes of "Ignorance," "Humility," "Covetousness," "Good Deeds," "Riot," and so on. They are nowhere near as
sensational as the sufferings of the saints and less meaningful to most
people than the Bible-history plays. But you might find the characters
of the Devil and Old Vice entertaining, even if for the wrong reasons.

Akin to the morality plays are some of the mummers' performances and other "disguising games" put on at Christmas and other
feasts. In these the emphasis is not so much on words and scripts as
on roles, exemplified by the masks ("mumming" is another word for
"disguising"). Heroes are pitted against "evils" such as the Cardinals of
Rome or the legendary giants Gog and Magog. Hence men must dress
up like these "evils." Edward III is very keen on such disguising games,
and he makes them into spectacular events. For Christmas 1338 he
places an order for "eighty-six plain masks, fourteen masks with long
beards, fifteen baboons' heads of linen . . . and twelve ells of canvas
to make a forest, with a wooden pillory and a cucking stool."[12] Nine
years later (Christmas 1347), for the games held at Guildford, the king
orders "fourteen masks with women's faces, fourteen with the faces
of bearded men, fourteen with the silver faces of angels, fourteen
painted cloaks, fourteen dragons' heads . . . fourteen pheasant heads,
fourteen pairs of wings for these heads, fourteen tunics painted with

the eyes of pheasants' wings, fourteen swans' heads, fourteen pairs of wings for the swans, fourteen painted linen tunics, and fourteen tunics painted with stars."[13] In 1348, you can even see the king himself take part in one of these mummings, dressed as a giant bird.[14]

Mumming does not always involve a play. Witness the procession that takes place before the ten-year-old Prince Richard at Kennington in late January 1377. One hundred and thirty London citizens "disguised and well horsed in a mummery" ride out of the city via Newgate, with trumpets, sackbuts, cornets, shawms, and other instruments and "innumerable torches of wax." They pass over London Bridge and ride through Southwark to Kennington, where the young prince is staying with his mother, his uncles, and many other lords. They all ride two by two, in red coats and gowns, with masks on their faces. Forty-eight of them come as esquires, and forty-eight as knights. Then follows one "richly arrayed like an emperor" and another man "attired like a pope." After these follow twenty-four cardinals and "eight or ten men with black masks, as if they are legates from foreign princes." When they have all entered the courtyard, they alight from their horses and enter the hall. The prince and his mother and the lords come out of the chamber into the hall, and the mummers salute them. The leading mummers place a pair of dice on the table before the prince and wager him a golden bowl. There is quiet . . . The prince rolls the dice . . . He wins! Next the mummers wager a golden cup. Young Richard rolls . . . He wins again! Thirdly they bet a golden ring. And yes, you've guessed. The dice are loaded in the prince's favor. The mummers give gold rings to everyone present, and so begins a feast, and music sounds, and the prince and the lords dance with the mummers.[15]

No account of playacting would be complete without mentioning satire. Just as sarcasm is an essential element of everyday humor, so too reversing the order of things is considered a worthwhile and telling joke. In many great households satirical games are played at Christmas. Household roles are reversed. Chief officers are forced to act as menial servants for a short while, and a kitchen servant might be set up as a steward or lord. What is interesting is that underlying all this mockery is an acute awareness that at any moment the order of things really might be reversed. The Wheel of Fortune—which lifts men up only to set them down in their pride—is a familiar image to all medieval people. And it is this understanding of vainglory that powers medieval satire.

One of the best and most entertaining examples you will see of this is a street show mocking the Church in general, and the Premonstratensian Order in particular—its chief monastery being that of Sempringham. The Premonstratensians are most famous for having both male and female canons in one double monastery, under one roof. Sniggering in some secular quarters is inevitable. In 1348 a group of players pull up their wagon in the streets of Exeter and set about performing their play about the "Order of Brothelyngham." The authorities' reaction is shock. The bishop writes immediately to his archdeacon:

> We have heard, not without grave disquietude, that a certain abominable sect of evil-minded men, named the Order of Brothelyngham, has lately arisen by inspiration of him who sows all evil deeds. These men . . . have chosen for their head a certain crazy lunatic, of temper most suitable to their evil purpose. This man they call their abbot; they dress him in monastic garb, set him up upon a stage, and adore him as their idol. Then, at the sound of a horn, which they have chosen instead of a bell, they lead him through the streets and lanes of the city of Exeter with a great throng of horse and foot at their heels. In this procession they lay hold of any clergymen or laymen whom they find in their way—even taking some from their own houses—and hold them with rash, headlong and sometimes sacrilegious spirit until they have extorted from them sums of money by way of *sacrifice* . . . And though they seem to do this under colour and cloak of buffoonery, it is without doubt nothing but theft . . . [16]

In medieval theater, it is not so much bad reviews which you need to fear but excommunication.

Jousting

If any spectacle from the fourteenth century can be said to be essential viewing, it has to be the joust. Where else, in all history, can you see the richest, most powerful, and most privileged members of society risk injury and death for the sake of your entertainment? Where else in all history can you find rich and powerful men *paying* for the privilege of breaking their necks and goring one another in public? One cannot imagine Roman emperors and senators fighting publicly. Nor Elizabethan seadogs, nor Jacobean courtiers. As for our modern political leaders, business leaders, and aristocrats, forget it. There is something intrinsically medieval about the practice of the great and the good risking injury and death for no other reason but to prove themselves worthy of their status through public demonstrations of their courage, strength, and skill.

In case you have any doubt about the level of danger, let it be stated unequivocally. Jousting is dangerous. A late-fourteenth-century knight will be wearing armor weighing eighty to one hundred pounds. He himself weighs perhaps two hundred pounds. He will be seated on a high saddle, charging toward you with a closing speed of about forty miles an hour on a destrier weighing more than a thousand pounds, and carrying a lance in which all the force is concentrated on a steel tip. Even if the tip is capped or blunt, the point of impact will be no more than a few square inches. The force exerted through that small area is enormous. If your opponent makes contact with your helmet, the blow may be likened to being knocked about the head with a hammer weighing half a ton, wielded at a speed of forty miles an hour. If you could not fall off your horse under such circumstances, you would not survive. Of course, falling off still means crashing to the ground from a galloping horse, in heavy armor, which is sometimes fatal in itself.

This form of joust—knights tilting at each other—is a refinement of a much older form of tournament, the *behourd* or *mêlée*, which is even more dangerous. It reflects the origins of tournaments—a means of training knights to charge together, in formation, to sweep an enemy off the battlefield. When introduced in the late eleventh century it stuns Christendom: a Byzantine princess, seeing a massed charge of Frankish knights for the first time, exclaims that they could punch a hole in the walls of Constantinople. The massed charge of knights continues to dominate warfare throughout the twelfth and thirteenth centuries. But in 1314, at Bannockburn, the Scots come up with a solution. They use an arrangement called a "schiltrom." This is a group of a few dozen men with very long pikes—sixteen feet long—all radiating outward. Those in the schiltrom all dig one end of their pikes into the ground and let the horses run towards them, holding the pikes steady while the horses impale themselves. In the same battle the Scots king, Robert Bruce, uses caltrops: small spheres of metal with four sharpened points emanating, so one point is always directed upwards. These make it harder for horses to charge along roads and stay in formation, as the caltrops stick in their hooves and cause them to stumble. With these developments, the massed charge is nearing the end of its useful life. When the English perfect the use of massed longbows in formation in the 1330s, the massed charge can no longer be seen as a significant strategic advantage, and the *behourd* is no longer a useful training exercise.

Even if you do witness a *behourd* in the fourteenth century, it will be unlike those of old. In the thirteenth century they are little more than battles without a cause. Men are frequently killed: in 1241 eighty knights are killed in a single tournament. But you need to remember that in those days it is said that a man "is not fit for battle unless he has seen his own blood flow, and heard his teeth crunch under the blow of an opponent."[17] A fourteenth-century *behourd* is gentle by comparison—undertaken for the benefit of the spectators rather than actual military training. One takes place at the tournament to celebrate the marriage of Edward III and Queen Philippa in 1328 at York. This is one of the last. After 1330, tilting, with all its chivalric rules, takes over.

In the mid-1330s, in the Marches of Scotland, the English and the Scots develop the joust of war. These are solo jousts—tilting with sharpened steel lances—not just for the sake of sport but also to kill the opponent. At one such joust held in front of Edward III at Roxburgh in 1341, Henry, earl of Derby, takes part in a joust of war against William Douglas and mortally wounds him. At a similar joust held shortly afterwards at Berwick to celebrate Christmas, the same earl leads a team of twenty English knights in a series of jousts of war against twenty Scottish knights. Only three men are killed, although many more are badly injured, including some who cheat by wearing armor *underneath* their clothes. What, you say—surely one wears armor on top of one's clothes? Not in this case. Astonishingly, both sides agreed before the joust not to wear any protective clothing.[18]

The jousts of war held in Scotland differ from a proper battle in one important respect. Killing your opponent is part of the sport. Prizes are given out by heralds afterwards to those survivors who have performed well, so it clearly has the character of a sporting event. One cannot say the same for the jousts of war held on March 27, 1351. On this occasion thirty English and Breton knights and esquires meet thirty French and Breton knights and esquires in a great *behourd*. Nine of the thirty on the English side are killed. On this basis, jousts of war might be considered the only sport in history with odds worse than Russian roulette. However, an armed struggle in which men are trying to kill one another is normally called war. This *behourd* comes to be known as the Battle of the Thirty. There is a very thin line between staging a joust of war for sport and the prosecution of an international armed conflict. Basically it comes down to handing out prizes for style.

Jousts of peace—jousts with capped lances—are normally only occasionally fatal. Sometimes a knight breaks his neck falling from his horse, or the strap on his helmet breaks, or a lance finds a chink between two pieces of his armor, but most injuries amount to no more than serious bruising, loss of teeth, and broken bones. Hence they are joyous occasions. Huge crowds attend them. People flirt, eat lavishly, and drink copiously, and they watch their aristocratic champions fight one another. When the great tournament of St. Inglevert takes place in spring 1390, very large numbers of Englishmen cross the Channel just to watch. For forty days, three French knights try to hold their own against all comers—from England, Spain, Germany, Hungary, and Bohemia—and the three of them manage it, despite having to fight more than a hundred visiting knights, some of them with uncapped lances. Of course all three Frenchmen are repeatedly injured in this extraordinarily uneven contest and have to have days off to recover, but all three survive. The kingdom of France is overjoyed at their success, which must be considered the greatest international sporting fixture of the century.

Hunting and Hawking

If the aristocracy are keen for the common folk to attend their jousts, then the opposite applies to their hunting parties. Hunting is one of the favorite occupations of the rich, and it is a carefully guarded privilege. All the designated forests are reserved as the hunting grounds of the king. Although the Charter of the Forest allows for lords to hunt a deer or two if they are passing through, this does not apply to anyone else. Very heavy fines are levied on any commoner who kills the king's deer. The same applies to lordly chases. If the king makes a grant of a chase to one of his lords, then this is tantamount to allowing him to have a private forest, where he and his friends can hunt roe deer, fallow deer, and red deer. If he grants him only "free warren," then he may keep a pack of hounds but only hunt foxes, hares, coneys, and pheasants with them, not deer or boar.

A huge amount of money is spent on hunting. In the 1360s, Edward III spends about £80 per year on keeping a pack of dogs and maintaining the huntsmen to look after them and train them.[19] His pack numbers between fifty and seventy dogs, and while lordly hunting packs are normally between a quarter and half this size, keeping them is nonetheless expensive. This is especially the case as aristocratic ladies also like to hunt, and they often do so together, so their packs of hounds need to be transported around the country.[20] Costs include food, huntsmen and fewterers (those in charge of the pack), and transportation. And of course the purchase price of the dogs themselves: greyhounds, mastiffs, alaunts (the heaviest and most vicious), spaniels (so called because they are believed to come from Spain), setters, and lymers (scenting hounds). Of course you need to add the cost of such trinkets as silver collars for the favorite dogs and silver-rimmed hunting horns. Even the costume in which to go hunting is expensive. In 1343 the king pays for green Turkish cloth to make the tunics and courtpieces for eleven earls and knights to accompany him on a hunt, plus mulberry Turkish cloth for his mother, his wife, and four other ladies for the same hunt, and more Turkish cloth for tunics for the fifteen esquires accompanying them.[21]

What people choose to hunt depends on personal taste as well as the law. The acknowledged expert, Edward, eldest son of the duke of York, will assure you that, while the hart (red deer) is the best to hunt, the buck (fallow deer) is the best to eat. He also praises the wild boar as a quarry, on the grounds of danger; according to him a boar can rip a man in half with its tusks. Sadly, it is unlikely you will be able to chase after wild boar. They have been hunted nearly to extinction in Britain: to see them you really have to be with the king, as his royal cousins on the continent send them as occasional presents. So, if you would take Edward of York's advice, hunt the hare instead. Although he is the son of a duke, he actually prefers hunting hares to deer, wild boar, and everything else. The reason, he explains, is that you can hunt them all year round, in the morning as well as in the evening. The hare is a clever, watchful, and swift quarry. It can run for miles and so can give the hounds a good long chase before being caught. Rabbits and coneys by comparison are good for nothing but trapping in nets, so they can be skinned, eaten, and turned into fur-trimmed hoods.

If you think hunting with dogs is an expensive business—and it most certainly is—then you will be astonished to realize how much money is spent on falconry. In 1368 Edward III's falconry expenses exceed £600—more than most lords' annual incomes. Although this is exceptional, even in a normal year he spends more than £200. He employs forty falconers, each at 2d per day, and spends up to 1½d feeding each of his fifty to sixty birds.[22] In 1373 he orders all the bridges in Oxfordshire to be repaired, simply because he wishes to go hawking. His fanaticism for the sport leads him to introduce legislation protecting trained birds of prey. From 1363, if you find a falcon, tiercel, lanner, or any other lost hawk, you must hand it over to the sheriff so it may be reclaimed by its owner.

With royal patronage on this scale, you might think that you will have no chance of pursuing this sport yourself. But even a moderately prosperous townsman may have a bird of prey, as revealed in the inventory of William Harecourt of Boston (see chapter 7). William has two hawks and "a gentle falcon," altogether worth £10. There is a whole social hierarchy to bird ownership. The rarest and most splendid breeds are deemed suitable for kings. Golden eagles are considered suitable only for emperors—although, as there are only two emperors in all of the known world (the Holy Roman Emperor and the Byzantine Emperor), there is some flexibility on this. For a king, a gerfalcon is considered appropriate. These magnificent hunters are used to catch large birds, like herons and cranes. Edward III has several and spends more on them than he does on most of his servants. A lord is supposed to hunt with a peregrine falcon, a knight with a saker, an esquire with a lanner, and a yeoman with a goshawk. Sparrowhawks are usually associated with priests (the clergy hunt with birds as well as dogs). In practice, lords are not too fussy about what they hunt with. The young Edward II hunts partridges with sparrowhawks and spaniels, and Edward III keeps goshawks, tiercels, lanners, and several other lesser birds, not just gerfalcons.[23] William Harecourt's birds are probably goshawks or sparrowhawks. The reason his falcon is called "gentle" is not on account of its behavior to other birds—it rips those to pieces—but because it is suitable for a gentleman.

You will see hawks and falcons in all sorts of places. People have special perches made for them in their bedchambers. They have silver chains made for them. In the streets you will frequently see men walking along with falcons on their arms, or a woman accompanied by a servant holding her bird. This is not just to show off; if you own a valuable bird you want it to become familiar with the noise of the street and your surroundings, so it does not become scared and fly away. Problems arise when young men take their birds into church to attend Mass, or into the law courts. Even the clergy are reprimanded from time to time for paying too much attention to their birds of prey. You might have thought that the abbot of Westminster would be above such things. Not at all: in 1368, worried that his favorite falcon might die, he pays 6d for a wax image to be made of the bird, which he places on the altar of the church as a votive offering for its recovery. The following year he has a special collar made for his greyhound, called "Sturdy."[24]

Popular Games

If you wander through the streets of any town or city, you will come across children playing familiar games. Some will have odd names, such as "pinch me" or "hoodman blind," but basically they are the same as modern playground games. Hoodman blind, for example, is blind man's buff but without a blindfold; in the fourteenth century all one has to do is to turn the child's hood back to front. Catching butterflies in nets and pilfering eggs from birds' nests are perennial favorites, as are "follow the leader" and "heads or tails." Froissart mentions playing these as a child, as well as "hare and hounds," "cow's horn in the salt," spinning tops, telling riddles, and blowing soap bubbles in a pipe.

Most popular amusements are concerned with contests of some variety. At a fair you will be able to watch wrestling competitions, with the traditional prize of a ram for the winner.[25] As you would expect, clergymen do not approve. According to a Dominican preacher, wrestling is "a foul and unthrifty occupation." Thomas Brinton, bishop of Rochester, puts wrestling matches in the same category as gluttony, chatting idly in the market, and anything else which distracts the populace from listening to his sermons.[26] Realistically, the wrestling is far less likely to offend your sensibilities than the baiting competitions. Men and women enthusiastically crowd around to watch bearbaiting and bullbaiting (chained bears and bulls being beaten with sticks and attacked by mastiffs and alaunts until they are driven near crazy with rage). Boys and girls love cockfighting and traditionally organize their own contests on Shrove Tuesday, asking adults to bet on their birds.[27] They also love cockbaiting. This involves throwing sticks and stones at a tethered chicken. If you are a hungry boy, killing the bird with a well-aimed stone is only part of the fun; taking it home for supper is equally satisfying.

As you travel around medieval England you will come across a sport described by some contemporaries as "abominable . . . more common, undignified and worthless than any other game, rarely ending but with some loss, accident or disadvantage to the players themselves." This is football.[28] Although that description might sound a little negative, when you watch your first match, you too might think it is nothing more than a *mêlée* without weapons. Shrove Tuesday is when a large number of football matches are held. The captains of the two sides meet and decide how many people are going to play: dozens or even hundreds might take part in a celebratory game between two parishes. It is the number of people involved which determines the size of the playing field. If more than a hundred people are playing, the goals (two at each end) might be several miles apart. If only two tithings are competing, there might be only a few hundred yards separating them. Balls range in size from small, stuffed leather ones, not dissimilar to a modern cricket ball, to large ones, made of stitched pigs' bladders filled with dried peas.

Rules in football (or "campball" as it is normally called, a "camp" being a field) vary from place to place and from match to match. There is no offside rule—or any other rule for that matter. For much of the century the only law relating to football is the one banning it. In 1314 the mayor of London forbids the game being played anywhere near the city. Edward III bans it throughout the kingdom in 1331 and again in 1363. It creates a lot of noise. It distracts people from practicing their archery. It results in damage to property and crops; many people are injured and some are killed. The case of William de Spalding is perhaps the most famous. In 1321 William petitions the pope for an indulgence on account of the fact that, during a game of football, a friend of his died from running into him so hard that his knife went through its sheath and into his friend.[29] When medieval people roll on the ground during a football match, you can be sure they are not feigning an injury in the hope of being awarded a penalty.

Other outdoor games you are likely to see include bowls, ball-and-stick games (especially hockey), quoits, and tennis. Lawn tennis is not wholly a nineteenth-century invention; its earlier "real tennis" form comes to England in the late fourteenth century. Chaucer refers to it as being played with racquets in *Troilus and Criseyde,* and it is also mentioned in *The Second Shepherds' Play,* the most entertaining of the Wakefield Cycle of mystery plays. Do not expect to see a neat rectangular court marked with lines. You might not even have a racquet. The word "tennis" refers to the server's exclamation as he serves. When played without a racquet it is called handball or *jeu de paume.* Some towns have bylaws banning it from being played in their high streets or in their guildhalls. Your fellow players will sling a net across the road and *that* will become your court. You score extra points for hitting the ball through someone's window. Blocking the street with a net and hitting around a hard projectile is hardly the way for young men to endear themselves to the urban authorities.

The foremost popular sport is archery. When Edward III prohibits football, it is very much with the idea that men should spend their time shooting longbows. From 1337 archery becomes almost the only legal sport for commoners. There is a rather extreme proclamation in that year that the penalty for playing any other game is death.[30] In 1363 this proclamation is reissued in a slightly more lenient form, forbidding men playing quoits, handball, football, hockey, coursing, and cockfighting on pain of imprisonment. Archery is once more emphasized as the sole sport approved by the king. There is good reason, as you will realize when someone puts a longbow in your hand. It is about six feet long, made of yew, with the springy sapwood on the outside and the harder exterior wood facing you. The handle is six inches in circumference. A hemp string is looped over notches in each end, or over horn nooks. The arrows, made of poplar or ash, are about three feet long and an inch thick, tipped with a three-inch-long iron arrowhead, and fletched with goose or peacock feathers. In order to draw a longbow to its fullest extent, and shoot the arrow for five hundred yards, you have to bend it so far that the flight of your arrow is beside your ear. The string at that point should make an angle of ninety degrees. The draw weight is 100 to 170 pounds.[31] That requires huge strength. In addition, archers in battle are expected to repeat the action of shooting this weapon between six and ten times *per minute.* Men need to start practicing with small bows from about the age of seven in order to build up the muscles necessary and to continue practicing in adulthood—hence the king's proclamations of 1337 and 1363. Before long, men are trying to split sticks standing in the ground at a distance of a hundred yards or more and telling tales of Robin Hood as a folk hero.[32] And England has the most powerful army in Christendom.

When the weather keeps you from playing bowls, and when archery practice is over, what indoor games might you play? Cards are unlikely. Although there are card makers in France in the fourteenth century, card games have yet to catch on in England—although they soon will. Alternatives are "cross and pile" and dice. The former you know as heads or tails (all medieval silver pennies have a cross on one side and the king's head on the other). Dice games are enormously popular. Many members of the aristocracy lose large sums on a regular basis. Even Edward III is prone to losing at dice, paying out nearly £4 on a single day in 1333.[33] The same goes for his much more conscientious grandson, the future Henry IV, in 1390.[34] If you want to join in, the most popular versions are raffle (using three dice) and hazard (two dice). Remember that, despite the huge popularity of these games, not everyone looks kindly on those who play. People have been known to gamble themselves into poverty and even nakedness—their clothes left in pawn with the tavern keeper who advances them the money for their last bet. For this reason, several towns ban dicing altogether.

Chess, tables (a form of backgammon), draughts (checkers), and merrils (nine men's morris) are the most popular board games. Chess is the preferred indoor game of the aristocracy. Some sets contain

carved pieces of the most exquisite workmanship. In 1322 Lord Mortimer has a nutmeg gaming table and a gold-painted chess set, and his
wife has a set of ivory chessmen.[35] Henry IV commissions new chess
pieces while he is in Venice in 1392.[36] Edward III, his mother, and sister
all have crystal and jasper chessboards, with carved crystal (white) and
jasper (black) pieces to match.[37] If you challenge any of these lords and
ladies to a game, bear in mind that the modern rules have not yet fully
evolved. Although it is accepted by about 1300 that pawns can move
two squares on their first go, the queen (normally called the prime
minister) can only move *one* square in each direction. Also, the bishops
(or elephants, as they are still called) can only move two squares along
their diagonals, although they can jump over other pieces.

Pilgrimages

Let us say you find yourself out at sea in a storm. The small ship is
pitching and rolling terribly, falling forty feet or more with each huge
wave. The wind is blowing incessantly, and it is beginning to grow
dark. The ship's captain has already cut down the mast, and over the
noise of the wind you hear a shout that water is pouring into the hold.
The horses down there in their panic have kicked at the caulked timbers and are now swimming, terrified, in the bilge. The ship is beginning to break up. All the lanterns are out, the spray and sea fret having
extinguished every flame. You are cold, soaked, in utter darkness. You
have no idea in which direction the nearest land is. At such moments
there are only two things you can do. The first is to tie yourself and
any members of your family with you to a large piece of wood, so that
when your bodies are found, you can all be buried together—which is
what the earl of Warwick decides to do in the fifteenth century. The
second is to pray. If you go for the latter option, then the chances are
that your conscience will enter into a sort of bargaining arrangement
with God in which, in return for your being returned to dry land
safely, you will promise to go on a pilgrimage. Or two pilgrimages. Or
five, as Edward III does when caught in a storm at sea in 1343.

Reasons for going on pilgrimage vary greatly. You might do so
because of a pact with God, or the saints, along the lines mentioned
above. Or you might want to confess to a particular sin. If you have

committed adultery, for example, you might not wish to confess to the priest if he happens to be your spouse's brother. Traveling a long way to confess, and atone, is the perfect answer. On the other hand, if you need to get away from where you live—if you *wish* to commit adultery, for example—what better way is there of leaving the gossips in your home town? Chaucer's Wife of Bath, who has "thrice been to Jerusalem" and has also visited the other major shrines of the Three Kings at Cologne, Santiago de Compostela, and Rome, is well versed in the art of love. She is only too happy to conflate "wandering" geographically with "straying" morally. On a more conscientious level, a man who has fought in a battle might wish to undertake a pilgrimage in order to give thanks to God for his survival. A man or woman whose spouse is extremely sick might wish to leave his or her side to make a pilgrimage to a nearby shrine, to ask for the help of a local saint. The merchant in Chaucer's "Sea Captain's Tale" remarks to his wife that failed merchants go on pilgrimages to escape their creditors.

As that motley crew who set out with Chaucer on his journey to Canterbury indicate, you do not have to wear any special clothes to be a pilgrim. The knight—returning from a military expedition—wears a coarse tunic besmirched with rust from his chain mail. His esquire wears a short, embroidered gown, with sleeves cut long and wide, in the latest fashion. The knight's servant, a yeoman, wears his coat and hood of green, carries a bow, arrows, sword, and dagger and wears a leather bracer on his arm. The merchant is adorned in a multicolored tunic with a fashionable beaver hat from Flanders. Thus everyone is wearing their usual attire, from the sea captain in his knee-length woollen gown to the Wife of Bath and the physician, "dressed in Persian blue and scarlet, lined with taffeta and fine sarsenet." It is true that you will come across the odd die-hard pilgrim wearing the traditional long, wide-sleeved cassock of russet, patched with crosses. No doubt he is also carrying a staff and wearing a wide-brimmed hat adorned with scallop shells and pewter badges from all the holy places he has visited. But such stereotypes are the minority and more like traveling hermits than pilgrims.

If you set out on a pilgrimage, the chances are that very soon you will fall in with other pilgrims heading in the same direction. It is a good idea to stay with them, for the sake of company and entertainment as well as the extra security. As the theologian Wycliffe points

out to the archbishop of Canterbury, when men and women go on
pilgrimages they sing "wanton songs" and play bagpipes, so that

> every town they pass through, what with the noise of their singing
> and the sound of their piping, and the jangling of their Canterbury
> bells, and the barking of dogs after them, they make more noise than
> the king would, if he were to come that way, with all his clarions and
> minstrels.[38]

Interestingly the archbishop does not deny such accusations, but
rather explains that the reason why the pilgrims have pipers and sing-
ers in their company is so that, if one of them should strike his foot
upon a stone and make it bleed, the musicians can take away the pain
with mirth.

Where should you go on your pilgrimage? For the truly dedicated
there are the great pilgrimage destinations of Santiago de Compostela
in northern Spain, Rome, the shrine of the Three Kings in Cologne,
and Jerusalem itself. However these journeys are expensive, time-
consuming, and dangerous. For most people, keen to go on a pilgrimage but reluctant to sail abroad, the greatest draw is not a particular
church but the choicest relics. Just as God, Jesus, and the saints are the
stars of the mystery plays, so the shrines of the saints are the most
holy destinations. Chief among these is the shrine of St. Thomas
Becket in Canterbury Cathedral. It attracts about two hundred thousand pilgrims every year, each one of them paying 1d or more to see
the sights: the place where Becket was struck down, the point of the
sword that killed him, his tomb, and so on. This generates more than
£900 yearly, not to mention the many gifts from visiting dignitaries.[39]
The shrine itself is entirely covered with plates of pure gold and studded with sapphires, diamonds, rubies, balas rubies, and emeralds, with
carved agate, jasper, and cornelian reliefs. The most stunning jewel of
all is one particular ruby, no larger than a man's thumbnail, embedded
in the wall to the right of the nearby altar. Even though the church is
quite dark, especially near the shrine, this ruby radiates an intense red
light, which causes everyone who sees it to marvel at it.[40]

With treasures like this on display, the fame of Canterbury spreads
even farther, across Europe. And so more visitors come. If you visit
you may be encouraged to buy lead and pewter ampullae: small

vessels supposedly containing holy water mixed with St. Thomas's own watered-down blood. This water is supposed to have a wide range of medicinal and spiritual properties. Alternatively, you may buy a pewter badge showing the sword that killed Becket, or a badge showing him being killed.[41] So the fame of the saint and the church is spread farther by pilgrims proudly taking these souvenirs back home. It is big business—and so is the pilgrim trade in all the other major churches where there is a saint's body. You may not be familiar with the name of St. William of Perth but income from pilgrims visiting his tomb in Rochester Cathedral pays for the central tower to be rebuilt in 1343.

Most English saints' remains may be considered "real" relics: they are actually what they purport to be. They are not pigs' bones (to use Chaucer's expression), nor are they the bones of a nondescript corpse sold on the ecclesiastical relic market. It is only to be expected that the body of St. Hugh, bishop of Lincoln, lies in his shrine in Lincoln Cathedral: he died in 1200. Even the Saxon saints' bones have, in many cases, been carefully preserved in their churches down the centuries. However a few of the major pilgrimage destinations require more explanation. Why does Walsingham Priory have a reconstruction of the house of the Virgin Mary? The reason is that someone dreamed of it, and started to build it, and miraculously the stones were moved to this site. As the priory grew in importance, the relic of the Virgin's milk was purchased by a benefactor, as was a famous image of her. You might say, therefore, that the shrine of Our Lady of Walsingham has nothing to do with the actual Virgin Mary. But this is the second most visited place of pilgrimage in England—second only to Canterbury. How does one account for this?

In order to understand the power of such places you need to understand pilgrimages from a subjective point of view: scientific objectivity will not help you. Look at the effect on those who make the journey to Walsingham. Having traveled for days—perhaps weeks—all the way from their homes, the pilgrims come at last to the Slipper Chapel, about a mile and a half from the priory. It is the first stage in the culmination of a long journey. Here they take off their shoes, so they can walk the last mile and a half to the priory barefoot, in a penitential fashion. With their feet hurting but their anticipation heightened, they sing religious songs along the way. Then

The Principal Pilgrim Destinations in England[42]

Place	Main Attraction
Beverley Minster	The shrine of St. John of Beverley, bishop of York
Bromholm Priory	The Holy Rood (a portion of the True Cross)
Bury St. Edmunds	The shrine of St. Edmund, king and martyr
Canterbury Cathedral	The shrines of St. Thomas Becket, archbishop of Canterbury, and several other archbishop-saints, including St. Dunstan
Chester Abbey	The shrine of St. Werburgh, abbess
Chichester Cathedral	The shrine of St. Richard de Wyche, bishop of Chichester
Crowland Abbey	The shrine of St. Guthlac, hermit
Durham Cathedral	The shrine of St. Cuthbert, bishop of Lindisfarne
Ely Cathedral	The shrine of St. Etheldreda, queen and abbess
Glastonbury Abbey	The shrine of St. Dunstan, abbot of Glastonbury and archbishop of Canterbury (although he is actually buried at Canterbury); King Arthur and Queen Guinevere (supposedly); this is also believed to be the first Christian church, said to be built by Joseph of Arimathea
Hailes Abbey	The Holy Blood
Hereford Cathedral	The shrine of St. Walter Cantilupe, bishop of Hereford
Lichfield Cathedral	The shrine of St. Chad, bishop of Mercia and Lindsey
Lincoln Cathedral	The shrines of St. Hugh, bishop of Lincoln, and St. Hugh of Lincoln, martyr
Norwich Cathedral	The shrine of St. William, martyr
Oxford Priory	The shrine of St. Frideswide, abbess of Oxford

Ripon Cathedral	The shrine of St. Wilfrid, bishop of Hexham
Rochester Cathedral	The shrines of St. William of Perth, pilgrim and martyr, and St. Paulinus, bishop of York and Rochester
Walsingham Priory	The replica of the house of the Virgin Mary in Nazareth, together with her image and some of her milk
Westminster Abbey	The shrine of St. Edward the Confessor, king of England
Winchester Cathedral	The shrine of St. Swithin, bishop of Winchester
Worcester Cathedral	The shrine of St. Wulfstan, bishop of Worcester
York Minster	The shrine of St. William, archbishop of York

they come to the narrow pilgrims' gate in the walls of the precinct. Inside, they enter a small chapel where, on making an offering, they are allowed to kiss a great bone, called the finger bone of St. Peter. They are then conducted in solemn silence to a thatched building where there are two wells, famed for their medicinal properties and for the rumor that they have the power to grant pilgrims whatever they truly desire. Having made such wishes, the pilgrims are led to the chapel of the Virgin. By this stage, they are in a state of religious ecstasy. They enter the chapel, one by one. At last they pass before the famed relic of the Holy Milk. That the milk itself is solid, and probably made of chalk, mixed with egg white, is unimportant to them.[43] What matters is not whether the relic is genuine or not but the spirit of the pilgrimage itself—a demonstration of commitment and faith.

Most great religious houses have substantial collections of relics, Canterbury Cathedral has several shrines besides that of St. Thomas Becket, including the bodies of three other archbishop-saints: St. Oda, St. Anselm, and St. Dunstan. Similar assortments of holy body parts are to be found in many lesser houses. Wimborne Minster, for example, is not one of the principal pilgrimage destinations, having

Relics in the Church of Wimborne Minster[44]

A piece of the True Cross
Part of Christ's robe
A large stone from the Holy Sepulchre
A piece of the altar upon which Christ was lifted up and offered by
   Simeon
Some hairs from Christ's beard
A piece of the scourging pillar
A shoe of St. William
Part of the thigh of St. Agatha
Some bones from St. Catherine
Part of St. Mary the Egyptian
Part of Christ's manger
A thorn from Christ's crown of thorns
One of St. Philip's teeth
Some blood from St. Thomas Becket
St. Francis's hair shirt

no famous miracle-working saint's corpse with which to draw the crowds. But nevertheless you may consider going there, if only to see "St. Francis's hair shirt." And the relics at Wimborne are mere dust compared to some dazzling artifacts preserved in overseas churches. What about going to see the sponge which was soaked with vinegar and lifted to Christ's lips while he was on the cross? Or the finger with which St. Thomas touched the rib of the risen Christ? Or some of the earth from Calvary saturated with the holy blood? All these are kept together, in the church of Santa Croce, in Italy. The same church claims also to have a piece of manna—the food with which God fed the starving Israelites. Quite extraordinary. But such claims show the confidence of the church. Few pilgrims who make the journey to Santa Croce will even imagine asking the obvious question: why was this heavenly food not eaten at the time?

Literature and Storytelling

Shocking though it may appear to you, you have something in common with these people who believe in relics, fight tournaments, and hunt with falcons. Books. Many of them see literature as a satisfying and enjoyable way to spend time. Of course, they might not actually pick up a book themselves; lords and their families, together with members of their households, are accustomed to having books read to them as they sit in the hall or chamber of an evening.[45] Nevertheless the music of a tale told well is as popular as any other form of minstrelsy and as enjoyable as literature in the modern world.

Leading this move towards the enjoyment of literature is the royal family. All the fourteenth-century kings and their spouses are keen on books. Among the many volumes in Edward II's personal possession are a Latin history of the kings of England, a biography of St. Edward the Confessor in French, a Latin prayer book, and a "romance" in French.[46] "Romance" is the term for all fiction; it does not necessarily relate to a love story—although many romances do incorporate love stories. Edward's consort, Queen Isabella, is an enthusiastic book collector. She has many volumes of religious devotion, including a spectacular apocalypse; a two-volume Bible in French; a book of sermons in French; two books of Hours of the Virgin; and various antiphonals, graduals, and missals for use in her chapel. She also owns an encyclopedia (Brunetto Latini's *Trésor*, in French) and at least two history books: *Brut* (bound with the *Trésor*) and a book about the genealogy of the royal family. She also owns at least ten romances. Among them are *The Deeds of Arthur* (bound in white leather), *Tristan and Isolda*, *Aimeric de Narbonne*, *Perceval and Gawain*, and *The Trojan War*.[47]

Ten romances suggests that Isabella is keen on reading. But this is not the full story. Not only does she borrow books from her friends, she takes books from the royal lending library. This contains at least 340 titles and is housed in the Tower of London.[48] As a younger woman, she borrows romances for herself and titles such as *The History of Normandy* and Vegetius's text on warfare for her sons. Edward III is not a bookish man but he can read and write and values books highly. Once, in 1335, he pays a hundred marks (£66 13s 4d) for a single volume. Various people give him presents of books throughout his life, and these are added to the royal library. A member of his house-hold fetches one when the king calls for something to be read to him in his chamber.

This is what book ownership means for the aristocracy: hundreds of valuable secular manuscripts in English and French, and religious manuscripts in Latin being lent, borrowed, and read aloud. Joan, Lady Mortimer, has four romances with her at Wigmore in 1322. Thomas, duke of Gloucester (youngest son of Edward III), has forty-two religious books in his private chapel at Pleshey in 1397 and eighty-four other books elsewhere in the castle, including romances such as *Le Roman de la Rose (The Romance of the Rose)*, *Hector of Troy*, *The Romance of Lancelot*, and *The Deeds of Fulk Fitzwarin*.[49] Thomas's wife is from the Bohun family, earls of Hereford, who are among the greatest patrons of book illustration of the whole century, so these are not just books which are good to listen to—many of them are wonderful to look at too. Many bishops are similarly surrounded by reading material. Richard de Bury, bishop of Durham, has so many books in his library that you have to climb over stacks of them to get to his desk. It takes five carts to take them all away after his death in 1345.[50]

Literature is a means to delight the mind and embolden the spirit. It is therefore not surprising that it is available outside noblemen's households. Pick up a book like the Auchinleck manuscript, written in the 1330s; it contains no fewer than forty-four texts in English for a well-educated Londoner to read to himself or to his wife, or for a well-educated wife to read to her husband. Flick through at random: you will come across a short account of *The Assumption of the Blessed Virgin*, then the story of *Sir Degaré*, *The Seven Sages of Rome*, *Floris and Blancheflour* (a romance), *The Sayings of the Four Philosophers*, *The Battle Abbey Roll* (a list of names of Norman knights who fought at Hastings), and the famous romance *Guy of Warwick*. Later you might read the short poem *In Praise of Women*, or the romance *Arthur and Merlin*, or *Sir Tristrem* (Tristan and Isolde), or *Sir Orfeo* (Orpheus and Eurydice). Perhaps historical tales are more to your liking? In which case you can turn to the life of Richard the Lionheart, or the life of King Alexander the Great. The whole book is a veritable library in one volume, with entertaining texts for all the family.[51]

Although literature is something shared across the centuries, the way people actually read varies considerably. All medieval books are

manuscripts—printed books do not arrive in England until the earliest imports in the 1460s—so it is worth paying the extra money for
a really good, clean text which you can read clearly, whether it be in
English or French. Because they are manuscripts, they all tend to be
valuable, so they are not the sort of things you pick up lightly. Ladies
may have reading parties in the gardens of aristocratic houses, being
read to as they sit on the grass surrounded by flowers and trees. But
reading otherwise takes place indoors. Communal readings may take
place in the hall, but private readings to the lord and his family alone,
or with invited guests in the lord's solar chamber, are also common.
Those doing the actual reading may well be hampered by the lack of
light. Candles certainly put a strain on readers' eyes. Because of this,
some wealthy individuals have wooden-rimmed spectacles (invented
by Italians in the late thirteenth century). The studious bishop of Exeter, Walter Stapledon, who dies in 1326, leaves a pair of spectacles in
his will.

The result of all these difficulties with light, text, audience, valuable
manuscripts, and spectacles is that reading is not something idly done.
Literature has more of the character of a performance than a moment
of quiet reflection. This is where the enjoyment of storytelling comes
in. As only a twentieth of the rural population can read, literature is
still a minority activity. Most storytelling is done by minstrels, or story-
tellers traveling with minstrels, who recite their stories from memory.
Nor can you separate this oral tradition from written culture and say
the two are different. Lords might listen to a story being read to them
from a book, or they might equally listen to a minstrel in the hall
recite a tale from memory. And just as some stories move from the
written word to being performed from memory, so there are stories
which begin as oral tales told at fairs and end up being written down.
The stories of Robin Hood are a good example. If you wander around
the forests of Yorkshire in the years leading up to 1318, you will meet
people who appear to be of the Robin Hood fraternity. You may even
meet an outlaw called John Little, who, in 1318, takes part in a robbery
with members of the Coterel gang.[52] You may even meet a real "Robin
Hood"—real in the sense that several men of that name are living in
and around the manor of Wakefield in the decade before 1318.[53] Probably none of these men will live up to your expectations of a bunch
of expert archers, clad in green, led by a smiling hero with a highly

refined social conscience. But within fifty years of the Coterel gang turning to crime, the deeds of Robin Hood and Little John are being celebrated up and down the country. The poet William Langland describes one of his characters in about 1377 as being able to recite rhymes about Robin Hood and the earl of Chester. Not until the next century will any Robin Hood stories be circulated in a *written* form. Thus literature and the oral tradition swap stories, to the benefit of both, and to the entertainment of the people who cannot necessarily afford books themselves.

PLEASURABLE PROSE

History books are popular in the fourteenth century—especially those written with their prospective audiences in mind. First and arguably foremost of such works is the chronicle composed towards the end of the century by Jean Froissart, a Hainaulter who spends much of his life in England. He knows Edward III and Queen Philippa personally, and he writes poems as well as history (all in French). His great chronicle is written to celebrate the extraordinary deeds of English and French knights. No other writer summons up the flavor and romance of chivalric deeds quite as well. Another entertaining writer is Jean le Bel, Froissart's compatriot and inspiration, whose work details the early part of the reign of Edward III. Similar compelling knightly histories are to be found in books by Sir Thomas Gray, who writes a chronicle while imprisoned in Scotland in the 1350s; by Robert of Avesbury, who writes about the deeds of Edward III; and by an anonymous herald, who writes about the Black Prince.

Most popular of all the available history books is the *Brut*. This racy chronicle, first written in French in about 1300 and translated into English towards the end of the century, is a history of Britain from its legendary origins to the fourteenth century. It incorporates a great deal of romance literature. For example, a large portion of the book consists of stories of Merlin and King Arthur. But actual events start to creep into this wonder-filled narrative with the coming of St. Augustine in 597; by 1300 the book has assumed the form of a series of tales of recent history, reported reasonably faithfully and written in an informative but entertaining fashion. It becomes so popular that several of those who get hold of copies start keeping them up to date, effectively writing their own chronicles. Hence the book spawns a whole new tradition of history writing. Hundreds of manuscript copies of this work are in private libraries by the end of the century, in the original French, in English, and even a few in Latin. Only one historical work is anywhere near as popular: the *Polychronicon* of Ranulph Higden, a monk of Chester, whose multivolume history of the world appeals to the laity as well as to the clergy, especially after John Trevisa translates it into English in 1387.

There is one other form of nonfiction which is also read for pleasure. Travel writing is a narrow genre which has great fascination for people as they sit around their fires of an evening. If you should join them you might be surprised to realize that it is not the late thirteenth-century journey of Marco Polo being related—manuscripts of his travels are relatively slow to reach England—but that of Sir John Mandeville. Mandeville is supposedly an Englishman from St. Albans, whose travel book is circulated in French in the second half of the century. Like Polo, he also claims to have visited the Far East, but really his knowledge comes from other writers and his own imagination. Or, rather, the imagination of the man who dreamt him up, for "Sir John Mandeville" is the literary creation of a French cleric, who invents the character and fleshes out his travels with details from older Arabic works. His relationship with his readers is like that between a saint's relics and the pilgrims who venerate them. The real value is not a matter of objective truth. When esquires and knights hear how they may find their way to Constantinople and Jerusalem, to Babylon, Egypt, Tartary, Persia, and ultimately China and India, they are drawn in. They imagine that they too can visit these wonderful places and see these fantastic riches. They picture four thousand barons drawn up in the presence of the great khan. They wince at hearing how, in the market of Cairo, men and women are traded like beasts. They shudder on hearing that, when a man dies on the island of Rybothe, the custom is for his son to decapitate his body and for priests to chop his corpse up into small pieces to feed to wild birds. Such tales are really romances; they play upon the willing suspension of disbelief as much as any tale of King Arthur. But they are important for the same reason that Arthur's tales are important. They are inspirational as well as enjoyable. Columbus will one day acknowledge his debt to Sir John Mandeville. And within a hundred years of Mandeville's travels being translated into English, an English ship will land on the shores of North America. The captain, John Cabot, will announce he has found the land of Mandeville's "great khan."

POETRY

The fourteenth century is not just the cradle of English poetry, it is its first golden age—or, at least, its first since the Conquest. Early in the century the most popular French pieces, like the old Breton lays, are translated into English versions. These are normally about a thousand lines in length and deal with a tale of King Arthur's court. The most popular titles are the anonymous *Sir Orfeo, Sir Tristrem*, and *Sir Degaré*, and Thomas Chester's *Sir Launfal*. The much-loved French classic *Roman de la Rose* is translated into English a little later (in part by Chaucer). But the real glory lies in the original English poems. These really are of quite an extraordinary range, especially considering how recent the idea of writing in the English language is. On the one hand you have the clumsy poems of the ardent nationalist Laurence Minot: hymns in praise of Edward III's military victories in Scotland and France between 1333 and 1352. On the other you have the technical brilliance of the author of *Gawain and the Green Knight*. In between you may come across devout writers like Richard Mannyng. His twelve-thousand-line poem, *Handling Sin*, has a powerful literary directness—"the tavern is the devil's knife"—and is much more than a vehicle for mere moralizing.

Such is the wealth of talent that it is difficult to know where to begin to describe the century's greatest literary creations. But one way to proceed is to draw up a shortlist for the title of the most creative writer of them all. So, with due acknowledgment of the high quality of many writers who do not fall among the top four of the century, the following should give you something to go on when looking for great literature in fourteenth-century English.

JOHN GOWER

A friend of Chaucer, who describes him as "moral Gower," he is from a family of Kentish knights—although not a knight himself. He comes to London at a relatively young age and dedicates himself to writing.

What is remarkable is that he does not just write in English, he also writes poems in French and Latin—and these are not just occasional pieces to show off. His satirical Latin poem *Vox Clamantis* (The Voice of One Clamoring) extends to more than ten thousand lines, commenting on the state of England. It takes the form of a great dream-vision in which the Peasants' Revolt is likened to a terrible apocalyptic night. All the world is turned upside down. Tame animals become wild, wild animals become frenzied, domestic animals become disobedient, and the peasantry rises. The poet flees from London as they advance, hacking and slaying people with their farm implements. As for his French poems, these include his two books of ballads and his earliest full work, *Mirour de l'Omme* (Mirror of Man). The *Mirour* extends to nearly thirty thousand lines on the origin and nature of sin and the spread of corruption through the world.

Gower's great achievement as far as English literature goes is his *Confessio Amantis* (Lover's Confession). Part of the reason for his success is his attentiveness to his audience's tastes. Although you might think that writing a poem more than thirty thousand lines long is no way to endear himself to his readers, he has a good theme—a complaint about the discord of love—and he elaborates on it in a series of elegant stories and digressions. He states in the prologue that those who try to write pure wisdom manage only to dull men's wits, and for this reason he declares his intention is to write a book "somewhat of lust and somewhat of lore, that of the less or of the more, some may delight in what I write." This is good advice to writers in all ages.

The whole great work is begun because of a chance meeting between Gower and King Richard II. As their boats pass on the Thames, Richard beckons Gower on board and asks him to write something for him personally. Of course, Gower is hugely flattered and immediately starts writing "a book for King Richard's sake, to whom belongs my allegiance, with all my heart's obeisance." After a few years, however, Gower realizes he has made a big mistake. The king is turning into a despicable tyrant and deserves no respect from Gower, let alone the dedication of his greatest literary work. Thus he scrubs out his lines promising allegiance to Richard and writes instead a dedication to Richard's cousin and rival, Henry of Lancaster (the future Henry IV). From then on until the end of his life, he is an ardent Lancastrian supporter and pours out poems in all three languages, praising the new king.

WILLIAM LANGLAND

Next on our shortlist is the writer who epitomizes medieval social criticism. William Langland is from Shropshire, born around 1325, poetically gifted and haunted by his religious conscience. He is the very opposite of a court poet like Gower. He would not be seen dead praising the king or his nobles. His *Piers Plowman* is a dream-vision on one level but it is more accurately described as a passionate and savage indictment of hypocrisy, self-aggrandizement, greed, and corruption, especially with regard to the clergy. Like much fourteenth-century English poetry, it is written in alliterative verse—that is to say that the lines are not sewn together with rhymes but with alliteration, a balanced line of two halves, with an alliterative pair of syllables in each half. A good example is the melodious first line, "In a summer season when soft was the sun"; another example is the famous line in which he sees "a fair field full of folk."

As soon as the poem begins to be copied in the 1370s it is recognized as a masterpiece. Langland's personal conviction and sense of injustice, combined with a commensurate literary skill, guarantee its success. He directly addresses the sinful ways people live their day-to-day lives. Their own characteristics and foibles are personified and addressed. He is unstinting in his criticisms of the wealthy who "in gaiety and gluttony themselves gulp down their wealth, breaking no bread for the beggar." As for the growing tendency for lords and their families to withdraw from the hall and live more private lives in their apartments, he rails against it, declaring:

> Dull is the hall, each day of the week
> When the lord and his lady like to sit elsewhere.
> Now the rule of the rich is to eat by themselves
> In a private parlour, avoiding the poor,
> Or in a chimney'd chamber, leaving the chief hall
> That was made for meals and men to eat in
> And all for sparing what will be spent by another.

In this he is like an earlier social commentator, the author of a poem called *Winner and Waster,* in which it is stressed how important it is for lords to maintain a great household (and thereby maintain their servants and the poor). In contrast, self-made men like lawyers and doctors are selfish, for they do not spend anything on anyone but themselves. But Langland's literary skill is far superior to every other social-protest poet and almost every other writer of alliterative verse. "We have no letter of our life, how long it shall last," he declares, meditating on those who take long life for granted, as if it could be conferred by royal charter, or "letter." His criticisms of the clergy for their hypocrisy are stinging:

> I teach every blind buzzard to better himself
> Abbots, I mean, and priors, and all kinds of prelates
> And parsons, and parish priests, who should preach and instruct
> All men to amend themselves, with all their might . . .
> Unlearned men may say of you that the beam lies in your eyes
> And the speck of filth has fallen, by your fault, mainly
> Into all manner of men's eyes, you maledict priests![54]

A second edition of the poem follows in the 1380s (following the Peasants' Revolt) and a third about 1390. Chaucer clearly knows of it, and several other poems are written imitating it. By the time of his death, William Langland might not be rich, and he might not have eradicated priestly hypocrisy, but he certainly has his supporters and is famous.

THE *GAWAIN* POET

If Langland has any rival as the greatest writer of alliterative verse then it is the third poet on our shortlist. Unfortunately we do not know his name. He comes from Lancashire or southern Cheshire and is well read in French romances. He knows the *Roman de la Rose,* quotes from Sir John Mandeville's travels, and is familiar with the operations of a great household, so he is almost certainly connected to a knight or a man of higher rank. But in many ways his actual identity does not matter. In four poems—*Sir Gawain and the Green Knight, Pearl, Cleanliness,* and *Patience*—he has left a body of poetry which has a timeless appeal, so that his most famous work has become his name. Consider this description of Jonah entering the body of the whale:

Like a speck entering by a minister door, so mighty are its jaws,
Jonah passes by the gills, through slime and gore,
He reels in through a gullet, that seems to him a road,
Tumbling about, yes, head over heels,
Till he staggers to a place as broad as a hall,
. Then he finds his feet and gropes all about
And stands up in its belly, which stinks like the devil,
His is a sorry plight, amid grease pungent as Hell.

The greatness of this poet lies in his range. He can describe the inside
of a whale in a vivid poetic manner. And he can describe, with great
tenderness, a little pearl, neatly enclosed in gold, which is beyond
comparison with any to be found, even in the East.

So round, so radiant in each array,
So small, so smooth her sides were,
Wheresover I judged gems gay,
I set her singly above them all.
Alas! I lost her in a garden,
Through grass to ground she fell away.
Wounded by love, by love forsaken,
I mourn that pearl without a flaw.

And only as you read the following stanzas do you realize, with a
tender but painful shock, that he is not talking about an actual pearl
but about his infant daughter, Marguerite, who has died although
not two years old. She is the one who has fallen "through grass to
ground." Now she lies in that garden, amid flowers, under a mound
of earth. And it is heart-wrenching "to think of her colour, clad in
earth—oh earth, you mar a merry jewel." As he mourns her, he grows
chill with cold, and a terrible grief touches his heart, and despite the
power of his reason and belief in the comfort of Christ, he is overcome. In the dream-vision which follows he sees his daughter as a
little queen of Heaven, and, from the far side of a stream, she speaks
to him, teaching him through faith to accept her death. But he cannot
resist going forward, to try and touch her. On entering the cold water
of the stream, he awakes suddenly—only to find himself stretched on
her grave.

Pearl, together with *Cleanliness* and *Patience*, would be enough to secure a place on this shortlist for this poet. However, a still greater work may be ascribed to him: the greatest Arthurian poem of them all: *Sir Gawain and the Green Knight*.

The setting is the New Year feast at Camelot, and Arthur and all his knights are looking forward to some new event, when in strides a huge knight clad entirely in green. This knight is carrying an axe, and he challenges any man dining at Arthur's table to exchange blows with him. He will accept the first blow and then, after twelve months, the man who wielded it must seek him out at the Green Chapel and accept a blow from him in return. Sir Gawain, Arthur's youngest knight, accepts the challenge and steps forward. "Take now your grim tool," the Green Knight says, "and let's see how you knock." "Gladly, sir, forsooth," says Gawain, as he lifts the axe. The Green Knight exposes his neck, ready for the blow, and remains steady as Gawain brings the axe down and cuts off his head. To the astonishment of all, the knight's headless body does not fall. Instead it steps forward, reaches down, and lifts his head (which has rolled under the table). Laughing loudly, the head repeats the grim challenge. Sir Gawain must accept a blow from the knight at the Green Chapel in twelve months' time.

At this stage, it looks as if Sir Gawain's readiness to accept the knight's challenge was a big mistake. Nevertheless, when the time comes he does not flinch. He rides off on his horse, Gringolet, "far from his friends a forsaken man, scaling many cliffs in country unknown," challenging the guardians of river crossings to duels and winning them all. On Christmas Eve, after many days searching for the Green Chapel, he comes to a castle. He asks for accommodation, and the lord of the castle allows him to stay for three days, telling him that his quest is over, for the Green Chapel is just two miles away. The only condition of his stay is that Gawain must share with the lord everything he receives in the castle.

The lord goes hunting each day, leaving Sir Gawain in the company of his beautiful wife. Despite her ardent attempts to seduce him, all he gives her are kisses. Mindful of his promise to share everything he receives, he exchanges these kisses with the lord each evening, receiving in return the game caught during the day's hunt. On the third day, the lady gives him her girdle as a token of her desire to sleep with him. This Gawain conceals from his host, exchanging only the day's kisses.

Then he goes to the Green Chapel. There he meets the Green Knight and, true to his promise, Gawain lays his neck bare to the axe. The Green Knight swings his axe and brings the axe down suddenly. But he gives him just a nick with the blade. The Green Knight then takes off his helmet and reveals himself to be Gawain's host, the lord of the castle. He is fully aware of the secret gift of the girdle. The whole episode has been a test of loyalty and courage, and Gawain has come through in style, with nothing against his honor but the concealment of the lady's love token.

Any prospective traveler in medieval England will be delighted by this poem. It is not just the narrative structure and the subtlety of the twists of the plot, the commentary on men being snared by feminine charm, nor even the full characterization of the main players. Fourteenth-century England comes alive more in this poem than perhaps any other single work of literature. Small evocative details come across as tapestry-like delights, such as the point where Gawain is seated on a chair beside the fireplace in the castle, with cushions beneath him and a large fur-lined mantle thrown over his lap. Or the evocative description of the morning in the castle:

> In the faint light before dawn folk were stirring
> Guests who had to go gave orders to their grooms
> Who busied themselves briskly with the beasts, saddling,
> Trimming their tackle and tying on the luggage.[55]

That this writer was the same man who described the inside of Jonah's whale and the poignant loss of an infant daughter is deeply impressive. Not many poets have the ability both to convey intense personal emotion and to write entertainingly and meaningfully on a popular subject for a wide audience. That an unknown man can do both so brilliantly is something of a marvel. And so it is astonishing that almost no one knows these works. If you wish to pick up a copy of *Pearl* or *Gawain and the Green Knight,* you will ask the copyists in the London and Oxford bookshops in vain. Just one manuscript survives down the centuries, in the dark and quiet, keeping this poet's genius alive.

GEOFFREY CHAUCER

Finally we come to the man himself, a true genius of the English language, the great poet of love between men and women, of carnal desire, of men's talents and follies, of the virtues and foibles of women, and—above all else—of good-humored wit. Without Chaucer, any visit to the fourteenth century would be a less enjoyable experience.

He is a Londoner by birth. His father is John Chaucer, a vintner, who sails to the Low Countries in Edward III's household in 1338. Because of this link with the royal family, Geoffrey is placed in the household of Elizabeth, the king's daughter-in-law. He does not go to university, and from this he no doubt takes his healthy skepticism of scholarship (as he puts it, "the greatest clerks be not the wisest men"). At about the age of eighteen, in 1359, he goes to France in the king's army. There he gets captured. Fortunately Edward III comes to his rescue and pays £16 towards his ransom. In the mid-1360s he marries Philippa de Roët, sister of Katherine Swynford. Soon afterwards he begins a series of journeys to France and Italy on behalf of the king. In this way he acquires a great familiarity with Italian vernacular literature—particularly the works of Dante, Boccaccio, and Petrarch—as well as the metrical rhymes of French poetry. These give him the necessary forms and structures in which to create an English style which is harmonious to listen to and completely flexible, enabling him to express wit, observation, emotion, and ideas.

It is the human interest in his poetry which places Chaucer at the very pinnacle of English medieval literature. In his *Book of the Duchess,* written about 1369 or 1370, after the death of the young duchess of Lancaster, he writes very movingly of her loss, of her "goodly sweet speech," and how she was "the chief mirror of all the feast," and how a gathering in her absence was "like a crown without jewels." This is no mere forelock tugging—he knew the duchess well—it is genuine elegy. When you read his description of her countenance—where he describes her eyes as "good, glad and sad"—you know he is recalling the way she looked at him and remembering her presence with great affection.

Chaucer writes many works in English, and into all of them he breathes his skill, his love of people, his generosity of spirit, and his lively interest in the ideas and stories of the world. Particularly recommended among his middle period works are *The House of Fame, The*

Parliament of Fowls, and *Troilus and Criseyde.* The lament of Anelida, betrayed by her lover in *Anelida and Arcite,* is heartrending.

> Alas what has become of your gentleness,
> Your words full of pleasure and humbleness,
> Your observance in so modest a manner,
> Your waiting, and your close attendance
> On me, whom you called your mistress,
> Your sovereign lady in the world here?
> Alas, is there neither word nor cheer
> You vouchsafe upon my heaviness?
> Alas your love, I buy it all too dear.

Chaucer is not just a poet of swooning heartbroken women and beautiful dead duchesses. He is also a poet of the living. In what is by far his most famous work. *The Canterbury Tales,* he takes you through the houses of the poor as well as the rich. In "The Nun's Priest's Tale" we see "a poor widow, somewhat stooping with age, dwelling in a narrow cottage, beside a wood, standing in a dale." We hear of her simple life, "for little was her cattle and her rent," and how she kept herself and her two daughters, with three pigs, three cows and one sheep. We see inside her cottage: "full sooty was her bower, as was her hall, in which she ate many a slender meal." Thus he conjures up a picture of her two-roomed cottage, with an open central fire and smoke that gets everywhere. Then he turns to the widow herself:

> Her diet matched the cottage where she lived
> Repletion never made her sick.
> A temper diet was all her physic,
> And exercise, and heart's sufficience . . .
> No wine she drank, neither white nor red,
> Her board was served with white and black—
> Milk and brown bread—in which she found no lack,
> Fried bacon and sometimes an egg or two.

This is great description, but readers' delight in Chaucer's poetry lies in his descriptions of people. For example, among the Canterbury pilgrims there is a nun, a prioress

That in her smiling was full simple and coy
Her greatest oath was but "By St. Eloy!"
And she was called Madame Eglentyne.
Full well she sang the service divine,
Entuned in her nose full sweetly . . .
In eating she was well taught withall;
She let no morsel from her lips fall
Nor wet her fingers deep in her sauce.
Well could she carry a morsel and ensure
That no drop of it fell upon her breast . . .
Her upper lip she wiped so clean
That in her cup no grease was seen
When she had drunken up her draught . . .
But then to speak of her conscience
She was so charitable and so piteous
She would weep if she saw a mouse
Caught in a trap, if it were dead or bled.
She had small lap dogs, which she fed
With roasted meat, and milk, and wastel bread.

Such images of character are a real strength of Chaucer's writing: sometimes he can describe a man in just a few words, as in the brilliant image of "the smiler with the knife beneath his cloak." And yet he also has the ability to put thoughts into the mouths of the characters he so vividly describes. This is where he goes beyond the readers' expectations. Not only can he illustrate the backdrop, and not only can he describe the character, he can make the people come alive, with all their desires, fears, deceitfulness, lustfulness, and cheating. In words he paints their souls. Moreover he can do this for any group he chooses, rich or poor, men or women, without prejudice. Just listen to the speech he gives to his Wife of Bath, addressing one of her husbands:

You say that leaking roofs and smoke
And chiding wives make men flee
From their homes. For heaven's sake!
What's wrong with you, so to speak?
You say we wives our vices hide
Until we're wed, and then we show them—

> Well, that's the proverb of a shrew.
> You say that oxen, mules, horses and hounds
> Can be tried out at the sales stands
> And basins, lavers, and things men buy
> Like spoons and stools, and such utensils
> As pots, and clothes and dresses too—
> But wives you're not allowed to try
> Until we're wedded. Old, dotard shrew!

It's lively stuff, and it gets livelier, far livelier, as the wife declares that, because she pleases her husband every night in bed, he would be a miser to deny another man "to light a candle at his lantern." Chaucer even has her go so far as to admit that she seduced a twenty-year-old lad on the day her fourth husband was buried. He shows you the character without judging her. And it is all to good purpose, for, having created such a strong character, he can then put into her mouth all sorts of home truths that cannot possibly be said by a man:

> For trusteth well, it is impossible
> That any clerk will speak good of wives
> (unless they be saints' holy lives).
> Who drew the picture of the lion? Who?
> By God! If women had written stories
> As clerks do, within their oratories,
> They would have described more wickedness
> Than all the sons of Adam might redress.

And so he hits his mark. The question of "who drew the picture of the lion" is an allusion to one of Aesop's fables, in which a lion, seeing a picture of a man killing a lion, remarks that the picture would have been different if the lion had drawn it. And it perfectly suits Chaucer's wit to use a strident woman to argue on *his* behalf that women have been badly portrayed in literature because most stories are written by men. There is a certain irony that it is a man writing this, in the Middle Ages—hardly an age of sexual equality.

Chaucer's brilliance is not lost on his contemporaries. Gower, in his *Confessio Amantis,* has the goddess Venus address Chaucer as "my disciple and my poet." Another contemporary calls him "the most noble philosophical poet in English" and praises him for his "goodness of gentle manly speech."[56] All three kings in his lifetime, Edward III, Richard II, and Henry IV, appreciate him and give him presents—income, wine, employment, and a free house to live in above Aldgate. His manuscripts are regularly copied and widely circulated; even French writers praise him. This gentle man with a love of good women and good men, and a ready wit and a fluent pen, with an understanding of lust, covetousness, cowardice, envy, guilt, and all the less desirable traits of his contemporaries, is able to win hearts and entertain minds everywhere, and seemingly without effort. How many writers can describe sex in such a way that you know they are smiling as they compose the lines?

> They go to bed, as is meet and right
> For although wives be full holy things
> They must, patiently, undertake at night
> Such manner of necessities to please
> The folk who wedded them with rings
> And lay a little holiness aside.

Picture him in the 1390s, standing about five feet six inches high, with a paunch, and a forked white beard, walking along the street to his house above Aldgate, with a pile of vellum rolls under his arm, as people pass by in their hoods and motley clothes.[57] When he gets there, there is no wife waiting for him. Philippa has died a few years earlier. Instead he goes up to his chamber alone, and, as he puts it in his earlier poem, *The House of Fame*, "there, dumb as any stone, you sit before another book, till fully dazed is your look, and there you live a hermit's life." But as he sits there, working out *The Canterbury Tales*, he has the most incredible vision. For what survives today of his great work is just a small portion of what he envisages writing. He plans that his thirty pilgrims will each tell two stories on the way from Southwark to Canterbury and two on the way home again. That is a total of 120 "Canterbury tales." As it stands, he only completes one tale each for twenty-two of the pilgrims and two for himself. On this basis, it is the greatest unfinished work in the English language.

Envoi

So we come to the end of the fourteenth century. From first setting out on the road and seeing Exeter Cathedral rising high above the city walls, and smelling the smells of Shitbrook, we have encountered all manner of things: irregular measures of time, roast beaver and puffin, medicinal baths of boiled puppies, and traitors' corpses cut into quarters. We have discussed how young the people are, how credulous and how violent. We have seen the precarious state of justice and how people live constantly on the verge of starvation, illness, and death. We have caught glimpses of the clothes, the musical instruments, and what people do for fun. Although there are many more things we could say about fourteenth-century England, probably enough has been said for you to have an idea of what it is like, prior to setting out. Only one question remains to be answered. Why should you want to set out in the first place? Or, to put it more bluntly, why should you actually want to see the living past? Is the fourteenth century not better left for dead, a pile of parchments, monastic ruins, and museum artifacts?

This book began as a "virtual reality" description of a faraway country. In actual fact it has touched upon a more profound subject, namely the way we see the past. How does a vision of medieval England as a living community differ from one in which it is described as dead? In traditional history, what we can say about the past is dictated by the selection and interpretation of evidence. Paradoxically, this same evidence imposes a series of boundaries, limiting the research questions we can ask and what we can claim to know about the past. Academic historians cannot discuss the past itself; they can only discuss evidence and the questions arising from that evidence. As postmodernist philosophers have repeatedly pointed out—to the great frustration of many historians—the past has gone, never to return. Knowledge of it *as it actually was* is impossible.[1]

That is all very well. But, as this book has shown, there is no reason why we cannot consider medieval England as a living community. It is just another place in time, like France in the twenty-first century, or Germany in the twentieth, and so on. Knowledge of it *as it actually was* might be difficult—impossible even—but so is knowledge of England as it actually was yesterday. If we accept that the evidence available to us in writing about any place in any time is always going to be partial and incomplete—including a modern country which could be physically visited (for you cannot see all of it at once, or meet everyone)—then certainly one can write a guidebook to medieval England which in theory is as comprehensive and accurate as a guidebook to a modern country.

This is the crux of the matter. If medieval England is treated as dead and buried, what one can say about it is strictly limited by the questions arising from the evidence. However, if treated as a living place, the only limits are the experience of the author and his perception of the requirements, interests, and curiosity of his readers. We can ask any question we like about the past and set about answering it to the best of our knowledge and ability. The implications of this for understanding the nature of history itself, and for transcending the postmodern questioning of historical knowledge, are huge. History is no longer just an extended academic exercise—it can be anything you want it to be. If the limits of history are set by the questions that people (not just historians) ask about the past, then history is as wide as the public imagination. As stated in the introduction, the result is a new way of conceiving history—"free history" as I have described it in a theoretical essay, "What Isn't History?" written alongside this book.[2]

There lies an even more profound implication of the "living past." What does it reveal about us individually and collectively in relation to time? This is perhaps the most interesting aspect of the whole concept. Through it we can see ourselves collectively living for hundreds of years, and in so doing we can see ourselves change. Cast your mind back to the different standards of hygiene and justice in the fourteenth century. If we look at these aspects of life and judge them as dirty and cruel, we are really only describing our own perceptions as viewed from the modern world. There is nothing wrong in doing this, it just is very present-centered. It says more about us *now* than it does about us in the fourteenth century (or any other age for that matter; the past is all dirty and cruel in the modern popular imagination, with the exception of the Romans, who are just cruel). However, if we start to consider medieval people as alive—the women cleaning their houses, for instance, gathering up the dirty rushes in the hall, putting new ones down, shooing the dogs outside, wiping the table, laying out the tablecloth, rinsing the wooden bowls, scouring iron and brass pans, scrubbing the family's tunics and linen, polishing the silver spoons, and sweeping the yard—we can begin to see these people in relation to their contemporaries. Of course they are not all filthy. Many are proud of the clean state of their houses—like their modern counterparts—regardless of the judgments of people in six hundred years' time. We may consider them excessively cruel for beating their children and dogs, but this is judging them by our standards, not their own. As we have seen, fourteenth-century parents who do not beat their children are thought to be acting irresponsibly.

In this way we can begin to appreciate the changes in almost every aspect of life, from the age structure of the population to the changing nature of the diseases we suffer. Everything changes. What does not change? Only that these people, like us, are human, and have urges, needs, and challenges; and that these are continually shifting. If we really want to understand what humanity is, and how adaptable we are, we must see ourselves as a constantly living, evolving race—always on the very cusp of a vast and unimaginable future, whether we live in the fourteenth century or the twenty-first—and in no way dead until the whitened bones of the last human being lie abandoned on the sand.

Over the course of the century described in this book, more than ten million people live and die in England. Many die in infancy. Many die young. Some die twitching on the end of a rope. Some die screaming in smoke-filled rooms. Some perish in battle, many in pain and terror. Some die fighting so furiously that, in their moment of glory, they *want* to die heroically. Many more die alone, shivering, scared, and feverish with plague. Whatever the manner of their deaths, at some point in their lives there is also some joy, be it the childhood treat of a spoonful of jam or the thrill of an illicit kiss, or seeing a grandchild. At the end of the day—at the end of the century—this is what history is. History is not just about the analysis of evidence, unrolling vellum documents or answering exam papers. It is not about judging the dead. It is about understanding the meaning of the past—to realize the whole evolving human story over centuries, not just our own lifetimes.

Somewhere in the 1370s, a beautiful young noblewoman is looking at Geoffrey Chaucer. She is teasing him, looking him in the eye, smiling, and laughing. She will remain there like that, forever, just like the Canterbury pilgrims will forever be riding along together on their way to Canterbury, never to return. Men are gathered around the poet, listening as he describes the woman, her smiling laughter, so fresh and fair and free. They can tell he still feels the sadness of her death. What they hear is what we hear. We might interpret the lines differently, and we might misunderstand a few words (we are, after all, strangers in this century), but some inkling of Chaucer's affection for this woman comes across to his audience—to them, to us, and everyone in between. Whole centuries of us are there in the echoing hall of time, listening to Chaucer's poem. If Gower takes the storyteller's place, we may hear about the terror of the Peasants' Revolt; if Froissart, the chivalric gloss of knightly warfare in France; if Langland, the injustice of the clergy; if the *Gawain* poet, his grief for his little girl, his pearl. And in listening we may offer all these men, women, and children a degree of recognition: the sort of dignified memory and sympathy which today we offer to those who gave their lives in war.

You may not agree. You may think that living for the here and now is all that matters. Or you may think that judging the past as dirty and cruel in some way establishes our superiority over our ancestors. But if you believe that we are the inheritors of a living, vibrant past, and that an understanding of what we have been is vital to an understanding of what we are today, and what we will be in the future, then you may find yourself becoming a thoughtful time traveler, setting out on the highway of human history, guided by Chaucer down all the alleys of fourteenth-century life. You might even consider joining him and his companions in that tavern, the Tabard, in Southwark, and yourself becoming a pilgrim. At the very least you will hear some good stories.

Notes

1. The Landscape

1. These cries are from the early fifteenth-century poem "London Lick-penny," once attributed to John Lydgate. A similar series of fourteenth-century cries appears at the end of the prologue of Langland's *Piers Plowman*.

2. The figures in this table come from the poll tax returns of 1377 as tabulated in Hoskins, *Local History*, pp. 277–78. The population estimates are drawn from the fact that in sixteenth-century England about 32 percent of the population was aged below fourteen, and that this figure is a reasonable estimate for the late fourteenth century. In addition it allows for two other facts: (1) that clergy and beggars were exempt from paying, and (2) some of those who ought to have paid did not. As a result, the approximate population figures are based on the estimate of 6 percent of the total civic population being taxpayers, the remainder being children under fourteen (32 percent), clergy (2 percent), beggars and evaders (6 percent collectively). The areas of doubt are the proportions of beggars and evaders. If 10 percent of the population evaded, and another 10 percent were beggars, then taxpayers amount to only about 46 percent of the population, and the estimates given here should be increased accordingly. Some cities have been ascribed much larger populations than these tax-based figures indicate. Winchester has been calculated to have had a population of about 7,000 to 8,000 in 1400, three times this estimate for 1377. See Dyer, *Standards*, p. 189. The figure for Plymouth is no longer extant; 1,700 is Professor Hoskins's estimate. Note: Gloucester and Oxford did not become cities until the sixteenth century.

3. If the population of England was 2.5 million, and at least 170,000 lived in these thirty cities, and the two hundred other towns and cities have

an average population of 650, the proportion is 12 percent. Other writers have suggested that as little as 5 percent of the population were urban dwellers in the fourteenth century (e.g., Platt, *Medieval Town*, p. 15, drawing on the work of Lawrence Stone) but these figures are based on the assumption that only 150,000 people lived in towns. About 190,000 people lived in just the largest forty (as listed by Hoskins). So the figure is much more likely to be nearer the one in seven (14.3 percent) in Dyer, *Standards*, p. 23, or even the one in five (20 percent) suggested in Dyer, *Everyday Life*, xv.

4. Riley (ed.), *Memorials*, p. 279.

5. Riley (ed.), *Memorials*, p. 67. The other details in this paragraph are from the same source.

6. Brown, Colvin and Taylor, *History of the King's Works*, I, p. 534.

7. Second only to Edward III's work at Windsor Castle. See Brown, Colvin, and Taylor, *History of the King's Works*, I, p. 157.

8. This example dates from the thirteenth century. See Scott (ed.), *Every One a Witness*, p. 42.

9. Henry III was importing fir boards from Norway in the previous century. See Wood, *Medieval House*, pp. 395–96.

10. Details on the trees have been taken from Salzman, *Building* (mainly from chapter 16), Esmond and Jeanette Harris, *Guinness Book of Trees*, and Cantor, *Medieval Landscape*, p. 63. The reference to elm (which is otherwise not noted in these books) is due to the reference in Riley (ed.), *Memorials* to an elm too near the walls of London being cut down in the year 1314. Elms also apparently grew in the twelfth century at Smithfield (Morley, *Bartholomew Fair*, p. 9) and, most famously, at Tyburn.

11. Quoted in Coulton (ed.), *Social Life*, p. 2.

12. Dyer, *Standards*, pp. 258–60.

13. Hoskins, *English Landscape*, p. 118.

14. Barnwell and Adams, *House Within*, p. 4.

15. This figure has been extrapolated from (a) the area of the county as described in Lewis, *Topographical Dictionary*, and (b) a population figure derived from the poll tax returns of 1377 on the same basis as the figures for the towns. It presumes that 40 percent of the population was thirteen years of age or less, or clergy, or avoided the tax illegally or were destitute. It is not possible directly to compare these figures with modern ones, as the definition of a town is differently composed in the modern world (motor transport and the railways having changed the relationships of towns and rural areas). Surrey—which had a rural density of about 40 people per square mile in 1377—now has in excess of 2,000 for those areas that have *not* been swallowed by Greater London.

It may be of interest that Norfolk, Suffolk, and Huntingdonshire (all of which remain largely rural) have between 381 and 442 people per square mile (according to the 2001 census); Rutland has 243 people per square mile, Dorset 389, Devon 273, and Cornwall 378. Cumberland and Westmorland, combined as Cumbria, have 218. The population density of modern counties is determined to a far greater extent by the towns and industries within them, rather than the nature and landscape of the county itself.

2. The People

1. See Hatcher, *Plague, Population,* pp. 13–14, 71. The poll tax of 1377, supposedly leveled on all the population over fourteen, with only the clergy and the naked poor excepted, shows 1,386,196 taxpayers. If one uses the same estimate used above—that this represents about 60 percent of the total population—then the total would be about 2.31 million. Earlier estimates are normally extrapolated from this, taking into consideration the level of plague-related mortality in 1348–49, 1361, and 1368. The population was continuously falling for a whole century, to the 1440s. See Hatcher, *Plague, Population,* p. 27.

2. Dyer, *Standards,* p. 182.

3. Hatcher, *Plague, Population,* especially p. 71. The age-related statistics here are estimates based on the sixteenth-century figures in Wrigley and Schofield, *Population History,* especially table A3.1 on p. 528. These statistics relate to a life expectancy at age twenty-five of about thirty-two more years, which is in excess of the estimates of between twenty and thirty years at age twenty in both Dyer, *Standards,* p. 182 and Harvey, *Living and Dying,* p. 128 (both based on fifteenth-century data). Hence the slight revision downwards in average age from the figures in Wrigley and Schofield's table A3.1. Modern figures have been taken from the website of the Office of National Statistics.

4. Dyer, *Standards,* pp. 316–17. See also Roberts and Manchester, *Archaeology of Disease,* p. 57, which gives 171.8 cm (5 ft. 7 in.) for men.

5. Greene, *Medieval Monasteries,* p. 161.

6. Roberts and Manchester, *Archaeology of Disease,* p. 75.

7. Coulton, *Chaucer,* p. 13.

8. Cokayne, *Complete Peerage,* V, p. 629.

9. Very briefly there is also the rank of marquis. Robert de Vere was created marquis of Dublin in 1385, a title that he technically still held after being created duke of Ireland the following year and did not become extinct until his death in 1392. In addition, John Beaufort was created

marquis of Dorset by Richard II in 1397; his brother Henry IV stripped him of the title on his return to England in 1399. It was then declared "un-English."

10. For Isabella, see Mortimer, *Greatest Traitor*, p. 171. For Gaunt, see Dyer, *Standards*, p. 36, where his income is given as £12,474; Goodman, *John of Gaunt*, p. 341 gives his income for the years ending at Michaelmas 1394 and 1395 as "about £10,000 net (£11,750 gross)."

11. See Dyer, *Standards*, pp. 30–31 for incomes of the knightage and lesser gentry.

12. The number of parliamentary prelates varied greatly. In 1307 fifty-four were summoned. In 1399 just twenty-six: the abbots of Peterborough, Glastonbury, St. John's Colchester, Bury St. Edmunds, Abingdon, St. Mary's York, Waltham Holy Cross, Crowland, Bardney, St. Benet Hulme, Malmesbury, Reading, St. Albans, Selby, Thorney, Battle, Westminster, St. Augustine's Canterbury, Cirencester, Evesham, St. Peter's Gloucester, Ramsey, Hyde by Winchester, Winchcombe, and Shrewsbury. In addition, the prior of Coventry was regularly summoned. Note that all the prelates in Parliament are given precedence over the earls, even though dukes are given precedence over archbishops. See *PROME*, 1399 September, introduction.

13. The medieval English dioceses are Bath and Wells, Canterbury, Chichester, Coventry and Lichfield, Ely, Exeter, Hereford, Lincoln, London, Norwich, Rochester, Salisbury, Winchester, and Worcester. The Welsh ones are Bangor, Llandaff, St. Asaph's and St. David's.

14. Dyer, *Standards*, p. 36.

15. This estimate is based on the large proportion with £50–£500 in *Valor Ecclesiasticus* as noted in Knowles and Hadcock, *Medieval Religious Houses*.

16. Dyer, *Standards*, p. 119, quoting E. A. Kosminsky, *Studies in the Agrarian History of England in the Thirteenth Century* (Oxford: 1956), pp. 216–23.

17. Coulton, *Medieval Panorama*, p. 76.

18. Finberg, *Tavistock Abbey*, p. 77.

19. A 1279 lease of a whole manor to its chief tenants is printed in Fisher and Juřica (eds.), *Documents*, pp. 102–103.

20. Dyer, *Standards*, pp. 193–94.

21. Quoted in Coulton (ed.), *Social Life*, p. 433.

22. Quoted in Leyser, *Medieval Women*, p. 97.

23. Leyser, *Medieval Women*, p. 114.

24. There are a few exceptions to this. Edward I campaigning against the Scots in his sixties is perhaps the most obvious. Roger, Lord Mortimer of Chirk, took arms against Edward II in 1322, at the age of sixty-six. Sir Thomas Erpingham took part in the battle of Agincourt (1415) at the age of sixty. Henry Percy, earl of Northumberland, rebelled several

times against Henry IV in his sixties, dying in battle at the age of sixty-six.

3. The Medieval Character

1. The story appears in Riley (ed.), *Historia Anglicana*, I, pp. 418–23. It is probably propaganda, as the outrage is terrible and yet the nunnery not mentioned. No nunnery of this size in the vicinity can be identified. Richard Barber in his *ODNB* article on Sir John Arundel points to some corroborating details though. Either way, Walsingham believed that these outrages took place. They are therefore indicative of the violence people believed was inherent in society.
2. Furnivall (ed.), *Babees Book*, p. 46.
3. Bradley (ed.), *Dialogues*, p. 9.
4. Coulton (ed.), *Social Life*, pp. 519–20.
5. Hamilton, "Character of Edward II," p. 8.
6. Mortimer, *Greatest Traitor*, p. 214.
7. Coulton (ed.), *Social Life*, p. 470.
8. Woolgar, *Great Household*, p. 1.
9. Few fourteenth-century churchwardens' accounts survive. According to the list in the appendix to Hutton, *Rise and Fall*, pp. 263–93, the earliest are Bridgwater (1318), St. Michael, Bath (1349), St. James, Hedon (1350), Ripon (1354), St. John, Glastonbury (1366), St. Augustine, Hedon (1371), St. Nicholas, Hedon (1379), and Tavistock (1392). That these cover both the north of the country and the southwest (from Yorkshire to West Devon) is a good indication that the format was more widely known in the fourteenth century than the few extant accounts suggest.
10. Kaeuper, "Two Early Lists of Literates."
11. For comparison, it has been estimated that the overall literacy level in England in 1500 was about 10 percent (Stephens, "Literacy," p. 555). An urban literacy rate of 20 percent and a rural one of 5 percent would equate to 6 percent overall, based on the 12 percent of people living in urban areas mentioned in chapter 1. As the main force of the revolution in record keeping and education was a thirteenth-century development, this 6 percent figure seems commensurate with the estimate of 10 percent in 1500, prior to the significant developments in education and literacy of the sixteenth century.
12. Hingeston (ed.), *Royal and Historical Letters*, I, pp. 421–22.
13. Mortimer, *Perfect King*, p. 360.
14. Simek, *Heaven and Earth*, pp. 61, 86.
15. "The spherical shape of the Earth was taken for granted and had been

so since Aristotle. This fact had been an integral part of scholarly knowledge since the Carolingian renaissance of the eighth century . . . By the
thirteenth century the spherical shape of the earth . . . had found its
way not only into scholarly but also popular literature." Simek, *Heaven
and Earth*, p. 25.

16. Simek, *Heaven and Earth*, pp. 88–89.

17. Simek, *Heaven and Earth*, p. 83.

18. Coulton (ed.), *Social Life*, p. 522.

19. Quoted in Gimpel, *Medieval Machine*, p. 193.

4. Basic Essentials

1. Ruffhead (ed.), *Statutes*, I, p. 311.

2. This is adapted from R. L. Poole, quoted in Cheney, *Handbook of Dates*,
p. 3.

3. Chaucer wrote a treatise on the astrolabe for his son. Henry IV's accounts refer to repairs to his astrolabes when he was earl of Derby. See
Mortimer, *Fears*, p. 154.

4. Smith (ed.), *English Gilds*, pp. 370–409. This is certainly the case in the
fifteenth century; at what date it commences is unclear; these ordinances predate Edward IV's reign but the terminology may be contemporary.

5. Dilley, "Customary Acre."

6. Finberg, *Tavistock Abbey*, p. 11*n*.

7. Hindle, *Medieval Roads*, p. 31.

8. The statistics in this paragraph are from Finberg, *Tavistock Abbey*, pp.
30–31.

9. Aspects of repute, manners and politeness have largely been taken from
Furnivall (ed.), *Babees Book*, especially "The Babees Book," "Stans Puer
ad Mansam" and John Russel's "Boke of Nurture." The notes on female
behavior are largely from "How the Good Wijf Taughte Hir Doughtir"
in the same volume.

10. Wylie states Jean de Hangest, lord de Hugueville, shook hands with
Henry IV after his audience with him at Windsor in 1400 (Wylie, *England under Henry IV*, IV, p. 263). Le Roy Ladurie refers to the unusu-
alness of handshaking among thirteenth-century French people in
Montaillou, p. 140.

11. Bradley (ed.), *Dialogues*, pp. 4–5.

12. Fisher and Juřica (eds), *Documents*, pp. 237–38.

13. Coulton, *Medieval Panorama*, p. 302.

14. I have followed *The Cambridge Urban History of Britain* in using the

spelling "guild merchant" as opposed to the more usual "gild merchant." As is well known, some of the most important cities never had
a guild merchant (London and Norwich are the most frequently cited
examples). However, as the subject is complicated, and to describe the
relationships between guilds, guild merchants, and the administration
of incorporated towns would take more space than can be warranted
here, the description of town administration has been kept simple.

15. See Bolton, *Economy,* chapter 4, "The Growth of the Market."
16. These are all from fourteenth-century cases noted in Riley (ed.), *Memorials.*
17. Mortimer, *Perfect King,* p. 210.
18. Bradley (ed.), *Dialogues,* pp. 15–16.
19. Rowe and Draisey (eds.), *Receivers' Accounts,* p. 7.
20. Dyer, *Standards,* p. 210.
21. For the carpenter and laborer, working on the estate of the bishop of
Winchester (eight manors, average), see Bolton, *Economy,* p. 71; for the
thatcher and his mate see Dyer, *Standards,* p. 215; for the royal masons
see Salzman, *Building,* pp. 70–77.
22. Erskine (ed.), *Fabric,* pp. 182–83; Salzman, *Building,* p. 72 (tilers).
23. Salzman, *Building,* p. 74.
24. Woolgar, *Great Household,* pp. 31–32.
25. This applies to building work too. See Salzman, *Building,* p. 71.

5. What to Wear

1. Riley (ed.), *Memorials,* p. 20.
2. *PROME,* 1363 October, nos 25–32; Ruffhead (ed.), *Statutes, I,* pp. 315–16.
3. TNA E 101/386/9 m. 12.
4. TNA E 101/386/18 m. 59.
5. TNA E 101/385/4 m. 28; E 101/386/18 m. 59.
6. Newton, *Fashion,* p. 4.
7. By 1334 buttons were being used on royal garments, as shown by TNA
E 101/386/18 m. 58: "fifty-six pearls delivered to the prince's tailor to
make buttons for the prince's surcote" (March, 30 1334).
8. The change in design seems to draw its inspiration from the aketon, a
quilted jacket which usually fits between the shirt and the chain mail
covering the chest. Because the aketon has to fit the body closely (as
looseness will result in rips), the sleeves cannot be cut from the same
fabric as the rest of the garment. So they have to be cut separately and
sewn onto the quilted body of the aketon (which is laced up the back).
From about 1330 the narrow-sleeve principles on which aketons are

made are applied to items for civilian dress. When Edward III ordered aketons for those who helped capture Roger Mortimer in 1330, he gave them also to two noncombatants, a physician and a clergyman (Shenton, 'Coup of 1330', pp. 23–24). Therefore the aketon by this time had a nonjousting purpose. In February 1333 Edward ordered payment of an account with his armorer, John de Cologne, which mentions "an aketon of purple velvet embroidered with a rose of pearls" and "two aketons covered in vermilion velvet and embroidered with images of parrots and other decorations" (TNA E 101/386/9). Obviously, these were meant to be seen. With regard to the purple aketon, if it served a practical function rather than a ceremonial one, it would not have been encrusted with pearls. We know that as early as 1327 Edward's own practical tourneying aketons did have gold embroidery, and so they did have a high level of decoration (like the Black Prince's extant jupon or aketon at Canterbury Cathedral). Nevertheless, the evidence that aketons were given as personal gifts to men who would never be expected to joust (let alone fight), coupled with the fact that they also might be bedizened with pearls, shows that quilted jackets were being used for noncombative purposes by 1333, and moreover they were made by a linen armorer, a member of the Guild of Tailors and Armourers to whom Edward granted a charter in 1327 (Davies and Saunders, *Merchant Taylors' Company*, pp. 13, 50). This suggests that tailored garments were being made for civilians at exactly the right time to be the impetus for the new fashion. This is supported by contemporary references to aketons being "open over the chest" (Newton, *Fashion*, p. 15). The transition was complete by 1338, for the roll of liveries of cloth and furs made by the clerk of the great wardrobe during the year September 1337–September 1338 records "fourteen ells of green taffeta and 1½ lbs of cotton in order to stuff and line a short robe made of mixed red cloth of Cologne, spattered with black dye, as well as silver, gilded, enamelled buttons, to be fashioned in the style of a doublet for the king's person . . . fourteen ells of red taffeta and 1½ lbs of cotton to line and stuff an identical garment of mixed red fustian and black spattering, which was to have similar buttons and was to be fashioned as a doublet in the same way" (TNA E 101/388/8). Having said all this, it is just possible that the credit for the new style should in fact be ascribed to Edward II, for the king's tailor Henry of Cambridge was paid in 1327 for "eight cotehardie tunics at 14d each": this predates the earliest previously noted appearance of the front-buttoned cotehardie by six years (Cunnington and Beard, *Dictionary*, p. 54).

9. Brie (ed.), *Brut*, II, pp. 296–97.

10. Courtpieces do date from much earlier than this, though they seem to be rare before the late fourteenth century. The earliest example I have

come across is the *"curtepye"* given by the king to the queen in 1334–35. This was made of brown scarlet *"oneree des gargulottes dor de les elees de soie de diverses coloures"* (TNA E 101/386/18 m. 59). Although this is clearly a female garment, and presumably was worn over a tunic (to cover the legs), it was adopted by men by 1344. The royal accounts for 1342–44 mention courtpieces for eleven earls and knights to go hunting with the king (TNA E 101/390/2 m. 1).

11. Harvey, *Living and Dying*, p. 132.

12. Some contemporary images of Richard show him completely beard-less: for example, the portraits in Westminster Abbey and the Wilton Diptych, and the image of Philip de Mezières presenting his manuscript to Richard (see plate 4). Even Richard's funeral effigy, made during his lifetime, shows him with the smallest imaginable beard and hardly any mustache. The tiniest forked beard and mustache are shown in Creton's illustrations (painted 1401–1405). Just a little more hair is visible in the illuminated initials in the Book of Statutes (St. John's College, Cambridge: MS A7) and the Shrewsbury charter.

13. Cunnington and Cunnington, *Underclothes*, p. 33.

14. Most of the descriptions of the peasant clothing of 1340 are from the illustrations in the Luttrell Psalter and, to a lesser extent, the Smithfield Decretals (both in the British Library).

15. Sources for peasant clothing for the end of the century are nowhere near as rich as the Luttrell Psalter. In addition to various British Library manuscript images online, see Basing, *Trades and Crafts*; Cunnington and Lucas, *Occupational Costume*.

16. For cosmetics see Woolgar, *Senses*, pp. 136–40, 175.

17. In 1341 a London apprentice is found with money in his two pockets. See Sharpe (ed.), *Letter Books 1337–1352*, pp. 249–75, at fol. ccxviii b.

18. All the references in this paragraph come from TNA DL 28/1/6 fol. 22r–23v (goldsmiths), fol. 24r–v (jewels).

19. See for example the famous illustration of the men at an inn in Glasgow University Library, MS Hunter 252, fol. 70. Reproduced in Thorp, *Glory of the Page*, p. 31.

20. Duby (ed.), *Private Life: Revelations*, p. 525.

21. Duby (ed.), *Private Life: Revelations*, p. 525; Woolgar, *Senses*, p. 35.

22. Mortimer, *Perfect King*, p. 100.

23. Woolgar, *Senses*, p. 35.

6. Traveling

1. See Milles, *The Gough Map*.

2. Fisher and Juřica (eds), *Documents*, p. 289.

3. Bradley (ed.), *Dialogues*, pp. 49–50.

4. Hindle, *Medieval Roads*, p. 31.

5. Henry IV did visit Devon, at least three times. However, the first two were before he was king and the last after the end of the fourteenth century. Edward II and Edward III avoided the peninsula altogether.

6. Mortimer, *Perfect King*, p. 460.

7. Hindle, *Medieval Roads*, p. 20. Another example, from 1499, is given in Coulton (ed.), *Social Life*, pp. 426–27, in which a glove merchant was drowned in a clay pit dug in a road near Aylesbury by a miller. Chaucer mentions the same problem befalling a student in "The Miller's Tale."

8. Hindle, *Medieval Roads*, pp. 41–43.

9. The Boke of St. Albans, quoted in Reeves, *Pleasures and Pastimes*, p. 103. There is a similar quotation in the book of The Menagier of Paris, according to Bayard (ed.), *Medieval Home Companion*, p. 108.

10. Woolgar, *Great Household*, p. 190.

11. Lyon, Lyon and Lucas (eds.), *Wardrobe Book*, pp. 313–27.

12. Henry IV, before his accession, purchased a St. Christopher for his messenger going to the king. See Mortimer, *Fears*, p. 154.

13. Ohler, *Medieval Traveller*, p. 97.

14. Chaplais, *Piers Gaveston*, p. 23.

15. TNA DL 10/253.

16. The actual timing of this message is a matter of inference, not precise recording. See Mortimer, *Fears*, p. 216.

17. Hill, *King's Messengers*, p. 108.

18. Woolgar, *Great Household*, p. 193.

19. TNA DL 28/1/9 fol. 6v, 7r.

20. Woolgar, *Great Household*, pp. 181–82.

21. Jusserand, *Wayfaring Life*, p. 95.

22. Jusserand, *Wayfaring Life*, p. 101.

23. Johnes (ed.), *Monstrelet*, I, p. 30.

24. Hutchinson, *Medieval Ships*, pp. 50–55.

25. Hutchinson, *Medieval Ships*, p. 44.

26. Hutchinson, *Medieval Ships*, pp. 60–61.

27. For the sake of an integrated description of a ship I have conflated the archaeological evidence of the Bremen cog (built in 1380) with a brief description of a similar ship in Boston harbor in 1373. For the Bremen cog, see Hutchinson, *Medieval Ships*, pp. 16–19. For Richard Toty's ship, see *Calendar of Inquisitions Miscellaneous*, IV (1377–1388), p. 125.

28. Hutchinson, *Medieval Ships*, p. 59.

29. Coulton, *Medieval Panorama*, p. 325.

30. Smith, *Expeditions*, pp. 23, 26.

31. The descriptions of personal hygiene on board a boat are taken from the late-fifteenth-century writings of Felix Faber, quoted at length in Duby (ed.), *Private Life: Revelations*, pp. 587–88.

7. Where to Stay

1. This is adapted from a contemporary dialogue book's passages on staying at an inn. See Bradley (ed.), *Dialogues*, pp. 49–50.
2. Woolgar, *Great Household*, p. 26; Chaucer, trans. Wright, *Canterbury Tales*, p. 149.
3. Kingsford, "London Merchant's House," pp. 137–58.
4. Eleven coconut cups survive from medieval England. See the Eton College example in Marks and Williamson (eds.), *Gothic*, item 190. As that entry makes clear, such items were very rare.
5. Riley (ed.), *Memorials*, pp. 199–200. The assumption that Hugh le Bever was a taverner is based on his valuable drinking vessels and the fact that he had six casks of wine.
6. *Calendar of Inquisitions Miscellaneous*, IV (1377–1388), p. 128.
7. Greene, *Medieval Monasteries*, p. 154. The license was granted in 1317.
8. Harvey, *Living and Dying*, p. 131.
9. Prescott, *Medieval Hospital*, pp. 137–38.
10. The dozen here refers to Queenborough (started 1361), Farleigh Hungerford (1370), Nunney (1373), Shirburn (1377), Bolton (1378), Wressle (1380), Sheriff Hutton (1382), Wingfield (1385), Bodiam (1385), Lumley (1389), Brancepeth (1391), and Penrith (1397).
11. The great hall at Ludlow Castle, dating from the end of the thirteenth century, is 60 feet by 30 feet; that of Caerphilly Castle, dating from 1326, is 70 feet by 35 feet. See Wood, *Medieval House*, pp. 62–66, for other examples.
12. Emery, *Dartington Hall*, p. 153.
13. Emery, *Dartington Hall*, p. 268, quoting TNA C 145/278 no. 37. Certain items not pertaining to the household have been omitted, e.g. the lord's armor.
14. Woolgar, *Great Household*, p. 12 (Arundel); information from English Heritage's display panels at Okehampton Castle (earl of Devon). Note that the latter differs substantially from the figure computed on the basis of bread allowances for the earl's household; it seems to be based on the livery roll.
15. Given-Wilson, *Royal Household*, p. 11. This is based on the list published in Tout, *Place of the Reign of Edward II* p. 244–81.

16. Society of Antiquaries of London, *A Collection of Ordinances and Regulations* pp. 3–4. This includes those under the authority of the controller of the household, sergeants-at-arms, esquires of the household, officers, and minstrels but does not include artificers such as builders and carpenters or serving men-at-arms. The list also seems to omit the steward, the chamberlain, and the treasurer, so is not complete.

17. Woolgar, *Great Household*, p. 8.

18. Given-Wilson, *Royal Household*, p. 278.

19. Many pictures of beds from this time do not show curtains. Some do, however, such as the early fourteenth-century Tickhill Psalter. See Woolgar, *Great Household*, p. 77. Henry IV paid for curtain hooks for his bed at the end of the century. See Mortimer, *Fears*, p. 128. The fourteenth-century French book, Wright (ed.), *La Tour–Landry*, p. 6, describes an emperor's daughters sleeping in a bed with curtains.

20. Bayard (ed.), *Medieval Home Companion*, p. 106.

21. Furnivall (ed.), *Babees Book*, pp. 179–80.

22. TNA DL 28/1/5 fol. 29r. The earliest entry for a close-stool in the *Oxford English Dictionary* is 1410.

23. The description of the toilet here is taken from the early fifteenth-century account in Furnivall (ed.), *Babees Book*, pp. 179–80.

24. In Chaucer's "Reeve's Tale," the Miller's wife leaves the room in order to answer a call of nature in the night.

25. Dyer, *Standards*, p. 170, quoting P. D. A. Harvey (ed.), *Manorial Records of Cuxham* (Oxfordshire Record Society, 1976), pp. 153–59.

8. What to Eat and Drink

1. Dyer, *Standards*, p. 262.

2. For the close relationship between harvest failure and petty crime see Hanawalt, "Economic Influences," pp. 281–97; Platt, *Medieval England*, p. 110.

3. At the peasants' feast at North Curry (Somerset) in 1314 each man of the hundred should have received two white loaves, as much ale as he could drink, a mess of beef, bacon with mustard, another mess of chicken, cheese, and candles "to burn out while they sit and drink." On Christmas Day 1347 at Hunstanton (Norfolk), Sir Hamon le Strange and his household consumed bread, two gallons of wine (12d), one big pig for the larder (4s), one small pig (6d), a swan (a gift from Lord Camoys), two hens (given as rent), and eight rabbits (two of which were a gift). See Fisher and Juřica (eds.), *Documents*, pp. 406–408.

4. Dyer, *Standards*, pp. 153–54 (Worcestershire and Norfolk), 159; Finberg, *Tavistock Abbey*, p. 98.

5. Langland, *Piers Plowman*, passus VI (B Text), lines 280–95; Langland, trans. Tiller, *Piers Plowman*, p. 81.

6. This recipe is a paraphrased version of "Hares in Padell" in Society of Antiquaries of London, *A Collection of Ordinances and Regulations*, p. 428. Although the publication of the volume as a whole relates to the royal household, not a peasant home, this section of recipes is not necessarily an exclusively royal one. It has been used here as indicative of the form of a contemporary recipe for hares. The peasant version would not include the spices.

7. Dyer, *Standards*, p. 157.

8. Riley (ed.), *Memorials*, p. 312.

9. Smith, *Expeditions*, pp. 5–34, esp. p. 19.

10. According to the *OED*, the term *"vin clairet"* originally denoted "white" or yellowish wine. No medieval accounts refer to Gascon wine as claret. A date of circa 1600 is given for it being associated with red wines from this region.

11. Creighton, *Epidemics*, I, p. 50. This should be compared to 1,334 individual brewers of ale.

12. TNA DL 28/1/9 fol. 21v (two turbots for 14s).

13. TNA E 101/388/2 m. 1.

14. Carp were purchased along with pike by Henry of Lancaster when in Venice in the 1390s. See Smith, *Expeditions*, p. 217. The Franklin in Chaucer's *Canterbury Tales* keeps pike and carp.

15. Smith, *Expeditions*, p. 97. He paid five nobles and eleven scot (Prussian) for one fresh sturgeon and one porpoise. The same account notes that two porpoises were worth twelve scot. At twenty-four scot to the noble, the sum paid for the sturgeon therefore was about $5\frac{1}{4}$ nobles, or 35s sterling.

16. For these carving terms, see Furnivall (ed.), *Babees Book*, pp. 140–48, 265.

17. TNA E 101/394/17 m. 1.

18. Harvey, *Living and Dying*, p. 69.

19. Harvey, *Living and Dying*, pp. 40–41.

20. Bradley (ed.), *Dialogues*, p. 48.

21. Harvey, *Living and Dying*, p. 54.

22. Coulton (ed.), *Social Life*, p. 405.

9. Health and Hygiene

1. Talbot, *Medicine*, plate III.

2. Quoted in Rawcliffe, *Medicine and Society*, p. 82.

3. Scott (ed.), *Every One a Witness*, p. 132, quoting John Mirfield, *Breviarum Bartholomei*.

4. Scott (ed.), *Every One a Witness,* p. 132, quoting John Mirfield, *Breviarum Bartholomei.*

5. Rawcliffe, *Medicine and Society,* p. 53.

6. Talbot, *Medicine,* p. 132.

7. Woolgar, *Senses,* pp. 118–19.

8. See the case of William Wombe in Woolgar, *Senses,* p. 129.

9. Coulton (ed.), *Social Life,* p. 45.

10. Woolgar, *Senses,* p. 132; Vigarello, *Concepts of Cleanliness,* p. 17.

11. Duby (ed.), *Private Life: Revelations,* p. 525 (Cluniacs); Harvey, *Living and Dying,* p. 134 (Benedictines).

12. Salzman, *Building,* p. 276; Woolgar, *Senses,* p. 135.

13. Furnivall (ed.), *Babees Book,* pp. 182–83.

14. This is based on the thirteenth-century French example of Montaillou. See Le Roy Ladurie, *Montaillou,* p. 142.

15. Talbot, *Medicine,* p. 112.

16. Riley (ed.), *Memorials,* pp. 400—1.

17. *Calendar of Inquisitions Miscellaneous,* IV (1377–1388), p. 72.

18. For his soap on crusade see Smith (ed.), *Expeditions,* pp. 63, 85, 164. His laundress, Isabel, was paid 6d for her hire of a washtub and board at Calais. Wylie, *England under Henry IV,* II, p. 51.

19. Woolgar, *Senses,* pp. 133–34.

20. Duby (ed.), *Private Life: Revelations,* p. 361.

21. Roberts and Manchester, *Archaeology of Disease,* pp. 48–49, 53, 58.

22. Coulton, *Social Life,* p. 507.

23. Harvey, *Living and Dying,* p. 128. The comparative figure is based on later statistics, for those few years when there were both parish registers and monastic records.

24. Quoted in Zeigler, *The Black Death,* p. 19.

25. Hatcher, *Plague, Population,* p. 22; Gottfried, *The Black Death,* p. 64.

26. The population of the United Kingdom at the time of the 1911 Census was 45,221,615. The proportion of those under the age of seventeen was about 40 percent. The official 1922 War Office report recorded total deaths, including civilian men, women and children, as 702,410 (1.55 percent of the total).

27. Hatcher, *Plague, Population,* p. 59.

28. This is taken from Agnolo di Tura's famous description. He was from Siena, but the bells were banned in England too. His description of burying his own children is one with which many English people would have been able to sympathize.

29. Creighton, *Epidemics,* I, p. 105.

30. Ormrod, "Personal Religion," p. 863.

31. Hatcher, *Plague, Population,* p. 58.

32. Evidence of pre-1492 endemic and venereal syphilis is rare and open to question. See Roberts and Manchester, *Archaeology of Disease*, p. 158.

33. Shorter, *Women's Bodies*, p. 98. The figure is drawn from sixteenth-century Aldgate, the nearest figures available in this study.

34. This figure is taken from the sixteenth-century figures in Wrigley and Schofield, *Population History*, p. 249.

35. It is often said that the Black Prince died from dysentery; this is almost certainly incorrect. Dysentery kills within a matter of weeks, as with Henry V. The Black Prince's wasting disease, which struck him in his late thirties and carried on for several years, was probably similar to that suffered by his nephew, Henry IV. See Mortimer, *Fears*, p. 435 n. 14.

36. Creighton refers to the first recorded ergot case in Britain as 1762 (Creighton, *Epidemics*, p. 57). This is surprising given that rye was certainly eaten in rye bread and in maslin bread, especially in the early fourteenth century.

37. Dyer, *Standards*, p. 209.

38. Mortimer, *Perfect King*, p. 332.

39. Talbot, *Medicine*, pp. 173–76.

40. Talbot, *Medicine*, pp. 129–30.

41. Coulton (ed.), *Social Life*, pp. 506–507.

42. Rawcliffe, *Medicine and Society*, p. 58.

43. Berkeley Castle Archives: Select Roll 39.

44. For the household ordinances of Edward II (1318) see Tout, *Place of the Reign of Edward II*, p. 251. For those of Edward III (1344–47), see Society of Antiquaries of London, *A Collection of Ordinances and Regulations*, p. 3.

45. Rawcliffe, *Medicine and Society*, p. 135.

10. The Law

1. Summerson, "Structure of Law-Enforcement," p. 314.

2. Cam, *Hundred Rolls*, p. 186.

3. Woolgar, *Senses*, p. 74.

4. Pugh, *Imprisonment*, p. 194.

5. Cam, *Hundred Rolls*, p. 71.

6. Ruffhead (ed.), *Statutes*, I, pp. 190–91 (1 Edward III cap. vii), which orders an inquiry into gaolers forcing prisoners to appeal guiltless men.

7. This typical example is from Pugh, *Wiltshire Gaol Delivery*, p. 96.

8. Summerson, "Structure of Law-Enforcement," p. 326.

9. Cam, *Hundred Rolls*, p. 137.

10. Cam, *Hundred Rolls*, pp. 70–71.

11. McKisack, *Fourteenth Century*, p. 206. A very similar series of events is found in the thirteenth-century case of William de Lisle, sheriff of Berkshire and Oxfordshire. See Cam, *Hundred Rolls*, p. 63.

12. Cam, *Hundred Rolls*, p. 135.

13. Bennett, *Life on the English Manor*, p. 203.

14. The Statute of Marlborough (1267) established that no freeholder was bound to attend his lord's manorial court unless this was specifically required of him by his charter. Bennett, *Life on the English Manor*, p. 202.

15. Bennett, *Life on the English Manor*, pp. 246–47.

16. There is widespread confusion on this point. I have followed *The Oxford Companion to Law*, p. 616.

17. Bennett, *Life on the English Manor*, pp. 197–98.

18. Bennett, *Life on the English Manor*, p. 196. As Henry of Lancaster's accounts show, when buying eggs in bulk, a dozen cost a penny. Even a retail price double this would mean sixteen eggs are less than 3d.

19. Lister (ed.), *Wakefield Court Rolls* [1313], p. 14.

20. Riley (ed.), *Memorials*, pp. 195–96.

21. These ordinances are taken from Moore (ed.), *Borough Ordinances of Cowbridge*. This roll dates from 1610–11. It is based on an earlier set of ordinances, however, and forty-five of the fifty are in the same order as the ordinances of Kenfig, Glamorgan, written in 1330. It is highly likely that the Cowbridge ordinances therefore date from the fourteenth century. While Cowbridge and Kenfig are not in England today, in the fourteenth century they come within the lordship of Glamorgan, which was in English hands, and the template for these ordinances was the set for Hereford. Cucking stools are mentioned in *OED* from the first decade of the fourteenth century.

22. Smith (ed.), *English Gilds*, pp. 370–409. These ordinances were drawn up in the reign of Edward IV. However, they are based on earlier sets of ordinances, as made clear from some statements within the document itself and by comparison with fourteenth-century ordinances from other towns. The wording has been considerably simplified.

23. Scott (ed.), *Every One a Witness*, p. 227, quoting *Calendar of the Coroner's Rolls*.

24. *PROME*, October 1399, item 16.

25. Hardy and Hardy (eds.), *Waurin 1399–1422*, p. 40.

26. *PROME*, October 1399, Introduction.

27. Jewell, *English Local Administration*, p. 141, quoting W. C. Bolland, *The Eyre of Kent*.

28. Riley (ed.), *Memorials*, pp. 492–93.

29. Wylie, *Henry V*, I, pp. 31–32.

30. Harding, *Law Courts*, p. 95.

31. Wylie, *England under Henry IV,* IV, p. 318. This event actually dates from 1410 but it may be considered indicative of the security afforded to transfers of money generally.

32. Hanawalt Westman, "The Peasant Family and Crime," p. 13.

33. Hanawalt Westman, "The Peasant Family and Crime,"pp. 14–15.

34. Platt, *Medieval England*, p. 110.

35. McKisack, *Fourteenth Century*, p. 207.

36. Details of the Folville and Coterel gangs here have been drawn from Stones, "The Folvilles of Ashby-Folville" and Bellamy, "The Coterel Gang."

37. An example is Henry Beaufort, bishop of Lincoln and later bishop of Winchester. He had a daughter, Joan, by Alice Fitzalan. See *ODNB*.

38. Woodcock, *Ecclesiastical Courts,* p. 61.

39. Cam, *Hundred Rolls*, p. 193.

40. Coulton (ed.), *Social Life,* p. 320.

41. Brie (ed.), *Brut*, II, p. 442.

11. What to Do

1. Prestwich, "Court of Edward II,' p. 61.

2. Wright (ed.), *La Tour–Landry*, p. 1.

3. Chaplais, *Piers Gaveston*, p. 78.

4. TNA E 101/387/9 m. 7.

5. TNA E 101/389/8 m. 19.

6. TNA E 101/396/11 fol.19r.

7. Society of Antiquaries of London, *A Collection of Ordinances and Regulations*, p. 3.

8. Smith, *Expeditions,* p. 137.

9. Illustrated in Reeves, *Pleasures and Pastimes*, p. 46.

10. Coulton, *Medieval Panorama*, pp. 98–99.

11. This list is from the Cambridge University website Medieval Imaginations, downloaded November 1, 2007: http://www.english.cam.ac.uk/medieval. Exeter has been added in view of the performance of the satirical *Order of Brothelyngham* play there.

12. TNA E 101/388/8 m. 4. The "cucking stool" here is actually described as a "shelving stool," the old word "shelving" here meaning "tipping" (*OED*).

13. TNA E 101/391/14 mm. 8–9.

14. Mortimer, *Perfect King*, p. 259.

15. Coulton (ed.), *Social Life*, pp. 391–92, quoting John Stow.

16. Coulton (ed.), *Social Life*, p. 493.

17. Keen, *Chivalry*, p. 88, quoting Roger of Hoveden. The detail of eighty killed at the tournament of Neuss in 1241 is from Keen, *Chivalry*, p. 87.
18. Barber and Barker, *Tournaments*, p. 34. There is uncertainty as to the places of these jousts of war. I give a different reading in Mortimer, *Perfect King*, p. 191, drawing on Lumby (ed.), *Knighton*, II, p. 23. Another version again appears in Maxwell (ed.), *Scalachronica*, p. 112.
19. Given-Wilson, *Royal Household*, p. 61.
20. Woolgar, *Great Household*, p. 193.
21. TNA E 101/390/2 m. 1.
22. Given-Wilson, *Royal Household*, p. 61.
23. Hamilton, "Character of Edward II," p. 61.
24. Coulton (ed.), *Social Life*, p. 396.
25. Chaucer's Miller "always won the ram at wrestling matches up and down the land." Chaucer, trans. Wright, *The Canterbury Tales*, p. 15.
26. Reeves, *Pleasures and Pastimes*, p. 96.
27. Woolgar, *Great Household*, p. 101.
28. Coulton, *Medieval Panorama*, pp. 83–84.
29. Coulton (ed.), *Social Life*, p. 400, quoting Froissart.
30. Coulton (ed.), *Social Life*, p. 397.
31. The description of the bow is mainly from the 1298 example described in Bradbury, *Medieval Archer*, p. 81. The note on the draw weight comes from Reeves, *Pleasures and Pastimes*, p. 98.
32. Reeves, *Pleasures and Pastimes*, pp. 98–99.
33. Mortimer, *Perfect King*, p. 103.
34. Smith, *Expeditions*, p. 107.
35. Mortimer, *Greatest Traitor*, pp. 118, 120.
36. Smith, *Expeditions*, p. 281.
37. TNA E 101/392/15 m. 1 (made for Edward III, 1360); E 101/393/4 (Isabella, 1358). Isabella had two such sets; one was given to her daughter after her death.
38. Heath, *Pilgrim Life*, pp. 43–44.
39. Heath, *Pilgrim Life*, p. 29.
40. Coulton (ed.), *Social Life*, p. 39, quoting an Italian *Relation of England* (Camden Soc., 1847).
41. Alexander and Binski, *Age of Chivalry*, pp. 222–23.
42. Alexander and Binski, *Age of Chivalry*, p. 206. Salisbury has been omitted as St. Osmund was not canonized until 1457.
43. Heath, *Pilgrim Life*, pp. 238–39.
44. Heath, *Pilgrim Life*, pp. 59–60.
45. Given-Wilson, *Royal Household*, p. 61, quoting Edward IV's Black Book, in which the custom is described as "of old."
46. Johnstone, *Edward of Carnaron*, p. 18.

47. TNA E 101/393/4 fol. 8r; Lewis, "Apocalypse of Isabella," p. 233.

48. Stratford, "Royal Library," p. 189.

49. Mortimer, *Greatest Traitor*, p. 120; Anthony Tuck, "Thomas, duke of Gloucester (1355–1397)" in *ODNB*.

50. Mortimer, *Perfect King*, pp. 34–38.

51. Shonk, "Auchinleck manuscript"; MS description on website maintained by National Library of Scotland, http://www.nls.uk/auchinleck/, downloaded November 15, 2007.

52. Bellamy, "Coterel Gang," pp. 700–701.

53. Holt, *Robin Hood*, pp. 40–50.

54. Langland, trans. Tiller, *Piers Plowman*, pp. 110–11.

55. Anon., trans. Stone, *Gawain and the Green Knight*, p. 64.

56. Douglas Gray, "Chaucer, Geoffrey (c.1340–1400)," in *ODNB*.

57. See his entry in *ODNB* for his height and appearance.

Envoi

1. Or, as Keith Jenkins succinctly puts it, "We can never really know the past . . . the gap between the past and history . . . is such that no amount of epistemological effort can bridge it" (Jenkins, *Re-thinking History*, p. 23).

2. Ian Mortimer, "What Isn't History?" pp. 454–74.

Full Titles of Works
Mentioned in the Notes

A few key texts have been of fundamental importance in writing this book. I feel obliged to single out books by Christopher Dyer, Barbara Harvey and Christopher Woolgar as particularly informative. I am also indebted to those older source-based books by G. G. Coulton, L. F. Salzman, Lucy Toulmin Smith and Henry T. Riley. But over the last twenty or so years I have looked at a large number of secondary sources and manuscripts, and visited many museums and historical sites. To try to list them all now would be tedious as well as extremely difficult. It would also suggest I had given them all equal weight. For this reason, only those works cited in a short form in the notes are listed here.

J. Alexander and P. Binski (eds.), *The Age of Chivalry: Art in Plantagenet England 1200–1400* (London: Royal Academy of Arts, 1987).

Anonymous, *Sir Gawain and the Green Knight*, 2nd ed., Brian Stone, trans. (Harmondsworth: Penguin Books, 1974). p. 64.

Richard Barber and Juliet Barker, *Tournaments: Jousts, Chivalry and Pageants in the Middle Ages* (Woodbridge: Boydell, 1989).

P. S. Barnwell and A. T. Adams, *The House Within: Interpreting Medieval Houses in Kent* (London: HMSO, 1994).

Patricia Basing, *Trades and Crafts in Medieval Manuscripts* (London: British Library, 1990).

Tania Bayard (ed.), *A Medieval Home Companion* (New York: Harper Perennial, 1991).

J. G. Bellamy, "The Coterel Gang: An Anatomy of a Band of Fourteenth-Century Criminals," *English Historical Review* 79, 313 (1964), pp. 698–717.

H. S. Bennett, *Life on the English Manor: A Study of Peasant Conditions 1150–1400* (Cambridge: Cambridge University Press, 1967).

Maggie Black, *Food and Cooking in Medieval Britain: History and Recipes* (London: Historic Buildings and Monuments Commission for England, 1985).

J. L. Bolton, *The Medieval English Economy 1150–1500* (London: Dent, 1980).

Jim Bradbury, *The Medieval Archer* (Woodbridge: Boydell, 1985; reprint 1998).

Henry Bradley (ed.), *Dialogues in French and English by William Caxton: Adapted from the Fourteenth-Century Book of Dialogues in French and Flemish* (London: Early English Text Society 1900).

F.W.D. Brie (ed.), *The Brut*, 2 vols. (London: Early English Text Society, 1906–1908).

Edward Britton, *The Community of the Vill* (Toronto: Macmillan of Canada, 1977).

R. Allen Brown, H. M. Colvin, and A. J. Taylor, *The History of the King's Works: The Middle Ages* 2 vols. (London: HMSO, 1963).

Calendar of Inquisitions Miscellaneous, vol. 4, 1377–1388 (London: HMSO, 1957).

Helen M. Cam, *The Hundred and the Hundred Rolls: An Outline of Government in Medieval England*, new ed. (London: Merlin Press, 1963).

Leonard Cantor (ed.), *The English Medieval Landscape* (London: Croom Helm, 1982).

Pierre Chaplais, *Piers Gaveston: Edward II's Adoptive Brother* (Oxford: Clarendon Press, 1994).

Geoffrey Chaucer, *The Canterbury Tales*, David Wright, trans. (Oxford: Oxford University Press, 1985).

C. R. Cheney, *Handbook of Dates for Students of English History* (London: Offices of the Royal Historical Society, 1945; reprint 1991).

G. E. Cokayne, revised by V. Gibbs, H. A. Doubleday, D. Warrand, Lord Howard de Walden, and Peter Hammond (eds.), *The Complete Peerage of England, Scotland, Ireland, Great Britain and the United Kingdom Extant, Extinct or Dormant*, 14 vols. (London: The St. Catherine Press, 1910–98).

G. G. Coulton, *Chaucer and His England*, 2nd ed. (London: Methuen & Co., 1909).

————, *Medieval Panorama* (Cambridge: Cambridge University Press, 1938).

G. G. Coulton (ed.), *Social Life in Britain from the Conquest to the Reformation* (Cambridge: Cambridge University Press, 1918).

Charles Creighton, A *History of Epidemics* in Britain, 2nd ed., 2 vols. (London: Cass, 1965).

C. Willett Cunnington and Phillis Cunnington, *The History of Underclothes* (London: Michael Joseph, 1951).

C. Willett Cunnington, Phillis Cunnington, and Charles Beard, *A Dictionary of English Costume 900–1900* (London: Adam and Charles Black, 1960).

Phillis Cunnington and Catherine Lucas, *Occupational Costume in England from the Eleventh Century to 1914* (London: Adam and Charles Black, 1967; reprint 1968).

Matthew Davies and Ann Saunders, *The History of the Merchant Taylors' Company* (Leeds: Maney, 2004).

Robert S. Dilley, "The Customary Acre: An Indeterminate Measure", *Agricultural History Review*, 23 (1975), pp. 173–76.

Georges Duby (ed.), *A History of Private Life, II: Revelations of the Medieval World*, Arthur Goldhammer, trans. (London: Belknap, 1988).

Christopher Dyer, *Everyday Life in Medieval England* 2nd ed. (London: Hambledon Press, 2000).

———, *Standards of Living in the Later Middle Ages* rev. ed. (Cambridge; Cambridge University Press, 1989).

Anthony Emery, *Dartington Hall* (Oxford: Oxford University Press, 1970).

Audrey M. Erskine (ed.), *The Accounts of the Fabric of Exeter Cathedral, 1279–1353*, vol. 24, 26, (Torquay: Devon and Cornwall Record Society 1981–83).

H.P.R. Finberg, *Tavistock Abbey: A Study in the Social and Economic History of Devon* (Cambridge: Cambridge University Press, 1951).

H.E.S. Fisher and A.R.J. Juřica (eds.), *Documents in English Economic History: England from 1000 to 1760* (London: Bell & Hyman, 1984).

Frederick J. Furnivall (ed.), *The Babees Book*, Early English Text Society 32 (1868, reprint Woodbridge: Boydell & Brewer, 1997.

Jean Gimpel, *Medieval Machine: The Industrial Revolution of the Middle Ages*, 2nd ed. (London, Wildwood House, 1988).

Chris Given-Wilson, *The Royal Household and the King's Affinity: Service, Politics and Finance in England 1360–1413* (New Haven: Yale University Press, 1986).

Chris Given-Wilson (ed.), *The Parliament Rolls of Medieval England, 1275–1504*, CD ed. (Birmingham: Scholarly Digital Editions, 2005).

Anthony Goodman, *John of Gaunt: The Exercise of Princely Power in Fourteenth-Century Europe* (Harlow: Longman, 1992).

Robert S. Gottfried, *The Black Death* (London: Hale, 1983).

J. Patrick Greene, *Medieval Monasteries* (Leicester: Leicester University Press, 1992).

J. S. Hamilton, "The Character of Edward II: The Letters of Edward of Caernarfon Reconsidered," in Gwilym Dodd and Anthony Musson (eds.), *The Reign of Edward II: New Perspectives* (Woodbridge: York Medieval Press, in association with The Boydell Press with the Centre for Medieval Studies, University of York, 2006), pp. 5–21.

B. A. Hanawalt, "Economic Influences of the Pattern of Crime," *American Journal of Legal History*, 18 (1974), pp. 281–97.

Barbara Hanawalt Westman, "The Peasant Family and Crime in Fourteenth-Century England," *The Journal of British Studies*, 13, 2 (1974), pp. 1–18.

Alan Harding, *The Law Courts of Medieval England* (London: Allen and Unwin, 1973).

Sir William Hardy and Edward L. C. P. Hardy (eds.), *A Collection of the Chronicles and Ancient Histories of Great Britain, Now Called England, by John de Wavrin, Lord of Forestel, 1399–1422* (London: HMSO, 1887).

Esmond and Jeanette Harris, *The Guinness Book of Trees* (Enfield: Guinness Superlatives, 1981).

Barbara Harvey, *Living and Dying in England 1100–1540: The Monastic Experience* (Oxford: Clarendon Press, 1993).

John Hatcher, *Plague, Population and the English Economy 1348–1530* (London: Macmillan, 1977).

Sidney Heath, *Pilgrim Life in the Middle Ages* (London: Unwin, 1911).

Mary C. Hill, *The King's Messengers 1199–1377* (London: Edward Arnold, 1961).

Paul Hindle, *Medieval Roads and Tracks* (Risborough: Shire, 2002).

F. C. Hingeston (ed.), *Royal and Historical Letters During the Reign of Henry IV, King of England and France and Lord of Ireland*, 2 vols. (London: Longman, Green, Longman and Roberts, 1860; reprint, 1964).

J. C. Holt, *Robin Hood*, rev. ed. (London: Thames and Hudson, 1989).

W. G. Hoskins, *Local History in England*, 3rd ed. (London: Longman, 1984).

———, *The Making of the English Landscape* (Hammondsworth: Penguin, 1955; reprint 1985).

G. Hutchinson, *Medieval Ships and Shipping* (Leicester: Leicester University Press, 1994).

Ronald Hutton, *The Rise and Fall of Merry England: The Ritual Year 1400–1700* (Oxford: Oxford University Press, 1994).

Keith Jenkins, *Re-thinking History*, rev. ed. (London: Routledge Classics, 2003).

Helen M. Jewell, *English Local Administration in the Middle Ages* (Newton Abbot: David and Charles, 1972).

Thomas Johnes (ed.), *The Chronicles of Enguerrand de Monstrelet,* 2 vols. (London: H. G. Bohn, 1853).

Hilda Johnstone, *Edward of Carnarvon 1284–1307* (Manchester: Manchester University Press, 1946).

J. J. Jusserand, *English Wayfaring Life in the Fourteenth Century* (London: Ernest Benn, 1889).

Richard W. Kaeuper, "Two Early Lists of Literates in England: 1334, 1373," *English Historical Review*, 99 (1984), pp. 363–69.

Maurice Keen, *Chivalry* (London: Yale University Press, 1984).

C. L. Kingsford, "A London Merchant's House and Its Owners," *Archaeologia*, 74 (1924), pp. 137–58.

David Knowles and R. Neville Hadcock, *Medieval Religious Houses* (London: Longmans, Green, 1953).

Emmanuel Le Roy Ladurie, *Montaillou: Cathars and Catholics in a French Village 1294–1324*, Barbara Bray, trans. (London: Scholar Press, 1978).

William Langland, *The Vision of Piers Plowman*, Terence Tiller, trans. (1981).

Samuel Lewis, *A Topographical Dictionary of England*, 7th ed., 4 vols. (London: S Lewis & Co., 1849).

Suzanne Lewis, "The Apocalypse of Isabella of France: Paris, Bibl. Nat. MS Fr. 13096," *The Art Bulletin*, 72, 2 (1990), pp. 224–60.

Henrietta Leyser, *Medieval Women* (London: Weidenfeld and Nicolson, 1995; reprint 1997).

John Lister (ed.), *Court Rolls of the Manor of Wakefield*; vol. 3, 1313–1316 and 1286, Yorkshire Archaeological Society Rec. Ser. 57 (1917).

J. R. Lumby (ed.), *Chronicon Henrici Knighton, vel Cnitthon, monachi Leycestrensis*, 2 vols. (London: HMSO, 1889–95).

Mary Lyon, Bruce Lyon and Henry S. Lucas (eds.), *The Wardrobe Book of William de Norwell* (Brussels: Palais des Académies, 1983), pp. 313–27.

Richard Marks and Paul Williamson (eds.), *Gothic: Art for England 1400–1547* (London: Victoria and Albert Museum, 2003).

Sir Herbert Maxwell (ed.), *The Scalachronica: The Reigns of Edward I, Edward II and Edward III as recorded by Sir Thomas Grey* (Glasgow: n. p., 1907; reprint Felinfach: Llanerch, 2000).

May McKisack, *The Fourteenth Century, 1307–1399* (Oxford: Clarendon, 1959).

Kate Mertes, *The English Noble Household* (Oxford: Basil Blackwell, 1988).

Nick Millea, *The Gough Map: the Earliest Road Map of Great Britain* (Oxford: Bodleian Library, 2007).

Patricia Moore (ed.), *The Borough Ordinances of Cowbridge in Glamorgan* (Cardiff: Glamorgan Archive Service, 1986).

Henry Morley, *Memoirs of Bartholomew Fair* (1859; reprint London: Hugh Evelyn, 1973).

Ian Mortimer, *The Fears of King Henry IV; The Life of England's Self-Made King* (London: Jonathan Cape, 2007).

——, *The Greatest Traitor: The Life of Sir Roger Mortimer, 1st Earl of March, Ruler of England 1327–1330* (London: Jonathan Cape, 2003).

——, *The Perfect King: The Life of Edward III, Father of the English Nation* (London: Jonathan Cape: 2006).

——, 'What Isn't History? The Nature and Enjoyment of History in the Twenty-First Century," *History*, 312, 93 (2008), pp. 454–74.

Stella Newton, *Fashion in the Age of the Black Prince* (Woodbridge: Boydell Press, 1980).

Norbert Ohler, *The Medieval Traveller*, Caroline Hillier, trans. (Woodbridge: Boydell Press, 1989; reprint 1995).

W. M. Ormrod, "The Personal Religion of Edward III," *Speculum*, 64 (1989), pp. 849–911.

The Oxford Companion to Law (Oxford; Oxford University Press, 1985).

ODNB: The Oxford Dictionary of National Biography (online edition).

OED: The Oxford English Dictionary (online edition).

D. M. Palliser, *The Cambridge Urban History of Britain*, vol. 1, *c. 600–c. 1540* (Cambridge: Cambridge University Press, 2000).

Colin Platt, *The English Medieval Town* (London: Secker & Warburg, 1976; reprint 1988).

———, *Medieval England* (London: Routledge & Kegan Paul, 1988).

Elizabeth Prescott, *The English Medieval Hospital* (Melksham: Seaby, 1992).

Michael Prestwich, "The Court of Edward II," in Gwilym Dodd and Anthony Musson (eds.), *The Reign of Edward II: New Perspectives* (Woodbridge: York Medieval Press, in association with the Boydell Press with the Centre for Medieval Studies; University of York, 2006), pp. 61–75.

PROME: Chris Given-Wilson (ed.), *The Parliamentary Rolls of Medieval England, 1275–1504* (CD edn, 2005).

Ralph B. Pugh, *Calendar of London Trailbaston Trials under Commissions of 1305 and 1306* (London: HMSO, 1975).

———, *Wiltshire Gaol Delivery and Trailbaston Trials 1275–1306*, vol. 33 (Trowbridge: Wiltshire Record Society, 1978).

T. B. Pugh, *Imprisonment in Medieval England* (Cambridge: Cambridge University Press, 1968).

Carole Rawcliffe, *Medicine and Society in Later Medieval England* (Stroud: Alan Sutton, 1995; reprint 1999).

Compton Reeves, *Pleasures and Pastimes in Medieval England* (Stroud; Alan Sutton, 1995).

Henry Thomas Riley (ed.), *Chronica Monasterii S. Albani: Thomae Walsingham, quondam Monachi S. Albani, Historia Anglicana*, 2 vols. (London: Longmans & Company, 1863–64).

Henry Thomas Riley (ed.), *Memorials of London and London Life in the XIIIth, XIVth and XVth Centuries* (London: Longmans, Green, 1868).

Charlotte Roberts and Keith Manchester, *The Archaeology of Disease*, 2nd ed. (Ithaca, N.Y.; Cornell University Press, 1997).

Margery M. Rowe and and John M. Draisey (eds.), *The Receivers' Accounts of the City of Exeter 1304–1353*, (Exeter: Devon and Cornwall Record Society, 1989).

Owen Ruffhead (ed.), *The Statutes at Large, from Magna Charta to the end of the Last Parliament, 1761*, 8 vols. (London: M. Basket, 1763–64).

L. F. Salzman, *Building in England down to 1540: A Documentary History* (Oxford: Clarendon Press, 1952; reissued 1992; special edition 1997).

———, *English Life in the Middle Ages* (Oxford: Oxford University Press, 1926).

A. F. Scott (ed.), *Every One a Witness, The Plantagenet Age* (London: White Lion, 1975).

Reginald R. Sharpe (ed.), *Calendar of the Letter Books of the City of London, F 1337–1352* (London: John Edward Francis for the Corporation, 1904).

Caroline Shenton, "Edward III and the Coup of 1330," in J. S. Bothwell (ed.), *The Age of Edward III* (Woodbridge; York Medieval Press in association with The Boydell Press, 2001), pp. 13–34.

Timothy A. Shonk, "A Study of the Auchinleck Manuscript: Bookmen and Bookmaking in the Early Fourteenth Century," *Speculum*, 60 (1985), pp. 71–91.

Edward Shorter, *A History of Women's Bodies* (London: Allen Lane, 1983).

Rudolf Simek, *Heaven and Earth in the Middle Ages*, Angela Hall, trans. (Woodbridge: Boydell, 1996).

Joshua Toulmin Smith (ed.), *English Gilds* (Oxford: Early English Text Society, 1870).

Lucy Toulmin Smith (ed.), *Expeditions to Prussia and the Holy Land made by Henry Earl of Derby . . . in the Years 1390–91 and 1392–93* (London: Camden Society, 1894).

Society of Antiquaries of London, *A Collection of Ordinances and Regulations for the Government of the Royal Household* (London: Society of Antiquaries of London, 1790).

W. B. Stephens, "Literacy in England, Scotland and Wales 1500–1900," *History of Education Quarterly*, 20, 4 (1990), pp. 545–71.

E. L. G. Stones, "The Folvilles of Ashby-Folville, Leicestershire, and Their Associates in Crime, 1326–1347," *Transactions of the Royal Historical Society*, 5th series, 7 (1957), pp. 117–36.

Jenny Stratford, "The Royal Library in England before the Reign of Edward IV," in Nicholas Rogers (ed.), *England in the Fifteenth Century: Proceedings of the 1992 Harlaxton Symposium* (Stamford: Paul Watkins, 1994), pp. 187–97.

H. R. T. Summerson, "The Structure of Law-Enforcement in Thirteenth-Century England," *The American Journal of Legal History*, 23 (1979), pp. 313–27.

C. H. Talbot, *Medicine in Medieval England* (London: Oldbourne, 1967).

Nigel Thorp, *The Glory of the Page* (London: Miller, for Glasgow University Library, 1987).

TNA: The National Archives, Kew (formerly the Public Record Office).

Thomas Frederick Tout, *The Place of the Reign of Edward II in English History*, 2nd ed. Manchester: The University Press, 1936.)

Georges Vigarello, *Concepts of Cleanliness: Changing Attitudes in France since the Middle Ages*, Jean Birrell, trans. (Cambridge: Cambridge University Press, 1988).

Westman: see Hanawalt Westman

Margaret Wood, *The English Mediaeval House* (London: Phoenix House, 1965; reprint 1981).

Brian L. Woodcock, *Medieval Ecclesiastical Courts in the Diocese of Canterbury* (Oxford: Oxford University Press, 1952).

C. M. Woolgar, *The Great Household in Late Medieval England* (New Haven, London: Yale University Press, 1999).

————, *The Senses in Late Medieval England* (New Haven, London: Yale University Press, 2006).

Thomas Wright (ed.), *The Book of the Knight of La Tour–Landry* (London: Early English Text Society, 1868).

E. A. Wrigley and R. S. Schofield, *The Population History of England, 1541–1871: A Reconstruction* (London: Edward Arnold, 1981).

J. H. Wylie, *The History of England under King Henry IV*, 4 vols. (London: Longmans, 1884–98).

————, *The Reign of King Henry V*, 3 vols. (Cambridge: Cambridge University Press, 1914–29).

Philip Zeigler, *The Black Death* (London: Collins, 1969).

Illustrations

All the images in this volume have been kindly provided by the British Library, from manuscripts in their collections. The author is grateful for permission to reproduce them.

Section 1

Wheel of Fortune, from a mid-fifteenth-century copy of Lydgate's *Troy Book* (Royal 18 D. II fol. 30v).

Alexander the Great given white elephants, from an early-fifteenth-century romance (Royal 20 B. XX fol. 82v).

Lady at her toilet, from the Luttrell Psalter, *c.* 1325–40 (Add. MS 42,130 fol. 63r).

Woman wearing a wimple, from a philosophical tract illuminated in Paris, *c.* 1300 (Burney 275 fol. 166r).

Women reaping at harvesttime, from the Luttrell Psalter, *c.* 1325–40 (Add. MS 42,130 fol. 172v).

Woman being beaten by a man, from a German manuscript of 1446 (Add. MS 17,987 fol. 88r).

Woman beating a man, from the Luttrell Psalter, *c.* 1325–40 (Add. MS 42,130 fol. 60r).

Lady shooting at a hare, from the Taymouth Hours, *c.* 1325–35 (Yates Thompson 13 fol. 68v).

King John of England does homage to King Philip of France, from an early-fourteenth-century *Chroniques de France* (Royal 16 G. VI fol. 362v).

Philippe de Mezières presents his treatise to Richard II of England, *c.* 1395 (Royal 20 B. VI fol. 2r).

Queen Guinevere and the maiden sent by the Lady of the Lake, from a French romance, *c.* 1316 (Add. MS 10,293 fol. 90v).

Two images from *De Claris Mulieribus*, early fifteenth century (Royal 20 C. V fol. 5r).

Plowmen, from the Luttrell Psalter, *c.* 1325–40 (Add. MS 42,130 fol. 170r).

Builders, from the Bedford Hours, *c.* 1414–23 (Add. MS 18,850 fol. 17v).

Women spinning and carding wool, from the Luttrell Psalter, *c.* 1325–40 (Add. MS 42,130 fol. 193r).

Women spinning and carding wool in the early fifteenth century, from *De Claris Mulieribus* (Royal 20 C. V fol. 75r).

Boy being birched by his teacher, from *Omne Bonum, c.* 1360–75 (Royal 6 E. VI fol. 214r).

Burning of the Templars, from a late-fourteenth-century *Chroniques de France* (Royal 20 C. VII fol. 44v).

Section 2

World map of Ranulph Higden, from a late-fourteenth-century *Polychronicon* (Royal 14 C. IX fol. 1v-2r).

Map of Great Britain, from Matthew Paris's *Abbreviato Chronicorum Angliae,* 1250s (Cotton Claudius D. VI fol 12v).

Royal traveling coach, from the Luttrell Psalter, *c.* 1325–40 (Add. MS 42,130 fol. 181v–182r).

Early fourteenth-century cogs, from the Smithfield Decretals, *c.* 1340 (Royal 10 E. IV fol. 19r).

Late-fourteenth-century cogs, from Jean Creton's *Histoire du Roy d'Angleterre Richard II, c.* 1401–5 (Harley 1319 fol. 18r).

Richard II dining, from Jean Waurin's *Chronique d'Angleterre,* illuminated in the late fifteenth century (Royal 14 E. IV fol. 265v).

Alexander the Great dining, from an early-fifteenth-century French romance (Royal 20 B. XX fol. 88v).

Gallows, from a 1487 edition of *Chroniques de France* (Royal 20 E. III fol. 28r).

Executions, from a late-fourteenth-century *Chroniques de France* (Royal 20 C. VII fol. 133v).

Monk and woman in the stocks, from the Smithfield Decretals, *c.* 1340 (Royal 10 E. IV fol. 187r).

Diagnosis through the inspection of urine, from a late-fourteenth-century *Chroniques de France* (Royal 20 C. VII fol. 78v).

Physicians administering medicine to a king, from an early fourteenth-century *Chroniques de France* (Royal 16 G. VI fol. 310v).

Clergymen with the plague, from *Omne Bonum, c.* 1360–75 (Royal 6 E. VI fol. 301r).

Leper with a bell, from a Pontifical, *c.* 1400 (Lansdowne 451 fol. 127r).

John of Arderne performing a fistula operation, from a late-fourteenth-century medical text (Sloane 2002 fol. 24v).

Two musicians and a female acrobat, from the Smithfield Decretals, *c.* 1340 (Royal 10E. IV fol. 58r).

Carol of love, from an early-fourteenth-century copy of the *Roman de la Rose* (Royal 20 A. XVII fol. 9r).

Bear-baiting, from the Luttrell Psalter, *c.*1325–40 (Add. MS 42,130 fol. 161r).

Index